PHILOSOPHY OF
THE FILM

PHILOSOPHY OF THE FILM

Epistemology, ontology, aesthetics

Ian Jarvie
York University, Toronto

Routledge & Kegan Paul
New York and London

First published in the USA in 1987 by
Routledge & Kegan Paul Inc.
in association with Methuen Inc.
29 West 35th Street, New York, NY 10001

First published in Great Britain by
Routledge & Kegan Paul Ltd.
11 New Fetter Lane, London EC4P 4EE

Set in 10 on 12pt Times
by Pentacor Ltd.

Printed in Great Britain by
T.J. Press Ltd., Padstow, Cornwall

Library of Congress Cataloging in Publication Data

Jarvie, I. C. (Ian Charles), 1937–
Philosophy of the film.

Bibliography: p.
Includes index.
1. Moving-pictures–Philosophy. I. Title.
PN1995.J36   1987   791.43'01   86–26226

British Library CIP Data also available
ISBN 0 7102 1016 7

To Suzanne and Max

Kant led investigation back to the human intellect, and inquired what the latter had to reveal. Not without reason, therefore, did he compare his philosophy to the method of Copernicus. Formerly, when men conceived the world as standing still, and the sun as revolving around it, astronomical calculations failed to agree accurately. But when Copernicus made the sun stand still and the earth revolve around it, behold! everything accorded admirably. So formerly reason, like the sun, moved round the universe of phenomena, and sought to throw light upon it. But Kant bade reason, the sun, stand still, and the universe of phenomena now turns round, and is illuminated the moment it comes within the region of the intellectual orb.

(Heine 1882 (1833), p. 114)

our belief in real *things* . . . seems[s] to withstand criticism, and to win in competition with other theories. And even when [optical illusions] do mislead us, as in a cinema – especially in cartoons – they do not lead adults to assert seriously that we have before us a world of things. Thus we are not (as Kant and Hume thought) . . . forever the prisoners of our minds. We can learn to criticize ourselves, and so to transcend ourselves.

(Popper 1983, p. 154)

CONTENTS

Contents

PREFACE

At the 1951 Venice Film Festival the Grand Prize – the Golden Lion – went to a Japanese film made the previous year, called *Rashomon*. Early in 1952 the same film gained an Academy Award Oscar as Best Foreign Film. *Rashomon* tells a story of banditry, rape and violent death; yet those things are not what it is 'about'; rather, a standard textbook tells students that

> *Rashomon* is a film about the relativity of truth in which four conflicting versions of the same event are offered by four equally credible (or equally incredible) narrators. . . . Kurosawa seems to suggest that reality or truth does not exist independently of human consciousness, identity, and perception. (Cook 1981, pp. 557–8)

Thus at the mid-century films had artistic status. They could sustain an annual international festival at Venice; the festival was competitive, implying that standards were available by which to make comparative judgments of quality; and the prize winning film was 'about' philosophical matters of truth or reality:

> Great works of art revolve around the meaning of life, the conditions of the *conditio humana*, the price of an existence worthy of a human being. They ask questions about the validity of values which may serve to distinguish the good from the bad, the better from the worse. They owe their significance not to the answers they give but to the questions they ask. (Hauser 1982, p. 558)

It is appropriate, writing in the mid 1980s, to use the past tense about the 1950s. An overtone of affirmation in that past tense must, however, be disavowed. It is not quite true to write that films 'had' artistic status, standards 'were' available. *Rashomon* was 'about' philosophical matters. These assertions would in 1951 have been news to most intellectuals who concerned themselves with the arts, with standards or with philosophy. News they would have been inclined to doubt. Some would have denied that films had any status remotely comparable to the traditional arts; others, who might have conceded that point, would have said that it was precisely the lack of established standards that prevented films from being on a par with the traditional arts. And few if any philosophers would have allowed that films contained recognizable philosophy. As recently as thirty-odd years ago, then, only very small groups of intellectuals took films seriously as art or as thought.

The artistic status of films as such and of any particular film are concerns of philosophical aesthetics; these matters, and the use of films as a vehicle for philosophy and philosophizing, are topics to be discussed only in the second and third parts of this book. Part 1 will consider the film as it presents a problem for philosophy.

Even before 1950, a handful of philosophers had written monographs about film (viz. Munsterberg 1916, Harms 1926, Adler 1937, Cohen-Seat 1946; and, subsequently, as my bibliography reveals, articles have proliferated. Why are films of philosophical interest? To point to *Rashomon*'s concern with reality or truth is an answer that confuses the vehicle with the passenger, the singer with the song. How so? It is obvious that films, like books or scholarly journals, can be used as vehicles by philosophers. But we do not usually assume that the media of books and scholarly journals are of philosophical interest. Why, then, is film of philosophical interest? I shall argue that the medium itself raises philosophical questions concerning reality or truth; perhaps even that our experience of film can be deployed as a counter-example to the widely-held philosophical view that appearance and reality are hard to distinguish or to the view that we cannot be in the world and conceptualize it and its objects as external to us.

A brief explanation of this is needed. The cinema-goer watching *Rashomon* is, let us assume, an educated, comfortably off, middle-class occidental. His true (or real world) situation is to have set aside a couple of hours, paid some money, settled himself down in a darkened hall and concentrated his eyes and ears on a powerful source directly in front of them. While the film rolls we may speak of his being transported to medieval Japan, where there unfolds a drama in another language, entirely in shades of black and white, played out by persons of a most unfamiliar mien, underscored by strange music. Yet we can say that at a cognitive level the occidental grasps much of what is going on, is curious to find out what will happen next, or, even, what 'really' happened; and meanwhile at the affective level is excited, shocked, moved, upset, thrilled and so on.

Pinpointing the case of the occidental watching an oriental film is only a means of dramatizing what experiencing films always involves. There is much to wonder at in the successful reception of an American film by English schoolboys (my personal experience); or of a Hollywood film in New York; or even of a film set in contemporary Los Angeles and showing in Los Angeles. The point is not the geographical or cultural distance between the world of the viewer and the world of the people on the screen: it is the contrast between the real conditions of the viewer sitting in the dark, looking at and listening to a powerful source in front of him and what that source is conveying. Film was invented as recently as 1879, so we know that the medieval Japanese world of *Rashomon* was not photographed when it might have existed. Besides, the story it tells is a fiction and so it could never have been photographed as it happened. Furthermore, the concept of photographing things as they happen is, to anyone who knows how films are made, scarcely intelligible. The entire drama enacted before us in *Rashomon* never happened, either in real-life medieval Japan, or in real-life Japanese film studios in 1950. *Rashomon*'s world is an artifact, an entity that transcends the sum of its parts.

So in viewing *Rashomon* we cognitively 'know' and affectively 'feel' in relation to a series of events that never took place, that are not real, that are 'only a film'. Furthermore, as the very first philosopher to write about film, Hugo Munsterberg, argued, we experience and feel the film world all the while knowing it is not real; knowing that its apartness from our world is absurd, yet enjoying it. We are not fooled. How can this be, and what is the nature of the suspension of credibility that allows cognition and affect to work, but not so as to deceive us into mistaking the film's world for the real?

Two negative features of this book need highlighting, ways it deliberately differs from much current writing about films. Under the influence of literary close-reading and deconstruction a whole new political manner of interpreting films has grown up, one which treats film texts with great seriousness. Interesting though much of this is, it only fitfully overlaps with philosophy as defined by the great problems that stand at the centre of the subject. More important, its method is frequently promiscuous: sucking in from the surrounding culture widely different and even contradictory theoretical ideas. Thus in essays on a single Hollywood film one might find deployed not just Marx but some special versions of Marx say Althusser; not just psychoanalysis but some esoteric variant say Lacan; plus an obsure feminist theorist. In so far as the present book interfaces with that body of writing about films, it does so at the methodological level, arguing that that is no way to argue. Until the ideas are laid out in a critical manner there is no way that discussion of them can avoid the fate of Barthes, who in *S/Z* succeeded in generating hundreds of pages of commentary on a text about thirty pages long.

At a simpler level, film students have always been prone to certain sorts of obscurantism, pretentiousness and promiscuity of reference. To try to prevent my own efforts falling into these traps I have set up five rules to which I have tried to conform my text, and which I commend to film students in general.

In the preface to his classic work *The Story of Art*, E.H. Gombrich tackles the problem of pretension and the problem of readability by outlining several rules he imposed upon himself as he wrote his book. Taking my cue from him in this, as in much else, I set out the rules by which I have been trying to abide.

To counter name-dropping and title dropping I propose the rule:

(RP 1) Make the sense of your argument turn on citation of only a handful of names and titles, mostly ones the reader can be expected to be familiar with or can relatively easily become so.

The other arts are a vast repository into which we all dip; only those instances familiar to everyone are legitimately cited otherwise there is an exclusion effect; highbrowism generally and in film studies in particular is a vice not a virtue. In general, avoid displays of intellectuality. This does not prevent me from using other citations, especially in notes, but it does allow the reader to follow what I am saying without having to have read everything I have read or to have seen everything I have seen.

To counter Frenchspeak I adopt the rule:

(RP 2) Forswear esoteric vocabulary; it is not worth the exclusion it entails.

To counter obscurantism I adopt the rule:

(RP 3) Make every sentence transparent; if something will not come clear, delete it; nothing in the main argument to turn on obscurity.

The obscure but seemingly profound is pseudo-profound: what is not clear cannot be assessed; it is the writer's, emphatically not the reader's, work to see that the prose says what he means, neither more nor less. The purpose of writing or reading discursive prose is to engage certain problems and to move discussion of them along. Cleave to that aim at all times and cut away everything extraneous; readers' time and patience are limited. Above all, do not cast yourself as a mighty man of taste and erudition offering gems of enlightment to those around you. Indeed:

(RP 4) Eschew so far as possible all evaluative terms.

As we shall see in Part II, only the poorest of arguments exist for categorical evaluative judgments. They are easy to controvert, but hard to discuss rationally. To minimize them is to minimize the exclusion of the reader and also to minimize the reliance on weak arguments.

Above all:

(RP 5) Take as models for how to do philosophy and how to be profound such examples as Plato, Berkeley and Russell rather than Hegel, Husserl and Heidegger.

And finally, following Gombrich all the way, I operate with a meta-rule that says do not impose these rules inflexibly or unreasonably. Violation of them is not merely a matter of human

xiii

weakness, lack of self-control. It is the recognition that, generally, good rules are not always good rules, that there are occasions when making an exception will help the argument along, or be acceptable to the reader.

Rules of Procedure*

(RP 1) Make the sense of your argument turn on citation of only a handful of names and titles, mostly ones the reader can be expected to be familiar with or can relatively easily become so.

(RP 2) Forswear esoteric vocabulary; it is not worth the exclusion it entails.

(RP 3) Make every sentence transparent; if something will not come clear, delete it; nothing in the main argument to turn on obscurity.

(RP 4) Eschew so far as possible all evaluative terms.

(RP 5) Take as models for how to do philosophy and how to be profound such examples Plato, Berkeley and Russell rather than Hegel, Husserl and Heidegger.

*See pages xii–xiv

ACKNOWLEDGMENTS

The writing of this book was made possible by a John Simon Guggenheim Memorial Fellowship and a coincident leave from York University, Toronto. In addition I received a Research Grant (410-82-0879) from the Social Sciences and Humanities Research Council of Canada. The ideas in this book have been tried out on successive classes of students at York since 1981-82. Joseph Agassi, Brian Baigrie, Evan Cameron, Allan Casebier, Jagdish Hattiangadi and Iris Mor read the first draft and made many suggestions. They are in no way responsible for my response.

I.C.J.
Toronto 1986

INTRODUCTION: ON THE VERY IDEA OF A PHILOSOPHY OF THE FILM: *CASABLANCA*

Don't worry what's logical. I make it go so fast no one notices.
(Michael Curtiz)

1 PHILOSOPHY AND THE FILM

The aim of this Introduction is to clarify what might be expected of the philosophy of film, offering thereby a framework into which can be fitted the scattered and diverse efforts of others. All the arguments and theses will be illustrated with the help of one film: *Casablanca*. This will, I hope, seem an unlikely choice: in taking up the challenge to show its appropriateness I may diminish that sense of unlikelihood. In a banal sense there is plenty of philosophy in films. We can all recall, 'Johnny, Johnny, why don't you stop fooling yourself', and countless other deathless aphorisms. Some of these may be true, though not original; culling them from films is more likely to be a satirical than an enlightening exercise. Most of the canonical works of academic philosophy were written before films existed and are, therefore, unlikely to discuss them. Nevertheless, film may be embraced within some of the things philosophers do, whether mentioned or not.

We call a certain sort of thinking, taking as its object anything under the sun, 'philosophical', as when we speak of philosophy of life or a philosophical attitude to things. Films are full of that. Such very general thinking is not confined to philosophers. What sort of thinking do philosophers call 'philosophical'? One answer,

1

a highly self-conscious one, can be attributed to Kant, or to his influence. That answer is: thinking about thinking. Can this apply to film? On this view philosophy of the film is thinking about how we think about film; is, so to speak, thinking about the very possibility of thinking about film. Kant pushed his argument all the way, and concluded that the purest form of philosophy concerned itself with thinking itself, and in general, the possibility of thinking about anything at all. I am uncertain whether that leaves any room for film.

While not necessarily endorsing Kant's stipulation of what constitutes philosophy, I shall, for the purposes of characterizing the subject of philosophy of the film, utilize it as a starting point. If film is to be an object of thought, one question involved in thinking about it at all might be, what sort of a thing is film that we can think about it? Questions framed in such a way – using 'thing language' – are characteristically answered by telling us that the thing is a material object, in this case celluloid on spools, created by a photographic process and then realized by a reverse process – instead of light coming through a lens to strike film, light is thrown through the film to go out through a lens on to a screen (a more circumspect answer would add parallel clauses about sounds going through microphones and, as electricity, through photo-electric cells and so, as light, to film, and light through film sent out through photoelectric cells as electricity to loudspeakers to become sound). But as material object the film is only one among many – sticks and stones, trees and people, dynamos and cameras – and does not pose any peculiar philosophical problems. *Casablanca* considered as several reels of celluloid in cans is just one material object among many.

Philosophers variously theorize that our very capacity to think of material objects – things – can be explained because they are accessible to our senses, or intellects, because they fit the categorial apparatus; they participate in universals, because they have both primary and secondary qualitites; and so on. Each is an attempt to specify what it is about material objects that makes it possible for us to think about them. Films *qua* material objects – like books – are uninteresting because they do not create special problems for any of these (problematic) theories.
(problematic) theories.

So it is not the material object that is being addressed when we

2

consider the very possibility of thinking about the film in general, about *Casablanca* in particular. What is being addressed is something we loosely speak of as 'on' the film, or 'contained in' the film; namely the content, or meaning – usually a form of narrative. Such an object of thought as narrative is not material; yet it is at the same time not immaterial or mental. It is in a metaphysical limbo in much the same way as are relationships. People are concrete but the relationships between people, equally real, are abstract. The stories, plots, themes or meanings, in short the content of films, are also abstract objects.

How then is it possible to think about the film in general as abstract object, as meaning; about *Casablanca* in particular as an abstract object? This is a question; how does it become a problem? What is to stop us thinking about abstract objects? This is to misunderstand. 'How is such thinking possible?', asks, 'how is it done?', not, 'how on earth can it be done?' What then are the conditions that make it possible to think about film as abstract object? As with physical objects, thought can be construed as a relation between the thinker and what is being thought about. There must then be capacities in the thinker to discern, identify and understand the object of thought which, in its turn, must at least partly possess features that make it accessible to the thinker. The thinker about film content, I suppose, is not different from the thinker about mathematics or motor cars. In so far as philosophy has any theories of the thinker (viz. empiricism, associationism, rationalism, phenomenalism, Kantianism) these need not find the thinking part of thinking about the film problematic. However, when it comes to the object of thought, such as a book, a film, or *Casablanca* in particular, the philosophy is more problematic. There are philosophical theories of material objects or physical substance, and of mental entities or mental substance, and reductions of the one to the other. But the field of relations, meanings and of abstractions in general is contested at such a fundamental level that narrative in general, never mind narrative film in particular, still less *Casablanca*, has scarcely been theorised about at all. Hence what follows will be crude.

The most general answer to how it is possible to think about the film *qua* abstract object is that film's contents, which are information stored in retrievable form on rolls of celluloid, can be actualized so that those who experience the film build up from it an intelligible content, one we even might be tempted to call 'a world'. The real world includes among its contents things, people, relations, abstractions; so does the world on film; the world we can discern on film simulates the real world so closely that we can speak of a resemblence, even of a continuity, between the two. Yet since the film world is a world contained on celluloid, it is philosophically important to discuss whether we know in principle how to demarcate this imaginary world from whatever we take to be the real world that it resembles. Only if we can demarcate the film world from the real world can we ask the question of whether the presuppositions involved in making the contents of film intelligible to ourselves resemble those presuppositions we need for intelligibility in general and hence whether film is a useful way to think about thinking and making sense in general.

A basic condition enabling us to think about film, then, is that it is such that we are able to discern in its content something resembling a world; something, that is, like the world, but yet in some definite way not the world, merely like it. 'World' here could be expanded: it connotes order not chaos, contents not void, intelligible not meaningless. So we can redescribe what is presupposed by our discerning a world on film by saying that it permits us to impose order, to make intelligible, to individuate and to identify things. What we might call the project of constituting a world on film is merely a small part of the wider project with which we are constantly engaged; that is, imposing intelligibility, order, individuation and identity on the world in which we live. Precisely because film in some way replicates locally what we are constantly engaged in globally there is the possibility that we may learn from our constitution of the film world about our world-constituting activities in general.

The overwhelming majority of the intelligibles, the ordering forces, the individuals and the identities to be found in the film world are people; or, as some philosophers prefer to call them, persons. Each narrative film such as *Casablanca* has what we may call a cast of persons. But films in general also have casts of persons, persons who reappear in one film after another – shifting their personae from one story to another, changed yet the same. I am referring to stars, a by no means trivial variant of the notion of a person. Here then we have a feature of the world on film that both differs from and resembles our world. Stars provide points of continuity and recognition across or between films. They may be a principle or cause of whatever reality we decide the films have, as well as another clue to the very possibility of thinking about the film.

Why not now go on to explain how it is possible for us to discern a world on film? This Kantian question is better avoided here, for the simple reason that it is too ambitious. Our understanding both of thought and of the objects of thought is rudimentary, no more so than when we try to tackle world constitution. We have only the dimmest idea of how infants build up their picture of the world from the undifferentiated manifold of experience, especially when all our communication presupposes our results being coordinatable. It is possible that studying how it is done with films may illuminate that murky area. If world constitution from films is to illuminate world constitution *tout court* we have some way to go as yet.

Not only do we discern a world on film, but that world resembles our world. Here again the theory of resemblance is bitterly disputed territory – ironically, since none of the competitors has strength to do much more than throw a punch or two at their opponents before collapsing.

For the present, then, I take it that thinking about film is possible because we have the physical and mental equipment and they provide the materials for us to constitute something it is natural to write of as a world, both resembling and differing from ours, differing in particular because the world on film is an artifact, not a natural occurrence. Furthermore, although resembling our world, it differs from it decisively in being known not to be real (see Part 1).

2   FILM AS PHILOSOPHY

Having discerned a world on film we now have an artifact with a meaningful content about which we can raise the question: is it beautiful? This too is Kant's question, and to ask it is to look at something under its aesthetic aspect. I am uncomfortable with the terminology, since it seems obvious enough that there are works – *Taxi Driver* comes to mind as does *1984* – that want discussion as aesthetic objects but which are far from beautiful. Also, since films are artifacts so recently arrived, there is a possibility that they are unlike any other form of the aesthetic experience and hence require separate consideration, consideration that may lead us to revise our appreciation of the other arts. These topics will be our concern in Part II: Movies as an Aesthetic Problem.

Having asked of the film, 'is it real?', and 'is it beautiful?', the other obvious question that can be asked of the meaningful contents of the film is, is it true?

To this it could be replied, is *what* true? The world on film is not the world, even when it sets out to resemble or reproduce that world, and even when it is successful, it still isn't the world. So if its being true means identity with the world then it is never true. But 'is what true?', raises other possibilities such as: is the resemblance postulated between the film world and our world a true resemblance? Do people in our world behave as do the people in this film world? Are the ideas uttered by the characters in this film true ideas? Is this verbal summary of what seems to be the message of this film a true message (as well as truly the message of this film)? Is the attitude the film adopts towards its message a correct one? Here we go beyond the Kantian concern with how thought is possible by raising the question of whether what we think is true.

Perhaps this is the point to look closely at our example of film, one that is well known, rich in content, yet not usually analysed intellectually, *Casablanca*. [1] Let me try to show how we can separate out at least four layers of philosophical address in the film, of all of which we can ask, 'is it true?' twice. The first time we think we can ask it, we ask it of the interpretation: i.e. is it true that the film will bear this interpretation; the second time we ask it we assume the interpretation is plausible and we proceed then to ask whether what the interpretation says is true. Let me give names to the layers:

> layer 1: quest
> layer 2: attitude
> layer 3: thesis
> layer 4: framework

A *quest* will usually take the form of a central character who searches for an answer to a *problem*: in the case of *Casablanca*, what is the morally correct action to take. Towards both this problem and its hero's quest the film can adopt an *attitude*, e.g. approving, critical, or, in this case, romantic-ironic. Then the film can itself, as it were in its own voice, be said to offer a *thesis*. In the case of *Casablanca* this is reasonably clear. Cynicism and opportunism are presented as attractive but immoral philosophies; individuals caught up in these philosophies can redeem themselves, indeed will redeem themselves, when the issue is presented to them in the right terms and someone exerts leadership.

Finally, all intellectual production, indeed all cultural products, do not question the most general presuppositions that make their culture what it is; Collingwood called these Absolute Presuppositions, I call them the *philosophical framework*. In *Casablanca* both individualism and romantic love between individuals are unquestioned values. By contrast, the total absence of connection to families of origin or to social class appears not to worry the characters or the film makers. Values exist independently of social context. Yet the real people watching the film are rarely so rootless. A complex inference must be made from our capacity not only to tolerate but to enjoy dramas set among the rootless to the possibility of tensions within the culture between the individual's connections to the rest of the society and the value attached to self-containedness. Furthermore, all the characters display one or more degrees of loyalty to nations, to France, to America, or to Germany. This is nuanced but unquestioned. The characters are, still further, committed to bourgeois morality, which hardly means anything in the circumstances. For example, can one display loyalty to a friend to no avail and yet at the cost of life? Early in the film Rick refuses to display such loyalty (to Ugarte, Peter Lorre), yet at the end he does, and it means everything and he gambles everything – and wins his moral worth back. Both the hero – the neutral if not isolationist nightclub owner and former gun-runner, Rick – and the detached, loyal official of Vichy, Louis, set out (in the symbolic act of bringing their countries) into war. These are only some of the presuppositions of the framework; there are many others, especially regarding value (what is funny, what is wrong, how to treat employees, etc.).

Before going on to explicate all these elements in this one film in detail, some methodological points. Philosophy, whatever conception of it we have, is a cognitive activity carried out in discursive language. Films are complexes of sounds – including spoken language – and images, including images of speech and of writing. But non-linguistic sounds and images also contain a good deal of information, including philosophical information. Through its sounds and visuals the film can convey disapproval, celebration, irony, apprehension and many other attitudes towards its characters, the situations they are in, and the courses of action on which they embark. It is, for example, hard to isolate all the overtones of irony, romance, ruefulness and cliché that flow from the use of the popular song 'As Time Goes By' in *Casablanca*. When the philosophical documents under discussion are themselves purely words on the page this problem of overtones is much less. It is true that Plato, writing in dialogue form, uses dramatic elements of character manipulation and rhetorical elements of speech to add to the overt level of the clash of views between his speakers – not to mention his use of myths and his borrowing of poetic verse. Notoriously, he has left us with an insoluble problem, namely, when, if at all, does Plato speak for himself? Plato never appears in his own dialogues, the dialogues contain no commentary to prompt the reader except when put into the mouth of one character or another, and the character who does best the others more often than not is given the name of a historical personage – Plato's teacher Socrates. The same problem, 'when does the film speak?' besets us here.

Analysis being a mode of using words, before we can begin to analyse out the quest, attitude, theses and framework of *Casablanca*, we have to transform the film into words; not the film as reels of celluloid but the meaningful entity we take to be contained on them must be put into forms of words suited to philosophical analysis. The usual way of doing this is to paraphrase the plot and/or to describe scenes in a manner that highlights the analytic points that are going to be made. If we see interpretation as something imparted to a film, our practice of building it into the paraphrase will make it impossible for us to check the interpretation against the paraphrase. And if we cannot check it against the paraphrase, can we check it all? And unless we can check it at all, how can we improve our interpretative efforts?

One solution might be to strive for a 'neutral' paraphrase; a description of the film that does not favour any particular interpretation, much the way that in science we look to a body of facts neutral to contesting theories and hence usable to adjudicate between theories. In search of such I turned to consumer guides, those mass-produced paperbacks that rate movies to be shown on television. Here are three:

Paraphrase A

Casablanca (1942) 102m. ****D: Michael Curtiz. Humphrey Bogart, Ingrid Bergman, Paul Henreid, Claude Rains, Peter Lorre, Sydney Greenstreet, Conrad Veidt, Dooley Wilson, S. Z. Sakall, Joy Page. Everything is right in this classic of war-torn Casablanca with elusive nightclub owner Rick (Bogart) finding old flame (Bergman) and her husband, underground leader Henreid, among skeletons in his closet. Rains is marvellous as dapper police chief, and nobody sings 'As Time Goes By' like Dooley Wilson.

(Leonard Maltin *TV Movies*)

Unfortunately this is inaccurate – the city of Casablanca is not 'war-torn'; try again.

Paraphase B

Casablanca (1942) ***½ Humphrey Bogart, Ingrid Bergman, Paul Henreid. This one is famous for the song, 'As Time Goes By', plus a wonderful cast but try not to forget that overall it's a very dull melodrama of intrigue. You'll enjoy it if you can overlook its faults and keep track . . . of its stream of characters. Oscar as Best Film. (Dir: Michael Curtiz, 102 mins)

(Steven Scheuer, *Movies on TV*)

This is worse. *Casablanca* is hardly a 'melodrama of intrigue', and inaccuracy is now compounded by value judgment ('dull') and aesthetic judgment ('melodrama'). This paraphrase B will hardly serve to check interpretation, since it is full of it.

Paraphrase C

Classic story of an American expatriot [*sic*] who involves himself in romance and espionage in North Africa during World War II.
(The Penguin Video Home Entertainment Guide, 1983)

C is short yet squeezes in again value judgment ('classic') and inaccuracy ('involves himself').

Our quest, then, for a neutral authority against which to test interpretations is not such an easy one. Consider two slightly longer examples.

Paraphrase D

Humphrey BOGART, as the cynical yet vulnerable owner of Rick's Bar in war-time Casablanca, discovers that a Resistance worker whose escape to the US he is aiding is the husband of his lost love. **Casablanca** has all the qualities of romantic Hollywood films at their best: a tightly worked out plot, crisp dialogue, satisfying predictable characterizations, and the polish of a well-knit studio team working together. Bogart's tough-guy qualities were admirably teamed with Ingrid BERGMAN's luminous beauty, and Claude RAINS gave an excellent performance as the devious French police captain.

Bogart's much quoted 'Play it again, Sam' is incorrect; he in fact says 'Play it, Sam'. . . .

(Oxford Companion to Film, 1976)

Although longer, this abounds in inaccuracies.[2] Inaccuracy, it would seem, is produced under the pressure not just of compression, or faulty memory, but of interpretation. Another example:

Paraphrase E

Casablanca captured the mood and the immediacy of a war-time situation involving political refugees from Nazi-occupied Europe and their desparate attempts to attain exit visas to Lisbon and freedom. Set in Rick's Café-Américain, owned by Richard Blaine (Humphrey Bogart . . .), a man who once fought with Spanish loyalists and smuggled arms to Ethiopia but now refuses to stick his neck out for anyone, its plot centered on the unexpected arrival at the café of Victor Laszlo (Paul Henreid) and his wife Ilsa (Ingrid Bergman . . .), the only woman Rick has ever loved. Their affair, which began and ended in Paris shortly before the Nazi occupation, starts all over again, shines through the film's numerous and somewhat far-fetched sub-plots, and ends – as it did once before – unhappily, when Ilsa and her husband, having obtained the necessary exit visas for which they came to Casablanca in the first place, board the plane leaving Rick to resolve his inner conflicts by again sticking his neck out and working on the side of peace.

(Hirschhorn, 1979, p. 238)

This is much more scrupulous but, we notice with dismay, it is full of interpretation and value-judgment.

Most bizarre of the interpretative plot summaries discovered in my search was by Richard Corliss, who playfully suggests its hidden agenda is a romance between Rick and Louis. He ends it thus:

Paraphrase F

In **Casablanca** the Howard and Davis roles are taken by Bogart and Rains, and the de Havilland and Knowles parts by Bergman and Henreid. Bogart chooses Rains over Bergman less because he finds a fellow cynic more compatible than an inexperienced idealist than because, in wartime, the man of action must accept comradeship (i.e. pragmatic patriotism) over love (i.e. political idealism). To a nation that had just entered the war and was considering the prospects with some reluctance if not resistance, *Casablanca* acted as both an explanation of its causes and an exhortation to America's young men to pack up their sweethearts in an attic trunk and smile, smile, smile – wryly, of course. The men (Bogart and Rains) would do the fighting while the women (Bergman) and idealists (Henreid) would keep the home fires of freedom burning until their return.

(Corliss 1974, p. 105)

Such fun and games aside, my last hope was that some academic treatment of the film, where detachment is encouraged, might turn up a neutral paraphrase. In a dissertation about the work of the film's director Michael Curtiz, the author's discussion of each film is preceded by a summary:

Paraphrase G

In December of 1941, Casablanca swarms with refugees desperate for exit visas. Ugarte (Peter Lorre), a petty crook, has murdered two German couriers and stolen the powerful 'letters of transit' they carried. He asks Rick (Humphrey Bogart), owner of Rick's Café Américan, to keep them until he can sell them, but Captain Renault (Claude Rains), prefect of police, arrests him under the approving gaze of Nazi official Major Strasser (Conrad Veidt). Rick, unmoved by Ugarte's capture, is upset by the entrance of Victor Laszlo (Paul Henreid) and his beautiful companion, Ilsa Lund (Ingrid Bergman). A flashback reveals that Ilsa and Rick were lovers in Paris and planned to leave together when the Germans invaded. But Ilsa stayed in Paris, sending Rick a mysterious note saying she could never see him again. In Casablanca, Laszlo learns from Ferrari (Sydney Greenstreet), a black marketeer, that Rick probably has the stolen letters of transit. But Rick refuses to give them to Laszlo. Later, Ilsa confesses that she still loves Rick, explaining to him that she was married to Victor during their Parisian affair, but thought him dead. The day they were to leave she learned he was alive and therefore had to abandon Rick to help her husband. Rick now agrees to resolve the triangle. He tells Renault to arrest Laszlo when he gives him the letters, but when Renault tries to do so, Rick orders him to take them all to the airport. Rick puts Ilsa on the plane with Laszlo and the letters, and shoots Strasser when he tries to prevent its take-off. Instead of arresting Rick, Renault decides to leave Casablanca and join the Free French forces with him.

(Rosenzweig 1978, pp. 148–9)

This is a careful paraphrase of the events of the film, not of the motives and moods, still less of the philosophizing of which it is full. It is also accurate and artful, being written in the present tense, except for the flashback, which is paraphrased in the past tense. My point in quoting these various paraphrases should be clear. Just as in science there are no theory-free facts, every fact is a fact only for a particular theory, [3] so there are no paraphrases without interpretation; a film means partly what we take it to mean. Therefore no paraphrase can be neutral, whether it is long or short. Does it follow that interpretations and hence paraphrases are mere matters of inclination or taste? That there are no

13

uncontroversial 'facts of the film' to check paraphrases against and refute some? Not quite. Refutation is the strongest form of criticism and hence the most powerful engine of progress, but it is not the only one. My deployment of multiple paraphrases itself demonstrates how interpretation makes them vary; their inaccuracies are themselves criticisms, their being juxtaposed and analyzed is itself progress.

Discussing the philosophy in films, then, is a bit of an interpretative mine-field. In paraphrasing films for purposes of philosophical discussion we must force ourselves to look at the film as a whole, including all its non-verbal elements, rather than just attending to overt statements made by the characters or to what can be unravelled from the shape of the plot. Mere plot summary is far from sufficient, even though it is an obvious place to begin. It is an obvious place to begin because the *quest* is a good deal easier to identify than either the *attitude* or the *thesis* of the film. It is not sufficient because the content of a film is not exhausted by its plot summary, and this is true even when referring to the cognitive aspect of 'content'. Indeed, I suggest that no one plot summary or paraphrase can exhaust the philosophical content of the film. Works of imagination build in ambiguity and sometimes draw their strength from it. I see no reason for insisting on a single correct interpretation of a film like *Casablanca*. Cogent cases may be made for several interpretations, some of which may not be consistent with each other. Even stating the plot accurately is very difficult. And all this should not surprise us. Stating things in words is a tricky business. In philosophy we wrangle endlessly about the interpretation of the classics – which, after all, are usually written texts.

Before proceeding to close scrunity of *Casablanca* a comment on the scope of the inquiry. It is trivially true that every film is philosophical in the popular if not in the Kantian sense. Any film is grist to the Kantian mill, however, since we can pose it as a case at which we can direct the question: how do we manage to make sense of this? and we could, were we so inclined, interrogate in turn this sense-making to illuminate how we think about thinking. Nevertheless, not all films are equally philosophically interesting, from the popular *or* the Kantian point of view. Since films are products of specific cultures there are always implicit in them the presuppositions of that culture. Yet they may embody them in an uninteresting manner; they may not address them as problem or difficulty. These conceptions of (something) being philosophical or interesting are more general than, and hence they incorporate the whole of, the Marxist conception of ideological meaning – such as interpreting an American film as embodying the 'contradictions' of the capitalist system. For, the interpretation of the alleged contradictions may interest Marxists and non-Marxists alike. This is not to exclude, however, other possible interpretations that may also be interesting, including non-Marxist and anti-Marxist philosophical interpretations. Roughly speaking, what is philosophically interesting is the revelation of an unnoticed consequence of a philosophy. The production of a new criticism, the detection of inconsistency within a philosophy, or between it and another philosophy not hitherto seen as contradictory, and, perhaps, a new way of formulating a philosophy.

Before returning to *Casablanca*, a word about non-fiction films. Since every film is made within a cultural framework there is a trivial sense in which it is informative about that framework. This had led Sarris, for example, to suggest that all films are documentaries. In the sense in which this is trivially true, the following is also true, though somewhat less trivial: not all documentaries are equally interesting as informants. Being interesting, unlike being true, is a relativized concept; what is interesting is relative to point of view; what is true does not vary. Our interest in problems, theories, evidence, contradictions, constantly changes, and so films that may once have been dismissed as uninformative on what now are thought to be interesting matters (the real issues of the war), turn out to be informative on what are now thought to be interesting matters (the culture in which *Casablanca* was made). To explicate all this fully would require recapitulating the entire view of the nature of intellectual concentration and change that I espouse, my own most general framework. For that the interested reader will need to go elsewhere (see Jarvie 1964, 1972).

3   *CASABLANCA* AS PHILOSOPHY

Now to the philosophy of *Casablanca*. Let us start from the plot, or at least a summary of the plot. What is required to do this right? First and foremost one tries, of course, to get it right; that is to say, to make true interpretative statements rather than false ones. Moreover, one also tries to present the plot in interesting rather than uninteresting statements; in simple rather than complicated ones; in straightforward rather than pretentious ones. Further, one tries not to mislead one's reader by psychological terminology. Writing 'one tries' does not imply some sort of effort of will, although I have no objection to that. Rather is that a shorthand way of saying we do better to operate inside social institutions designed to promote these ends, especially the social institutions of methodological rules. The individual or social effort to speak the truth does not ensure that one does so; our interpretations are always hypothetical or putative truths. We remind ourselves and our readers of that point if we explain how our interpretations were reached, how they solve problems, what difficulties they contain and hence how they can be criticized – we can even be self-critical and attempt to criticize them ourselves.

Here is my interpretation in a paraphrase:

Paraphrase H

Casablanca is the story of two lovers (Rick and Ilsa, Ingrid Bergman and Humphrey Bogart) who stumble across each other after he thinks she has abandoned him. Their desire is rekindled but she now travels with her husband (Victor Laszlo, Paul Henreid), whom she had thought dead at the time of the affair. Despite her pleas, Rick, feeling that Victor is an anti-Nazi hero deserving support, decides he deserves his wife and that he, the hero, should sacrifice his own inclinations.

H centres *Casablanca* on a quest: to find the right thing to do both in relation to his personal desire for this woman, and in relation to the world situation. At one stroke Rick resolves both problems, enabling the resistance hero to flee with his wife, assassinating a high German officer, and setting off with the prefect of police to join the Free French. Yet H could be criticized on any number of grounds. It presents the dilemma of the hero's quest in a cut-and-dried manner that is false to the manner in which the film is experienced. For the structure of the plot is one of

16

gradual disclosure. Much time is spent on establishing the setting, and then on introducing us to Rick in a manner that plays his ostensible cynicism off against clues of deep sympathies (he refuses to allow an official of the German Bank into his private gaming room; he plays cat and mouse with the German Major Strasser (Conrad Veidt); yet he turns the murderer Ugarte over to the authorities). We also see him cool in love, refusing to sympathize with a woman eating her heart out for him, and indeed, summarily packing her off home. He seems secure in himself and invulnerable. But the biggest disclosure begins when Ilsa walks into his cafe with the underground leader Victor Laszlo. Although shattered by her reappearance, Rick congratulates Laszlo on his 'work'. But memory hurts and we see him hit the bottle, feel sorry for himself, and flashback in memory to his Paris affair with Ilsa. In the present they resume their affair. He schemes to flee Casablanca with her.

Rick's quest, then, is not disclosed to us as such at once, but is rather something the film uncovers slowly: formerly a man of action on the right side, disillusioned in love, he has become indecisive and impotent and only the reappearance of his lover and the highlight it throws on the public issues that surround him restores him to action. His ostensible cynicism is a disguise.

Another criticism of paraphrase H is that it draws only on the narrative. That is to say, it ignores the music, the atmosphere, the way the film is acted, above all the way it is directed and cut – as though these factors did not contain any philosophical content. I accept this criticism. Indeed I have invited this criticism with my analytic separation of a film's attitude and a film's thesis. These are often carried by just those factors paraphrase H ignores. The overall attitude the film strikes towards Rick and his quest is romantic: with all his faults he is a big man, adored by the people around him, capable of handling himself in difficult situations. Rick is revealed as only seemingly tough on the outside, in private vacillating, and not so much tender as sentimental. The film pictures him as real and admirable, it does not ironize him as a weakling or an amoral cynic. Those who know him best, such as Sam the pianist, or Carl the waiter/bookkeeper, offer acceptance, not criticism. The film does not second guess these people and it does not invite us to judge Rick differently from them. Hence, when he does the right thing at the end the spectators' feelings have been orchestrated into a bitter-sweet surge (unhappily he is right to renounce Ilsa), not unlike what the characters can be presumed to be feeling. At this point Rick and Louis walk away from us into the fog as the camera cranes up so that we look down on them. Both dilemmas are now resolved and both are behaving admirably. This shot exports them from the concluded narrative to the beginning of a new and disjointed one.

Such touches are very artful, as is the way the director contrives to conceal the fact that Bogart was quite a small man, smaller than several others in the cast, by constantly shooting and framing him so that his presence looms over the others. Bogart's manner as actor is alternately detached and preoccupied, or involved but ironic, epitomized in his catchphrase, 'here's looking at you, kid'. His line readings are always hard-boiled, ignoring the ends of sentences and delivered in a rhythmic monotone, slightly lisped. These mannerisms draw attention. The two other principal male characters are Claude Rains as Louis, the Chief of Police, and Paul Henreid as Victor Laszlo. Laszlo is always presented as right and brave, but also as intense and humourless, whether facing the fact of his wife's infidelity or in crossing swords with Germans. He radiates goodness; he embodies the values that Rick had formerly fought for – yet he depends on Rick throughout. Louis, on the other hand, played by an English actor with humorous detachment and nonchalance, explicitly denies having convictions, says he swings with the prevailing wind. He, with his opportunism, corruption and methodical seduction of women is much more the cynic than Rick. His humour makes him more attractive than Laszlo. Yet it is Laszlo, through Rick, who offers him grace and a chance at being decent.

It would not be unreasonable, then, to interpret Victor and Louis as two facets of Rick's own character, each exaggerated and projected into the field of action and conflict. In siding with Victor, Rick affirms his better self, and it is his example which draws Louis to his side as they set off to use their derring-do to fight for what is right. Unlike Bogart's performance, which embraces both extremes, Henreid and Rains concentrate their performances consistently, each in his allotted narrow range.

Ingrid Bergman's Ilsa, meanwhile, allows us to see her feelings as she glows in her Paris scenes with Rick and again after the affair resumes, while in other scenes she withholds herself so that she is an enigma. In her intense desire for Rick she embodies also the romantic view of him, described by Louis, who declares that if he were a woman, and he (Louis) weren't around, he should be in love with Rick. Now all these aspects of the movie's mechanics are missing from paraphrase H so before trying to improve it I will consider more such points.

How much one can make of it I am not sure, but Laszlo is usually dressed in white, as is Ilsa; Strasser in black; Louis alternately black and white; Rick in white dinner-jacket and black trousers. These matters are anyway slight compared to other atmospheric or attitudinal matters, especially the music and the direction. Rick's faithful piano player functions as a refrain, particularly his songs, 'It Had to be You' and 'As Time Goes By'. These link the film together, as Sam is alluded to as the atttraction at Rick's club: Rick's rival Ferrari tries to buy him; Sam is present when Rick and Ilsa begin their affair, and he resists the requests of both of them to repeat the songs he played when they were in Paris. At times the sound-track lets him sing; at others Max Steiner's score picks up the melodies and orchestrates them for mood.

It is the direction, however, not the narrative, which imparts to the film a thick romantic atmosphere. The direction is by the prolific Hungarian (in Hollywood from 1926) Michael Curtiz, whose speed and malapropisms were legendary. He shot the film consistently in the third person, that is, with the camera looking at people who look to the side of the camera where, the viewers know, there is someone else. Almost every scene has Bogart in it. The exceptions are interviews at Renault's office, street scenes, and Victor and Ilsa's quest for exit visas, which takes them from the police station to Ferrari's club. In all these other scenes not more happens than is required to let us know what is going to affect Rick. That his is the lead point of view of the film, despite the consistent third person technique, is clear from the major flashback to Paris, which occurs when he is drunk and sorry for himself. It dissolves to a view of the Arc de Triomphe, and to Ilsa and Rick taking a car ride. It includes genuine newsreel footage of the Nazi advance, and ends at the railway station when Ilsa does not turn up. A note she has sent him is shown in close-up, from Rick's point of view, the only point of view shot in the film, the lettering dissolving under raindrops.

Curtiz's direction, then, is crisply to the point, not afraid to use clichés and symbols (raindrops on a letter, spilled glasses, popular songs, costuming, unflinching shots of people's faces as emotions pass over them, catch-phrases, even, shamelessly, a tower with a searchlight on it for Rick and Ilsa's sexual reunion), and, above all, the established strengths and personalities of his stars to move the narrative along. Clichés and banalities, combined and intensified, are a means of deftly stirring complex emotions in the audience, since they draw on a reservoir of associations, and so can add up to more than the sum of their parts, being neither clichéd nor banal.

The film editing is of the style known as 'seamless'. That is, cuts are at the natural ends of scenes, and usually introduce scenes with a telling detail (Rick's hand signing a chit, the neon sign on Rick's cafe). Within scenes cuts are made time and again on action-reaction cues: one character says something meaningful while looking at the other and we cut to a matched shot of the other, matching eyelines and usually distance, moving back for the more expansive gesture, moving forward for the emotionally powerful detail. A noticeable feature of this is the cut on meaningful glances exchanged between Rick and his head waiter as to who should come into the gaming room; between Rick and his bandleader on whether to play the 'Marseillaise'; and, of course, between husband and wife, lover and beloved, even piano player and customer. These make us aware of Rick's control of things in a way known only to him and his employees, reinforcing the sense that the point of view of the film is his all the way, for him and against him, as the case may be. Seamless editing ensures that the *attitude* and *thesis* of the film remain implicit, subordinated to the demands of the narrative.

The movie is thus all in one tightly controlled style. An interesting feature of this seamless style is that it assumes what we may call the unflinching gaze, which is third person even though oriented around one person's point of view. Director and editor allow us to gaze at people as they experience moments of intimacy and of stress, moments that in life we might be shy of overhearing and which we might flinch from if we were involved. This filmic permission to go close to people in a manner not permitted in our culture presumes our invisibility and hence our ghostly detachment. We can come close because we cannot be seen, and because we cannot intervene: we do not affect the course of events. We are thus encouraged to think that our fixed gaze at the screen is making us ubiquitous to the events being watched but their reality seems tangible to us because they go on as though we were not there – as indeed we are not. Dr Johnson's notorious test of whether a stone was real was to kick it. Were we to advance on the screen or to talk to it there would be no kick back, the film would be immovable in its course, a seemingly real thing, oblivious of the seemingly unreal us.

It is not hard to see what is being offered. The events of the plot are being presented to us as a reality, a possible world realizing itself. The incorporation of maps, narration and newsreel serves to authenticate time and place. The narrative structure itself, showing a line of cause-effect connections between the actions of the *dramatis personae*, makes this possible world causally self-contained. The camera and hence the audience are never there as causal factors. And the film's concentration of *quest* and *attitude* on Rick renders him a causal principle. Impotent when the film opens, a centre of confusion as it unfolds, he is explicitly named as the one who must act to precipitate a resolution.

All these technicalities are absent from paraphrase H. This makes it deficient. As an excuse I might say, perhaps, that these are mere frills. Not so: they constitute the very texture of the film and embody its implicit philosophy.

Let us bring out this philosophy. The film romanticizes and ironizes the hero's *quest*. He is the hero, he is admirable, but he is also mixed up. Becoming less mixed up he also becomes no less romantic and attractive, even though he now seems to be venturing into a phase of life without women – as is Louis too. Women may deflect one from one's true goals, make one feel sorry for oneself, but, when you think it through, women can also clarify one's mind and assist one to regain balance – for their sake. The affairs of three people may not 'amount to a hill of beans in this world of ours', but the fate of this world matters, so one makes oneself matter by acting to that end.

Scripted and shot during 1942, the only date visible in the film is 2 December 1941 on the chit Rick okays early in the film. Pearl Harbour was 7 December 1941. Rick and Louis's decision to take sides coincides exactly with America being forced willy-nilly to do so. If we interpret the film in terms of those contemporary events, which the opening maps and commentary and the inserted newsreel footage encourage us to do, then it becomes a drama of isolationism. Isolationism seems a droll and sophisticated position, compatible with the individualism of Rick's line, 'I stick my neck out for nobody'. Sooner or later, though, events of such magnitude impose themselves and force the isolationist or neutralist to choose sides, to follow the values known to be right. Neither individualism nor romantic love is more important than such a decision.[4]

All this is a very complex philosophy. The individualism and romanticism are very strongly felt. Yet they are contradicted when we are told the affairs of three people don't 'amount to a hill of beans in this world'. This final scene also denies the romanticism. Rick's speech to Ilsa in effect says that they do desire each other intensely, but that desire fades and that if he yielded to her wish that she leave Victor and stay with him she will eventually regret it. He is now going where she cannot follow so, thinking for both of them, for all of us, as she asked him to when they were reunited, he sets aside desire and inclination and elevates thought and long-term considerations. The speech has strong echoes of a most famous speech in the Bogart canon, where he tells the villainess/heroine of *The Maltese Falcon* that even though he desires her, indeed perhaps because he desires her, he is going to turn her over to the police for the murder of his partner, that there are limits to the indulgence of self.

We have come across contradictions so perhaps others should be mentioned since Marxists hold that all films of high capitalism must in some way reproduce the contradictions of the capitalist system. In this film all the characters are without any past or any ties to the wider networks of society and family. Only the vaguest of allusions are permitted, and the one flashback finds them equally disconnected. Yet the impetus of the story is that these characters are pursued by their past, relentlessly. So they both lack a past and are hounded by the past. This is a highly Marxist message. The past from which we wish to be free haunts and controls us. Another contradiction is that in all their private dealings the characters are trapped in bourgeois morality, yet that morality is futile as it cannot guide one in the unusual and complex war-time conditions of semi-neutral Casablanca. (Even Ilsa's affair with Rick is reconciled with bourgeois morality since it began when she thought Victor dead.) Yet another contradiction is that the film implies it is about politics, but it is in fact about choosing sides. Vichy is not a political arrangement, it is a compromise – in the pejorative sense of a bargain with the wicked. The war is presented in Marxist terms as the great anti-fascist struggle, not as a complex and temporary political coalition between three nations with highly diverging political interests: America, Russia and Great Britain. Marxism is characteristically anti-politics. And, of course, the conflict between bourgeois morality and political morality is the heart of the film, and politics wins; it is for political reasons that Ilsa must stay faithful to her husband. In the war the bourgeois West was absolved by Marxists when it joined Soviet Russia in the anti-fascist struggle and so ethics and politics resolve their contradiction and bourgeois society was redeemed – for a time. The romantic vision wins: hard times give us an occasion to exceed ourselves.

We have, then, two layers of philosophy exposed: the hero's *quest* for the right thing to do when desire has turned to self-pity and rekindled desire conflicts with manifest duty. The answer is to sort out priorities, think things through and accept the sacrifices required. Console the pain of loss with memory: 'We'll always have Paris.' We show strength in our capacity to renounce. The implicit attitude of the film is to *romanticize* this dilemma, to fill us with yearning and sorrow, and intimate that we should accept and approve of the outcome.

The film is more ambiguous in its *thesis*. As stated, it could be an allegory for the plight of isolationist America, implying that when events are of a certain magnitude and a certain evil one's (correct) instinct to get involved will not go on being denied. It can also be taken as representing in its drama another of the contradictions of capitalism: it contains conflicting values and only a vision of the coming struggle and the emerging future make rational choice of action possible. Rick and Ilsa are trapped by their bourgeois morality: about betrayal of love, of Rick by Ilsa (false appearance); betrayal of marriage, of Victor by Ilsa (inadvertent in Paris, deliberate in Casablanca). At the same time Rick is in a situation – the anti-fascist struggle – where bourgeois morality doesn't apply. For example, Rick effectively hands over Ugarte who we learn has been killed while in custody, and Louis cynically sits deciding whether to call it suicide or attempted escape. Both Rick and Louis are witty and admirable throughout, despite such behaviour, and are wholly redeemed in the ending. This is an interesting non-bourgeois morality: even those who have murdered, never mind been corrupt (Louis takes sexual and monetary bribes, Rick's roulette wheel is fixed), are redeemable in the right circumstances. Rick murders a German and Louis covers it up.

Two purposes are served by bringing all this to the surface. One, which will count with film scholars, is to understand something of the emotional power of the film, its grip on the audience. It deals with issues that are not hard to understand, it operates on several levels at once, and it blends problems of cognition and action into emotional states such as mood, desire, pain, etc. The other, which will count with philosophers, is to penetrate the ideas being put forward in items of popular entertainment, to endeavour to state them and subject them to the test of truth. To do this they have to be paraphrased out of their originating context – in which, of course, they are made to seem true, even inevitable, in that the film unrolls the same way each time – into a context of assessment. We have to be able to identify and label the philosophical components, isolate the arguments implicit in their incorporation in the film, then bring to bear philosophical skill and expertise in assessing these ideas and their argumentative support. When we do this we may come up with somewhat different conclusions than the film offers, but our tribute to the film consists in its having forced us to think things through for ourselves.

Indeed, in Chapter 15, we shall look at some work of Woody Allen, who constructed an entire work, both play and film, around a character who tries to solve his problems in life by thinking about what Bogart would do in *Casablanca*. The hilarity comes from the incongruity of the project, but the power also comes from our affection for this film.

Of all the philosophy in the film we can ask whether it is true, whether its morality is moral, and whether such arguments as the film presents are valid. Its romanticizing attitude is both offputting and appealing. Since so much tension and despair is experienced over love, it is pleasant to have a film endorse our feelings, our sense of weakness, our sense of foolishness. However, the contrast that is drawn between love and duty, desire and work, pivots on treating women as objects of love, as support staff to men, not as

24

themselves directly capable of duty, work. Women are to be loved, but to love them is dangerous for they may let you down and make you impotent in your work. Only when you discover a misunderstanding is your capacity to act restored. Such a philosophy is at best pathetic. The thesis that the pressure of events will bring one back to the right, that Germany and Vichy's aim to detain or kill Victor will galvanize Rick, that Pearl Harbour will galvanize America, is shabby and corrupt. 'Only when things affect you personally can you bring inclination into harmony with action', is hardly an elevated principle of morality. This litany could go on, exposing contradictions as well as falsities and moral equivocations. The opening sequence of the globe and the refugees, the shooting of the Free Frenchman, the conspiring in the cafe, intimate that what is at stake are world issues, political questions. The narrative then concentrates on the romance, encouraging us to place it at the centre of our attention, only at the end to have Rick say that the affairs of three people don't amount to a hill of beans in this world. So world affairs dominate explicitly, but personal affairs dominate implicitly. The film can't have it both ways as philosophy, although its drama and emotional force may come from precisely such clashes.

Casablanca was reviewed in *Variety* in December 1942. It won Oscars for best film and best direction in 1943. Thirty years later it was so established a part of popular consciousness that Woody Allen could centre a whole play round it (*Play It Again, Sam*) and even incorporate brief extracts into the screen version of the play. This brings us to the general *philosophical framework* of our culture, the broadest aspect under which we can consider philosophy in film, and the one remaining manner of looking at *Casablanca* we have not undertaken. What are the broad philosophical presuppositions taken for granted in *Casablanca*? We get different answers if we take different perspectives. *Subspecie aeternitatis*, as it were, we get the metaphysics of the person, distinct from the machine, capable of acting freely and perhaps contributing to the course of history. Rick admires Laszlo's work, never suggesting that history is a mere product of forces grander than the individual. We get a classless utopia, where drinking, smoking, gambling and sexual adventures are a normal part of the lives of decent people as well as of criminals. We get a notion of the world as interconnected: events in remote places, whether Paris or Casablanca, may have consequences elsewhere. So, although the individual is defined without background, he is enmeshed in a surrounding of world scope. We get a metaphysics of love; the importance, pleasure and pain of an intense feeling between men and women which is not ruled by marriage and almost refuses to be ruled by world war. We have a world of nation-states and colonies to which attach intense patriotic emotions, a world virtually without government and politics. The issues are ones of right and wrong, not choice under uncertainty. We have a world conflict in which neither communism nor Jews are mentioned. A world which seems to have a future. These people know how to do right without the help of politicians or priests – no-one brings in God.

These are not theses of the film, they are premises in the absence of which the film could not advance to its theses. The object, therefore, of exposing them is only to show the pervasiveness of philosophical matters, and how much of what we do and think and enjoy takes for granted a philosophical background. They cannot be incorporated in a brief plot outline, hence I offer the schema on p.27.

4 CONCLUSION

Being unable to draw on any well-established theory of how thinking is possible, and hence of how thinking about thinking about the film is possible, I first tried to argue that the film as a material object poses, as such, no special problems for philosophy. As an abstract object the film seems to contain philosophy and we are able to think about it philosophically. Revealing the philosophical content of *Casablanca* and thinking about it does not show *how* it is possible, but it does show that it *is* possible. On the whole the assessment of the level of philosophizing in the film was not very high. This is not surprising; the philosophically inclined would not seem likely to choose films as a vehicle for their efforts. So why is it done? Why do writers, directors, etc. put philosophy on to film? The anwer is simple: they do not. *Philosophy puts itself in their films*. That is to say, behind such a work there always lurk the personal or cultural presuppositions about reality, morality, etc. implicit in our thought and action. One job of philosophy is to expose and to criticize those presuppositions.

PHILOSOPHICAL ANALYSIS OF *CASABLANCA*

	Is it true?	
	Of the film	In general
Quest: Rick's moral dilemma, how to act in love and war	All other characters in the film face versions of this dilemma	There are other issues
Attitude: romantic-ironic	Permeates	False and self-deceptive
Thesis: self-sacrifice is redeeming	Highly ironic	False
Frame: individuals without families, nationalists, romantics, etc.	Unquestioned	Highly contentious

PART ONE

MOVIES AS A PHILOSOPHICAL PROBLEM

One general principle seemed to control the whole mental mechanism of the spectator, or rather the relation between the mental mechanism and the pictures on the screen. We recognized that in every case the objective world of outer events had been shaped and molded until it became adjusted to the subjective movements of the mind.

(Munsterberg 1916, p. 58)

In the cinema, what is 'given' to us is a sequence of stills, but what we see, or observe, or perceive, is movement; and we cannot help seeing the movement, even if we *know* that we are seeing only photographs of (say) an animated cartoon.

(Popper 1983, p. 45)

1

KNOWLEDGE AND EXISTENCE

Experiencing a movie we *allow* ourselves to be deceived; we *suspend*, as the cliché has it, our disbelief; we *play* with our sense of reality. This activist thesis is the short answer to the problem: what is philosophically interesting about films? In experiencing films people solve philosophical problems without thinking about them, thereby accomplishing what some philosophical theories do not.

Everyone is a philosopher in the sense that they have general views of the world. Film-goers among them regularly accomplish what many philosophical theories wrestle with and are defeated by; and this rehearsal of their powers is a source of great pleasure, perhaps because the human capacity to model the world and to play at modelling possible worlds is greatly to our evolutionary advantage. Professional philosophers cannot help being fascinated by the spectacle of ordinary people playfully accomplishing what the philosophers theorize about. Play is voluntary and fun. Playing at it and with it is how children come to terms with the world they have entered. Since, even for adults, the world is always changing and hence being entered anew, play does not cease to have value and to give pleasure with the end of childhood.

Writing of allowing ourselves to be deceived seems to imply that at some level we are not deceived. Is this correct or are we film-goers genuinely deceived? Do we momentarily slip into a state of mind where we take the scenes that appear to be happening for real happenings and hence become excited, afraid, happy and so

on just as though we were witnessing the real thing? Phenomenologically this would be a mistake. The texture and intensity of our
feelings in situations of danger, happiness, puzzlement and so on
are a good deal more intense and long-lasting than the simulacra of
these emotions we experience at films. Most film-goers, for
example, 'recover' from any feelings experienced in the cinema
within quite a short time. Only a few have nightmares or are
otherwise shaken up. People who go through real-life crises of,
say, threats to their life, sometimes never retrieve their emotional
equilibrium. Events of such importance in our lives or the lives of
those close to us have lasting emotional impact even though their
immediate impact varies greatly. The effect of films is transient.

What goes for emotion also goes, I think, for cognition. Writing
about depth perception, Munsterberg says:

> If the pictures are well taken and the projection is sharp and we
> sit at the right distance from the picture, we must have the same
> impression as if we looked through a glass plate into real
> space . . . . *Nevertheless we are never deceived; we are fully
> conscious of the depth, and yet we do not take it for real depth.*
> (Munsterberg 1916, pp22–3)

Some evidence suggests otherwise:

> *L'Arrivé [sic] d'un train en gare* . . . was a visual tour de force,
> and audiences are said to have stampeded at the sight of the
> locomotive barreling toward them from a distant prospect into
> the foreground on the screen. (Cook 1981, pp.10–11)

L'Arrivée was made by the Lumière brothers in France in 1895.
Further evidence that we are, or at least, can be, deceived is
provided by anthropologists reporting that primitive peoples
worry about the chopped-off appearance of people on the screen
(Wilson 1961); or by observing children poking the television or
going round the back in search of what they can see.

To reiterate Munsterberg: while we do have the same impression as though we were looking through a glass plate into real
space, most of us are not deceived into believing that that is
actually the case. The simplest explanation of why some are fooled
and others are not comes from children, who very rapidly learn
that neither poking nor going round the back of the television set
does any good: there is nothing there. It is from this notion that

there is an element of learning in our cognitive and emotional responses to film that the unfortunate metaphor 'film literacy' derives.

The key mechanism here seems to have to do with a 'discount' (Friedson 1953) we are able to place on deceptions and illusions through familiarity with them. You may not be able to 'see' what the prestidigitator or illusionist is doing, but you 'know' the egg is not coming out of the ear, the lady is not being sawn in half, and you are able to discount the cognitive and affective shock of its seeming to happen. No doubt sculpted busts or statues without arms look like mutilated people when first we encounter them, as do head-and-shoulders close-ups and partial views. But familiarity breeds contentment. New devices with which even experienced cinema-goers are unfamiliar can retrieve the unguarded reaction, as when the audience flinches at a stereoscopic movie when an object looms forward, or when a powerful sense of vertigo is induced by large screens such as Cinerama or Eymax.

Film makers like to tease us by testing the strength of our learned disbelief in the difference between the real world and the screen world. They show characters watching films and then stepping into the screen. Buster Keaton does it in *Sherlock Junior* (1924); Olsen and Johnson do it in *Hellzapoppin* (1941), Steve Martin and Bernadette Peters do it in *Pennies From Heaven (1982)*; Jeff Daniels does it in *The Purple Rose of Cairo* (1985). Both Elmer Rice (1930) and Gore Vidal (1974) have toyed with the idea in novels. Stephen Spielberg and Tobe Hooper used the idea for scary purposes when they had a character sucked into the television set in *Poltergeist* (1982).

This should alert us to a very important point about the phenomenology of film-viewing: suspension of disbelief is not the same as hallucination. The latter, I take it, is where we take for real something that happens not to be real; we cannot tell the difference. It seems that with film watching we are able to *play at* taking on-screen events for real. We learn not to be fooled as small children are, and we continue to enjoy movies despite no longer being fooled, even to the point of accepting the idea that on-screen characters will be fooled and fool us in ways we have learnt not to be. It is this playful distance, perhaps, that allows us to become cognitively and affectively enthralled by movies. Being enthralled by movies does not visit upon us all the consequences of real-life events. We are not usually cognitively exhausted and emotionally ravaged by movies; rather, we emerge feeling good. Part of that feeling good comes from the vigorous philosophical exercise that experiencing film represents.

This brings us back to philosophy. Two of the central problems in the Western philosophical tradition are, what do we know (epistemology), and, what exists (ontology)? They are very troublesome problems over which philosophers are deeply divided. Not least of the troubles with them is their mutual relation.

It can be argued that before we can answer the question of what exists, we have to solve the problem of what we know. Since knowledge is what we know of what exists, it is what we know about what exists that allows us to move towards articulating what we know of what exists. The tantalising Kantian possibility always remains, however, that what we know of what exists is not all that exists. Philosophers who give knowledge precedence over existence include Bertrand Russell, the logical positivists, and Karl Popper. By parallel reasoning it can also be argued that before we can solve the problem of what we know we must first solve the problem of what exists, because when we ask what we know, what we mean is what do we know of what exists, and how can we assess any claim to know something or other exists if we have not solved the problem of what exists and hence can adjudicate our claims to know that it does? Martin Heidegger and his followers give precedence to existence over knowledge.

Another and somewhat different trouble with these two problems is this. The problem of knowledge seems to be about 'us', since it queries what 'we' know. The problem of ontology, though, in asking what there is, leaves out any reference to us and appears only to speak about 'the world'. The question arises of the relation between 'us' and the world, whether knowledge is a state of 'us' or some other sort of thing and if that, what sort of thing? Various ways of overcoming this trouble have been tried. 'The world', it has been argued, can only mean 'our world' and so the reference to 'us' is implicit, if disguised. The problems then of whether we can know about what exists, or whether the world is different from our knowing about it, cannot arise. 'Knowledge', by contrast, can be regarded as a hot line between mind and world into which we tap with differing degrees of success. Success is measured not by us but by some extra-human criteria which humans at best may dimly perceive.

Cutting through this thicket is not a task for an essay on the philosophy of film. It is enough if we can see how films enter into the debate about these problems. My own preference as a philosopher of science is to adopt a deceptively naive solution to these problems as a first approximation and to effect refinement to the extent that its simplicities prove inadequate. To the problem of, 'what do we know?', I should suggest the answer (a) not very much and (b) the cream of what we think we know is contained in science and mathematics. From this flows a relatively straightforward answer to the problem of what exists: (c) what exists are those entities disclosed or postulated by the current theories of mathematics and science.

The position is not as counter-intuitive as at first seems. It does not reduce the world to atoms and molecules. There is plenty of room for pink string and sealing wax, kind hearts and coronets. What it offers is a criterion. If the question is raised, 'is this, that or the other real, does it exist?', we may try to answer by means of the following question, 'do our current scientific theories of the world require it, postulate it, have a place for it, seem as though they could be made consistent with it?'[1] Sometimes ordinary or common-sense knowledge clashes with science, e.g. the view that disease is caused by entities called 'germs', or that movies appear to move because of 'persistence of vision'.[2] In such cases science may displace the putative entities of common sense from their explanatory role, perhaps even eliminate them altogether, while explaining why such common-sense views seemed tenable.

Now to locate this wilfully naive epistemology – we don't know very much, what little we know is science, and science is the best arbiter of what is real – in relation to the troublesome issue of which is prior, knowledge or existence, and the equally troublesome isssue of what we are talking about, is it the way the world is or our grasp of the way it is? This will inaugurate a gradual programme of expanding on the idea and showing that, despite its simplicity, it is sufficient to solve many of the philosophical problems raised by films.

(a) We don't know very much. Faced with problems needing an answer, we guess. Guesses are sifted by assessing them: (i) as solutions to the problem; (ii) for internal consistency; (iii) for consistency with other, independent, ideas already assessed; (iv) for consistency with those guesses so seemingly unproblematic we call them 'facts' (Popper 1959, 1963, 1972, 1983; Bartley 1961). This eliminates the problem of priority between knowledge and existence. Neither comes first; what comes first is the problem to hand. If it is a problem about our knowledge, then guesses about that will have to be checked against what there is, which will have to be, for the purposes of the discussion, taken as unproblematic; if the problem is about what there is, our guesses will have to be checked by means of what we know, which in its turn will then have to be, for the purposes of the discussion, taken as unproblematic. Neither knowledge nor existence is a secure base from which to build a bridge to the other. Both are part of our philosophical predicament. The possibility that we know nothing of what there is, or, that there is nothing, cannot be ruled out; but that is not a reason for ruling it in. This method is not new: science, mathematics and philosophy are all quite familiar with the method of working with two uncertain things to learn more about each; and this pretty well sums up the situation on knowledge and existence. The answer to the sceptical impasse argument is the progress of science.

(b) Science and mathematics are certainly created by human beings, 'us', but when we find and correct mistakes in them it seems we are making contact beyond ourselves, with the real world. At all events, whatever is disclosed by or constructed for science is the nearest thing we have to 'knowledge' about the things which 'exist' in the world. Certainly common sense won't do. Yesterday's science is today's common sense, and if we are going to treat science as our best approximation to knowledge we must exclude defunct science.[3]

(c) Scientific discoveries can reasonably be claimed as transcendental, that is, as representing contact with the world beyond our act of cognition just as beyond all known time and space. 'Transcendental' here not implying once and for all true, a final breakthrough to things in themselves, but only that we have a method of making contact with the world, at points, here and there. That method is the method of experience; the method, that is, of deriving experiential consequences from science and then checking them out. Experience is a curb on science rather than a source of it. A simple name for this philosophy of knowledge and existence is 'realism': the claim that science vouchsafes us glimpses of how the world is.

Other metaphysics than realism can make sense of science, it is true, especially pragmatism/instrumentalism: which treats the entities of science much like the microchips of computers – useful to do calculations but telling us nothing about the way the world being calculated is. Popper opposes it, yet has shown (1963, ch. 2) that instrumentalism can be consistently maintained. Many views, however, can be consistently maintained that are not all consistent with each other. So consistency is at best a minimum or necessary condition for seriously entertaining a view. Perhaps the strongest argument against the pragmatism/instrumentalism alternative is this: it makes us hostage to the ad hoc adjustment. Since the instrumentalist criterion of admission to science is that a theory have predictive success, and since predictive success can often be obtained merely by adjusting the calculations or adding a lemma, there is nothing to prevent us piling up epicycles into an incoherent but still working muddle. This argument gains force from the availability of the alternative of interpreting science realistically. Realism has been the dominant interpretation of science until this century, and can thus be claimed to have been fruitful. At all events it will be adopted in this book.

Once we put science in place as our best claim to knowledge about the world, we can interpret it realistically as knowledge of a real world extending beyond our mere consciousness of it, a world of things and processes which, when we attempt to act, will curb our guesses by making some of them go wrong. Realism then faces serious problems of its own: if there is a real world of which we are a part but which extends in time, space and sorts of entities well beyond any possible experience of ours, or even of the entire human race, how do we find out what it is like? We can have our own ideas or opinions about it, but they become falsified. How can we know that they are not all mistaken and that even the idea that there is a real world is not itself a mistake?

We find this problem posed in very early philosophical texts as the problem of the relation between knowledge and opinion. In the Greek world the temptation to collapse knowledge into just a variant of opinion was resisted because of the discovery of mathematics. Mathematics seemed like an insight into the structure of the world, of doubtful application to human beings and other living creatures, but of immense application elsewhere.

Unlike opinion, which was personal, mathematics was impersonal: what was correct was not necessarily what people thought was correct.

As the Ancient Greeks looked to mathematics, we in the age of film look to science. Not that science for a moment proves or demonstrates or puts beyond doubt the idea that there is a real, external world. To argue thus is to put the cart before the horse. Rather it is a metaphysical presupposition of science that realism is true. However, it is a valid argumentative stratagem to proceed in this way: assume what you want to show, carry out calculations as though it were true, and, if these calculations seem correct and no anomalies or troublesome cases crop up, claim that you have given an argument forwarding the original assumption. Only if the same results can be achieved under other assumptions is the force of this argument undermined.

Science does presuppose realism, I would maintain, makes lots of hypotheses and deductions on that basis, and hence makes a case for its assumptions. There have been in this century distinguished scientists who have dissented from this, and tried to show how science actually confounds realist assumptions and who in their place have put instrumentalist or even idealist assumptions. It is enough to signal awareness of these matters since turning aside to argue them through would ensure never getting anywhere near the philosophical problems of the film.

Let us take it then that our scientific knowledge is knowledge of a real external world, a world in which there are many sorts of things, and that science is our best effort to reach knowledge of that world and to catalogue those sorts of things. Included in this world are films, persons, and the process of persons experiencing films (not 'viewing' because that leaves out hearing). These persons inhabit a real world of things and processes, they know that they do, and some have a little knowledge of how the world works. Most, however, do not know how the cinema works its magic on them; that is, cannot give a scientific account of what natural laws and physical conditions make it possible for them to experience films. This is no different from their inability to give even a first approximation to the manner in which they see, hear, conceptualize and think about their everyday real world.

Yet they do have one very important piece of knowledge: the knowledge that there is a difference between the world on the screen and the world they inhabit. As already indicated, there is a phenomenological texture and durability missing from the cognitive and affective enthralment in which films hold us that is detectably different from that of real events. This is not to deny what is sometimes called the power of the world films project. Unlike reading, the pace of which the reader can control, unlike the theatre, the pace of which the actors can control as they respond to their sense of the audience, films unspool inexorably in real time, not to be stopped, slowed down or speeded up. The only choice is to give attention or not to give attention. And when we give attention we have the sense that we have been looking through a plate glass window into a world (Gibson 1979, p. 301).

Notice that I write 'a' world rather than 'our' world or 'the' world. Once experienced, there is a sense in which the land of Oz becomes part of our world, but only in the sense that our contact with it is vicarious: through the little girl Dorothy as central character, or perhaps through the transparent point of view of the overlooking camera, we have experienced that world and have stored it into our memories. When we have experienced many movies and have become familiar with their conventions, their depiction of typical streets and interiors, their ways of showing how people behave, the stars they use again and again, the manner in which space and time transitions are elided, we build up a rough and ready map of the world on film, one we can talk of, retrieve, describe, and refer to in the course of discussing matters in the real world.[4] But, like Alice, however familiar or however curious that world gets, we do not lose track of the benchmark of the real world to which we actually belong.

Indeed, I would claim that it is only the implicit contrast, however submerged the recognition of it, between the real world we inhabit and the film world we do not that makes the film world so enthralling and satisfying. Things work out so interestingly there, there is so much order and coherence, in contrast to the world as it actually is.

The world on film is most of the time a recognizable world. It contains people, buildings, furniture, motor cars; there is talk and music and noise, people have relationships, problems, emotions; events connect and disconnect one with the other. If I am right, though, none of these is mistaken by us for the real thing. Or, to be a trifle more guarded, those few people among us who begin to react to the film world as if it were real, and try to enter into relationships with it that are more appropriate to those in the real world, get classified as in some measure disturbed ('neurasthenic', as Munsterberg says). What in particular is disturbed is precisely their sense of reality, their knowledge – which we want to take for granted – of the difference between the real and the unreal.

The problem of the difference between the real and the unreal takes many forms in philosophy. One of the most approachable is when it is formulated as the problem of the difference between appearance and reality. The problem has two facets. The first is that of deception.

Appearances can deceive us as to the true nature of things. What looks simple can turn out unmanageably complicated, Colourless, harmless looking liquid can be deadly poison. A gorgeously coloured creature can be dangerous. What properties things have is not always apparent at first or second glance. Our most intimate acquaintance with this truth has to be in regard to other people. It seems to be a characteristic feature of our society that people dwell behind well-established facades that make for certain kinds of social ease but that may deeply conceal the person underneath.

The second facet of the problem of appearance and reality is that of superficiality. Appearances are surface, we tend to think; realities are depth. What a person, institution or thing is, and what makes it what is is, are buried deep.

An example of the worry that appearances are misleading is a simple optical illusion such as the appearance that a straight stick thrust into water looks bent, hence has become bent. What happens when we turn our attention to film? As Munsterberg noted (1916, pp. 19-24), what is on a cinema screen is in two dimensions, yet we perceive events on it to be taking place in three. But here the superficial appearance of depth is a mistake: screen depth is discontinuous with theatre depth: we cannot walk into the world that recedes from the screen.

An example of the problem of superficiality would be an acorn, apparently a small, hard, and inert piece of matter, not much different from a stone or a piece of baked clay. Such character-ization is superficial because what the innocuous surface of an acorn conceals is the enormous potential in the right conditions to become a full-fledged oak tree. A film certainly is not just rolls of celluloid, nor is it merely some distraction for idle moments. This celluloid distraction conceals within it the enormous potential to enthrall us both cognitively and affectively; to inform, persuade, record, galvanize, delude and possibly even invade the consciousness of living people inhabiting the real world.

What I seem to be moving towards via this line of argument is the conclusion that films are an awkward wrench thrown into the machinery of philosophers' ways of handling the problem of appearance and reality. Bishop Berkeley, in the eighteenth century, gave one of the most thorough and radical examinations of this problem ever. Consider this: how can we be sure that the world continues to exist when we turn our backs on it? Never for a moment did Berkeley doubt that it does continue to exist. But, he reasoned, everything that we know is a construction from the data that flow into us through our sense organs. It is, as it were, sustained by that flow of data. If we turn our back on the world then we have no data at all, unless there is a conveniently located reporter who can call out to us when asked whether the world we were momentarily receiving data from still endures. Arguing that, 'to be is to be perceived' – or, as it might better be put, 'to be is to be perceivable' – Berkeley concluded that someone or something had to be perceiving, receiving the data all the time from all the things we think are real in order to guarantee that they are enduring. Thus God, the Supreme Perceiver, able to do it everywhere from all angles at once, becomes necessary for there to be a perceivable world at all. Very neat and not at all plausible.[5]

Films present something of the same sort of problem. If we turn our backs on the screen and stop our ears, are the things we were seeing and hearing in any sense still there? When we pick up a can of rolled celluloid in what sense is the film that we have just experienced or can later experience there present in the can? Or is the can of celluloid, like an acorn, a little bundle of potential which, when mixed with the right conditions – not of soil, air, and water, but projection machinery, electricity, light, and a human perceiver – yields for all those who will attend to it the experience of a film? By Berkeley's reasoning this will not do. We need to postulate an Eternal Spirit who is as it were continually viewing all the movies ever made, as well as all those yet to be made in order to sustain them in their potential for realization when we do finally turn our attention to experiencing them. God is the Supreme Movie-goer. The one exception to this would be *King Kong*, a monster movie of 1933 that is so phenomenally popular that it is said there is no time of the day or night, no day of the year, when it is not playing somewhere in the world. Always being perceived, it is always in being with or without God!

Even without *King Kong* as a counter-example to Berkeley's God, films seem to be a trouble to his philosophy since it is very much the case with them that 'to be is to be perceived' yet what we perceive and enjoy we sharply and playfully discriminate from those perceptions of things we consider real. Berkeley's God is not, of course, a solution to the problem of sense-illusions, but rather to the possibility that all sensing is illusion, that nothing is there when we don't attend to it and when we do attend to it we are imagining things. This extreme idealism ('the world is my dream') is one by which many people are tempted once they come to grips with the problem of appearance and reality. It has in its turn such grotesque internal problems (how can it be articulated without contradiction, how can it be communicated without contradiction, how, if it were true, would it make any difference to our action in, and thinking about, the world – perhaps in this latter resembling the zero content yet plausible hypothesis that everything in the world is shrinking at a uniform rate?) that most of us cannot be bothered with confronting it. More to the point is what Berkeley did to explain how to avoid or correct piecemeal sense-illusions. Berkeley's arguments are very simple. First, he reasons, the ideas of

> Sense are more strong, lively, and distinct than those of the Imagination; they have likewise a steadiness, order, and coherence, and are not excited at random, as those which are the effects of human wills often are, but in a regular train or series. (Berkeley 1710, Part First, Section 30)

His second argument is that each sense (sight, sound, touch, taste, smell) is an independent channel which may offer information in conflict with that from another channel. So my eyes see a stick that bends at the surface of the water, while my hands feel a stick straight along its length. Both are correct. Each is a perception we have been caused to have. A mirage of water to the eyes is different from the arid ground trodden by the feet. What could have caused such conflicts of information? Not, Berkeley reasoned, a unified world of material objects which were both bent and straight, wet and dry.

Once upon a time Berkeley's views were considered an extreme and perverse form of subjective idealism, despite his strenuous denials. Today we think they are better interpreted as a consistent working out of phenomenalism, the doctrine that we construct the seeming objects of the world out of the flow of information that comes in through the senses (hence 'sense data' in the jargon). Clearly, the coordination of the senses then becomes a highly sensitive point for phenomenalism: why do we construct single objects that range over several senses, rather than different objects, even different worlds, for each of our senses?

Precisely the same question can be posed about films. The entities we see and hear while experiencing a film have no corresponding touch, taste or smell. They are not purely imaginary, since machinery, electricity and so on are required to call them forth. But they do disappear when we turn off the apparatus.[6] While the apparatus is on, however, it is an open question whether the sensations we have are not stronger, more lively, distinct, steady, orderly, coherent, and regular than those of the real world. And yet, as I shall argue below, we do make a phenomenological discrimination between the screen world and the real world. Meanwhile, if to be is to be perceived, the creation of films and their being exhibited makes the inventory of the things in the world rise and fall in an untidy way as projectors start and stop – unless we bring in the Supreme Film-goer.

2
PLATO AND THE CAVE

Berkeley is what we call a modern philosopher, although he was active in the eighteenth century. His approach to the problem of appearance and reality and his religious phenomenalistic solution to it were stimulated by the science of his time, which meant above all the theories of Sir Isaac Newton. Berkeley did not gainsay the immense power and elegance of Newton's ideas, and the capacity of some of them to give us accurate predictions about the course of events. What he objected to were what he considered the shaky metaphysical foundations of the work, especially such 'occult' concepts as gravity and such 'fictions' as the infinitesimal. He subjected these to severe scrutiny and found them wanting. In their place he wanted an acknowledgment that science be grounded in perception, that it aims at prediction, and it leaves deep matters like the nature of the world to religion.

However, the classical formulation and discussion of the problem of appearance and reality was laid out nearly twenty-one centuries before Berkeley, and twenty-three centuries before movies by the greatest and most influential of all philosophers in the Western tradition, Plato of Athens. In his book *The Republic*, which is much concerned with the kind of thing the State should be, the sorts of duties it should undertake, Plato finds it necessary to solve in summary fashion both the problem of knowledge and the problem of existence, because these bear on the forms and content of education. He is particularly exercized to ensure that citizens of the Republic are immunized against both deception by appearances and superficiality of appearances. He did not think it was easy to buy this insurance. Indeed, he argued that it was possible only in a properly organized Republic. Only in a properly organized Republic was education carefully controlled for deception and superficiality and only in a properly organized Republic were those talented enough to recognize the difference between appearance and reality in positions of sufficient status and power to guard the rest against these evils.

Not only was Plato writing before movies, he was writing before science also. As noted before, the Greeks looked to mathematics for the kind of guidance and exemplar that we now seek from science. Yet, in the course of his discussions in *The Republic* Plato wonders how it is that we know the difference between appearance and reality, how it is that we build up a true picture of the world we inhabit. To highlight the problems we face he tries to imagine man's condition under systematic illusion or deception, such that the boundaries of what he sees and hears constitute the boundaries of his world. In the course of this he produces the simile of the cave, the most potent image of man's epistemological and ontological predicament in the whole of Western philosophical literature.

imagine men to be living in an underground cave-like dwelling place, which has a way up to the light along its whole width, but the entrance is a long way up. The men have been there from childhood, with their neck and legs in fetters, so that they remain in the same place and can only see ahead of them, as their bonds prevent them turning their heads. Light is provided by a fire burning some way behind and above them. Between the fire and the prisoners, some way behind them and on a higher ground, there is a path across the cave and along this a low wall has been built, like the screen at a puppet show in front of the performers who show their puppets above it.

– I see it.

– See then also men carrying along that wall, so that they overtop it, all kinds of artifacts, statues of men, reproductions of other animals in stone or wood fashioned in all sorts of ways, and as is likely, some of the carriers are talking while others are silent.

– This is a strange picture, and strange prisoners.

– They are like us, I said. Do you think, in the first place, that such men could see anything of themselves and each other except for shadows which the fire casts upon the wall of the cave in front of them?

– How could they, if they have to keep their heads still throughout life?

– And is not the same true of objects carried along the wall?

– Quite.

– If they converse with one another, do you think that they would consider these shadows to be the real things?

– Necessarily.

– What if their prison had an echo which reached them from in front of them? Whenever one of the carriers passing behind the wall spoke, would they not think that it was the shadow passing in front of them which was talking? Do you agree?

– By Zeus I do.

– Altogether then, I said, such men would believe the truth to be nothing else than the shadows of the artifacts?

– They must believe that.

(Plato, The Republic, trans. Grube)

Astounding though this anticipation of the cinema is, we must be careful in interpreting it. Plato was engaged in a thought-experiment that had a purpose. Its purpose was to show that if we imagine that the five senses are sources of knowledge we will have no defence against arguments from deception and superficiality. We may be like the prisoners in the cave mistaking shadows and echoes for real things. The world of appearance may be a delusion and totally different from the real or true world.

Source: *Random House Encyclopedia*

Figure 2.1: *Plato's Cave*

Naturally, in the course of twenty-three centuries of discussion, interpretations of Plato have abounded and so what follows has to be understood as not necessarily uncontroversial. Trying to pinpoint in a less metaphorical way the key property that knowledge of truth should have as opposed to delusive opinion Plato seems to have hit upon change. A truth, and hence knowledge, must be something that doesn't change, that is fixed once and forever. We may not at any point have full knowledge of the truth, but each piece that we acquire we acquire once and for all. The inspiration of mathematics is apparent here. All around us the world is in flux, but the truths of mathematics are fixed and eternal. Their fixed character does not at all preclude their relevance and application to the changing world, but does mark the difference between superficiality and depth, between deception and true insight.[1]

Plato's argument, then, is as follows. If you think we gain knowledge from our senses consider the possibility of a set-up that systematically deceives us. Would we then be able to see through the deception? His answer is, with the unaided senses, no. If we covet access to the truth, an access we call knowledge, the senses may be of use but they cannot be relied upon. His own answer, which need not delay us here, was that certain highly talented intellectuals, after long and rigorous training, could develop a capacity to 'see' the truth about things. Their input was essential if an edifice of delusion rather than knowledge was not to be built into the Republic's educational curriculum.

Let us notice now how close Plato comes to describing the experience of a film. Cinema-goers are not fettered, but they do concentrate their attention on the frontward source of light and sound and attempt to exclude 'distractions'. There is a single source of light above and behind them that casts shadows on the front wall. The shadows are artifacts, only some being reproductions of objects in the real world. Sounds are generated that appear to come from the direction of and hence out of the shadows. We are, then, re-enacting Plato's thought experiment every time we experience a film. Yet, as I have suggested, if one of our film-goers comes to 'believe the truth to be nothing else than the shadows of the artifacts' we wonder about their losing contact with reality. Sometimes we treat it seriously, if their capacity to function in our world is impaired; at other times we may indulge it as a harmless fantasy, no worse than hanging on to a teddy bear. Those whom Sklar (1975, ch. 8) calls the 'Guardians of Culture' have not always been sanguine. From the time films were first publicly exhibited down to the television-saturated times of today, these Guardians have worried that ordinary people will substitute the false reality of the films for the true reality of life in our world. At the very least people may take knowledge selectively from films, knowledge that conflicts with what are accepted as truths in the society at large. This was why the onscreen mores of film people were closely scrutinized and, when appropriate, censured by the Guardians. Films might suggest that fun rather than hard work was an appropriate aim in life; that the senior generation is not necessarily the wiser; that the upper class is not necessarily worthy of its status; that all of life's problems solve themselves if one can find true romantic love. Having done battle with the legacy of these Guardians in other works (1970, 1978a) I want to side-step them here.

'Guardians' of culture is an appropriate label, since Platonist elitism pervades our society. By Platonist elitism I mean the anti-democratic idea that insight into the true (and the good) is vouchsafed only a few individuals and it is the place of the rest of us to hearken unto them. Hence a small part of society's members arrogates to itself the position of passing judgment on the rest. My own view is somewhat different. The ordinary movie-goer, I have contended, routinely has no trouble in keeping in mind the difference between the real world and the film world. The film world, while enthralling and eagerly sought, is regularly dis-counted when life as it is is confronted. It is the Guardians whose contact with reality is shaky: they convince themselves that while they are not fooled, other, lesser creatures are.[2] Hence the others must be protected against themselves. (In the apocalyptic vision of Nathaniel West, for example, the deranged film-goers will eventually riot and tear apart those who displease them (West 1939; see also the film *The Day of the Locust* 1975). Some of us are more desirous of protection from the Guardians: *quis custodiet ipsos Custodes?*)

To make arguments of this kind against film the Guardians must have exposed themselves to a certain amount of film. And, one cannot but assume, they will have experienced a certain amount of everyday life. Whence then comes their delusion that some people (not themselves) are being deluded, or corrupted, or deranged by films? I fear the answer has to be that it comes from the artificial insulation of their lives from those of ordinary people. The man on the Clapham omnibus has a more mature and sophisticated adult discount of the film world than he is given credit for. This is probably to be explained by affluence and leisure. If movies are a pleasant interruption from an uncomfortable life full of pressing problems there will be little advantage to mistaking the film world for the real world. Rather the opposite advantage. The affluent and leisured intellectual, however, can allow his imagination full play during and after a film; he lacks that short sharp shocking return to the real world attendant upon earning a living by enervating labour.

Plato takes the argument one stage further. In the continuation of the passage quoted, he envisages one of the prisoners escaping and making his way painfully up towards the light, out of the cave. At first blinded, gradually his vision returns and he is able to apprehend the world of things the way they are, rather than as they seemed in the cave of shadows. Possessed now of compassion for his deluded fellow-prisoners he makes his way back into the cave and endeavours to persuade them as to how the world really is, and that what they know is only a shadow-world. Of course, Plato being a good scenarist, the escapee does not succeed; his account of the real world is taken as preposterous.

Plato's epistemological despair is thus very deep. Not only are ordinary people systematically deluded into taking shadows for things, appearances for reality, opinions for knowledge, they are also convinced of their own clear-sightedness. So only the rare individual will ever be able to crawl out of the cave and escape the world of delusive opinion. Only if those who know what the real world is like are put in charge of the education of the very young will they be able to free mankind of the fetters on its mind. One finds echoes of this attitude in discussions of the danger that movies present to the individual and society that begin as soon as they come to public attention (Sklar 1975; Jowett 1976; Jarvie 1978a).

This digression on the pervasive Platonism of so many who ruminate on film in our society aside, let me take up the principal assertion I want to defend: movies show that there is something wrong with the cave argument. Film-goers are regular attendees at Plato's cave. Yet only a sprinkling of them, those we call 'disturbed', treat the world they encounter there as other than imaginary.

It is easy to see what a spokesman for Plato would say. The people in the cave have been there all their lives and know nothing else. The film-goer is not confined but rather moves back and forth between an existence in the real world and visits to the world to be experienced from films. He thus keeps experiencing whatever differences there are between the real world and the film worlds and this enables him to discriminate between them. Such a reply on behalf of Plato is plausible, always assuming there are experiential differences at the interface between the real world and the film world. Suppose, then, that we are men of two worlds, moving effortlessly between the two. How do we manage to designate one as the real world, the other as unreal? Why would we not, on the cave analogy, come to regard both as parts of the real?

This is a serious conundrum, precisely because of what is often overlooked: the film world is in fact part of the real world. It is a fact of the real world that its inhabitants can subject themselves to sources of stimulation that give them a sense of entering another world organized on somewhat different principles. They do not cease to be real and their experience of the movie is real. So our problem thickens: how do we differentiate that part of this real world that is unreal and recognize it as such? It is not so much that we can shift back and forth between two adjacent worlds, but rather that we conceive of our real world as wholly incorporating or encompassing a sub-world that is as such real, but which creates in us the experience of inhabiting a world different from this one, a difference that is not real, not really there.

What I am arguing is that there is a sense in which we never leave the real world; cinema, chair, darkness, light, sound, are all quite real. Hence, in film-going, we do not in any literal sense move out of our real world and into an unreal one. What we do is to create real conditions in our real world that allow us in imagination to experience a world that we know, both cognitively and emotionally, not to be real. This makes the contrast argument less plausible as the means by which we mark and sustain the boundary between the real and the unreal.

Disposing of the contrast argument is not, however, enough. There is some sort of contrast between the real and the unreal worlds, which is not the cause of our being able to distinguish the two, but is rather the reason we want to cross over and why we enjoy doing so. Imagination, it seems to me, is a form of release from our cave-prison, a chance to alter the constraints of our world a little or a lot and to work out the consequences.[3] It is because we know that things in the real world are not altogether like those in the unreal world that the latter is so interesting. Were we unable to distinguish real from unreal, were it all homogenized, then the cave problem would hardly arise.

Here we are beginning to expose the hidden transcendental assumption that is built into Plato's simile of the cave. The people talking about it (Socrates and Glaucon in the dialogue) are detached observers, able to describe the human condition from the outside and hence to raise the question, are these people aware of their true condition, the real state of things? To obtain a cinematic parallel for the perspective of the cave simile we need to bring in the reflexive camera: the film-goer experiencing the film is himself now being filmed by a camera that is invisible. Why invisible? For the same reason that the men fettered in the cave cannot hear Socrates and Glaucon talking about them. If they could overhear, they would have a means of becoming aware of their true situation. If the film-goer noticed he was being filmed he would, on viewing the film, have a record of the true situation he was in during the elapsed real time that he allowed himself to be in the screen world.

The cave metaphor, then, makes no sense unless there are those standing outside able to be condescending towards those fettered. Is not perhaps the human epistemological condition in general like this? That is to say, is not the situation decisively changed, not by our being able to show that we are not fettered in the cave-prison of our senses, but by our raising and hence being aware of the possibility? We cannot dispose of the thought that we are subject to systematic delusion but, aware of the possibility, we can qualify all our claims to true knowledge and be vigilant to the possibility of correcting them.

Let us bring this back to film and film-going. They are an improvement on the simile of the cave because they reassure us that our epistemological predicament is not as the cave suggests, but rather as movie-going suggests. We are subject to illusions, some of them voluntary, others involuntary, but we are also aware of this danger which we confront not by agonizing about it but by playing with it. In being film-goers we tease ourselves constantly by imaginatively breaking out of and re-entering the real world, thus alerting ourselves to the possibility that what we naively think of as the real world may itself be a nested illusion inside some wider, real world. We know this because the enhancement of our imaginations by mechanical apparatus makes obvious the possibility of an infinitely nested and receding series of cameras filming cameras filming people.

My claim that film shows our epistemological predicament to be less dire than is suggested by the simile of the cave will not easily be accepted. The cave simile is by no means the only reason deployed by Platonists or indeed by idealists in their campaign to reject realism. Furthermore, my construction of film into an argument is not decisive. I have not proved realism; I have not disproved either Platonism or idealism. All this I would readily concede. At the start I made it clear that realism seemed to me a reasonable hypothesis which I would assume, and whose conse- quences I would then work out. A test of it would be whether the consequences were such that the assumption should be sustained. Were the consequences to take the form of insuperable contra- dictions and difficulties one might trace back the source of these contradictions and difficulties to the assumption of realism and hence reconsider, possibly even abandon, it. So far, however, no consequences remotely so grave have turned up.

By arguing from assumption I side-step the demands to prove realism or to disprove Platonism or idealism. These are tasks which, for philosophical reasons, I believe cannot be fulfilled. These doctrines are metaphysical and hence irrefutable; and no amount of verification proves them.[4] Instead of proof and disproof we can argue the plausibility and fruitfulness of what can be called the hypothetical realistic alternative. On the plausibility: consider the alternative. The possibility is that the entire claim to knowledge which we rest on the data of the senses, and hence the entire world and its contents constructed on that base, is a total illusion. Such a possibility may be uncomfortable to contemplate but it is in its turn a hypothesis or supposition. Whatever the difficulties of realism this alternative seems implausible. We would need strong reasons for accepting it rather than common-sense realism. On the fruitfulness: common-sense realism seems to underlie science, seems to make pretty good sense of the world, does not flounder in self-contradictory formulations, does not divide mankind into an 'insighted' elite, needed to guide, and the rest of us; in short, it is a fruitful basis for proceeding. These arguments, none of them conclusive, have, nonetheless, a certain weight.

If I am right, then thinking about film from a realistic point of view has made possible an interesting move. We have seen through the cave simile in a new way. The cave simile will not do its argumentative job because of the very fact that it can be posed: it presents us with two men, able to discuss the predicament of these prisoners in the cave, and to suppose that they themselves can distinguish, what the prisoners cannot, namely the real from the shadow world. Logically, Plato does make this point in passing when Socrates responds, 'they are like us', to the remark that these are 'strange prisoners'. In the reading of the simile in *The Republic*, however, and in the great bulk of discussion devoted to this image, the problem of the observer picturing this scene is not addressed. Films, which regularly show us situations at an intimate distance yet allow us to be invisible, alert us to this problem of framework. And defuse it at the same time.

We discuss Socrates discussing the prisoners in the cave; the regress exactly parallels an event, photographed for a film, and the viewer of the film being filmed. Is this regress vicious? That is, does our failure to cut it off render all our knowledge, the very sources of our knowledge, hopelessly suspect? That is, after all, what Plato wants the cave to achieve. How precisely does film prevent it? My answer is, if we toy with the boundary between appearance and reality we must have a certain confidence in our ability to handle it. We must, that is, feel sure there is little possibility of our being fooled. If the world on film, different as it is in so many respects from the one we inhabit, could infect our thinking and feeling in the real world, to such an extent that we acted inappropriately and dysfunctionally, would we be so sanguine about crossing and recrossing the boundary? Would we not rather shy away from it? Think of our behaviour in relation to severe sense illusions. The person lost in the desert does not toy with the mirage, knowing that the mirage may induce trekking in a direction that leads nowhere. Furthermore, films are a mass medium; it is ordinary people who so cheerfully pay to be fooled – and yet who are not for a minute fooled. They can master the art of crossing into and out of reality without the aid of elites.

Phenomenologically what I am saying amounts to this. The attraction of the film to the viewer/listener is not a case of delusion. It is voluntary illusion. It is not an escape into unreality, because there is a state of suspension of disbelief while the film unrolls that is very hard to describe in such simple terms as reality or fantasy, belief or disbelief, as we shall learn from Munsterberg. Rather is it this: films contain a potential seeming-world that can be entered voluntarily partly because of the way it contrasts with the real world. One might argue that films heighten our sense of, and sensitivity to, reality just because they differ from it so much. Contrast is one of our major means of mapping the features of the world. Without offering any grandiose suggestions about the function of imagination in general, I simply want to remark on its all-pervasiveness. Stories, day-dreams, dreams, drama, vary considerably in the degree to which they contrast with reality; that they exist, that we have them, makes them part of the real world. Yet they have this special proto-filmic quality of being worlds nested within the real world and hence usable to highlight its features, to mark its differences.

In sum, we can use film to face and face down the metaphysical problem of appearance and reality. How do we know we are not prisoners in the cave? Answer: we do not know; it is a hypothesis, a hypothesis we keep constantly before our mind by testing our sense of reality. By confronting ourselves, that is, playfully, with the seemingly real and thereby limning the boundary-line between the real and the unreal. This does not dispose of the problem, since every putative boundary between the real and the unreal is itself a hypothesis, a hypothesis needing constant test and, sometimes, serious revision. Whereas with movies we play with the boundary, in science we attack it, constantly changing the inventory of the things we treat as real and, as the maniac in *The Shining* wrote, 'all work and no play makes Jack a dull boy'.

3
THE GOLDEN MOUNTAIN, USDA APPROVAL AND REALISM

Let me restate my general claim. Watching and listening to films has philosophical importance. It is a contemporary re-enactment of Plato's cave. But the inhabitants of the cinema-cave are not prisoners; they are, to a considerable extent, pleasure-seekers. They use film as part of the process of coming to terms with and understanding the world they inhabit, knowing at some level that the world on film contrasts with the world off film. So film rebuts Plato's use of the cave to undermine the senses of the ordinary person as guides to knowledge. In fact it shows that ordinary people are very sophisticated in relation to the problem of appearance and reality. Unlike philosophers, they do not fear it and worry how to solve it. They solve it regularly and without fuss: they play with it.

Now to turn the tables somewhat, even though Platonists and idealists are no doubt far from being satisfied with the argument so far. Their views are metaphysical, they might say, and one cannot resolve metaphysical issues by analysing a mass medium. This is so. Indeed, it is questionable if one can resolve metaphysical issues. My aim in this book is to be suggestive, to open issues rather than to close them, to provide sketch maps not ordnance surveys, to start hares not shoot them. Up to this point a preference for the metaphysics of realism has been backed by a few reasons, but nothing sustained. Here is the reason why. Films can as easily be treated as troublesome for any traditional realism

56

as they can be support for it. Far from establishing or buttressing realism they jeopardize it. How so?

Most realisms are fairly naive sensationalisms. They proceed, that is, from the information flow from the five senses which they treat as a grounded base on which to erect claims to knowledge and to existence. Apart from the obvious point that this manoeuvre presumes what needs to be shown, films also dramatically exemplify the dilemma of the golden mountain. That dilemma arises as follows. There is in the world no mountain made of gold. There are, however, stories in which golden mountains feature. Question: does the golden mountain in the stories exist? If the answer is no, what is the reality-status of the story and the objects in the story and how do we discriminate Mt Gold from Mt Everest, especially as, depending on the storyteller, we may 'Know' more about the non-existent Mt Gold than about the all-too-real Mt Everest? If the answer is, 'yet it does exist', does that mean that the inventory of things in this world is, so to say, a double infinity: an open class containing all the reals and all the supposed reals of all time? And how will we classify, explain and understand all these supposed-real real objects: for they certainly, like the golden mountain, do not obey the laws of regular physical nature?

This issue has already been brought up in our discussions of film. Films exist as cans of celluloid if as nothing else. When the celluloid is projected those attending to it will not describe the contents of the projection as merely a jumble of flickering shadows and random sounds. Rather will they describe places, people, events, conversations, moods. If the film takes two hours to run, can we say that there were extra places, people and events in the universe during those two hours, and that they have now, the projection having ceased, disappeared? A hard-nosed realist might deny this. But then what sense could he make of film? Perhaps the following: for two hours there were projected images and sounds to be experienced in the world, projected images and sounds contained in potential form in the combination of the celluloid and the projection apparatus. Attended to in certain conditions these images and sounds fill the consciousness of someone experiencing them, reducing their sense of contact with the real world towards zero, but not to zero. The places, things, people and events such viewers would describe in their account of this experience are not real things, but imaginary things, mental things. The mental events are real, the celluloid and projection apparatus are real, but the apparent objects they contain are not there. They have no tangible physical existence; they do not obey the laws of nature; they are not present if the machinery is switched off or the film breaks. In the real world *ex nihilo nihil fit* and mass/energy is always conserved. Since film things, places, people and events do not behave this way we know they are not real. Their existence is an illusion.

To begin with, notice the weakness in the argument. It is not true that all film objects disobey the laws of nature. Did they do so much of their plausibility would be lost. Objects and people on film much of the time behave as do their counterparts in the real world. Again, to say 'what is on film does not affect the real world' is quite false. Films do affect the way people think and behave, perhaps only a little but not zero. Film things do not drop from the mind when the film stops. They may linger in thought and memory for as long as any other sensory stimulus. In this respect their impact upon us and the world may be clear and direct. It matters little if my fear of spiders was induced by seeing or touching one, being told fearful stories, or seeing them on film, I still react aversively and with revulsion. So, shadowy though the world of film may be, it enters into the causal chains of the real world. And enters, be it noticed, not so much in the manner of its production (by consuming electrical energy or celluloid chemicals), but in its content, what the shadows signify to the receiver. Films play on our mindscreen just as other things (real-world stimuli) play on our mindscreen and, since what we then think and do is a result of that play on our mindscreen, they are very much involved in the chains of events of the real world.

What has happened here? Has the argument gone astray? Are fantasy, imaginings, unreal things infecting the hard world of solid objects, real people and natural laws? Quite so. Film is an awkward matter for realists. One might even notice the desperate move in the hard-nosed case of suggesting that film events take place in the mind. If they do, then part of the world is in our mind, and realism collapses towards the solipsistic version of idealism. At the very least a realist wants events to be an interaction between real mental things and unreal film things.

However hard-nosed the realist philosophical position adopted, films pose some troubling questions. Sitting in a cinema and drowning one's senses in the stimuli produced by the film is a thought-experiment to freak-out sensationalists. Sensationalists resort to the senses as sources of knowledge because they argue these are our points of contact with reality. Our senses directly perceive the world. It is true that the form in which the information comes may need processing to become coherent and intelligible because the raw data may only be a jumble. Nevertheless, if the brain is to control our manoeuvres in the real world it must have sources of contact with that world. Ordinary sense-illusions are troublesome, but since they are usually transitory and can be checked by other lines of enquiry, such as using the hands to feel the stick that to the eyes looks bent in water, they do not pose an insuperable dilemma. Films, however, not unlike sensory deprivation experiments (the subject of at least two films – *The Mind Benders* 1963, and *Altered States* 1980), are not so easily disposed of. Such illusion as they create can be sustained for quite a long time. Some people – who we may declare abnormal – begin to treat the world on film as though it were the real world. The mechanisms by which film achieves its effects can only be exposed as deceptive if one has, as it were, the prior idea that they may indeed be deceptive, an idea that leads one to test for deception. This is as though one were to declare the senses not sources of knowledge *simpliciter*, but possible sources of knowledge that are contaminated and so are being checked. Whence comes the knowledge that the senses may be contaminated sources? Since the senses are seats of raw data that need processing, the knowledge that they are contaminated means that the processing must proceed with the special caution needed to avoid deception, so it seems as though that knowledge (of contamination) cannot itself come from the senses. Hence sense-knowledge is secondary, not primary. As it is being received there are already assumptions in place against which it is being checked.

This argument does not stem from the existence of films, any more than the existence of films creates the error in the cave simile that suppresses the crucial question of the point of view of the teller of the story, the camera. In both cases film, our use of it, and hence ability to reflect on it, draws attention to ways of looking at things, or strengthens and focuses certain ways of looking that can become general and powerful argumentative difficulties for, in this case, sensationalist realism. We might have dreamed up these arguments without films; it is much easier with them.

How, if at all, can a sensationalist circumvent the difficulties highlighted by films? What devices can be introduced to authenticate sense data as coming from the real world, and to de-authenticate sense data actually coming from films? Possibly some Berkeleyan arguments from the vividness, texture, force and such like might be made. The suggestion being that sense data from the real world carry these properties much as certain meats carry a United States Department of Agriculture Grade A stamp, whereas film-generated sense data will not. Besides the objection to this already made in the previous paragraph, that it violates the basic canon of sensationalism that all knowledge comes through the senses, it is, unless very carefully phrased, even then a weak answer. All that is required to rebut it is a strengthening of the film thought-experiment, namely imagine film sense data that carry the USDA Grade A stamp; if sense data in general can be simulated by films, then any special or authenticated sense data can also be simulated.

Notice how subjectivist the argument has become. Because films simulate sense data, the question becomes, can we subjectively discriminate between true and false sense data? Even when it is suggested that the sense data may bear upon their face the USDA Grade A authentication stamp, that functions to assist our subjective discrimination by declaring it has an objective source. Sensationalists, hoping to be hard-nosed realists in direct sensual contact with the external world, end up, as Bertrand Russell (1927, ch. 37; 1940, ch. 8) was the first to notice, falling into one or another kind of idealism.

For those content with idealism this is of course no argument. Hence, when earlier dealing with Plato's so-called 'objective idealism', different arguments were used. The immediately preceding paragraphs tackling empiricism or sensationalism offered different arguments to expose the closeness of sensationalism to subjective idealism. Now to address a full-blown subjective idealism, although most of its adherents would rigorously deny that characterization, namely phenomenology. It is not my intention here to expound this in much detail; that will come later when discussing some of the phenomenological philosophers of film. It will suffice to make some parallels between the problems of sensationalism and the problems of phenomenology. In a way this has already been done. Faced with the delusive dilemma posed by the film experience, the natural move for the sensationalist is phenomenological: to hope that the sense data from the world will differ phenomenologically from the sense data from films. The slight difference would be the following. A sensationalist would hope to discover the USDA Grade A stamp already on the meat of the sense data. So his task is scrutiny of the sense data for a property they have been given out there in the world. The phenomenologist, by very subtle contrast, subjectifies the task. He scrutinizes the data of consciousness, with his consciousness, to decide where he will place the stamp. Data then do not come self-authenticated but must be authenticated by the reflective consciousness, a process Husserl goes into in complicated detail.

So complicated is pure phenomenology that very few of us can follow it to the extent of confidently offering criticisms that we can be sure do not involve misunderstandings. 'Phenomenology' is one of the buzz words of twentieth-century philosophy, to be used with a caution little short of avoidance. Husserl himself saw phenomenology as turning Cartesian doubt in the right direction (1960, Chapter 11) towards an unprejudiced intuition of those features of any given object without which it could not properly be said to be the object it is (Schmitt 1968, p. 139). Phenomenology engages in a process of articulating our intuitive recognition of phenomena, seeming to presuppose that what we are reflecting on is an external world containing other people. This, at least, is what I make of it, but I know of no arguments attributable to Husserl that help put to rest the sort of doubts raised by Plato's cave. Phenomenologists say they are scientific but not empirical; they scrutinize the data of consciousness to ground knowledge.

Films intrigue phenomenologists partly because they embody forms of free imaginative variation and bracketing of existence. Yet there is also a deeper attraction. Films are 'new', and arguably are 'phenomena', hence, in addition to being heuristic aids to reflecting on the phenomena they portray (people, things, etc.), they also present a challenge to be themselves subjected to phenomenological scrutiny. We can ask, 'what makes a film?', and proceed to add or delete predicates in a proposed description and see if the amended description still describes a film.

In this way we discover the necessary and invariant features of

a given kind of thing that the example must possess in order to be
an example of that kind of thing. We also discover which
features are accidental and hence irrelevant to the question
whether this object, as described, is or is not an example of a
certain kind of thing. What we discover is what
phenomenologists call the 'essence' of objects (Schmitt 1968,
p. 141).

As we shall see later in discussing Linden, the phenomenon which
is most intriguing to phenomenologists is the experience of
watching a film, as opposed to the experience of inhabiting the
Lebenswelt, or the experience of going to a theatre, the experience
of listening to music, and so on. Less kindly put, one could make
this point: unless the phenomenon of film can be discovered to
have an essence different from the phenomenon of experience in
general then phenomenology will be unable to discern a difference
between the real world and the film world.

My present concern is with the problem of appearance and
reality and the help or hindrance we get with this problem from
films. It seems to me that the idea that there are essences, whether
those essences are of universals to be specified in Aristotelian
definitions or of phenomena to be articulated in phenomenological
statements, is unhelpful.

None of us disagrees that there is a real world and a film world and
that the latter differs from the former in that it is imaginary. None
of us disagrees that the latter in some ways simulates the former
and hence creates illusion. But since we know they are different
there is a temptation to think there must be a core, a centre, an
essence of that difference. There must be some basic structure to
our experience of the real world that marks it as different from our
experience of film. Why must there be? Whence the necessity? To
explain, obviously, why we agree that there is a difference
between films and the world. What makes things different in
experience? Not merely some idle or contingent matter; for many
things that are fundamentally similar have minor or superficial
differences. But no difference is more basic and obvious than that
appearances are not the same as reality, films are not the world. So
if we recognize that there is a basic difference between the real
world and the seemingly-real world of the films we must penetrate
beyond the appearances of difference (or the appearances of

similarity, for that matter) to the essence of each, which, we assume, we will then find to be clearly different. Films thus confront the phenomenologist with the problem of appearance and reality.

Not all of the foregoing argument is plausible, in my view. Trying to solve the problem of knowing true from false sense data by asserting there is some essential, hidden and deep difference can, looked at closely, seem highly verbal. Simply a form of affirming that there is a difference – a table-banging argument. The whole issue is, is there a difference? To answer that there is by shouting is not very impressive.

Sensationalists are usually by conviction realists; phenomenologists fudge and redefine the issue but certainly do not want to be classed as idealists – usually because they see themselves as working on problems in the philosophy of Kant, who was himself accused of conceding to idealism (see section 7.24 below). I have declared myself a realist of a different kind, not a sensationalist, rather a critical realist. Is it not possible to turn film against this position also and create the same kinds of doubts as against sensationalist realism and phenomenology? It is not, I would hold. Critical realism adopts a different stance in relation to the issues, one that does not leave it so vulnerable.

How does a critical realist deal with the Golden Mountain? Mainly by not being dogmatic. If we are interested in whether there 'is' a Mt Gold we look for tests. What, for example, are its geographical coordinates? How would a mountaineer describe it? A critical realist employs empirical data, not as the sensationalist basis of his answers, but as tests of assertions. Basing ourselves on the metaphysics of a real world that can manifest itself to the senses in myriad ways, we test for its features by thinking through manners in which it will present itself to the senses, and hence allow us some access to its reality.

Perhaps I could crystallize the critical realist position thus: if the problem is, how do we know there is a, and how do we recognize the, difference between real-world data and film world data, the answer would be: we do not. Critical realism is appealing partly because it takes the problems posed by films seriously. To take a problem seriously is to acknowledge that it is a genuinely troubling matter. Not taking a problem seriously is to assume at once there is an answer and the only 'problems' are working out its details.

Until, it seems to me, we become aware of the assumption of point of view in the cave simile and the film process, until that point it is entirely possible that there is no solution to the question of whether there are discernible differences between the real world and the film world and, if there are, to the problem of how we recognize them. There may be no differences, or there may be differences which are inaccessible, and so no matter.

Once, however, we see how to pose the problem as in the cave discussion, or how to be a camera with its shutter open, literally or figuratively, we make a crucial breakthrough in setting up the problem, and can leave solving it for detailed discussion. But the breakthrough gives us a well-based hope that the problem is soluble. If we consider the attempts to recognize and sustain the difference between the real world and the film world we can also be critical as well as realistic. A critical realist can hold that, since the problem is very difficult, any proposed solution may eventually succumb to critical argument, be shown to be wanting in some way. The assumption that there *is* an essential difference, that it is the philosopher's task to pinpoint it once and for all, can be jettisoned.

What the critical realist has is a hypothetical position: assume that there is a difference between the real world and the film world, in what can this consist and how can it be detected? Sensationalist answers can be found wanting as either assuming or inviting prewrapped solutions to the problems they are supposed to be solving. Phenomenological answers can be essayed, assayed and found wanting because of their subjectivity: consciousness becoming its own criterion of the entities it is conscious of. We may be left with no very decisive answer. We have, after all, the case of those who are totally deluded by film, who take it as an extension of the real world, or who even substitute it for the real world. Most of us who are regularly exposed to a lot of films, for whom experiencing them is part of our real lives, undoubtedly engage in a good deal of feedback with them. We may even from time to time have the odd memory of an event and be phenomenologically quite unsure whether we experienced it, were told it, dreamt it or saw it in a film.

Needing, however, some rough and ready means to mark the difference, we work out our own ways, and we *play* with them: we cross back and forwards over a slippery terrain trying not to lose our balance. Notoriously, balancing on a slippery surface is learned yet is so subtle it can only be mastered by practical experience. Could it be that way with films? Perhaps critical realism is the common position of most people who are rarely, if ever, deluded by film, but who are not unaware of the possibility. By doing it and by constantly checking on ourselves, we solve it.

4

FILMS AND ACADEMIC PHILOSOPHY

Two central philosophical problems are the problems of knowledge and the problem of being; it is possible to argue that each is prior to the other, and it has been argued in the previous sections of this chapter that films bear in various ways on these problems and these problems bear in various ways on films. From the point of view of knowledge, films highlight sharply the issue of appearance versus reality, providing difficulties both for objective idealism and for naive sensationalist realism. From the point of view of existence or being, films restate the problem of the Golden Mountain, are a troublesome case since they are concrete physical objects which somehow also 'contain' meaningful content 'in' which there are (non-existent) objects, people, events. Furthermore, some of the things films contain were once, or are still, real; others have never existed in any other form than that seen on the screen. Descartes believed that the way to solve the problem of existence was to ask of every seeming-thing whether its existence could be doubted. He found that it was logically possible to do so for most things, even for his own self. So it looked to him as though, if there were a God, that God had made a world and put in it a creature such that the world was capable of systematic deception of man. This scenario struck Descartes as unlikely, since it was inconsistent with the properties of God. So, if he could prove there must be a God, which he did to his own satisfaction, then he could argue that even though it was logically possible to doubt his own existence it was not possible to attribute to God systematic deception. Hence, I think therefore I am, and God assures me that that move is sound. From this certain foundation in thought, Descartes rebuilds the world and our knowledge of it.

Without going so far as to say, I watch films therefore I am, we can play with its variations. The existence of films makes possible this question: How can I be sure that the world is not just a film, and that my watching films is only a nested version of that predicament? One answer to this could come from the late François Truffaut. In his film *La Nuit Américaine* (*Day for Night*, 1973), which is about making films, and in which he plays the role of the film's director, he asks the question, are films more important than life? His answer is a very clear – yes! Operating on this premise, the question of how can I be sure life is not just a film seems to be answered by saying, I cannot be sure, but let us hope it is.

Joking aside, I have in the text so far referred mainly to philosophers writing about the major philosophical questions without reference to film – Plato, Berkeley, Descartes. This was not done in order to claim that I have discovered the relevance of film to philosophy and will now pioneer the subject. Quite a few philosophers have written about film, in several languages. Yet there is no coherent sub-field, 'philosophy of film'. If I regard myself as a pioneer it will be in making the attempt to render philosophy of film a coherent sub-field. The way to do this most directly is to provide an overall structure for the field and to show how, within that, there are certain persisting intellectual problems which have given rise to rival solutions and lines of debate between these rival solutions. This is the way to get an intellectual map of the field, to 'place' different people's work in relation to the features of that map, and hence render their efforts coherent.

It is not that this task is such a difficult one, merely that it has been neglected. Hence writings in the philosophy of film tend to be scattered in diverse places, to be written by diverse people and hence stand against diverse backgrounds and assumptions (not to mention the chronic problem of the citation of diverse arrays of films as argumentative props). Such writing as there is tends to be dominated by phenomenology, usually phenomenology treated as a kind of idealism, something Husserl would not have acknowledged. A critical realist feels very isolated venturing forth. His normal allies in studies in science are positivists who usually have no place in their scheme of things for art. Those interested in art flirt with idealism,[1] and display woeful ignorance of science.[2] Most noticeable of all is that there are very few debates, and a large amount of writing that makes no reference to other, earlier writing and so gives very few markers for assessing whether the subject is making intellectual progress.

One conspicuous exception to this generalization about lack of debate is the theorizing about film that is usually classed as structural/Marxist/semiotic. Much of this stems from the Parisian intellectual milieux, in which there is a long tradition of philosophizing about film. French philosophy is dominated by the Cartesian, Hegelian, Heideggerian approach, which elevates the problem of existence/being above that of knowledge. The injection of Marxist and other ideas, usually treated as only marginally philosophy in the Anglo-Saxon world, has resulted in this line of thought and debate segregating itself and conducting intense internal struggles about small and large issues, while failing to engage in debate those philosophical positions that object to the premises of the tradition.[3]

It is noticeable that the English-speaking adherents of this French thought come primarily from literary studies. They shun and are shunned by their philosophical colleagues in the English-speaking world. The attraction is clear, French philosophers being quite reluctant to acknowledge any decisive boundary between their own discourse and those of politics, literature and social science. Hence they integrate closely with new work in literature and the arts. Such philosophy grants freedom to talk of existentialism, structuralism, post-structuralism, semiotics, Marxism, psychoanalysis and deconstruction.[4]

This discontinuity between French philosophizing in general, and that film theorizing influenced by it in particular, creates a problem when the approach is from another tradition, as is the case with the present book. Other things being equal, a tradition which vigorously encourages criticism and debate is one to be admired and engaged. But when the tradition has flagrant contradictions between the positions of its heirs, one may wish to stay clear. Some of the Marxism seems to stem from an idealist outlook, blissfully unaware that Marx was a materialist; some of it from materialism; the latter will often proclaim Marxism a scientific approach, indicating science as a positive value; the former more naturally displays a hostility to science and an anti-scientific approach. Even more serious for the fruitfulness of rational debate is the tendency to identify the self with the ideas: to write 'as a Marxist'. This says both that Marxist premises are outside the discussion and that non-Marxists need not listen.

Rationalist philosophy need not hold anything beyond discussion. It is about as appropriate to 'be a Marxist' when theorizing about film as it is to 'be a Lutheran'. Such designations can only mean commitment to ideas. Commitment raises another major objection. Philosophy as a rational enterprise strives to be open-minded and to proceed by reason. Commitment to any premise is to put it beyond the reach of reason. This, I believe, creates unnecessary difficulties for intellectual engagement.

So much for the intention behind this look at the academic literature. Theological discussions between *rive gauche* Marxists about films will be eschewed except where they throw up points of general interest. As for the rest, I shall centre discussion on two books with passing reference to others and to articles, the great bulk of which proceed as though predecessors and others did not exist. My aim will be to bring them to terms with one another by extending my framework around them, to show where they can be construed as arguing with one another without knowing it, or where they should be arguing with one another did they but know it. It may be that the participants have been unable themselves to map and make coherent this field because they were confused about it and their own position. I will not press that or any other diagnosis. Aetiology will not provide a framework. Although my framework may appear to be imposed, its status is hypothetical. It is a means of organizing and making coherent a lot of writing that should, I believe, be a literature. It will succeed not to the extent that it is accepted, but to the extent that it provokes questions and dissent that shows its weaknesses and so encourage the endeavour to replace it with a more comprehensive and better framework.

4.1   MUNSTERBERG

One philosopher, and one philosopher only, has an excuse for not engaging in debate, not referring to predecessors or contemporaries, but simply getting on with rumination on his problems. That philosopher is the first to write on these topics. Being the first, he has no intellectual obligations to others, since they do not exist. That figure in the philosophy of film is Hugo Munsterberg. Munsterberg's *The Photoplay: A Psychological Study* was published in 1916. It addresses the central epistemological and ontological questions raised by film. Its author was a distinguished member of the Harvard philosophy department. Fifty-four years later, another member of the Harvard philosophy department, Stanley Cavell, also published a short monograph on the ontological and epistemological questions raised by the film: *The World Viewed* (1971). Remarkably, Cavell nowhere mentions, still less discusses, his predecessor. Two other monographs, by George Linden (1970) and Paul Weiss (1975), will be discussed in this part; neither acknowledges any debt to, or even interest in, Munsterberg. Yet those who have written about Munsterberg (Wicclair 1978; Frederickson 1973; Andrew 1976) have found him prescient and full of insight, despite radical changes in films since his time (sound, colour, widescreen). How to explain this? One obvious answer would be that the writers publishing in the 1970s were interested in different things than Munsterberg and saw no sense in addressing his work. If the difference was considerable, a word to that effect would have been in order. So few people have addressed this field that a scholar would want to signal his lack of connection with anyone as much as his debts to others. But basically this explanation is not true. Cavell (and Linden and Weiss) both overlap with, and proceed further down paths begun by, Munsterberg. One might even try to make a case that Munsterberg did much of it better: clearly, succinctly and unpretentiously.

First of all, who was Munsterberg? That is, what prompted a Harvard philosopher to write a monograph about films? Munsterberg was a German psychologist and philosopher of some distinction who was recruited to the Harvard 'philosophical' department by the even more distinguished philosopher/psychologist William James (Hale 1980). The question of the relation of psychology to philosophy must be addressed at once. Intellectually and departmentally there was at that time no boundary between the two subjects. The mind was then, as it still is now, a central topic in philosophy. However, in those days the experimental and scientific study of the mind was taken to be continuous with philosophical reflection about it and hence was carried out by the same persons. The common root of philosophy of mind and of psychology in Kant's categorial apparatus was acknowledged. Nowadays many philosophers do not consider empirical work relevant to their entirely conceptual concerns, although they read a certain amount of psychology for its results. Psychologists who seek to become 'behavioural scientists' treat Kant as prehistory (Leary 1982).

Historians of philosophy would classify Munsterberg with the label 'neo-Kantian' both as philosopher and psychologist and this also needs a little explication. Kant was a philosopher of knowledge rather than of existence. Indeed, ontologists since Kant have had to tackle his devastating argument that there is little to be said about the way things really are – things-in-themselves – because there are epistemological arguments to show that that realm is in principle closed to us. Crudely put, and avoiding all Kant's apparatus and terminology, he could be construed as arguing like this. His predecessors in philosophy had argued one of two positions: either the world impresses itself on an empty mind (empiricism); or the mind contains within it pre-existing knowledge that makes sense of the world (rationalism). Kant tried to show that both models of the mind-world relationship break down. Empty minds cannot make sense of what comes in; pre-existing knowledge need have nothing to do with the world. What he proposed instead was an interaction model in which the mind comes partially prepared to classify and digest the information it receives from the outside world. The result is our knowledge of the world we inhabit. If, however, the question is raised as to whether the way we classify and act on the information is correct, that is, corresponds in some way to the way things ultimately are, the answer is not that we do not know but that we cannot know. The undifferentiated manifold of experience, things beyond our interaction with them, is a closed topic. We can but do our best with our given apparatus.

None of Kant's followers, never mind his critics, were too happy with his 'Copernican revolution' in philosophy, and they have been trying to unpick it ever since. In one way or another philosophers have tried to dispose of the unsolvable problem of a transcendental thing-in-itself and substitute an immanent thing-in-itself, one somehow present or potentially in the here-and-now.

71

Neo-Kantianism is a rather diffuse body of thought that divides roughly into two camps over whether to locate the immanent thing-in-itself in cultures, which will relativize it; or in the mind, and especially its basic ways of organizing information, as the thing-in-itself. Since we know the world only through our minds, the structures of our mind are the ultimate structures of our world. This does not lead to 'the world is my dream' solipsism. On the contrary, the structures of the mind are subject to empirical exploration and test. If, being quick on the uptake, we ask whether such a metaphysical realism towards the mind and the world is not presupposed rather than shown to be the case, the answer has to be 'yes it is'. One might say this is the problem of neo-Kantianism: how to ground the exploration of the mind so as to avoid the possibility that this activity is not in principle caught on the horn's of Kant's dilemma.

Munsterberg was very excited about film for a clear reason: he believed that films replicate in an external realm (outside the mind) the workings of the mind. Hence they give an unrivalled opportunity to study and test our ideas about the mind and they perhaps show us that the mind is capable of differentiating reality from illusion. It follows, in some way or other, that solipsism is false and that the structures of the mind are the terminating point for the quest for things in themselves.

Such a summary is bold as well as crude. Munsterberg did not quite manage to come out and say these things. But after we have looked closely at what he did say, I think this interpretation will take on a good deal of plausibility. Hooked into genuine problems of the philosophical tradition, Munsterberg's being intrigued by film was not slumming or casual, but intellectually serious: he saw there ways of approaching his major intellectual preoccupations. In writing the book he stressed other matters of more interest to his audience. Characteristically, Munsterberg wrote in two modes: a lengthy and scholarly mode for his peers; and a crisp popular mode applying psychology for the ordinary person.[5] *The Photoplay: A Psychological Study* is in the latter mode perhaps because he felt that, important though films were, his sense of their importance was esoteric and there were other senses in which they were important that would suffice to make his case that they should be taken seriously. We have only this one text to go by. Munsterberg was horriby split by the emotions of the Great War, especially as popular anti-German sentiment grew. He died suddenly in 1916, while lecturing, aged only fifty-three.

There are three sections to Munsterberg's monograph: an Introduction, followed by Part I, 'The Psychology of the Photoplay' and Part II, 'The Esthetics of the Photoplay'. I shall delay discussion of Part II until my own Part II, where I shall consider film in the context of the philosophy of art. At this stage I want to concentrate on films as a psychological/philosophical problem.

Munsterberg's aim, he confessed in the last paragraph of the work, was to prove the shallowness of the idea that films are unreal, commonplace and possibly a source of social corruption. On the contrary, he held the film to be a new art form with enormous but as yet barely realized potential. Thus his argument proceeded in this manner. The Introduction first sketched the 'outer' or technological development of the medium, as an extension of the ancient quest to reproduce movement in pictures. Secondly, the Introduction sketched the 'inner' development of the medium which consisted in the gradual realization that it was a new and independent art, not a version of, or substitute for, the stage, but a medium depending for its effect upon 'entirely new mental life conditions'. Part I then took up the explication of these mental life conditions and Part II drew out the aesthetic implications.

In a few short pages Munsterberg summarized the nineteenth-century history of toys and machines that reproduced movement. These were the 'outer' or technological developments of moving pictures. The impulse he saw behind them was scientific curiosity. It was scientists and inventors from Faraday to Muybridge who did the work. They seem not to have been consciously seeking anything like our present medium of mass entertainment and art. Perhaps the principal scientific impulse was to analyse and understand movement itself. Much movement in nature takes place either too slowly or too quickly for the unaided eye, so time-lapse and high-speed photography makes them accessible to our vision. Muybridge, for example, although Munsterberg does not mention this, settled with his photographs the long-standing dispute as to whether all four of a horse's hooves were ever off the ground together (they were).

In beginning with the mechanics of the medium Munsterberg was putting in place a very important component of his argument.

The technology of films owed very little to the stage and this paved the way for his later points that it took some time for the aesthetic-expressive potential of the new medium to become clear, and for the nature of its mental life conditions to become analysable. It has become a characteristic feature of textbooks about movies written since Munsterberg that they too begin with a section on motion picture technology, which is as though textbooks on poetry began with discussions of how people produce sounds and what sounds mean. The technology of pencil and paintbrush, or of chisel, is not normally addressed in books about painting or sculpture. Whereas Munsterberg's section had a clear place in his argument, it is hard to see what implicit question the technology section answered in subsequent books. If it is, 'How do motion pictures work?', it is easy to imagine the reader interested in films who replies, 'who cares?'. To appreciate a Leonardo, it is not necessary to know how it is done; why should 'how it is done' sections be part of film textbooks? The most obvious answer, and one I believe to be fraught with philosophical difficulties, is that technology can be used to demarcate film from theatre and the other arts: an art form's essence can be located in its technology. Careful exposition, development and critique of this thesis will also be more appropriate in Part II.

A less obvious answer would be this. Whereas in school we learn to write, to draw, to paint, and to shape, we do not (or did not) learn to photograph. The older art media are familiar to us from practice, the movies are not. Many are the families with snapshot cameras; very few of them know how to develop and print. This unfamiliarity is still greater with home movies, which almost no amateur develops and very few cut and rearrange. Hence those opening pages of textbooks about films may be no more than demystifying handbooks.

The inner development of moving pictures, Munsterberg allowed, consists in the dawning of an aesthetic idea: movies are an autonomous medium. The dawning of this realization breaks slowly. Topical events were the most obvious of subjects, but their novelty paled after a while. The life of nature was another obvious subject and thence a bold step to the illustrated magazine on the screen. But the chief road of advance was to democratize and cheapen the theatre. Despite being no more than 'the shadow of a true theatre' many plays were filmed. But films could be photographed in real settings, could flit instantaneously from scene to scene, and films allow the eye to track characters as they go from place to place. It is easy to splice scenes together so that we seem to observe what is going on at several places simultaneously. And beginning with slow cranking and fast cranking there develops the whole barrage of trick effects, some humorous, some dramatic, that are available only to films. And finally the development of the close-up, the ability to direct audience attention to detail, leads Munsterberg to the conclusion that it is a new art which ought to be acknowledged as independent of the theatre.

Munsterberg was aware that this is only preliminary. It would be easy to reply to him that despite these differences, films are not more than an enhanced form of the theatre; they are, after all, narrative dramas. This explains why he decided to rest his case not on these differences but on a totally new analysis of the 'mental life conditions' that made movies possible. He constructed a powerful argument to show that films are something utterly and excitingly new, a development of great interest not only to the aesthete, but also to the philosopher/psychologist. Although his book was popularizing, his argument was not simple and it has, I think, yet to be surpassed.

Before plunging into his Part I, a point or two about 'inner' development. It is important, I suspect, to accept his point that there was no destiny towards which nineteenth-century science and technology was working. The motion picture is not an endpoint to which its various sources are successive approximations. There was no hidden hand at work moving us along to reach movies, anymore than there is now a hidden hand moving us into television and through that to two-way interactive cable television. Similarly, there was no necessity to the discovery that film had aesthetic as well as informative and educational potential.

There is a dimension – both inner and outer – that is missing from Munsterberg's account of the rise of moving pictures. This is the social dimension. That he had a clue about it we can discern from his remark that it was cheaper to record a playlet on film and reproduce it many times than it was to stage it many times, and because it could be marketed cheaply it could democratize, make theatrical material available to many more people. The traditional arts have an elitist cast that was maintained in different ways. The barrier of literacy excluded many from reading poetry or novels, and made them customers for story-tellers. The cost of hiring players or musicians excluded many from those arts, as did the price of tickets when they became available to the public. Strolling players who begged, and religious performers for which one made offerings, were readier of access. Certain kinds of folk arts and crafts, which may not at the time have been categorized as aesthetic, rather, practical, served some aesthetic needs.

Society was changing very rapidly in the industrialized countries towards the turn of the nineteenth century. Factory and office work was drawing the population towards towns and cities, and this pressure was creating housing densities without much space for recreation or leisure. Just as space was more intensely used, so was time. Factory work operated not by the seasons but by the clock. Longish and regular hours created pressure for entertainment to be available immediately work stopped. This was the economic space into which mass entertainment was merchandized. It relieved the tired worker of the effort, it was inexpensive, it was available at the right time, it took place in a space of its own and it did not require skills or the collaboration of family or friends. If we consider the social situation of the newly urbanized masses, we can see how these social factors, external to moving pictures, also called forth another inner development, namely realizing the potential of this medium to cater to these needs. In order to be more precise we need the terminology of the economist. Whatever the 'needs' of the urbanized masses, they demonstrated a 'demand' for moving pictures by showing willingness to pay to see them, and to do it on a scale that surprised even those who went into the business, making the shrewder ones rich probably beyond their wildest dreams (Jarvie 1982).

This socio-economic argument should be set beside the aesthetic one. The idea is to avoid imagining that the movies discover their potential to realize D. W. Griffith's *The Birth of a Nation* and thus make art available to the masses. That teleology avoids the question of why the masses wanted art, why their previous modes of passing time and enjoying themselves were not sufficient. Perhaps they were sufficient. So let me phrase the question more carefully. The problem is, given that people had ways of spending their leisure time before they were offered moving pictures, why is it that when moving pictures were offered they switched their allegiance of time and money in that direction sufficiently to encourage entrepreneurs to offer more? My reasoning is that either their previous ways of utilizing their leisure time were not entirely satisfactory in the newly developing environment and way of life, or, that movies were not just a substitute for what had gone before but an improvement that displaced what went before when set in competition with it.

Sociology, then, comprises both inner and outer development. Social conditions had to make space, as it were, for the moving pictures, and the moving pictures had to be found suitable to, and capable of moving into, that available social space. Marxists go further and make all this a matter of necessity – when society needs or has use of some device that in itself will call forth its invention. This strikes me as largely verbal, since counter-examples can be dismissed by saying the 'need' was not strong enough or it was hidden. Living creatures have 'needs'; abstractions like society do not; human beings have needs but we do not know what they are. We do know what it is they 'demand'. Hence I stick to that.

Turning in his Part I to the psychology of the photoplay, Munsterberg set out to understand the mental means by which moving pictures impress us and appeal to us. What psychological factors are involved when we watch the happenings on the screen? He enquired into six topics: depth and movement; attention; memory and imagination; and emotions. Much of what he wrote remains fresh and thoughtful. Astonishingly, the Andersons (1980) report that, 'Little research has been done specifically with motion pictures, even in psychology (until very recently)' (p. 84). Warning the reader uninterested in physiological psychology to skip, Munsterberg launched into a careful distinction between the 'flat still pictures' of the photoplay and the three-dimensional 'plastic objects of the real world which surrounds us'. This lead him to a sharp conceptual distinction between objects of our knowledge and objects of our impression. Sitting in the cinema, he contended, 'We have no right whatever to say that the scenes which we see on the screen appear to us as flat pictures' (p. 19). He compared the problem to using the stereoscope. When we look through it at the two slightly different pictures side by side 'we cannot help seeing the landscape in strongly plastic forms', even though, 'we know very well that only two flat pictures are before us. . . . We feel immediately the depth of things' (p. 20). Whenever the eye is offered such pairs of views the mind must combine them into the impression of substance. Since knowledge of the flat character of pictures in no way excludes the actual perception of depth,

> the question arises whether the moving pictures of the photoplay, in spite of our knowledge concerning the flatness of the screen, do not give us after all the impression of actual depth. (p. 20)

Arguing that the impression of depth is created by a number of factors – apparent size, perspective relations, shadows and movements – Munsterberg compared the screen to a glass plate in front of an area of real space. Just as, looking through such a plate we would have the impression of depth continuing beyond it, so do we as we gaze at the screen.

> The photoplay is therefore poorly characterized if the flatness of the pictorial view is presented as an essential feature. That flatness is an objective part of the technical physical arrangements, but not a feature of that which we really see in the performance of the photoplay. (p. 22)

Yet films do not trade in illusion, *'we are never deceived; we are fully conscious of the depth, and yet we do not take it for real depth'* (p. 23). How so? Well, for one thing, he argued, if we sit to the side of the centre line there is a nagging slight distortion. For another thing the size of the frame and the whole setting are strong reminders. But, above all, there is the fact that we are looking at a screen. Hence both our eyes receive identical impressions and we have simultaneously to look at the surface and through the surface, just as when looking at our reflection in a mirror.

Here I want to interpolate an aside. It is not quite accurate for Munsterberg to write of the two eyes receiving identical impressions. Because we use two eyes, and because we usually are at an angle to the screen (most seats are both to one side of the centre line and either looking up or looking down at the screen), there are obviously slight differences between what reaches each eye. This may be idiosyncratic, if we are to judge by people's widely varying preferences for where to sit in an auditorium. Phenomenologically, my own observation is that all the apparent depth is in recession from the surface of the screen. That is, it is as though we were looking through plate glass into a real space. Three-dimensional movies enhance the plasticity somewhat, but their shock value comes from the limited-use property of being able to project that sense of plasticity forward: through the screen surface out towards the audience.

Moreover, the truly decisive addition that must be made to Munsterberg's analysis of depth is the use of sound. There are countless ways in which sound can contribute to and enhance the impression of depth and plasticity. By adjusting volume levels, echo, clarity of voice and sound effect the work of the eye is greatly assisted in building a plastic impression. All this utilizing only the one master speaker behind the screen. Some theatres are equipped for, and some films utilize, sound sources all around the auditorium. A relatively uninteresting film, *Earthquake*, was sometimes shown in theatres with special, very large rumble speakers at the back of the auditorium. During the earth tremor sequence, powerful low frequency rumbles were pumped through these sources, shaking the air and possibly the nearby seats to enhance the trembling image on the screen.

As I have argued earlier, it seems to me that we make a correction to such effects, both simultaneously – as Munsterberg allows – since there is interference of the single image and the angled screen surface, and also continuously over the long term. For example, the fright produced by the 'earthquake' rumbles does not linger. If it were to do so our ability to continue being drawn into the action of the motion picture would be spoiled. What happens is that we 'get over' the enhanced sense very rapidly, possibly by attending to our own reactions. This Munsterberg overlooks. If we jump, or scream, or cry in the theatre (laughing is another matter), our surroundings impinge upon us very rapidly, possibly because of slight changes of body position that remind us that we are seated onlookers not genuinely involved participants. Such a reminder offers a calming reassurance that we are suspending our disbelief, not witnessing actual events. The lingering tendency to cry after a film is over is not a counter-example; it may be explained by the film ceasing to offer us any source of distraction and so regaining our composure takes a little time. All this seems to me important to our enjoyment of moving pictures. While we can concentrate on and become engaged with events on the screen, our awareness of our bodies and our actual environment is not numbed, we are not as though sensorily deprived. These are the controls that prevent movies becoming either illusions or hallucinations. Munsterberg is right that experiencing movies is like nothing else. Movie space is not real space, movie persons are not flesh and blood.

> *We have reality with all its true dimensions; and yet it keeps the fleeting, passing surface suggestion without true depth and fullness, as different from a mere picture as from a mere stage performance.* It brings our mind into a peculiar complex state . . . a unique inner experience. (p.24)

Turning to movement, Munsterberg offered some enlightenment, but also a dead end. Marshalling a good deal of experimental research on persistence of vision he showed quite clearly that the movement of moving pictures is not a phenomenon of persistence of vision. It is a unique experience produced not by the succession of closely similar pictures, but laid over them by special activities of the mind. Perhaps the decisive experiment he cited for the independent character of perception of movement is staring at a rotating disk with a black spiral drawn upon it. If the gaze is shifted from the disk to a face, depending upon which way the disk was spinning, the face will appear to be shrinking or to be ballooning. Munsterberg said that this impression of movement resulted not from the stimulus (the unmoving face) but from the mind. We could equally well say: the mechanism of the eye, it having been excited by the spinning disk. Either way, movement does not here come from succession of images. He went on to give examples of how the mind constructs sights and movements that are not there. Put both lines of experiment together and motion becomes something super-added by the mind to motionless pictures. So with both the depth and the movement on the screen it is we who create it through our mental mechanism (p.30).

Having earlier signalled his great interest in the close-up, Munsterberg has prepared us for his discussion of attention and the role which that device will play there. Ordinarily, he contended, the act of paying attention involves the following: centring the object in consciousness; fading out the surroundings; adjusting our body in order to concentrate; and grouping our ideas, emotions and impulses around the object of attention. So far as I can see this characterization of attention straddles the distinction between voluntary and involuntary attention. Although the one comes from within and the other from without they are, he contended, intertwined in our daily activity.

Trying once more to pinpoint a unique feature of the motion picture experience, Munsterberg described the way we attend to a stage show. Although our very being there reduces the scope for our voluntary attention we can still attend to the drama in all sorts of ways, allowing our mind, like our eyes, to wander about. Of course, the stage craft of sets, lighting, voice, position, gesture, and so on, can and does direct the focus of attention to certain points. Our mind must follow these clues and fade down the surroundings. On the screen, by contrast, because of the close-up (and, obviously, cutting), the film does the work of the mind. The key point, the detail, the vital relationship, or signal, looms at the audience in a manner that cannot be missed. The act of attention which normally takes place in our mind.

> has remodeled the surrounding itself . . . . *The close-up has objectified in our world of perception our mental act of attention and by it has furnished art with a means which far transcends the power of any theatre stage* . . . . It is as if that outer world were woven into our mind and were shaped not through its own laws but by the acts of our attention. (1916 pp.38–9)

To this could be added another point of perception psychology reported by experimenters. We assist the act of attention-directing by the motion picture by gazing at the screen very differently from the way we gaze at the stage. In front of the stage our eyes actively roam and switch, for example to and from those entering or leaving, those speaking or silent. It is not inappropriate to attend the theatre with opera glasses to examine detail in the scenes. Such behaviour in a cinema would be absurd. Indeed, concentrating the attention on, let us say, the corner of the screen is something we almost never do. It seems as though we direct our gaze to a point near the centre of the screen and focused slightly in front of it. This allows us to 'take in' the whole of the image on the screen at once. We do not scan but fix; cutting and camera position do the rest. Such a gaze is easy to break, which may be one more physiological device we employ to remind ourselves, when the film is stressful, that 'it is only a movie'. As a child I hid under the cinema seat when the Wicked Queen in *Snow White and the Seven Dwarfs* became too frightening to bear. I have learned since that alteration of the gaze such as looking around the auditorium, or attending to a detail at the edge of the screen is almost equally as effective at defusing excess tension. More casual movie-goers may accomplish this with lots of body movement and lung exhalations but the result is much the same.

A thread now begins to be discernible in Munsterberg's prose, the thread that the movies have externally replicated otherwise internal mental processes. The theme that the world on the screen appears to be one shaped by the acts of our mind is worked through on to the topics of memory and imagination. The film maker, besides taking us near to things with the close-up, and far away with the long-shot, can cross time as well. The movie can shift from the apparent present to the apparent past, reverting to a scene viewed earlier, or to an earlier time not before seen but clearly signalled as before other events presently being shown. And this shifting into the past can be achieved symmetrically with the future; we can look forward into what is to come. Like the Ghosts of Christmas Past and Future in Charles Dicken's story *A Christmas Carol*, moving pictures take their viewer, as the Ghosts did Scrooge, through a time/space journey in a flash. And just as Scrooge is visibly present to himself in past scenes and palpably absent from future ones, and always invisible as ghostly observer, so are we the film-goers privileged to witness the past and future as well as present of screen characters while invisible ourselves. Sometimes, when memory or anticipation belongs to one of the very characters on the screen, it is as though we are privy to the working of their minds.

Munsterberg does not consider a more puzzling but equally exciting situation where the past or the future is seen as it were in the third person, from an objective point of view impossible of availability to any one character in the story. Who are we the viewers, then; whose mind are we privy to? *Rashomon* plays this trick especially well. We are shown four separate accounts of a series of events and as observers have been able to watch the tellers of those events in a manner they cannot watch themselves. We thus construct in our minds and imaginations an all-seeing point of view, a point of view never vouchsafed to any human being in any real series of events. We might use a Berkeleyan analogy and say it is as if the mental process we re-enact is in the mind of God. Less other-wordly, we could say we are participants in the detached mental process of the creator of the film itself. And this presents us with a nice conundrum: films are rarely the unaided creation of one person. To my students I usually describe them bluntly as the work of a committee. So the mind externalized in the unfolding scenes of a motion picture is very often the collective (and in a sense non-existent) mind of a committee.

Unlike Munsterberg, Cavell is highly interested in the way movies allow us to be present at scenes from which we or anyone else are absent. We will come to his views. One matter neither Munsterberg nor Cavell explicitly comments on is that the close-up and the invisibility of the spectator create in movies a powerful sense of intimacy. We movies-goers watch a kissing couple from closer than ever we could in real life, not only because in real life there are invisible boundaries keeping others at a distance (Goffman 1963), but also because at such close quarters in real life our presence would be an interfering factor. Few kissing couples would carry on regardless with a real person literally breathing down each of their necks in turn. Desire, even need, for intimacy is a powerful human sentiment. The attraction of its effortless achievement in movies seems to me to have less to do with scopophilia, than with social arrangements that discourage any psychological or physical intimacy much beyond the nuclear family. This capacity of the movies to make us feel intimate with other people may help explain both the role of stars and the dominance of the narrative film over all other forms.

Stars are fixed points in the flux of films. Cinema-goers see new films, new stories, set in new locations, with the persons changing too. This discontinuity is eased by the recurrence of stars, that is, the presence of actors and actresses who enhance the sense of intimacy by making it less fleeting. Instead of temporary intimacy with people never seen again, the star offers renewed and continued and hence more satisfying intimacy with the same person. Incautious film-goers are so taken in they start playing with the idea that they genuinely know, genuinely are intimate with, someone to whom they have been so close so many times. To an extent the stars and their studios contributed to this illusion by systematically confusing the onscreen persona projected by the star with their offscreen persona. Indeed, their offscreen lives became extensions of their onscreen roles in some cases (Walker 1966, ch. 7). [6]

As to the narrative form, that involves things happening to people. It is only to people that the viewer feels very close, having a sense of involvement with them. Instructional, scientific and documentary film can rarely, if ever, offer this effect and so is inescapably distanced from the audience.

The photoplay, then, to return to Munsterberg, acts as our memory and imagination act, for, in our minds, past, present and future are intertwined as are reality and imagination. The photoplay thus obeys the laws of the mind rather than those of the outer world. A good example is suggestion. Munsterberg wanted to differentiate suggestion from association by whether it is forced on us or not. It is not clear to me whether he makes his case at this point or not. His example of suggestion was uncompleted actions: a murder, or a girl taking off her clothes, need not be shown; if cut short the mind will do the work of completion. But more: the mind cannot avoid doing the completion. My doubts concern just how forced the processes of suggestion are, and whether they can be distinguished from association and symbolism. If the couple collapsing on the bed out of frame was enough to force the suggestion of coition upon us, why have film makers so often added trains entering tunnels, daggers sticking on the ground, or waves crashing against rocks? There seems to be a lot more to be said about audience inferences from what is not shown but variously hinted, suggested or symbolized than Munsterberg offers.

My doubts are not, however, directed against Munsterberg's principal point which is that at the movies '*The objective world is molded by the interests of the mind*' (1916 p.46). And yet, and at the same time, the movies disguise their mental origin and seek to suggest 'to the mind of the spectator that this is more than mere play, that it is life which we witness' (p.47). (Munsterberg's idea that movies simulate life or the real world and so disguise their true character as construction is regularly rediscovered, e.g., by John Ellis (1982), summarizing a decade of writing in *Screen*. That Munsterberg is not even in Ellis's bibliography is some indication of the state of film scholarship.)

One way in which motion pictures externalize and replicate mental processes is overlooked by Munsterberg: this is the movie that is about movies and movie making, sometimes about this very movie we are watching. Under the portentous label 'reflexivity' – a term from logic and linguistics indicating self-reference ('self-reflexivity' is a pleonasm) – this was 'discovered' in the 1970's. Because some artists of the twentieth century are acutely self-conscious (Shaw, Pirandello and Brecht in the theatre; any number of poets and novelists), it has been declared that films have become so also. A glance at the books *Hollywood's Hollywood* (Thomas and Behlmer 1975), *Hollywood on Hollywood* (Parish 1978) or *Movies on Movies* (Myers 1978) should be more than sufficient to indicate that – surely in a playful rather than a solemn way – taking film making as the subject of a film is an old idea. Some of the very best reflection on the relations and resemblances between the reel or the real worlds is to be found there.

But what else is this than self-consciousness: rather than film making being an invisible vehicle for a story, its operators draw attention to the process itself and playfully tease us with our knowledge of it. They show how differently stars behave on and off the screen, how magical effects are faked, how those who dream of walking into the screen world can do so. So, mimicking the mind, which can think and also think about itself and its own thinking, movies can externalize their own processes.

Concluding Part 1 on the psychology (i.e. philosophy) of the photoplay, Munsterberg has a chapter on emotions. 'To picture emotions must be the central aim of the photoplay', but, alas, one where the photoplay has limitations. In a word, words. The absence of spoken words limits the resources of the actor for conveying emotions to us. The face, especially in close-up, can accomplish a good deal of the work of conveying emotion but going pale, blushing, perspiring, and the pulsations of the carotid artery are involuntary and unlikely to set in when the actor goes through the motions. The stage actor compensates with his voice, the film actor must resort to the exaggeration of pantomine. To compensate for this the photoartist can take time searching for exactly the right gesture, and can also cast the actor for visual rightness, possibly using real people. 'With the right body and countenance the emotion is distinctly more credible' (1916, p.50).

Just as costume, scenery and music can enhance the feelings of a scene on the stage, so can they be manipulated in the movies.

Visual metaphors are possible, as the dissolve from the girl reading the letter to the vision of the beloved, from the music maker to a landscape embodying the feeling of the sound.

Turning from the expression of emotions to their reception by the audience, Munsterberg distinguished emotions shared with characters on the screen and emotions connected to the scenes of the drama, the latter 'may be entirely different, perhaps exactly opposite to those which the figures in the play express' (1916 p.53). The former, *shared emotions*, was the larger group. The film-goer projects back the emotions aroused on to the character, the scenery and the background. The latter, *spectator emotions*, where the film-goer reacts in terms of his independent affective life, laughs at the pompous, fears for the unaware child, is indignant at villainy, was only tentatively suggested in the photoplay as yet. He was writing in 1915.

It is important to forestall a misunderstanding here. Munsterberg did not mean that motion pictures have tended to concentrate on enabling the audience to experience the emotions of the characters on the screen at the expense of the more distanced dramatic emotions stemming from our appreciation of the character's predicament in advance of or apart from their realization of what has transpired. Writing in 1915 surrounded by a sea of slapstick comedy, for example, the whole humour of which comes from the audience looking at the characters in ways that they do not look at themselves, he would have had to be a very selective movie-goer to overlook them. What I understand him to be saying is something rather different. In modern terms, we could say that he thinks the exploitation of the visual resources of the medium for conveying emotional colour to the audience has as yet scarely begun. The examples he gave were creating the effect of trembling in a person by cutting the frames in the order 1, 2, 3, 4, 5, 6, 5, 6, 7, 8, 7, etc., and jolting the camera. When such sensations stream into consciousness, new emotions seem to take hold of us. He also mentioned the idea of conveying the feeling of being hypnotized by making objects in the room tremble and change their shape. This would seem to be a case of the first group of shared emotions rather than the second group of spectator emotions. And with this example he rather abruptly broke off and looked to future developments.

There have been developments since 1916 along the lines he

suggested. There was much experiment with visual metaphor in the silent period; interpolation of scenes to give dramatic mood, not the mood of the characters necessarily. In the apparent present time of the framing story of *Rashomon*, in which two of the story-tellers shelter from heavy rain in an old gate, the film-goer's appreciation of an oppressive atmosphere is not necessarily shared by the characters in the drama. When at the end the rain stops and the sun appears, the characters get on with the business of living, just as we, leaving the theatre as the lights come up, do the same. To be confined in the gloom of a rainstorm, an interlude from active living, is a nice metaphor for story-telling, for reflection, and, of course, for movie-going (see Part III, Chapter 13).

A later example of metaphor might be the beginning of *The Wild Bunch* (1969) when some wanton children burn alive some scorpions, callously enjoying the spectacle. Scorpions may not be our favourite fauna, but there is something repellent about their being incinerated. As the film unrolls it becomes clear *The Wild Bunch* are scorpions, with many innocent victims. They are ambushed and hunted by an indigent society, gunned down with relish. The metaphor works through interestingly, since rather than wait to be destroyed, the remnants of the bunch choose the course of self-destruction in an act of honour and revenge for a murdered comrade, as scorpions in anger will sting themselves to death.

I have already mentioned the use of visual and aural trembles at showings of *Earthquake*. But, like Munsterberg's example, this has to do with the first group of emotions: those shared by the audience and the characters on the screen. Munsterberg's main point is the development of means to evoke dramatic emotions in the spectator by filmic techniques, not empathy. He suggests cutting and camera movement. Every film student knows there are other devices. The angle of a shot, depending on character placement and set dressing, can convey a great deal. Movement of the camera also. In a musical the camera flowing with the dance can create a very strong sense of exuberance, but perhaps we take that as coming from the characters expressing their feelings. A prowling camera, however, can make us feel dread or danger of which the onscreen character is oblivious. This may look like we are taking the emotion from the prowler or threat, but that is not the case. The prowler stalking the victim may feel anger or lust;

the victim may be innocently engaged in something else. As we, looking through the camera, prowl, our emotions of fear and dread are those of neither person on the screen: they are dramatic.

One device not mentioned by Munsterberg in this connection but widely used in the silent era was tinting the film, especially sepia. Later, in discussing aesthetics, Munsterberg, getting a bit carried away with his own arguments, set aside both colour and sound as possible enhancements of the expressive resources of the photo-play because they made movies too literal. Yet sound and colour have in the meantime been greatly exploited to fulfil precisely his programme. Music, for example, can of itself convey danger. The very simple, slowly accelerating two-note rif used in *Jaws* (1975) indicates the presence of the shark and gets the audience into a state of high anxiety while the characters on the screen are unaware, and the shark itself is merely a disinterested eating machine. As long as costumes, sets, and the film stock itself could only trade in shades of black and white, the possibilities of emotional colouring (if the reader will pardon the pun) were limited. Red, for example, has overtones of flamboyance and danger in Western cultures, but red things photograph as dark in black and white. Being the colour of blood, its absence for dramatic effect was sorely felt. Once colour arrived it enormously enhanced the grand guignol aspects of movies. Other colours and combinations of colours can be very clear indicators of mood drama, much as black hats and white hats can indicate hero and villain. And just as Griffith could consciously seek to make the photographic images of *The Birth of a Nation* (1915) evoke the famous Civil War photographs of Mathew Brady, drawing on the well of emotional overtones of those images of that war, so was John Huston able, in the colour era, in contriving the photography for *Moulin Rouge* (1952), to experiment with effects that evoked the surface of Toulouse-Lautrec's paintings.

So when Munsterberg remarked that this area is one into which photo playwrights have scarcely ventured, he was correct. In his time things were only beginning. Where he was mistaken, I think we could say, was in his attempt to argue that films were in his time in their finished final form as technology, and that their essence was the externalizing or objectifying of the mechanisms of the mind and that all that remained was fully to develop and exploit that nature. On the contrary films were in his time in a transitional state from which they were further to evolve. Indeed, the resources of silent film were insufficient for its ambitions. Marvellous though the achievements of the period are, it is instructive that no-one wants to make silent films now, any more than they want to paint icons or pictures without perspective. The notion of progress in art is a troublesome one, but the evolution of its technology does sometimes lead to irreversible changes.[7] The addition of sound to films seems to be such a change. Colour is still optional, as witness the fact that even today black and white is sometimes used (e.g. *Manhattan* 1979, *Raging Bull* 1980).

Given the limitations of the silent film it is not surprising that Munsterberg did not expatiate on the use of the photoplay to convey ideas as well as emotions. In the extended parallels he draws between the two media, he nowhere addresses this issue. The theatre of ideas was flourishing in his time, especially in the hands of Ibsen and Shaw, so it could hardly be something that would not impress itself on him. To a certain extent the possibilities turn on the dramatist's ingenuity in dramatizing the ideas. But without the spoken word it is not easy to embody ideas in a character and to work out the nuances of drama as a reflection on the ideas concerned. While I raise the issue here, it is not one on which opinion is presently made up. Alexandre Astruc long ago (1948) claimed the challenge of movies was to put thought on film. Many and various ways have been tried, from the agit-prop exercises of the Soviet Union and the Third Reich, to the filmed harangues of Jean-Luc Godard.

No one will doubt that films can dramatize ideas and manipulate audience emotions in relation to them, much as live theatre can. Where there are problems is when they foray into disputed territory, which is often where the most interesting ideas are. Even when a conflict of ideas is effectively dramatized, let us say in the clash of two personalities, the need for dramatic closure and resolution tends to drive the film maker to pose answers. To show one side winning is to close an open question; to say it is an open question is hard to dramatize in such a way that it is distinct from that intellectual vice, fence-sitting. These dangers are lessened in intellectual discourse proper because the aim there is not to dramatize standing issues but rather to offer a contribution, a new move, that will clearly favour one or other side, or reframe the issue altogether. This sort of active participation in the struggle between ideas is closed to films. [8]

Before concluding this review of, and commentary on, the first of the great contributors to the emergent subject of philosophy of film, I want to bring up the matter of the problematic character of movies for the philosopher/psychologist. On psychology the question is simple: has Munsterberg made his case for their unique character, namely the externalizing of mental functions and hence the strong resonance between movies and the mind? He laid down in this argument a basis for the long-standing claim that films were a peculiarly powerful and threatening new force. Even while allowing that they have potential to inform, educate and entertain, there have always been voices pointing to the dangers movies represent, to their capacity to misinform, morally corrupt and distract from reality. If in some special way they resonate with the mind, this would explain why they are felt to be a greater danger, and hence arouse in their critics even greater levels of anxiety than did the media of print or the radio. [9]

The anxiety seems to stem from the belief in the power of images. This belief is expressed in the phrases, 'seeing is believing', and 'a picture is worth a thousand words'. On reflection neither strikes me as obviously true; but their status as clichés suggests that the idea that images have power is widely diffused in the culture. Images do, after all, it could be said, bear a relation of resemblance to that of which they are images, while words do not. Setting aside the awkward point that such an assertion employs a theory of resemblance that might be criticized (c.f. Chapter 8, below), let us take it that the assertion is widely believed. We can now explain why anxiety about filmic representation of the forbidden, whether violent, sexual, political or religious is greater than that aroused by written or spoken representations. We can also see why it was for so long thought that film could be utilized as a powerful new tool of education or propaganda.

Plato, however, as we have seen, took a sceptical attitude towards images, wondering if they could be distinguished from mere shadows. In this it is notable that modern science has tended to agree with him. Images are in the realm of appearance, and science finds appearance not a very good guide to reality. The shaping forces of our world are rarely part of visual appearance. The cinema-goer's playfulness suggests he also is not fooled by appearance. Munsterberg was torn by his view that images have unique power, and his aesthetic outlook which focused on the conventions or constraints on representation that themselves give scope for art. Art is not the imitation of nature, but the manipulation of feelings by conventional means. Hence Munsterberg argued carefully that it is the artificialities of the medium that give it the possibility of art, not its capacity to simulate reality. Its power, he thought, comes from the connection between the artificialities of film and the workings of the mind itself.

In this book I have been arguing that films are philosophically problematic. How does this tie in to Munsterberg's argument? Perhaps the major point would turn on his distinction between the real world and our impressions from the screen. We see depth on what we know to be a flat surface; we become familiar with characters who we know are shadows. As cinema-goers we are voluntarily incarcerated in Plato's cave in a test of our ability to know and experience things that are not real, responding to them in ways that resemble our response to the real, yet without becoming seriously disoriented about the boundary between the real and the unreal or the quality of the experience of one compared to the other. Whether one calls this a philosophical problem or a psychological one is of little importance. What is interesting is how we do this, and also, do we always do it successfully? Our ability to do it regularly and successfully, even to play at fooling ourselves a little bit, such is our confidence, points to an attitude we may then project on to the general philosophical problem of appearance and reality.

Among the many traditional moves in relation to this problem, which include the radical concession of declaring it insoluble, is a sophisticated version of declaring it no problem. One might capsule-summarize the solution like this: one man's appearance is another man's reality. Or, to objectify a bit: one theory's appearance is another theory's reality. So, whereas for common-sense theories the bulk of the ordinary objects in our world are both appearance and reality, for physics and chemistry our notions of density, or weight, or largeness are explainable as gross effects, appearances if you like, produced by deeper levels of reality such as atoms, forces, spin, charge and so on.

When we say of a film, 'it's only a movie', one of the things we are saying is: it is appearance, not reality. Despite the evidence of our senses and the response of our emotions, the real causal chain which has produced these reactions has to do with light on flat surfaces, isolation in dark rooms, opening of the imagination to beliefs, and so on. If we are cinematically sophisticated we may go one step further and show the shadows and sounds to be themselves caused by a complex but understandable kind of machinery linked back in time to a set of events that in many ways do not resemble the apparent events under most criteria of resemblance.

This then is a reformulation of the problem of appearance and reality that we can make with the help of film. It is an advance because it poses the problem better and solves it. Or, at least, so I would argue. The solution is along these lines. The distinction between appearance and reality is not an absolute. Not a fact of nature. This sounds like a Kantian argument, but it is not. Kant left the question of things in themselves open: if there are such things they are beyond our cognitive reach. As I pose it there are no things in themselves, there is no hard-and-fast distinction between appearance and reality. Rather, reality, or what we call reality, is the world and its objects as posed to us by our theories. What theories? Well, whatever theories we are talking about. Common-sense theories; the latest scientific theories; older refuted theories. Each defines appearance and reality, allows us to distinguish them, and in different ways.

Yet earlier I espoused a critical realism which was contrasted with subjectivism and idealism. I am not retracting that here. In the end our science demands that there is one unified, consistently describable world which, through chains of cause and structural configuration, can explain all appearances, and also all previous or variant attempts to explain. But our actual situation day-to-day is to be in possession of current or partial or at-best-for-the-moment theories which are far from offering a unified, consistently describable world that explains all appearances and previous and variant views. Our actual situation, then, is that while we might want to reach towards that world, the most we can manage is to penetrate beyond appearances – not being fooled by them. Posed philosophically this sounds daunting since ours is a world of sense-illusion, hallucination and deception. Yet we are so nonchalant that we construct within our world films – illusory further worlds that employ some of our own mental and sensory mechanisms in their own deception. And we are not deceived.

Why do we play like this, and with such vital matters? My guess is that it has to do with the urge to control the world, that is, to minimize its threat. Information about the world is useful, but being always incomplete needs supplementation by anticipation of possibilities. To think through possible scenarios is a means of planning what one will do when the scenario is real, not imaginary. Once a real scenario has been acted out, our pleasure in recounting it is a celebration of the overcoming of threat and danger. Films are only the latest versions of the cave-painting and camp-fire tales which we must assume were developed because they were functional; their secondary function of giving pleasure being related to their primary function of rehearsal, the function of rehearsal being successful accomplishment.

Before concluding this section I offer an argument for the realism that has been merely assumed. This argument is that any other assumption than that of an objectively real world creates for us problems that are too-easily soluble or insoluble. If we assume that the world is our subjective dream, the problem is why is it ever intractable and troublesome? We may experience danger in dreams but we wake up in the end. But in this world we sometimes do not wake up. So if we dream it, how can we die?

Far be it from me to claim that my position on appearance and reality is totally clear, or that it solves all problems. Like most philosophers, some of my enterprise consists of groping in a direction I hope is forward. Quite how there can be a real world to which our ideas are mere approximations, that never capture it, is not altogether clear. But we process information, we do anticipate and we do act. There then ensues an outcome. The outcome is not just what we wish or expect; it is best describable as the result of the interaction of our acts – which we predicate on how we think things are – with their impact and repercussions in a world that is the way it is.

Munsterberg's slim book has proved to be rich and provocative. He has shown us how to connect films to central philosophical concerns, and it has been possible to offer friendly criticism of his system, as well as to set aside his system and develop quite different lines of thought. Before leaving him one final context is missing from his work sketching which will help the further inquiries of this book. Munsterberg did allow that the spectator at the movie show is engaged in psychic activity, processing and making something new of the stimuli offered. What is missing is some sense of the social context of movie-going. A person going to a show comes armed with a set of expectations about pleasure for which he is prepared to pay money. The expectations are that the pleasure will be offered in ways that are intelligible, that conform to certain social conventions, knowledge of which constitute 'cineliteracy' (Eidsvik 1978). It is possible, then, that the workings of the photoplay are not solely derived from making concrete the workings of the mind, but are also partly derived from a set of social conventions held in common and in turn made concrete in the photoplay. It then becomes possible to say that films are not just the objectification of mental processes. They are also the objectification of social processes. It only needs one further step, the Popperian idea that mental processes derive from social processes to get right outside of Munsterberg's neo-Kantian framework.

So much for Munsterberg. This book is not a history of philosophical writing about films. It proceeds chronologically only for the reason that if there is hidden or muffled debate going on, the most obvious place to seek out the ideas and arguments that are being addressed and contested is among those already published.[10] But a debate can also have a logical structure that is independent of chronology, and also independent of publication. That is to say, there may be works published that are classified as within the field yet which may, with impunity, be passed over because they make no contribution. This is my attitude to two major figures of the inter-war years, Rudolf Harms (1926, 1927) and Mortimer J. Adler (1937). Harms achieves no more than Munsterberg, whom he does not cite. Adler is concerned to argue that movies do not break down the model of man as an active and rational agent capable of absorbing information and making prudential decisions. In this he is at one with Munsterberg in spirit, whom he often cites. Alder's work is monumental and deserving of an essay to itself. His overriding concern is the regulation of the arts. The issue of the passive mind, of movies' ability to short-circuit normal development and rational processes and induce socially undesirable behaviour and attitudes is an issue for the social sciences and I have debated it and reviewed the literature elsewhere (1970, 1978). The logical structure of the debate I am reconstructing, namely of films as a challenging embodiment of the dilemmas of Plato's cave, leads me to set both Harms and Adler aside. I also set aside those theories of the inter-war period who wrote treatises on the art of the film: Balazs, Arnheim, Rotha. The topics they addressed belong to Part II.

4.2 CAVELL

It was fifty-five years before another member of the Harvard philsophy (no longer 'philosophical') department wrote about film. Academic fashion having split psychology off into a separate department, we would not expect experimental results to figure in later work. And when Stanley Cavell subtitles his *The World Viewed* as follows, 'Reflections on the Ontology of Film', we may be inclined to think his slim book is about utterly different things than was Munsterberg's slim book. This would be a mistake. The remarkable fact is that despite being philosophy rather than psychology, conceptual rather than experimental, and talking of ontology rather than mental life conditions, Cavell's book addresses problems that overlap considerably with Munsterberg's. To see this we have only to ask, 'what is the ontology of film?'

Earlier in this book I made plain the usual meaning of ontology; it is, to use old-fashioned terminology, the science of being, that part of philosophy which addresses the problem of what exists – to use the modern terminology. Ontology is about what there is in the world. This leaves ambiguous the meaning of 'the ontology of film'. Does it mean the ontological status of celluloid in the inventory of the furniture of the world, or does it mean the problem we have already addressed, namely, the ontological status of the seeming things that are 'on film'. 'On' here in the sense not that emulsion is on celluloid but in the sense of meaningful material stored in its potentiality on the celluloid and accessible by running it through a projector.

Again, although this reduces the ambiguity, it is not altogether gone. We are back to the hoary problem for philosophers of whether the Golden Mountain exists. The Golden Mountain, a figment of our imagination, can here stand for the fictional content of all films. So the question is, does all material 'on' film exist? If it does, in some sense, are we expanding or obliterating the notion of existence? One simple distinction between the world we inhabit and in which there are reels of celluloid and the world 'contained on' films is to say that whereas the former exist, the latter does not; the latter is fiction, the former is fact; another way is to say one is real, the other unreal.

The introduction of this troublesome word 'ontology' can be traced back to an acknowledged influence on Cavell, a French film critic of the 1940's, André Bazin. His occasional writings were collected into four slim volumes in French, and selections have been translated into two volumes in English. The first selection of these translations to be published was his essay 'Reflections on the Ontology of the Photographic Image', which appeared in *Film Quarterly* in 1960. The argument of that piece goes as follows.

A photograph bears a different relationship to the object photographed than does a painting to the object painted. Perhaps painting originates in superstition, in the identity of an object and its image; perhaps the impulse behind it was to overcome death, to be a variant form of mummification. Even though such superstition and magic is no longer believed, painting has striven to produce resemblance, its original sin being the invention of perspective and its greatest crisis being brought on by photography. Painting's quest for realism was due to a confusion between the magical, psychological non-aesthetic quest for resemblance, and a true realism which presents both the concrete and the essence of the world. Photography frees painting from this confusion.

The relation between the photograph and its object is unique. We respond to a photograph as we respond to nature itself (or people themselves?). Photography uses a lens to strip away preconception, to present the object to us in its virginal purity, 'by a mechanical reproduction in the making of which man plays no part' (Bazin 1967, p.12). Faced with a photograph of someone 'we are forced to accept as real the existence of the object reproduced' (p.13)

> The photographic image is the object itself, the object freed
> from the conditions of time and space that govern it . . . it
> shares, by virtue of the very process of its becoming, the being
> of the model of which it is the reproduction; it is the model. (p.14)

So much for Bazin's argument. My acquaintance with it goes back to the time when, as an apprentice philosopher of twenty-three, I penned and published a critique of it (Jarvie 1960).

Looking back on my critique I see it as rather gentle, especially as I was uncertain of my footing around such continental philosophical buzz-words as 'being' and 'becoming'.

First, I pointed out a consequence of Bazin's view, that it would elevate neo-realism to the purest form of cinema. This conclusion I termed 'unpalatable', a characterization that in retrospect seems a lot more than a mere assertion of taste. But I directed the main thrust of my critique at Bazin's view of the history of painting as striving to achieve an objective view of reality; Gombrich (and Popper) had shown this not to be a feasible aim, rendering Bazin's reconstruction of the history of painting faulty. Further, it then seemed to me, the paint brush and pen were machines in exactly the same sense a camera was, and human manipulation is ineliminable from each. Hence man was not absent from photography. Films are, furthermore, entirely different from photography, especially in their ability to stylize, to move and to abbreviate (attenuate also, I should have added). As a medium, film combines means in which abstract articulation is highly developed and the representational poorly developed (such as music and lighting), with means in which abstraction is poorly developed and the representational highly developed (such as words and pictures).

Re-reading Bazin today to offer a further critique, I begin with utter incredulity that he is taken so seriously (Cavell 1971; Andrew 1976; Tudor 1973). Above all, that he is taken seriously by Cavell. Cavell cites Bazin a handful of times but I think the infuence is all-pervasive and helps explain much of the fuzziness and confusion that everyone complains of in Cavell.

To begin with, Bazin's article approaches films via painting and photography; the ontology of film is to be defined by contrast with the ontology of other things. Second, the argument from painting is speculative history. It begins in ancient Egyptian painting, speculating about sympathetic magic as the origin of painting. The cave paintings at Lascaux are older than Egyptian art and equally open to (different) speculation. The fact is we do not know what impulses produced these paintings, we can only guess; so far so good. But it is hard to control our guessing, as we cannot test. Hence arguments based on these guesses are pseudo-historical: logically weak and plausible only if the guessing strikes you as correct.

97

Even Bazin's history of recent painting is speculative. The quest for realism in painting continued long after photography appeared (1823), and I am referring to illusion, not to 'true realism'. *Trompe-l'oeil* and photographic realism emerge as schools as recently as this century.

The trouble here is that the other prong of the argument, that from photography, while not relying on pseudo-history, relies on something equally misleading: pseudo-analysis. Technologically, films employ photography. It does not follow that what films do is the same as, or even particularly resembles, what photographs do. In particular, films add at least two things to photographs: motion and sound. Neglect of this latter seems to me to vitiate much of what Bazin and his follower, Cavell, say, even down to their constant speaking of 'viewing' movies, a misleading usage. As Munsterberg would probably have it, while we may *know* that what we see in the cinema are series of two-dimensional still pictures, that is not the *impression* we have, that is not what we are watching. Bazin's analysis tries to reduce an experience *sui generis*, movie-going, to something related but different: photographs.

In delineating differences between photography and movies it is easy to overlook that the spectator's experience of a medium is as much a decisive difference as the apparatus. Considered as experience, movies differ from photography in their *size* – the movie screen has always been much larger than any photograph; in their *distance* – they are not little pieces of cardboard that can be held in the hand; and in their need of *darkness* – an absence of surround.

There is a third factor which is a resemblance between movies and photographs that yet creates a huge difference: montage. Montage in photography means a series of photographs close together – as on a page or a wall – that the photographer wishes the viewer to relate one to the other. Sometimes they may be of connected actions, other times not. The same French word, montage, is used for what is more usually called editing in film work. The difference is this: many photographs are displayed by themselves; but all films employ montage. Films thus necessarily demand of us that mental act of connection and completion as our attention crosses the cut from one shot to the next. This mental act makes for a decisive difference between photographs and films.

The deepest weakness in Bazin, however, is the ontological one, the attempt to connect the becoming of the photograph and the being of its object by way of the mechanical manner the one becomes the other (Lackey 1973; Blocker, 1977). No-one who has done photography, I should have thought, could conceivably play down the role of man in the process the way Bazin does ('in the making of which man plays no part'). Lenses no more work by themselves than do pencils or paint brushes. Of which more below. But even if they did, does that warrant such an assertion as that 'the photographic image is the object itself', it *is* the model of which it is a reproduction? What Bazin is asserting is the identity of the subject and the object, a photograph of someone *is* that someone. Can he really have thought this through? An object or a person can be photographed from many angles, in many ways. Is there an identity between all of these photographs and their original? Bazin's position requires the answer, 'yes'. Very well, what are we to make of those photographs taken from what are called unusual angles that pose grave problems of recognition? Do we continue to assert the identity, or do we confine identity to recognizable identity? If the latter, then some such notions as privileged angle of view will have to be invoked, namely an angle of view that permits recognition. This will be circular. So we are forced back to the former: no matter how unrecognizable, a photograph of an object shares the identity of its object. Then suppose we have a photograph of an identical twin, X, and before us stands the other twin, Y. Does the photograph X participate in the identity of Y? If we say yes, the problem can be exacerbated by further assuming Y has never been photographed. If we say no, we can then ask how can we tell the difference between the photograph of X and its apparent model Y? The answer cannot but take us beyond the photograph itself; the photograph itself is not perspicuous on this question. We should have to go back to the series of events we call 'taking the photograph' in order to find that Y did not participate in it (Snyder 1983)

So, if we know that someone is photographed, that can be a criterion for our assertion that they share their identity with the photograph; that is what we mean by their having been photographed. And this differs in some decisive way from what we mean when we say, 'so-and-so sat for a painted portrait', since apparently for Bazin, painted portrait and sitter do not share their identity the way photograph and subject do.

What, then, do we mean when we declare a photograph not to look like its subject at all? What weight do we give to our knowledge that a portfolio of very different looking photographs of a fashion model are all of the same girl? If we are a talent agent we may make use of the information: this girl can adapt to many different looks. If we are policemen we may throw up our hands in despair: which shall we choose for her wanted poster? Bazin seems to think that objects in the natural world have a look, or an appearance, and that photography captures that appearance in a way that is mechanical, hence verisimilar, hence credible. This is why we, or rather he, identifies photograph and photographed. If the problem of appearance and reality were so simple, I do not see how philosophers would have failed to spot this solution. It was always my understanding that it was precisely the deceptive character of appearances, or the possibility of their being deceptive, that makes us distinguish between appearance and reality. Bazin's doctrine relies on a notion of the real appearance of things, and this seems to me a confusion.

Bazin's hypothesis, then, that a photograph shares the *being* of its object because of its mechanical manner of *becoming*, is a pseudo-analysis resting on a quite superficial view of photography and an equally superficial appreciation of the problem of appearance and reality. Photographs do not solve the problem even partially; in some ways they exacerbate it. To have seen a photograph of someone is not necessarily to know anything about them, to be able to infer the first thing about their identity. It is sometimes, but only when we have other evidence to check that it is reliable. To make any claim from photograph to thing photographed is about as sensible as claiming that you know something about what a film star is like because you have seen many of their films. Films and photographs share this: they are artifacts, products far more of the conditions of their making than they are of their ostensible subjects.

Acknowledging the influence of Bazin, although never expounding his ideas or subjecting them to criticism, Cavell proceeds to attack the question, 'what is film?' (1971, p.15). Obviously, given his title, the answer is, 'the world viewed'. Not, be it noted, 'the world viewed *and heard*'. This may be a slip or an oversight, but it is not a trivial one, as we shall see. Nor, be it also noticed,[1] *a* world viewed'. Painting is apparently a world viewed; film is *the* world viewed. This sort of distinction, suggesting that film is a transaction with the world, whereas painting creates a world, shows the influence of Bazin. The argument comes from reflecting on photography. Bazin, and Cavell with him, and a great many other writers, are impressed by the idea that photography is a mechanical process of recording the world, what is in front of the lens. They think motion pictures do just that. By contrast, drawing or painting is taken to be non-mechanical; that is, human intervention is decisive whereas in photography it reduces towards zero. It is hard to formulate this argument without rendering it too naive. No-one, I take it, denies that photography involves some human intervention; or that drawing and painting employ mechanical means. Rather is it that once the shutter is pressed the image is recorded automatically, whereas every element of the painting or drawing goes on being produced by decision and intervention up to the last stroke. Or something like that. Bazin explicates himself with words like 'tracing' or 'death mask' or 'impression'.

Let me take attention away from the mechanics for a moment and try a different approach. Governments require that on passports we use photographs, not drawings or paintings. Furthermore, they usually specify that the photograph shall be a full-face close-up. This is what we might call a 'privileged point of view', supposed to be the most readily identifiable of all our aspects. Why is a drawing or a painting not acceptable? We cannot argue that they should be because some painters can paint a picture that looks exactly like a photograph, for this would beg the underlying question. What is it in a photograph that they are trying to capture when doing paintings exactly like it? What is the standard that photography sets? Obviously, the substitution of mechanism for human intervention is the *explanation* for the difference, not its characterization. What is the difference? What goes wrong if there is human intervention?

The simplest answer to this question would seem to be this: a painter paints what is in his mind, whereas a camera photographs what is in the world. Once there are photographs, painters can try to imitate them. But we need photographs as benchmarks against which to judge the paintings. When Cavell writes about this he distinguishes *the* world from *a* world (all italics in original):

The world of a painting is not continuous with the world of its frame; at its frame, a world finds its limits. We might say: A painting *is* a world; a photograph is *of* the world. What happens in a photograph is that *it* comes to an end . . . . The implied presence of the rest of the world, and its explicit rejection, are as essential in the experience of a photograph as what it explicitly presents. A camera is an opening in a box: that is the best emblem of the fact that a camera holding an object is holding the rest of the world away. The camera has been praised for extending the senses; it may, as the world goes, deserve more praise for confining them, leaving room for thought. (1971, p.24)

If a camera is an opening in a box, then a pencil is an elementary lever: emblem or not, the relation of box and pencil to the world they are being used to represent is more complicated than the distinction laid between 'is a' and 'of the'. Whether one contests Bazinian ontology directly, as I have done, or consequentially, as I have also done, it seems to me the ontology of the photographic image is not easy to resolve.

Three very worrying counter-examples come to mind. Recall, 'a painting *is* a world; a photograph is *of* the world'; what happens when we have films turning into paintings, and vice versa? if a painting is a world that ends at the limits of its frame, how is it possible for a camera to roam round the world, stop, and have its picture become a painting? How is it possible for a painting to come alive and be revealed as having a world beyond its frame? The examples I have in mind are as follows. In Vincente Minnelli's *An American in Paris* (1951) and John Huston's *Moulin Rouge* (1952) scenes open on paintings by Toulouse-Lautrec, dissolve into still photographs, then become animated. Five years later Minnelli reversed the experiment in *Lust for Life* (1956) when he had his camera capture landscapes that then turned into Vincent Van Gogh's paintings, landscapes that were very much not confined by their frames.

But there are other problematic matters here, and I want to focus on two: photography and sound. On the matter of photography I take my cue from the pithy remarks Alexander Sesonske (1974b) directed at Cavell's book. Arguably, cameras photograph objects in the world: Matthew Brady photographed bodies on Civil War battlefields. But films and photographs are not the same thing. Films are motion pictures, which may seem a trivial difference. They are also something else. Films are strips of motion pictures spliced together. Much ink has been spilled in film writing over the simple, and I would think incontestable, fact that two pieces of film spliced together add up to something different from the sum of their parts. Munsterberg would say that once this happens film externalizes our mental operations in a way that photography does not. If not two but three or umpteen pieces of film are spliced together, all resemblance to photography is lost. The world constituted by the mind of the viewer – to write in Munsterbergian terms – from the unspooling pieces of film need bear little or no resemblance to any state of affairs that ever existed anywhere in the real world. Just as a gramophone record by the Rolling Stones can be built up from separate tracks and sessions without the five members of the group ever having been in the studio at the same time, so can a film maker constitute a series of apparent events which we can, if we wish, call a world, a world nevertheless that never at any time existed in order to be photographed.

Sesonske tries to show this by analysing a sequence from *Jules et Jim* and differentiating between the scene as viewed in the cinema, the individual takes, the out-takes, the various actual days and dates of shooting versus the days and dates the action is supposed to cover, between the characters in the film and the actors playing them. Nothing much resembling what happens in the film ever happened anywhere. Then he pushes the argument one stage further by bringing in animation to show that a film may show what never could have happened anywhere. What is photographed in animation work are thousands of pictures painted on cels; a series, one might say, of worlds ending at their frame, although in motion pictures the frame often moves. But the film of *Snow White and the Seven Dwarfs* is not a film of paintings (unlike an art film such as Haanstra's *Rembrandt, Painter of Man*). What the Disney Studio enables us to constitute is a world, not in any sense *the* world.

Cavell's reply to this (1974) is to deny that cartoons are movies. Although this is his reply, he maintains that it is not an answer but an assumption. He all along took it that cartoons were not movies because of his own emphasis on reality (p. 169). He then proceeds to discuss the unrealities of the cartoon world – anthropomorphism, indestructability, epicene sexuality – as contrasted to the real world. This labour is not undertaken to convince us ('of course I cannot show this'), but to explain why he did not take movies to include cartoons.

This is an interesting way to deal with a counter-example. To say, first, the definition was never intended to include it and, second, there are reasons for ruling it out. Awkward counter-examples were christened by Imre Lakatos, 'monsters' and the strategy of declaring them outside the discussion, 'monster-barring' (Lakatos 1963-4). Cavell wants to bar the anthropomorphic monster of cartoons from his and Bazin's ontology of film. But film is what film does, and movies are what we all take them to be. For Cavell to invent a private language in which the word 'movies' does not include cartoons, to write about movies without telling us about this private usage, to tell us about it only when cartoons have been used to make fun of his ruminations about movies, is not to abide by the highest standards of philosophical argumentation.

Cavell, like Bazin, is intent on defending a hard connection between the world and film, a connection to do with its mechanical base.

> The material basis of the media of the movies (as paint on a flat delimited support is the material basis of the media [sic] of painting), is, in the terms which have so far made their appearance, *a succession of automatic world projections*. 'Succession' includes the various degrees of motion in motion pictures: the motion depicted; the current of successive frames in depicting it; the juxtapositions of cutting. 'Automatic' emphasizes the mechanical fact of photography in particular the absence of the human hand in forming these objects and the absence of its creatures in their screening. 'World' covers the ontological facts of photography and its subjects. 'Projection' points to the phenomenological facts of viewing, and to the continuity of the camera's motion as it ingests the world. (1971, pp.72-3)

Once more we must notice some oddities: a medium is to be specified by its material basis as though there is here some agreed rock-bottom on which an argument can be grounded. And yet the material basis is bogus. 'Paint on a flat delimited support' does not describe painting, and it is partly circular. 'A succession of automatic world projections', does not describe movies, since cartoons, scientific films, newsreels are all movies, and because the element of sound is left out. To say of movies, as earlier writers did, that they are a series of still pictures that give the illusion of movement is as useless as to say of speech that it is a series of vibrations of the vocal chords. 'Vibrations of the vocal chords' is not a description of speech, it is part of the physicist's explanation of how speech works. Similarly of the still pictures' apparent movement as a specification of movies: this is part of the answer to the question of how they work. What Cavell says about movies and about painting has no connection to physical or psychological questions about how movies or paintings work. It is rather an attempt to find a phrase which somehow incorporates his philosophy of movies within a commonsensical description of their mechanism. One could, I suppose, describe a motor car as a self-propelled conveyance, but it just seems like a fancy way of talking to no purpose. Other things than motor cars fit the phrase, and some motor cars may not fit.

Why then bother at all with 'a series of automatic world projections'? One answer is historical: the ancient Aristotelian quest for a science of being dealing with the essence of things. Hence the project of achieving definitions which capture the essence. To engage the reader in this quest it seems to me that the philosopher needs first to convince us that not just a science of essences but essences of themselves should be taken seriously.[11] One oddity about Cavell is that the two philosophers he cites most frequently – Heidegger and Wittgenstein (the devil and the deep blue sea) – hardly hold congruent views on these matters. Heidegger is an essentialist so deeply dyed that he seems unaware of the need of defence; whereas Wittgenstein was one of the foremost critics of essentialism in our time.

Cavell's obliviousness both to his own essentialism and to its need of defence puts him in the company of the vast majority of philosophers, past and present. It is rampant among the French thinkers so fashionable in film studies since the 1970's.[12] In his last book, *Camera Lucida*, Roland Barthes admits to being

> overcome by an 'ontological' desire: I wanted to learn at all
> costs what photography was 'in itself', by what essential feature

it was to be distinguished from the community of images . . . . I wasn't sure that photography existed, that it had a 'genius' of its own. (Barthes 1981, p. 3)

He proceeds on a metaphysical ramble around death (or, rather, Death) and depth, presence and absence, presentness and pastness to end up telling us that photography is 'that has been' (p.115):

> in the photograph, something *has posed* in front of the tiny hole and has remained there forever (that is my feeling); but in cinema, something *has passed* in front of this same tiny hole: the pose is swept away and denied by the continuous series of images: it is a different phenomenology, and therefore a different art which begins here, though derived from the first one. (Barthes 1981, p.78).[13]

As soon as a phenomenologist quits being programmatic and specifies what makes the thing he is investigating what it is and not another, the counter-examples flood to mind. In this case movies composed largely of still photographs such as Asch's *The Feast* or Kawelerowicz's *Passenger*, showing photography and cinema are not different arts. But does it make sense to argue with someone who says that because he did not know what photography's 'essential feature' was, he did not know whether it existed?

Here we may have come across a very troubling problem to do with our contacting reality. The fundamental reason for doing science, according to Popper, is to explore and explain the world we inhabit. The fundamental reason for demanding of ourselves that our statements about the world should be falsifiable is that only this is an indication that our statements connect with reality: when they clash with it (or, to be more precise, with statements about it). Empiricists always hoped that they could somehow show that through the senses we reach out and make direct contact with reality. Their views did not survive scrutiny. Those philosophers who describe photography and movies as having some privileged connection with the real world are latter-day inheritors of the empiricist view: the camera rather than the senses as a channel open to, or a contact point with, reality.

For Popper the weakness of untestable metaphysics is not that it may not be interesting or stimulating but rather that, because it is not falsifiable, because, that is, it is compatible with all states of affairs, the way reality is doesn't make any difference to it. It does not, despite appearances, have any content: it does not tell us anything about reality. In a famous article Worth (1975) argued that films show things and yet have no equivalent for the linguistic qualifier 'it is not the case that'. Hence they assert, but cannot deny and so are a kind of crystallized metaphysics: unfalsifiable, indifferent to the way the world is. Yet Cavell and others talk of films being 'the world viewed'.

To return to 'a series of automatic world projections', which may be no more than Cavell's attempt to sum up his philosophy of movies in a pithy phrase. Cavell's philosophy of movies is, as we have seen, derived from Bazin and the latter's reflections on painting and photography. Cavell holds in particular that the relation of the world viewed on movies to the world inhabited by me is to be specified in terms of presence and absence: that the movie world is present to me, but I am not present to it. When I gaze at a passport photograph I want to say that it brings the person shown into my presence; in looking at that photograph I am looking at the person himself. 'The reality in a photograph is present to me while I am not present to it' (1971, p.23). I shall try to show that this philosophy is naive and uncritical. Cavell conducts his discussion around a photograph of grandmother (p.18). He wants to say that looking at it brings grandmother, not just a photograph of grandmother, into my presence. I chose passport photographs as my example because even governments endorse some of them as 'true likenesses'. Yet all my readers know that people complain endlessly about passport photographs: not only that they are unflattering, but that they do not look like us. When reviewing photo albums, a characteristic remark is 'that's a good likeness', or 'that doesn't look at all like so-and-so.' At every point, then, those in the know make judgments about the relation of the photograph to the original. A photo of grandma taken at random may not at all bring her into my presence because I and/or others have judged this photograph to be not at all 'like' her. But what happens when we look at a photograph that has been declared a good likeness? Then, gazing at it, the presence of the person may be felt. What has this to do with the photograph? There is something misleading in thinking of a photograph as a photograph 'of' grandma. 'Grandma' is the generic name we give to a person (strictly speaking, in our kinship system, to two different persons). Can we possibly mean that this is a photograph of a person, because grandma is a person? Anyone inclined to answer in the affirmative should think again. A photograph is a form of reproduction that uses light and silver salts: persons cannot be reproduced by light and silver salts. We talk loosely when we speak of centring a person in the lens. What a camera photographs are appearances, in the case of persons their bodily appearances only, and the optical aspect of those bodily appearances only. (Cavell says photographs do not reproduce 'sights' (1971, p.23); how about 'sightings' then?) Cameras do not photograph the shape of bodies, their texture, their smell or the kinds of noises they make. And even were feelies or some other advanced system of recording developed, cameras would still not reproduce persons. Persons are not mechanical entities therefore I do not see how they can be mechanically reproduced. Philosophers dispute about what persons are and how they are to be identified, but none of them identifies persons with the bodies we say they inhabit. The simplest reason being that what a person is has much to do with his history, and history, being time past, cannot be captured on present film. Let us speak more cautiously. This photograph has been selected as representing grandma (Blocker 1977): we have felt able to project our sense of grandma into this photograph which thus serves to trigger an invocation of grandma. The photograph does not bring grandma into our presence; the photograph is a trigger or vessel that allows us to bring grandma to mind in a manner that we find appropriate. Grandma's presence is illusory; there is no presence. Rather, to use my terms, the *play* of our *mind* is *directed*.

Continuing our quest to grapple with Cavell's philosophy of movies, with the problem of the relation of the world on film to the world we inhabit, we must come back to his extraordinary assertion that photography means the human hand is absent in forming these objects. Literally false: the shutter has to be pressed, and that means at one moment not another. But to see how much deeper the human hand is involved one only has to look at the things that can go wrong. If the camera is not loaded or improperly loaded: no picture. If the hand shakes or the focus is wrong: no picture. If the f-stop is too high, or low, the film stock too fast or too slow, the light insufficient or excessive: no picture.

Snap. If the film is exposed to light before fixation: no picture. If the wrong developer is used; no picture. If the paper stock is out of date: no picture. And so on.

One obvious rebuttal available to Cavell is that all of these are automatic physical processes once set in motion, even if human triggering of each is required. So the chemicals of the developer do their work on the silver salts once the two are placed in contact. After all, every single step can be automated, as in the surveillance cameras in banks. Such a reply would be a bit like arguing that because computers can do jobs they can think for themselves. Computers are programmed to execute specified tasks and that programming can always be traced back to the work of human hands (and brains). Furthermore, the automatic character of, say, developer and silver salts interacting is no different from the interaction of pencil 'lead' with paper surface, of paint and oil, powder and water, and the absence of interaction between paint and canvas, as well as the interaction of paint and air to dry it: all these are automatic, that is, they are physical and chemical processes that need only be triggered to take place by themselves.

I do not want to press this line of argument all the way home. I do not, that is, want to contend that there are no significant differences between handcrafted arts like painting and drawing and mechanical arts like photography. But I question whether current technology, current understanding of natural processes, is a good basis for distinguishing the handcrafted from the mechanical. It might be sufficient to say of photography that it seems to minimize the intervention of the human hand and hence its likenesses are the most mechanical we can get.

The next obvious question is: what are these likenesses that we seek, and why do we seek them? Presumably the answer has something to do with truth. When we ask what a person is like, and our purpose is a serious one (let us say we want to apprehend him for a crime), then we seek a reply that is true. What do we mean by this? Usually, true means 'corresponds to the facts', so we can explicate the likeness question by saying we want a likeness that corresponds to the original in certain important ways. For example, that someone likes the person may be of little interest, similarly that the person was born under the zodiac sign of the crab. What we seek is a description, including a likeness, that is minimally subjective and personal: something like the common denominator of the way a person looks and is so that a stranger can recognize him. As we know from the difficulties of gathering such information for police purposes, no foolproof or exact recipe for this exists. Yet we strive for it. We want to minimize the human factor, maximize the mechanical factor. The trouble with the human factor is – what? That people see things, and especially other people, in ways that they colour. Painters, to speak crudely, paint what is in their heads as much as what is before them – even though they are striving to paint what is before them. Cameras, while positioned, focused, etc. by people and their minds, seem to photograph the world before them, not what is in the photographer's head.

To this I in turn reply that photographers can convey their thoughts and feelings to us through their work much as painters can. The point is that we seem to be able to press further the quest to minimize the human element in photography. Or perhaps it is that we more readily do so.

But if we can sustain the point that photographs are of the world and paintings of the mind, does it follow that the same is true of film? One of the reasons Bazin dislikes montage and prefers long takes is because he thinks the long take is a continuous photographing of something going on in front of the camera, a piece of the world viewed. On page 73 Cavell (1971) sits on the fence, a position, if we press down on his head, we can make rather uncomfortable. He writes that he does not follow either Bazin or Eisenstein in their views of what constitutes the essence of the cinematic, namely the long take versus cutting. This will not do. At the end of the longest take there must come a cut. With a cut comes a discontinuity: now at least two worlds are being viewed, one after the other (minutes or months or more may separate shots both in the film world and in the film studio). But the mind blends them into a single one, one that is certainly not being photographed. Munsterberg argues clearly that this world is supplied by, hence is 'in', the mind of the spectator. Thus, this admirable early film theorist never made the catastrophic mistake of thinking the experience of film is passive. Less acute observers have reasoned thus. A film projects a world, not the real world but an imaginary world: who is the author of this imaginary world? The answer they have come up with is, often enough, the director. So film students are encouraged to think of film as the intentional

act of the imagination of a film maker – the director for preference, with side arguments about the writer, the producer, the
studio, even.[14]

Here the analogy between film and language could come in
handy. To the extent that sounds and syntax are well-understood
conventions, speakers can exchange all kinds of messages, never
without ambiguity and misunderstanding. The more abstract and
complex the transmissions, the greater the possibilities for
receptors to get them wrong. Films use language, but they also use
sound, music, and imagery, including metaphors and cuts between
images. What is remarkable is how much control over audience
response and reception the film maker is able to exercise. But we
cannot conceal the collaboration: from the voluntary decision to
enter the cinema, to the continuing choice to be open to the film
and to concentrate on it, the participation of the viewer is
essential. Our own personal moods can make us immune to a film
we enjoy hugely on another occasion: the mood of an audience can
be resistant to a film in one place and receptive at another.

In short, the point I make is that film is unlike photography, in
that only the thinnest case can be made for it being photographs of
the world. Even leaving aside cartoons, it seems to me that from
the moment of the cut, film is creating a world, one bounded by its
frames, not extending beyond them in any sense. Cavell would not
accept this, and so I shall let him speak his piece.:

> The idea of and the wish for the world recreated in its own
> image was satisfied *at last* by cinema. Bazin calls this the myth of
> total cinema. But it had always been one of the myths of art . . .
>
> What is cinema's way of satisfying the myth? Automatically,
> we said. But what does that mean – mean mythically, as it
> were? It means satisfying it without *my* having to do anything,
> satisfying it *by* wishing. In a word, *magically*. I have found
> myself asking: How could film be art, since all the major arts
> arise in some way out of religion? Now I can answer: Because
> movies arise out of magic; from *below* the world. (p.39)
>
> I have spoken of film as satisfying the wish for the magical
> reproduction of the world by enabling us to view it unseen.
> What we wish to see in this way is the world itself – that is to
> say, everything. Nothing less than what modern philosophy has

111

told us (whether for Kant's reasons, or for Locke's, or Hume's is metaphysically beyond our reach or (as Hegel or Marx or Kierkegaard or Nietzsche might rather put it) beyond our reach metaphysically.

To say that we wish to view the world itself is to say that we are wishing for the condition of viewing as such. That is our way of establishing our connection with the world: through viewing it, or having views of it. Our condition has become one in which our natural mode of perception is to view, feeling unseen. We do not so much look at the world as *look out* at it, from behind the self. It is our fantasies, now all but completely thwarted and out of hand, which are unseen and must be kept unseen. As if we could no longer hope that anyone might share them – at just the moment that they are pouring into the streets, less private than ever. So we are less than ever in a position to marry them to the world.

Viewing a movie makes this condition automatic, takes the responsibility for it out of our hands. Hence movies seem more natural than reality . . . . *Reproducing the world is the only thing film does automatically.* (pp.101–3)

Setting aside the gnomic utterances (in what sense is either magic or movies below the world?), let us cleave to the main line of disagreement between Munsterberg and Cavell, one in which I am very much on the side of the earlier Harvard philosopher.

Cavell, in the second half of this passage, seems to have this line of thought: our present human condition in relation to the world is that we are alienated from it; we view it, we gaze out of it from behind the self. If this is so, then our viewing movies replicates this experience, and the way movies present the world to us, as invisible onlookers, nests the whole process in Chinese boxes. One finds much the same sentiment expressed by Merleau-Ponty (1945). This is philosophical psychology rather than ontology, but that is to be welcomed in the spirit of Munsterberg. Yet is it true? Since it is uttered in a phenomenological context the most that seems to be possible is introspective test – the least reliable of all, and one most present-day psychologists eschew.

If we can establish a contradiction, though, then at least we present the phenomenologist with a challenge hard to blink: both cannot be right. Let me centre my critique on the idea that we establish our connnection with the world through viewing it. This strikes me as similar to the idea that Munsterberg criticized, namely that we see depth. We do not see depth: what we do is construct depth with the help of such clues as apparent size and relation, movement, and the different information coming to each eye. One-eyed people learn to do it too, and some (Raoul Walsh, John Ford) have been successful film directors. This point about depth can be generalized to all viewing, to all connection with the world. It is incorrect to say our connection with the world is viewing it, however much we may feel that estrangement. We are part of the world, we embody some of it, it permeates us and our very act of viewing it is not one of sight, but is a construction using not merely sight but all five senses plus the variations of information produced by our moving around in and interacting with the world (Gibson 1950).

Here may lie an explanation of our ability to maintain distance from the world of movies, in the last resort. Although our minds and senses are active in constructing the world of movies, there are limits to our ability to act and interact in relation to it: it is somewhat impervious to us. We can cease to give it attention, but we cannot sway the course of events; we cannot alter the perspective. If something intrigues on the screen we cannot walk around behind it or reach out to touch in order to check it out.

Our connection with the world is *not* through viewing it; viewing the world is the outcome of our processes of connecting with the world. This contradicts Cavell. Just as Cavell oversimplified the automation of movies, he also simplified our detachment from the world and hence film's reproduction of it.

When Cavell says that by wishing we realize the myth of total cinema, that is recreate the world in its own image, he seems to be saying something a little like Munsterberg. A mental act, wishing, is externalized in the movies. Here he is making a deep mistake: movies, it is true, are created by our minds; but not by wishing, by work. That is, learning to experience movies, to make sense of them as a stimulus source, is a slow and elaborate process that we can watch happening both in children and in isolated cultures that have movies introduced to them (Notcutt and Latham 1937; Wilson 1961). Despite his frequent references to magic, Cavell fails to think through the accusation often levelled at the camera by people of other cultures, that it is the evil eye, the eye that steals something of the soul. Cameras are only the latest technology to be accused this way: drawings, statuettes and mirrors can be similarly threatening. When we introduce the child to movies one of the things we do is demystify them. We show how to impose coherence on elision, how to accept the ineluctability of what happens, how to make sense of our own invisibility and impotence to affect events. But we do not train children to imagine that what takes place takes place because they wish it. It only takes place because the film-goer has been trained to the point where he cannot introspectively reconstruct the state from which he started; the state, that is to say, of not being able to read movies.

In the ten years between *The World Viewed* and his second book on film, *Pursuits of Happiness*, Cavell published several essays on movies. With one exception these were studies of single movies, what are fashionably called 'readings'. Collected together and supplemented, they became *Pursuits of Happiness* (1981), of which more anon. The exception, 'More of the World Viewed', was a reply to critics of *The World Viewed*. Expanded and supplemented it became part of the enlarged edition of that book (1979). Adding an index (useful though insufficient because it is an index of names and what one needs of a convoluted writer is an index of subjects) and, as explained earlier, evading a counter-example, Cavell made some minor concessions and mostly simply expanded on his ideas. There is a strong sense in which Cavell is a social philosopher ruminating on the nature of life in society, 'alienation', etc. His second book was on Thoreau and he seems animated at times by Rousseauistic problems about wilderness and civilisation. Hence it is no surprise to find him writing of 'the human being's estrangement from the world' (p.213) and asserting that 'movies are inherently anarchic' (p. 214). By this he means that movie stories focus on love and happy endings that are often achieved despite society, even in the teeth of it. Hence the human love relationship has to be self-legitimated.

Pursuits of Happiness examines seven films made in America between 1934 and 1949 which are said by Cavell to constitute a genre, 'the comedy of remarriage'. Tricky as always, Cavell is using two, possibly three, technical words in this characterization. They are, 'genre', 'remarriage' and possibly 'comedy'; 'the' is used conventionally. To begin with 'comedy'. Not all of these films can properly be described as comic, e.g., *His Girl Friday*, which is reworking of the Hecht-McArthur play *The Front Page*, is a melodrama, albeit with wisecracks. 'Remarriage' troubles Cavell, since in not all of the films do the characters divorce each other and remarry, sometimes they don't divorce (*Adam's Rib*), and sometimes the first marriage is to someone else (*It Happened One Night*). In a sample of seven, two that do not fit is quite large, and when we add that in both *The Lady Eve* and *Bringing Up Baby* there is no remarriage at all only a first marriage, the simple-minded reader is liable to get confused. Cavell's ways with counter-examples and exceptions involve wafting them away or dancing around them with prose that rests on little more than the claim that if you demand a resemblance he can show you one. This feat, unlike prestidigitation, is not impressive, because every philosopher knows that everything is similar to everything else, in one way or another, and everything differs from everything else in one way or another. (Popper 1959, Appendix *). So it is very easy to argue resemblance; and not very convincing.

From 1934 to 1949 a finite number of films were made in America. Cavell might better have convinced us by offering a complete list of all comedies of remarriage and then argued that his deviant cases were added to highlight difficult points or because they took their devices from the majority. Empirical research, indeed scholarship of any kind, is not Cavell's *modus operandi*. Whereas Wolfenstein and Leites (1950) in a book which Cavell nowhere cites, and which therefore we can assume he has not read, tell us clearly where and when and how many films they saw in researching their thoughts on love and marriage in American movies.

But the most misleading technical term is 'genre'. In well-established film parlance, this French word for 'type' or 'kind' is descriptive of groups of films identified by the industry and the fans as belonging together, e.g. musicals, westerns, women's pictures, gangsters, horror, screwball comedy, etc. In the hands of film scholars these have been extended to include 'film noir', an attempt to characterize a certain kind of melodrama of the 1940's but not one the industry or the fans had distinguished for themselves. All the films Cavell is writing about could, at a pinch, be classed as 'screwball comedy', but remarriage is only an incidental topic within that genre.

Cavell has his own idea of genre, which begins in his idea of a medium. He believes that what can be achieved in a medium is something to be discovered (1971, pp.31–2); 'only the art itself can discover its possibilities, and the discovery of a new possibility is the discovery of a new medium . . . when such a medium is discovered, it generates new instances' (pp.32, 107). Consciously alluding to Kuhn's notion of a paradigm (n. 38), he seems to be arguing that some exemplary achievement in film provides a means by 'which something specific gets done or said' (p.32) and calls for new instances 'as if to attest that what has been discovered is indeed something more than a single work could convey' (p.107). Warning against the naive idea that because things are classed together they must share an essence in common (I), and finding that Wittgenstein's alternative analysis of 'family resemblance' fails to capture the sense of internal relations to the genre (1981, pp. 27-30), he argues that a genre is called into being by an act of criticism recognizing it as such.

This moves a long way from the received notion of genre. Most usages allow the film makers and the public to recognize the generic. But Cavell is doing something different. It is unfortunate that he wants to appropriate a word already spoken for, but this does not invalidate the notion he has. Putting it differently one might say: a film is made that marks some decisive new turn, either in its subject matter or the manner of its treatment. This then opens up a lot of new possibilities for cinematic expression. Successor films can be thought of as expanding and developing the possibilities contained in the original, to which they are linked by internal historical reference, and by the adoption of its conventions. Not all the conventions need be adopted but, where there is variation, some kind of compensatory device may be necessary otherwise the identification of the successor with the template will be broken. After a while such a new set of conventions seems fully worked out, and the genre peters out. The parallel with Kuhn's view of the role of paradigms in science is striking.

In my own work (1978a) I developed a similar idea to Cavell's which I called the cycle within the genre. There I analysed what I called the cycle of comedies about marriage (ch. II). I contrasted the idyllic depiction of marriage in vintage Hollywood domestic comedy with its gradual erosion in comedies during the 1960s and 1970s. I tentatively correlated this debunking of a sacred American institution with the reality of marriage breakdown and the separation of legitimate sex from marriage and love. Whether such a development is called a cycle within a genre (my terminology) or genre$_c$ (the subscript standing for 'Cavell') is no matter. The question is what problem is being addressed?

At the risk of some structural untidiness I shall digress to explore this now. I have assigned to Part III the problem of using films as a vehicle (Cavell would say 'Medium') for philosophizing, yet I cannot continue to discuss Cavell without coming at those issues, because that is what *Pursuits of Happiness* is about: film as philosophy. The advantages of continuously engaging with Cavell's thought rather than breaking off outweigh, I think, the untidiness.

It would be immodest to regret that Cavell overlooked my (1978a) and hence does not engage in a 'conversation' (more on this later) about the cycle of comedies on marriage. Less personal is a deep regret that he nowhere addresses the work of Wolfenstein and Leites. They were looking at films of 1945-46 and love, family, crime and solution, and performers and onlookers were the topics they discussed in detail. There are too many theses to summarize, but the central one is that American films of that time were preoccupied with the problem of false appearances; the problem, that is, that things and people seem at first to be one way but turn out in reality another. Their most famous exemplar is the 'good-bad' heroine, an alluring woman precisely because she is shady and possibly dangerous, but who always turns out to be blameless, usually selflessly protecting someone else. The reverse is also found, but more rarely. The *father*, a good person in myth, can turn out to be wicked and dangerous. The *person accused* will often turn out to be innocent; the *onlooker* will construe innocent events as compromising (very often a device of comedy); the *humble* but honest person will turn out to have the sparkling talent that the *arrogant* and pushy think they have.

Wolfenstein and Leites emphasize how often stories in American films are premised around people with no family background or connection, strangers in a strange land. They comment how this reflects American emphasis on the family of procreation rather than that of origin. This in turn connects up with the myth of America built by those who severed their ties with their family origins in the Old World and came to America for a new start, a

New Nation.

Compare their work with Cavell's. Cavell argues two main points, to do with the nature of marriage and the nature of woman. In short, he treats these films as meditations on these two matters and, in turn, he treats us to his meditations on the films and topics. While doing this he is also able to offer thoughts on the nature of film itself, particularly the manner in which, he claims, films incorporate a reflexive sense of their own processes of convention and illusion (1981, p.55). At several places he identifies particular characters as embodying the point of view of the film maker himself (he invariably and uncritically identifies this person with the director).

His theme seems to be that a loving marriage is central to human life and yet contains forces that threaten the social fabric. The solution is that couples create a kind of private world:

> What this pair does together is less important than the fact that they do whatever it is together, that they know how to spend time together, even that they would rather waste time together than do anything else – except that no time they are together could be wasted. (1981, p.83)

Remarriage is a device whereby the characters confront the nature of their life together, their need of it, their need to acknowledge it, hence their equality (the second topic), and need to renew the relationship constantly. Marriage involves a constant acceptance that it could end and needs work to be sustained.

All this is a very charming interpretation of these films, stated at somewhat excessive length and much too elliptically, and not very earth-shaking. As I shall discuss in the section on interpretation and on *Rashomon*, the question is whether Cavell shows us how to contest his views. That is, does he indicate to us the possibility that his readings are mistaken, and what sorts of argument would he accept as showing that? Consider the following. In American films, while the Hays' code was in force (see Jowett 1976), almost the only characters in films who had sexual relations were married people. Yet to writers one of the most enticing relations to write about is relations between the sexes. Hays' code, however, prevents one whole area being touched: non-marital sex. Now here is an ingenious solution: make the characters previously married, not just to anyone, but to each other. Presto, sexual knowingness between them is now permitted in allusion and nuance, without violating any of the code's provisions.

That is one kind of argument. Here is another. Cavell's philosophizing smacks of autobiography. He dedicates his book to his five-year-old son and writes in a manner which suggests strongly that he has pondered the nature of marriage in practice as well as philosophy. This would be consistent with his whole approach to philosophy where the philosopher's experience is its heart and soul. Thus in his solution to the problem of scepticism about reality he relies on his own acting and knowing and not being deceived, all of which 'acknowledge' reality. [15] But Cavell's rather romantic notion of marriage as a kind of disruptive but tolerated *folie à deux* might strike others as coyly connubial. Marriage is an important institution in this and other societies not for the sort of bourgeois individualistic reasons he gives, but because it regulates procreation, kinship bonds and property transactions. An outside observer might find the depiction of marriage in these films absurd, hypostatizing a notion of together-ness utterly at variance with the practice of most of mankind, including in America. Most of the couples in these films are played by film stars and one might hazard that the only place any of them inhabited marriages as Cavell imagines them to be is on these films. So these films are not in any sense drawn from or about the experience of the stars who play them.

There is no knowing how Cavell would react to such arguments. He - has, after all, 'faith in the authority of one's everyday experience' (1981, p.240). And there is a further reason which has to do with his conception of the nature of philosophizing. I have presented philosophy as merely a name for one branch of the continuous rational tradition of trying to solve problems and assess the truth of our solutions. Cavell's Introduction makes it clear that he has a different vision: philosophy for him is civilized conver-sation. Such a relaxed view is possible only if what one is puzzled about is not urgent and fascinating problems about the world, but puzzles about what other philosophers have said, or diagnosis of the mistakes people get into through careless use of words. This complacent and irrationalist model of philosophy seems to be in vogue in American philosophy as I write, with an academic bestseller – Rorty's *The Mirror of Nature* – entirely devoted to it.[16] The transition from frantic efforts by the profession to

119

demonstrate 'relevance' in the 1960s back to a 1950s posture of philosophy as cultivated chit-chat, needs the talents of a Gellner to explain.[17]

Most amazing of all, Cavell makes a connection between his idea of philosophy as conversation and his idea of marriage: drawing on Milton's phrase 'a meet and happy conversation is the chiefest and noblest end of marriage'. Anything but unaware of the sexual overtone (viz. 'criminal conversation'), Cavell is here once more juxtaposing if not identifying philosophy and sex. In *The World Viewed* (p.100) he remarked on the connection between philosophy and seduction and drew a parallel between sexual intimacy and 'one soul's investigation of another'. But whereas in philosophy teaching (all teaching?) an element of sexual attraction may be found, it is incidental to philosophy as problem-solving, which can after all go on in solitude. Furthermore, his idea of marriage as a long-running conversation (in the sense of talk, not sex):

> In adducing Milton's view of the matter of conducting a meet and happy conversation, I have emphasized that while Milton has in view an entire mode of association, a form of life, he does also mean a capacity, say a thirst, for talk (1981, p.152)

is very particularistic. It is not clear to me that partners in the vast majority of (happy) marriages on this earth engage in extended talk, or mutual investigation of souls. Hence I wonder at what does not bother Cavell: what on earth is this preposterous fantasy doing in so many American films?

I want to stress, before closing my discussion of Cavell, that I have raised two questions about film as a vehicle for philosophy. The first is, how do we challenge the philosopher's interpretations of the film? Second, equally important, is how do we challenge the film's philosophizing? These questions are different – although we can, by carelessness, collapse them into one another. Of course the philosopher in his work of interpretation is trying to articulate what he understands the film to be saying. To challenge his understanding is different from challenging what it is he under-stands. In my discussion of Cavell I have concentrated on the interpretations Cavell imposes, and the unclear procedure by which he does so. It only remains to say that if the philosophy of marriage he talks about is embodied in the films he studies then, as philosophy, those films are absurd.

4.3 PHENOMENOLOGY, LINDEN, WEISS

At the beginning of this book I indicated that I thought films had a significance in philosophy that made them more than of casual or applied interest. Trying to find their place in aesthetics may be merely a matter of applying or extending aesthetic theories to them. It may also be, as I shall argue in Part II, a little more than that. Films may explode many of the traditional ideas with which aestheticians operate and hence force a radical rethinking of that whole subject. With the use of films for philosophizing, the subject of my final part, it would seem that strictly applied interest is involved. Films can be used to broadcast philosophy in much the same way as print or the airwaves. Here again it may be possible to argue a little more strongly. I shall explore the idea that film is the harbinger of something new in philosophy as well as in art. Philosophy as we know it began in Ancient Greece among the affluent elite classes with leisure for reflection on transcendental matters. In other cultures such reflection is confined to the clerkly and priestly classes who kindly hand down their wisdom to the rest. Film, however, undertakes to philosophize through a mass medium in what is often called the age of the mass man. It follows that these efforts and the evaluation of these efforts is a far from casual or applied matter but rather one which may affect both the topics philosophy pursues and the forms within which it chooses to contain itself.

Coming towards the end of this part, I need to sum up what has been learned from the writers discussed, and press forward discussion of the problems themselves so that what I am saying overall, rather than in incidental remarks, becomes clear and criticizable. Such a taking stock will also ease the pains of transition to phenomenology.

Let us return then to the problems of knowledge and of being. Film, it seems to me, makes serious trouble for both these problems. Not only does it vary and illustrate standard arguments in intriguingly new ways, it also stands itself as a counter-example to widely-held views. In the field of knowledge it creates acute difficulties for any theory of direct perceptual knowledge. Stimulating strongly two of the senses, it presents us with the at first near insuperable problem of demarcating this film world from the real world. It further tickles us with the knowledge that this film world and our watching it is also in some sense part of what we call the real world. If Munsterberg is right it confronts us with our own mental processes and yet makes us less rather than more susceptible to illusion and hallucination. Moreover, it explodes the metaphor of the cave.

Be it recalled that the continuation of the cave story in *The Republic* is that one of the chained prisoners slips his shackles and crawls upward towards the light. Eager to enlighten his comrades he makes his way back into the cave and fails utterly to convince those still chained that they are victims of illusion and that the world of things is quite different from the shadows of their reality.

From this metaphor Plato draws a parable about the human epistemological condition. The knowledge of the senses is merely that of flickering shadows, faint traces and distortions of the real things. But most of us are cloistered in an epistemological darkness, literally quite incapable of seeing beyond the appearances to the way things are, the things in themselves. Luckily, there are those among us gifted with special insight that goes through the appearances, through the world of delusive opinion and penetrates to the true, real and unchanging essence of things, their Form. We must learn from the parable to listen to those so gifted among us, to be humble and to learn. Perhaps even, if *The Republic* is to be taken literally, to be ready to hand over the governance of our city to them because only they possess the wisdom to run it justly.

Munsterberg has shown us a basic flaw in this parable. Imprisoned in front of flickering shadows, unable to move our heads, unable to interact through the other senses with the world, we should most likely be able to make no sense whatsoever of the shadows and echoes that fill the cave. No-one need think Plato cheated; rather that psychology shows the flaw in his thought-experiment. Without contact with the tangible world we cannot construct it out of shadows. Shadows are shadows of the tangible; grasping the one without the other is impossible. One of the interesting things about feral children (subject of at least two movies)[18] is just how unable they are to recognize, enter and cope with our world. Hence Plato's escapee, far from seeing the light, as it were, about the true nature of things, is far more likely simply to die, unable to cope.

Growing up in human society, we as children have to learn to organize the interaction of our senses and our minds in order to build up a coherent and usable world picture. A world picture that enables us to function. This is an arduous process that takes at least fifteen to twenty years. In super-adding to the task, the challenge, which is playful not necessary, of similarly learning to organize the interaction of our minds and senses to enable us to make sense of movies, we also learn how to distinguish movies in our environment as not real. Thus, we all become as Plato's philosophers: we learn as a matter of course to map, and adjust and play with the boundary between appearance and reality. So complete is our mastery that we can reflect on it: having learned the difference between shadow world and real world we can, with some suspicion, address the claim that what we mistake for the real world is just a more elaborate shadow world, concealing the eternal forms of things in themselves. If there is anything to that suspicion we can address the evidence with confidence, having navigated the shadow/real line ourselves, and hence be suspicious of the possible self-serving that may be involved in the claim of privileged access made by the philosophers.

Films, then, bring back the problem of appearance and reality from the rarefied atmosphere of philosophical disputation, restore it to the people, who recognize it as a basic concern, and who learn to solve it on a routine and playful basis. Concretized and demystified, it involves a basic mental function, that of cognition, and while films do not show us how we do it, they do show us that we can and do do it. Thus the higher mysticism of the philosophers, the claim to deep insight into difficult matters, is quietly and rightly debunked. The clerks and the priests and educated elite have their privilege threatened, their claims to intellectual as well as social superiority undermined. A major legitimating device of social privilege – higher intellectual insight – is challenged at its very base by film.

Having looked at the difficulties films can create for sensationalism I shall now revert to my other contention about film's capacity to create discomfort for phenomenologists. At first it struck me as sheer coincidence that most of the philosophical works written about film since Munsterberg were phenomenological. In the case of the French it followed from the fact that virtually all French philosophy was dominated by German thought; that if they turned to writing about film, their work would be phenomenological. There was also the trivial reason that all phenomena are open to phenomenological investigation, so why not films? But all this did not explain the dominance of phenomenological writers in English writings about the philosophy of films too. It thus seemed to me that an intellectual explanation was called for.

I searched the books and articles for one, only to fail to find it. Phenomenologists have a tendency simply to announce that their aim is phenomenologically to describe the films. Why they should bother is not a question that makes sense. But Agassi has taught me to trust the slight odour sent up by such moves. Some topics, he notes, are pursued vigorously at a certain time, while others, in some ways crying out for discussion, are ignored. Rejecting the idea that such choices are arbitrary, he seeks in the case of science to trace back concentration of interest on a topic to underlying metaphysical concerns (Agassi 1964). His reasoning is the following: metaphysics lies behind all science but is regularly denied. Nevertheless, certain topics are in sensitive relation to current metaphysics. These are the ones that will tend to draw intellectual effort towards them. They are trouble spots that scientists sense the need to resolve even if they repudiate all interest in metaphysics. Applying this reasoning to films is straightforward. If members of a philosophical movement pay an abnormal amount of attention to a phenomenon then the chances are that phenomenon is in some way problematic to their ideas. Their attention is directed there in order to defuse the problem, to render the phenomenon harmless to their ideas.

Pinpointing the manner in which films are problematic for phenomenology is not an easy matter. There are two reasons for this: the phenomenological school is far from monolithic, and what can be said about one thinker or sub-group does not necessarily apply to others. Even more troublesome: the phenomenological philosophy is to a considerable extent programmatic. It consists, that is to say, of intellectual promissory notes about what can or will be accomplished.

Bearing these difficulties in mind we need to sketch a little background of phenomenology. Descartes' project, as already mentioned, was to found knowledge on secure ground. Taking the possibility of doubting something as a sign that it was not securely grounded, he was able to doubt everything around him. Reaching the question of his own thought-process, including his act of doubting, he wondered if that could be doubted away as well. Like a rabbit out of a hat he produces God, who must be a deceiver if he lets me think 'I think therefore I am' and be deluded. For Descartes, God cannot be a deceiver.

Husserl had less taste for God and chided Descartes for taking a wrong turn. Rather he argued that the secure foundation for all we know is in immediate experience. This is not sensation and hence empirical; not logical and hence analytic; but *a tertium quid*, phenomenological. The task of phenomenology is to describe the essence of phenomena as they present themselves to conscious-ness. In the usual method of phenomenology a crucial methodo-logical device is the practice of bracketing existence, that is, of reasoning by means of examples which might exist but need not and of examples which cannot exist but about which we can reflect. It is only by means of such examples that phenomenologists hope to get at the essence of what it is to be something or other rather than something else.

Husserl's solution to the problem of appearance and reality, if I may write in a way that would be rejected by his followers, is that it is badly formulated. As long as we think of images presenting themselves to the mind, and hence our problem being to tell images that correspond to things from images that correspond to nothing, he says we will remain trapped in weak responses like 'intensity', 'fullness', and the like (1982, p.263). His own theory, presented with the help of reflection on Dürer's etching 'Knight, Death and the Devil', distinguishes consciousness from the objects of consciousness and that somehow an image is a 'structure' of consciousness rather than an object of it, or a content of it. Perceiving a picture, we see some lines and shapes, some configurations of knight, death and the devil and we perceive, as it were, flesh-and-blood knight, death and the devil. This is a bit like saying, as the sense-data positivists did, that we perceive shapes and colours, also figures and ground, and also real things. In criticism of this it has often been said that what we perceive is objects and persons; when we look at a landscape that is what we perceive, a landscape, not coloured daubs. The problem is, what about when someone paints a landscape so accurate that we think we are looking through a window? or, as in the case of the sculptures of Duane Hanson, where we walk through the gallery and address the guard, who turns out to be a sculpture? Hoping for some enlightenment on this one looks to Husserl only to find him breaking off thus:

> For spontaneity there is an abyss here which the pure Ego can transcend only in the essentially new form of actualizing action and creation (where account must also be taken of hallucinating), (1982, p.263)

So by acting on or towards the deceptions or hallucinations we check the reality.

In a certain sense this is OK. Indeed, it is, as a matter of empirical practice, through the marshalling of ancillary evidence that we decide what is deceptive and what is not. But this seems to beg the question for Husserl, since it admits there to be no difference between the structuring of consciousness of reality and of illusion. Films create a lesser problem than *trompe-l'oeil* art, though, since instances where someone undertakes action in relation to them, as though they were real, is very uncommon. The case of Mr Hinckley (who failed to assassinate President Reagan), unable to differentiate Jody Foster the flesh-and-blood actress and student at Yale, from Jody-Foster-as-the-child-prostitute-Iris (in *Taxi Driver*) needing-care-and-protection, is manifestly pathological. Yet action is always in the real world and Husserl's method is supposed to bracket the real world while considering the pure essence of phenomena.

We are beginning, I think the reader should see, to make an oblique reapproach to the problem of existence, of being, of phenomena. Films are obviously a certain sort of grist to the mill of the phenomenologist because they provide a ready-made case where existence is bracketed. That is, things on film do not exist here and now in the manner that they appear to do. Yet they can give us enough data for phenomenological reflection closely resembling that which we would undertake when confronted by the *Lebenswelt*. At the same time they seem to present conundra. We will want to know what the essence of films is and to distinguish it pretty clearly from the essence of being-in-the-world. Of course, watching a film is a form of being-in-the-world, but it

126

also involves a phenomenon we might call being-in-the-film. It would be too simple to say this was a fancy name for identification. Rather might we consider the following: watching a frightening movie we, the audience, experience fear. Out in the world, we, the audience, sometimes experience fear. Yet in the cinema we, the audience, are not in any danger: our fear is imaginary. In most films that are frightening we are onlookers to actions and it is the characters on screen who are in danger. At times they know they are in danger and we share their fear; at other times they are oblivious to the danger that we are aware of and, so we fear for them. But whether we share their fear or fear for them, the question is whether our fear in the cinema is a phenomenon of fear or is it a phenomenon of cinema-going that is phenomenologically distinguishable from fear itself? By fear itself one might mean the emotion one experiences when in actual danger in the lived world, as opposed to observing danger in the illusion of the cinema.

With these preliminary forays into phenomenology it is, I think, appropriate to pass on to George Linden whose *Reflections on the Screen* (1970) is the longest phenomenological treatment of films in English. Linden characterizes the nature of the film experience as 'dyadic', consisting in 'the interdependence, coexistence, and synthesis of objective/subjective, outer world/inner world, universal/particular relationships . . . the spectator can participate in film'. The spectator's participation is described as an experience of 'excarnation or bi-association' (p.v). In simpler words, we experience the world as though we are outside our bodies, yet we do that experiencing through our bodies.

Unlike Cavell, who thinks that things present to us from which we are absent are past events, memories, Linden argues the movies are insistently in the present. In this he is at one with other phenomenologists:

> while one is viewing the film all places and moments are *present* when they are shown. Film has no past tense, no 'was'. The linguistic equivalent for cinematic presentation of the past is: 'That *is* how it was'; and for the future: 'This is how it will be.' (Kolker and Ousley 1973, p.391)

Much the same point is made by Weiss (1975, p.20), Danto (1979, p.5) and Sesonske (1980 *passim*). Linden declares:

127

> Most stories begin 'Once upon a time'. Films do not. They begin 'Once upon a now' . . . (p.2). The basic premise of theatre is 'What happens next?' The basic premise of the novel is 'What *has* happened?', the basis premise of film is 'What is going on now?' (p.7)

This is more colourful but less accurate than Kolker and Ousley. Phenomenologically, we are being told, the movies, or, more precisely, our experience of the movies, is always in the present tense, even when the narrative involves what are called flashbacks or flashforwards. We watch movies during an elapse of real time, but movie time, like movie space, is imaginary. This strong presentness affects the way film-goers relate to them:

> The motion picture can drive directly toward and record our ways-of-being-in-the-world, and hence it is more concerned with us as beings than personae. The motion picture does not provide us with a mere 'redemption of physical reality' [19]; it provides us with other voices, other worlds to be in. It is not primarily a representation, but a presentation. It presents us with an illusory world both livid and lived. It presents us man alive in the concrete circumstances of his being-in-the-world. (p.156)

Linden's thought needs help in articulation here. What he seems to be saying is that films are not tied to a single reality, namely that of this actual world, but rather that they open before us many possible worlds which present themselves so vividly that we have a sense of what it is to be in them. This distinguishes him from Cavell, who uses the definite article and thus seems to see 'the' (film) world viewed and the real world lived as continuations of each other. Yet it creates difficulties within phenomenology: if we have such a strong sense of being in the possible worlds of films, how will we bracket them from the real world in which we live?

Carried away with his enthusiastic immersion in movie worlds, Linden goes even further:

> The impact of presence, authenticity of illusion, the displacement of the body of the spectator, emotional infectiousness, the fusion of psychic levels, the disjunctive relations of the audience, and the individuate identification with the viewpoint of the camera by the eye of the spectator – all of these things are to be discovered in the experience

itself . . . The old newsreels did not lie. They claimed to be the
eyes and ears of the world. They were. (pp. 234-5)

Being careful to overlook the rhetorical excess of this passage (if
movies present possible worlds they cannot be the eyes and ears of
the world only *a* world), and the questionable points (the camera
shifts position and the film-goer often hears sounds that have no
visible source so whatever point of view is constructed is not
simply that of the camera/eye), we can see how Linden is lining
himself up to be baffled by the problem of differentiating not just
the real from appearances generally, but, within movies, the
fictional from the factual.

Seeing such a problem looming Linden takes a way out that is a
favourite of irrationalists of the last one hundred years: he suggests
that the problem is one created by (rather than formulated in)
words. Language somehow becomes suspect. In so far as language
is the embodiment of thought, this suspicion may lead on from a
distrust of thought or come back towards it. And since films
contain both thought and language, it follows that either they
should be distrusted, or that they should be lauded to the extent
that they do not utilize language:

> Like other theatrically oriented critics, Pauline Kael does not
> invite us to see along with her. What she does invite us to do is
> to think along with her. Thus she uses film as an occasion for an
> essay on some topic that may or may not be directly related to
> the film. In other words, a film provides her the excuse to discuss
> some topic which the film has initiated in her thought process.
> But a film is not thought, it is perceived . . . Films are not
> literature. They are at best image-writing. The literary film critic
> has a concept where his heart ought to be . . . (pp. 8-9)

> Words in films should be kept minimal, expressive, and
> concrete. Young children show and tell. Directors, like poets,
> should show. (p.10)

Philosophers, traders in words, should worry when they start
distrusting words. It is likely that the problem is not words but
what the words reveal about incoherence and contradiction in the
position they are espousing. Look at the juxtaposition in the last
three sentences quoted: speaking is contrasted with showing, and

poets – the skilled wordsmiths above all others – are declared showers not tellers.

There is no point in launching a general criticism of irrationalism. Not only is it all-pervasive but its shoddy tradition contains some ingenious argumentation that requires careful analysis and dissection to expose. Irrationalists are nearly always disappointed rationalists and hence tenacious, not to say ferocious, in their rationalist defence of their irrationalism. Where irrationalism is vague, incoherent, or unhelpful, as in Linden, that should be sufficient critique.

Linden contrasts thought and perception, apparently unaware of the possibility that perception is no more than a mode of thinking, namely thinking about what we call the external world. At a guess I imagine his idea is that perception is a causal process, that the stimuli in the world simply impact on our senses which then mirror or reflect the stimuli. Even without a philosophical education we can call on Munsterberg to explain carefully how this passive receptor view will not do, how the imposition of order on the undifferentiated manifold of experience is performed by the mind, by thought. We cannot *see* movies without *thinking* about them.

Munsterberg did defend film's silence, and could have said film is 'image-writing' and words 'should be kept minimal'. Indeed, he did say something of the sort. Linden, however, is writing in the later 1960s. No silent film had been made for forty years. He scarcely discusses any. He is inured, as are we all, to sound movies; movies, that is, in which the expressive resources of the creators encompass dialogue, narration, sound-effects and music deployed as a complement to images. The old prejudice that words necessarily spoil a film has succumbed to too many counter-examples to bother to list. We shall return, in Part II, to this astonishing love affair not with silent films as such, but with the quite prejudicial aesthetics developed for the silent photoplay. Recall that Cavell specifies movies as 'the world *viewed*', not viewed and heard'. Haig Khatchadourian similarly betrays what we can call the prejudice towards the visuals (1975, pp. 273, 277-8). So severe is the problem that I shall suggest in Part II that we declare silent film and sound film to be two different media, much as we differentiate movies from television.

To return to Linden and phenomenology. There is a thread

connecting Cavell, Linden, Weiss and some others that is independent of phenomenology, but not of the thinkers of that school and its existentialist branch. This is the idea that films assist us in contemplating what they sometimes call 'the predicament of modern man'. Quotes are around this phrase to signal my distrust of it. I am unclear who modern man is, and whether 'he' is in a predicament, never mind what 'it' is. This is sometimes seen as alienation, as isolation, as loneliness, as nausea, as self-conscious- ness (and hence modernism in art is a mode of this predicament). There is a vague line of argument that goes: since movies are the first new art of this alienated age they will embody, show and perhaps clarify the central predicament. The hunt is on.

> Like the rainbow, the film does not 'stand' anywhere. It is constituted not only by moisture and light but by sound and sight. It is a visible-aural object but intangible – one which inhabits a created space-time that is non-tangential to our natural standpoint – a kind of perpetual elsewhere that enters the presence of immediate experience. The film does not have the ordinary properties of physical things. It is a projector- amplifier-eye-ear-created image; a visual and sonorous monogram that emerges for perceptive engagement. As with the rainbow, we return again and again to perceive it with the ever- reborn hope that this time, at the end of it, we will find treasure.

> Motion pictures, like dreams or rainbows, are true myths that we tell ourselves so that we may try to come to grips with what life means in the living of it. Motion pictures, when understood, end in revelation. (pp. 278–9)

Elsewhere (p. 275) Linden affirms that by opening ourselves to the feelings of others, to a sharing of our community, we can overcome the alienation predicament.

Paul Weiss published *Cinematics* in 1975. I leave the reader to speculate about the coincidence of three books on the philosophy of film published in four years, none apparently aware of the progress of the other, and none bothering with Munsterberg. Weiss's is a less passive view than Linden's, a less reality-oriented one than Cavell's:

> A film is completed by the viewers before it; they are

transformed by the film into occupants of a world, part of which the film makes visible. (p.5)

Unlike Cavell, who delights in film's enabling us to be invisible and impossibly magical voyeurs of the reconstituted world, Weiss finds in movies a world of appearances that are both opaque (that is we can see them but not through them), and also translucent – because they point beyond themselves back to reality:

> Film creates appearances revelatory of Existence, and incidentally throws light on the other finalities . . . . *Film is a created (audio) visual ordered whole of recorded incidents*, providing one with a controlled emotional introduction, primarily to Existence, and secondarily to other finalities. (p.22)

The finalities in question are Death, Existence, God, etc.

Our predicament has, it seems, something to do with estrangement. Once upon a time men were in touch with the nature of which they are a part; they were integrated, felt part of the whole, were not self-consciously individualistic. Nowadays things are different. We stand apart from society, from other people, even from ourselves and we look to philosophy and art to articulate that predicament and show us either how to escape it (Linden's community) or at least come to terms with it. This, anyway, is the sense I make out of these writers. Neither the predicament nor the answer to it (e.g. Death, God) are things they agree about. Now comes film. Why film? Here's a stab at an answer. Husserl's way out of this predicament took him back to the pivotal philosopher of self-consciousness, Descartes. The self-conscious method of doubt, far from showing a way out of alienation and detachment is an embodiment of it. It encourages a sense of the self as an interior point of consciousness looking out at an 'external world' in which there are separate objects existing independently of me and of my contemplation of them. One line of criticism is to deny all the components of this picture: the division of self from world, of subject from object, of consciousness as interior intensity. The danger is a collapse either into a materialism that denies the differentiable person and the sense of individual self or into an idealism that takes everything into a dream world of the mind. Husserl's solution, so far as I can grasp it, seems in general to have been to attend to the very act of consciousness itself, bracketing, setting aside, or adopting the neutral modification towards the question of the reality of the world we live in. When we have achieved contact with the essence of phenomena we can take off the brackets and resume contact with the world, overcome alienation.

Our unreflective state he called 'the natural attitude', something obviously we break by 'bracketing'. The intriguing problem is how will we go back to the natural attitude? It is not that suspending the natural attitude is a way out of our predicament, but loss of all possibility of being in the natural attitude that is our predicament (Gellner 1975). We are Cartesian beings forever. Consciousness of our predicament, like self-consciousness induced in the child, is an irreversible state. As A. J. Ayer once said, it is perverse to make a tragedy of what could not be otherwise.

What of film? Notice how closely the Cartesian description of the self corresponds to film-going: the individual point of consciousness looking out from its interior, at a world that is given and separate, containing objects that permit us to see and manipulate them in their separateness from each other and us. No wonder Linden wants us to flow into an affectual union with the images on the screen: if we pour ourselves out there we may learn to pour ourselves out to others, to become permeable (p.275) and break down our isolation. It's just that it isn't possible; it is a fantasy comparable to those novelists I mentioned who dream of our entering the onscreen world. Our epistemological condition exactly parallels our film-going conditions; we are spectators who cannot become participants. We are in a permanent condition of bracketing, our *Lebenswelt* is one of standing outside it and ourselves reflecting; the whole world being trained in phenomenology (Husserl's dream) will no more change this than the whole world being psychoanalysed (Freud's dream) will result in the end of neuroses and unhappiness. Freud in his later writings accepted the idea that our condition is inherent; one might accept that, without accepting his particular explanation that it is inherent in upright posture and civilization. Films are a ready-made metaphor for lost innocence. We gaze into a world of people conscious of themselves but unconscious of us, therefore reflective to a limited degree. The power and flexibility of the medium emerges as, at first playfully and ever more seriously, film, without breaking its conventions, becomes able to portray the process of its own experiencing. Characters talk to the audience, pull the edges of the frame over towards them, push the 'The End' title back off in order to have more time; cartoon characters jump out of the inkwell and defy the hand that draws them; refusing to be confined, characters allude knowingly to, even step in and out of, other movies; and so on. Movies show us how to live with bracketing.

Ready-made illustration for phenomenology is one explanation for film's popularity with phenomenologists. But we are pressing the more intriguing possibility that films are troublesome. What if it proves difficult to distinguish fear at a film from fear out in the real world? What if films provide simulacra of immediate experience so powerful that reflection and intuition do not succeed in driving a phenomenological wedge between the two? Clearly, this would be a disaster. It would strand phenomenology in an idealist position, unable to distinguish the world imagined from the world real. Here we may begin to understand something of why Bazin and his follower Cavell are so concerned to forge a hard connection between the real world and the world on film. Hands-off mechanism or automatism is their guarantee that what is in film is continuous with, an extension of, the real world. Bazin, in his article, mentions his pleasure in a scene from a British film he otherwise did not much appreciate; *Where No Vultures Fly*. In this there is a sequence where a female lion leaves her cub and goes off. A little girl picks up the cub and begins to carry it home. The returning lion begins to follow the little girl, possibly to attack. At the climactic moment, when the little girl's father sees both his daughter holding the cub and the following lion, tells the little girl to put down the cub slowly then walk slowly towards him, and the following lion picks up the cub and slinks off, Bazin is thrilled because this is accomplished in one shot in which lion, child and father are all encompassed. Hence the reality of the scene is captured by the shot, whereas the sequence leading up to it is done in cut-aways. This is Bazin's argument for the long take as opposed to montage. We then know that what we are seeing is part of the world or, to speak more precisely, was at the time it was shot part of the real world.

Here also is the reason for an equivocation between, on the one side, invoking magic – photography allowing redemption of the lost past, bringing to my presence an object to which I am absent and such like – and, on the other side, the antithesis of magic, materialism – the material or mechanical nature of photography. Photography is for the phenomenologist material magic. If the world on film is an extension, recapitulation, time slice, or redemption of some past state of the world then its phenomenology is much simplified and the dangers much reduced. It is no longer a problem of appearance and reality, but rather it does and does not screen off the scenes beyond it, or on it.

There are other problems that films pose for the phenomenological attitude, less philosophically serious, perhaps, but nevertheless relevant. A common move of phenomenologists is to argue that the notion of intentionality, that consciousness is always consciousness of something or other, breaks down the idea of an observing subject hiding in Cavell's words behind the self looking out at an external world. The so-called external world is not external to the viewer, otherwise the very interaction of viewing, not to mention experiencing, would be unintelligible. Rather is bracketing merely a means of analysing the *Lebenswelt* in order to achieve a true integration with it. Films, unfortunately, preserve in the amber of experience the notion of a viewing subject and an experienced object, interacting it is true, but not in a manner that can break down the subject/object distinction. Only if they were to cleave to Munsterberg's argument about the interaction between the film and the mind would they be able to escape the conclusion that subject and object are separate in film as they are in life.

Unfortunately for Bazin and Cavell, the world of movies includes cartoons and abstractions, scenes shot in real time and others not shot in any time at all. Some directors use long takes, others montage; and most judiciously blend the two as they see the necessities of exposition. But they all cut, and once they cut, however frequently, the mind creates a world that is nowhere present and has never been anywhere present. As Sesonske puts it in his *reductio* argument about *Jules et Jim*:

> Spade and Archer never shared an office in San Francisco; Jules and Jim never shared a girl in pre-war Paris . . . . But suppose I were an experienced time traveller and wished actually to witness that brief moment in the projected world when Jules watches Catherine and Jim drive off the ruined bridge. To where would I go, and to when? To Paris in 1933? I wouldn't

135

find them there. Well then, Paris in 1961. I might indeed find Oskar Werner and Henri Serre, but Jules et Jim? What if I watched on Tuesday Morning, say, all seventeen takes of Oskar Werner by the river, from which three brief shots of Jules watching will be cut into the film? (1974b, p. 565)

And of course the answer to these rhetorical questions comes back that I will not find them *there*. Not just the camera, the film, the chemicals, the sets, the script, the projector, the cinema are humanly-made artifacts. Above all, the apparent world projected on the screen is a human artifact, an artifact of the mind, however much assisted by a lot of material devices. It is a world that is bounded by the frame, by the cut, by the opening and the closing titles. It makes no more sense to ask what becomes of things on film than it makes sense to ask of Hamlet, why did he not resolve his Oedipal feelings? I am not a censor and do not arrogate to myself any power to discourage such talk. All I want to stress is that it is sheer imagination: that is, it is a new imaginative material added to, even if inspired by, that already present to us. We can toy with there being a world beyond the frame if that pleases us, if that enhances the self-delusion of crossing from appearance into reality. But just as we get the impression of depth where there is no depth, we get the impression of a world where there is no world.

Perhaps we can even learn from films about philosophical matters. One idea that unifies the empiricists and the phenomenologists is the model of man as being an observer on the world, as acting on the world as object, he being a subject. Confronted with the doctrine explicitly, it is often disavowed, but both sides find it hard to replace it with a different model and it sneaks out in their talk. The problem is this: what is the relation of being to consciousness? In a way the answer is straightforward: consciousness is part of being, not a detached observation post that does not participate. What we need is a model of self and world that will mediate between being and consciousness and will not reify either nor reduce one to the other.

Does not film provide us with that model? From the start I have argued that through film we toy with the problem. At this point I can add the sharp point that this toying is itself a solution. What is the solution? To begin with, what is the problem? The problem is, how to differentiate appearance from reality? The solution then is, play with the problem, play with various attempts at different- iation. Or, if you like, the solution says: this is a problem that is not in some definitive way soluble. Doubts about the reality of things are bound to arise. Toy with them until they become urgent. When do they become urgent? When evidence shows that current theory is in some clear way mistaken. It then follows that all the entities postulated by current theory are up for challenge. Then the urgency becomes to find new theories that pass tests and which either replace current notions of what is real with a new set, or which target prior candidates for disposal and preserve others in the new regime.

The parallel with film is now complete. Developmentally we start as children looking behind the TV for the little people, or trying to stick our hands into the screen. Such naive realism yields gradually to a more sophisticated physics in practice (not in theory because very few children ever end up knowing enough physics to explain what happens on TV). More mature, a film invites us to take it for real, whether it is a fiction, a documentary, a scientific record, or a cartoon. This invitation is offered and accepted, knowing that reality is in fact sitting in a dark room with powerful light and sound sources that drench us. We, as film-goers, assess the putative reality we are offered just as we assess theories. A minimum requirement is that they be internally consistent – this is a very subtle matter sometimes, involving exactly which images must succeed each other if we are to maintain a consistent sense of the on-screen space. Next we require that it be consistent with other theories we hold or, if inconsistent, such as when Superman flies, minimally so. Third it must be consistent with its own evidence. When a documentary shows us, as does John Huston's *San Pietro*, a soldier throwing a grenade followed by a close shot of the grenade exploding, we are alerted to the worrying thought that the grim and realistic surface of this film may conceal a good deal of artifactual manipulation. Whether or not that will delegitimate the whole claim of the film is a matter for reflection.

PART TWO

MOVIES AS AN AESTHETIC PROBLEM

There is no such thing as art with a capital A, only artists.
(E.H. Gombrich, *The Story of Art*, 1950)

S.   Tell me, are there any film makers that influenced you in any way, that you learned something from, or do you feel completely self-made?

B.   No, no, no, no. I have grown up with a tradition. I don't think somebody just becomes a director, you know. We are like stones in a building, all of us. We all depend on the people coming before; I am just a part of this. So, I depend very much on a Swedish film tradition, Sjostrom and Stiller, and on the Swedish theater tradition – Sjoberg has meant a lot to me. He is my neighbour. He is marvellous. And then, you know, when I was young, nineteen or twenty years old, I saw the French pictures. . . . But then, of course, I have always seen pictures; I like to go to the movies. I'm a movie-goer.

(Simon 1972, pp. 19–20).

5

ART AND SCIENCE

Both the philosopher of science and the philosopher interested in films find much to dismay them in the branch of philosophy known as 'aesthetics'. Having both loyalties, I write this with some feeling. To the philosopher of science aesthetics looks poorly organized, showing little signs of progress, far more deeply Hegelian and anti-rationalist than other philosophical fields. To the philosopher of film the dismay comes from neglect: in the huge literature on aesthetics there is very little about films. Naturally, there is nothing whatsoever before 1889 and even for some time thereafter. But in the major journals and textbooks down to this day, films are as likely as not to be ignored. Six admirably rational works of recent vintage, Hospers' *Meaning and Truth in the Arts*, Wollheim's *Art and Its Objects*, Goodman's highly influential work, *The Languages of Art*, Scruton's *Art and Imagination*, Danto's *The Transfiguration of the Commonplace*, Sparshott's *The Theory of the Arts*, all fail to cite any film, still less to deal in general with film as one of the arts. In Danto's and Sparshott's cases, this despite the authors having written elsewhere about film. In another remarkable case of Harvard colleagues ignoring each other, Cavell's book mentions Goodman in neither edition, and Goodman returns the favour. Suzanne Langer appended a few pages on films to her classic work *Feeling and Form*. But the philosopher of art to whom I shall pay the greatest respect by attempting to work out ideas parallel to his for films, Sir Ernst Gombrich, scarcely mentions films in book after book, even when dealing with motion (1982).

141

Aesthetics traditionally concerns itself with the nature of beauty, and of understanding and appreciating those activities which aim at beauty, namely the arts. Hidden behind such an anodyne characterization is a pervasive problem that is regularly alluded to and evaded: the relationship between art and science. In an intellectual milieu divided into the two cultures there is a tendency for people to elect more interest in one or the other, and perhaps even to feign ignorance of the other. Yet the positivist rhetoric of so many scientists, and the idealist/relativist rhetoric of so many humanists, betrays prejudice disguised as lack of interest.

To map the nature of the conflict we need to add that people in the arts speak of their work as possessing not only beauty but truth; scientists, while consciously pursuing truth, will sometimes acknowledge that their work has beauty and that such a consideration may, other things being equal, affect their theoretical choices. A simple-minded solution to this rivalry would be to argue that the arts rank beauty above truth; the sciences rank truth above beauty. Once upon a time two further manoeuvres were possible. The first was to identify beauty and truth, to deny that there can be the one without the other; but ours seems to be an age when there is wide agreement that much of what seems to be true is ugly, and there are beautiful things that are false. The second manoeuvre was that beauty, because of its associations with refinement and the sublime, was taken without argument to be the nobler and more important value, truth tending to be identified with the mundane, possibly even the despised practical.

The advent of science in the modern world has, I think, changed all that. Proclaiming a devotion both to truth and to practice, science has taken on enormous cognitive weight. In transforming our world view it has devalued all previous world views, many of them expressed in and sustaining the greatest of past works of art; in transforming the thought and technology of our society, it has displaced the classes that formerly consumed and legitimated that art, as well as the classes which formerly produced that art. The ruler whose education trains him to master elegant calligraphy and the writing of poems in an archaic language is, in this modern age, 'out of touch'. Much of our world is a by-product of science and in it art is often reduced to the status of decoration. Is it any wonder that artists in their struggle to gain status have launched vitriolic attacks on science as the modern juggernaut, accusing it of being

142

dehumanizing, anti-life, lacking values and taste, elevating the common above the refined, desecrating nature, being, in some sense, unnatural?

Even when artists say little or nothing about science, it lurks in the background as a preoccupation (Agassi 1979). Once science exists art is forced both to compete with it, and, much more serious, to define itself in relation to it. If art does not produce knowledge, does not produce useful things, if it does not shape society and science does, then the obvious question is, 'what use is art?' This question, which a sociologist would see as seeking to legitimate the activities of art, preoccupies much art and many artists in the scientific age. We all need structures of rationalization for engaging in the activities that we do. If there is a powerful body of argument that suggests (however unfairly) that our activities are superfluous, parasitic even, making the counter-case is always (however implicitly) going on.

Just as the arts have reeled under the hegemony of science, so has science been turned to attack the arts. There are no Queensbury rules in intellectual battle that prevent kicking a man when he is down. Not content with their hegemony, some spokesmen for science have tried to show that all the pretensions of the arts to be other than icing on the cake are to be dismissed. I have in mind that extraordinary spasm in twentieth-century philosophy called 'logical positivism'. The older movement of positivism *tout court* took on a newly aggressive spirit in the twentieth century and identified all cognitive claims with science and mathematics. There were three sorts of things you could say: definitions and their unpacking, which included mathematics; empirical statements of fact and theory; and the rest. The rest, which included art and statements about art, morals and statements about morals, and religions and statements about religion, were either meaningless (e.g. '"goodness" is a non-natural property') or they were empirical reports. Thus, to say 'God exists' is to say something meaningless; but to say, 'Smith believes God exists' would be an empirical report on Smith's belief-state. What then of art? Statements like, 'Such and such a work of J.S. Bach is sublimely beautiful', is either meaningless since it cannot be checked against empirical evidence (public opinion polls do not verify it, only that people believe it), or it is an empirical report: a lot of people believe this. Aesthetic judgments then are, at best, matters of taste. This leaves things rather unsatisfactory. William Buckley tells us (*New Yorker* 31 January 1983) that he cannot accept that what the Rolling Stones produce is a beautiful sound. No doubt there are many devotees of the Rolling Stones who cannot see that Bach is a beautiful sound. One of the hoariest of Latin tags in this field is *de gustibus non est disputandum*: someone either likes chocolate or he does not. There is little point in dispute. Logical positivism forces this position on us.

This positivist line of attack is devastating indeed. In person most of the logical positivists were highly educated and refined men of impeccable taste. Deflating the claims of art was an unintended consequence of wanting to consolidate the hegemony of science: to rid the world of superstition and irrationality. Their argumentative machinery proved rather more powerful than it needed to be. If value in art, if judgments of beauty, are mere matters of taste then two very serious consequences follow. (1) Aesthetic judgments are removed from all possibility of rational assessment; one does not ask people to provide reasons why they like chocolate. (2) If there is no rational assessment of aesthetic judgments then all aesthetic judgments have equal weight (Jarvie 1967). Since people disagree in matters of taste, both in their positive and in their negative preferences, and since the traditional arts are a minority taste, the social position of the arts is by this reasoning placed in intellectual jeopardy. By the logic of positivism, the traditional arts are given low social valuation in the positivistic/scientistic society. Is it any wonder that, having been dismissed as beyond the rational, so many artists have savagely turned against the rational, which they proceed falsely to associate with science, thus swallowing the positivist pretence to speak in the name of science? The proper object of their criticism should rather be positivism than science, positivism in both its characterization of science and its characterization of art.

In indicating earlier that my aim is to try to apply the philosophy of art of Sir Ernst Gombrich to film as an aesthetic problem, I wanted to signal my vigorous dissent from positivism, a dissent that is stronger than that of many spokesmen for the arts. Despite protestations of anti-positivism, they often accept the positivist criteria of science and then repudiate science in the name of art. In a world dominated by science this is a form of spitting in the wind. In face of science that is genuinely, cognitively powerful, creative and to some extent exemplary, repudiating it is a form of know-nothingism hard to take seriously. The positivist picture of science is no more than that: one picture among many. Thoroughly to repudiate the positivist picture of art, it is not enough to reverse the valuation positivism gives to science and to art. It is necessary to offer a better picture, one that makes sense of their intimate ties in the past as well as in the present.

Ambivalence about science permeates criticism of the arts as well as the arts themselves. One strand in criticism accepts the positivist picture of both the arts and the sciences, and so abandons the traditional critical aims of assessing truth and aesthetic value. In their place, criticism is to concentrate on elucidating the work of art, elucidation that is under the control of a particular theory, and as an activity sufficient unto itself. Frye has gone so far as to claim that the arts are a language and one does not assess the truth or the aesthetic value of a language. An equally radical alternative criticism involves, in the first instance, repudiating positivism. Many literary people, unfamiliar with philosophy, imagine that the only opposition to positivism worth taking seriously is Marxist. They know idealists and Platonists oppose positivism but they will have no truck with them. Once Marx's ideas are supplemented, artistic works can be interpreted under them, with the bonus that Marxism describes itself as scientific, which makes criticism scientific even if it does not make art scientific. And then it is an obvious step to seek out Marxist (or radical) philosophies of science to complement the reading of the art works.[1]

At least such radicalism is preferable to the capitulation of Frye and others to a positivist view of science. At all events, both trends of thought see the interpretation of science – and hence of art in light of science – as central to the understanding of art. Their shopping list has on it a notion of science that leaves some conceptual scope for art. Thus not all cognition should be appropriated to science; and not all aesthetic factors should be removed from science. It then becomes possible to understand why science has so often been an inspiration to artists, and how art has been used to present ideas. It would not be hard, for example, to theorize that the advent of the novel had to do partly with the rise of industrial society and also with the notion of the human individual that had grown up and whose language – prose – could be used both to express truths and to embody the imagination. The very notion of imagination itself must have become individualized and so different from the collectively authored tribal myths and the divinely authored religious myths that preceded it.

Such a view of science already exists in the works of Sir Karl Popper. When he terms science the greatest spiritual adventure of mankind he chooses his words carefully. He wishes to assert a continuity in the works of the human intellect, whether they are now classified art or science. He takes it that science is simply the latest episode in man's quest to understand his world, completely continuous with all that went before it.

Like myself, Sir Ernst Gombrich is a follower of Sir Karl Popper, the major anti-positivist philosopher of this century. Popper has written very little about art, mostly about science. Neither positivistic scientists nor anti-positivist artists have seemed able to grasp his views. Positivism is so pervasive that it is taken for granted; it is not noticed that it is under attack. In writing about art Gombrich has not ignored scientific matters. Most art involves looking and seeing. This is a flourishing field of empirical psychology. Gombrich has brought this material directly to bear on his studies of what artists are trying to do and on how we can learn to look at their work. Art has a timelessness that overrides progress in its means (abstract inventions such as perspective, technological ones such as oil paint, or photography) and hence demands careful attention to the actual historical context in which it was created. So Gombrich essays a historical approach to the appreciation of art.

There are two principal points that Gombrich makes which permeate my own philosophy of the art of the film (1950, 1960). The first is his attack on the idea of the 'innocent eye', the idea, that is, that there exists a basic capacity in people to apprehend art provided their approach to it is open and uncoloured by prejudice. In place of the innocent eye Gombrich substitutes a developmental notion: both as children learning to appreciate art and as the human race learning to produce it, we have to build on a few physiological capacities and learn a great many rules and conventions. The second point I take from Gombrich is connected. He denies that the advance of art is an advance on truth; that is, the representations of people in Egyptian paintings are no less truthful than those of Rembrandt. The difference is rather in the means used to evoke what is seen, the means by which information is contained in the painting. Different sets of conventions enable different kinds of information to be conveyed. A difficulty here is that former sets of conventions once superseded are rarely revived. Reluctance to return to former modes of representation may have more to do with social change, with lack of interest any longer in the sort of information older conventions conveyed, than with an increase in truthfulness. This feedback loop, which Gombrich calls 'making and matching', is fundamental also to the aesthetics of film. Gombrich's more specific idea that painting is controlled by the eye-witness principle, namely that a painting shows only what an eye-witness could have seen from a particular point at a particular moment, is, I believe, quite false to film, where practice seems much more like the novelist's choices about 'voice' and point of view.

Pervasive in all this is an implicit Gombrichian point: the problem-structure faced by those making films is, like that faced by painters, historical in character. Film makers work against a background of tradition and in terms of an elaborate set of conventions. Both tradition and convention provide basic means for conveying information and stimulating the audience. They also provide a kind of challenge: setting limits and suggesting rules. To an extent film makers may be stimulated by the idea of going beyond those limits, or breaking those rules. Paradoxically, if they succeed, they merely add to the tradition and the stock of available conventions.

I can already hear the clamour of those who would argue that because art is timeless, the aesthetician should address the work as it stands now, and the response of the audience now – away with this historical structuring! To this it can be answered that the work as it stands now is surrounded by the real historical context of its creation and all those successive contexts in which it has been seen, appreciated, not appreciated, bought and sold, influenced other artists by attraction or repulsion. The present-day viewer's ignorance of those historical realities is not overcome by some magical interchange between his 'pure' sensibility and the work.

There is a simple *reductio* argument to show this. If the point is made that art is best appreciated by direct and unmediated contact between work and viewer, the 'innocent eye', the critic becomes redundant – including the critic making this point. If the idea is that mediation is an interference in the exchange between work and viewer, if the purer the contact the better, then the viewer with minimum preconceptions is the viewer who has not read any criticism or biography or history of this work. Perhaps even the viewer who strolls through the gallery and has his attention 'seized' by it. But if we want minimum preconceptions, why stop at eliminating from our throught-experiment writings about art? Why not have a viewer who does not have the category 'art' in his lexicon? The uneducated child of nature, as it were. Can we not, then, be sure of a pure response?

Unfortunately, it is obvious that children of nature will not wander around art galleries waiting to be 'seized'; they may not even know their way to art galleries, or that what they are to do in them is to look, rather than sleep, shelter, or break the paintings for firewood. But once we allow that some awareness of the category of art is necessary, and that the work is in that category, then it seems to me there is a valid slippery slope argument for saying that the more we know the better. Preconception being ineliminable, it follows that we would do best to attempt to articulate it, hence criticize it, hence improve it.

Included in the preconceptions which we should articulate, criticize and learn to improve are those we have about science, not just science in general and ignorant hostility towards, and misunderstanding of, it, but science in particular as it applies to the arts. In this, too, I try to be true to a Gombrichian attitude. He takes it for granted that psychology, particularly the physiological psychology of perception and recognition, is important because it corrects mistakes we make in trying to understand how art works and why it has developed in the manner that it has. It goes without saying that psychology depends on the hard science of physical optics. So far, then, from adopting the positivist idea of a separation of art and science, we should strive for a total integration of them. Not only are there intense and continuing historical links of which today's antipathy is merely a special case, but there are cognitive links in that science helps us avoid mistakes in understanding what goes on in art, and aesthetic considerations are not unimportant in science.

The science of seeing is a case in point. Sir Isaac Newton wrote a volume on optics which was an embarrassment to his followers because it treated light as particles, while the weight of opinion was that it was waves. In the case of movies we have so-called persistence of vision – the fact that we retain an image of a bright light source after it has been stopped. As Munsterberg showed, this may be a nice theory of the movies, but it is false. Those persisting images do not move, and superimposing one on the other does not create movement. Science, then, starts from problems to which it offers conjectures. These may be very appealing, either in their simplicity, their coherence with other ideas, their symmetry and elegance. Yet if counter-examples are produced those conjectures become part of the history of science.

6
AESTHETICS AND ESSENTIALISM

What are the problems films pose in philosophical aesthetics? To begin with, what are the problems of philosophical aesthetics? One way of talking is to say they are about, 'what is beauty?', and, 'is this beautiful?' Connected questions are, 'what does this mean, how is it to be interpreted?' Ambitious philosophers set out to say what beauty is before they discuss art. Less ambitious ones at least supply criteria for recognizing beauty before discussing art. This philosopher is not so ambitious. Not only would I be totally stumped if asked to say, 'what is beauty?', I have yet to come across a good argument showing that what the arts aim at is beauty. Besides, scientists do not say what truth is before they set out to find it, and some of them give very little attention to criteria for recognizing it either. There is the belief, which Popper has labelled 'the manifest theory of truth', that truth will make itself known, its light will glare forth once we have stumbled across it. I am not sure I believe in that theory either. Certainly I do not believe in the manifest theory of beauty, otherwise less art would be an acquired taste.

The problem with such questions as, 'what is beauty?' or, 'what is the meaning of this work?', is that they beg categorical answers of the form, 'beauty is such-and-such', or 'the meaning of this work is so-and-so'. But a philosophy of conjectures and refutations wants to avoid such categorical answers on the grounds that we may discover beauty where it had not been noticed before and we may discover meaning where we had overlooked it before. In other words, these are not prior questions to be settled before proceeding, but open questions to be explored in the course of thinking about other problems. My criticism of these traditional questions is methodological: the questions are objectionable because they presuppose certain kinds of answers. Perhaps a methodological approach to aesthetic problems is indicated.

To me the key methodological question about philosophical aesthetics is, 'how can we think, write and talk rationally about the arts?' This by-passes such essentialist forms of talk as in the set of questions above. If the arts aim at or produce beauty, that may be known not by a prior designation, but rather by a posterior recognition after much exposure. To say that beauty is the single quality that all meritorious works of art share strikes me as fairly vacuous, since the most obvious thing they share is all being, or all being called, works of art. Prior, then, to the question of what is beauty there must be some such question as, 'what is art?' Various highly obscure theories have been given in answer to this question, often enough implicit theories. For example, there is the theory of aesthetic experience. The idea that there is an experience different from that of the senses, or of love, or of the erotic, or of the spiritual, which attaches only to works of art. Art is one of the things that evokes this experience. In the post-positivist problem situation such a theory is little help. Just as those of us who deny religion can also deny that there is any such thing as spiritual experience, so can we ask how to characterize and recognize this aesthetic experience. The answer is usually little better than that you will know it when you have it (see Hospers 1946, p. 7). The manifest theory of aesthetic experience has little more to recommend it than the manifest theory of truth.

The post-positivist age has also produced its down-to-earth, no-nonsense empiricist theory of 'what is art?', usually called 'the institutional theory' (Dickie 1974). Summed up this could be expressed as, art is whatever the society cares to call art. The difficulty here is that the ancestor societies of our society often did not call anything art, and that there are members of the society now who scarcely call anything art, but if they do it is to denigrate it. There is a lot to be said for the institutional theory, if only because we can make things art by treating them so, leaving us only with the vexing question, are they good art?[1]

Another theory is that everything is art. This plays on the notion of aesthetic experience, arguing that it is not confined to works of art, but rather is a form of experience that is universally present. We can aestheticize a machine shop, a painting, a sunset, a concentration camp (*Night and Fog*), anything we want. All things have an aesthetic aspect. We may see in this theory a presupposition of functionalism in architecture and design where it is said that true beauty, hence the possibility of aesthetic experience, stems from the integration of the design of the work with the job it is intended to do. Not that efficiency and effectiveness are the same as aesthetic experience, but rather that aesthetic experience flows together with them.

What is beauty? What is art? What is aesthetic experience? Questions proliferate and so far scarcely a mention of film. Given unlimited claims on the time and attention of the reader, I might perhaps try to outline a whole philosophy of art and then, applying it to film, implicitly dispose of the problem of film and the errors of others in dealing with it. Such ponderousness imposes on the reader, something my Rules of Procedure (p.xiv) try to minimize.

Instead, I want directly to grapple with film and, as I go along, indicate the philosophy of art that best serves this end. Let me begin by clinging to generalities. Movies pose the following, very simple aesthetic problem: are movies art? This presupposes answers to the questions, what is art and what are movies? If they are art, what is their relation to the traditional arts? In particular, are they a version of older arts, a blend of several of them, or something entirely new? If they are art, what, if any, are their criteria of quality? If they are art, how do they take on meaning and how do we assess the truth of what it is that they mean?

If we take a straw vote, we find that the most fundamental question for philosophers writing of film is, 'what is film?' – no doubt on the supposition that before we know what it is we cannot answer such questions as whether it is art. In truth this strategy is question-begging because we can hardly ask what it is unless we know what it is: how else can we specify what we are talking about? There is a *faux naïveté* about the question, 'what is film?':

What is the power of the film that it could survive (even profit aesthetically from) so much neglect and ignorant contempt by those in power over it? What is film? (Cavell 1971, p. 15)

What, then, is a film? (Sparshott 1971, p. 321)

> . . . how can one decide what film really is and what an
> aesthetic of film might properly be? (Sesonske 1974 a, p. 33)

We could answer that film is what we call film, or, film is what we experience as film, or, film is its history. None of these answers occurs in the sources quoted. In fact these philosophers lean towards trying to identify film with its material base: with the machinery that produces it.

Sparshott (adapting Montague):

> A film is a series of motionless images projected on to a screen
> so fast as to create in the mind of anyone watching the screen an
> impression of continuous motion, such images being projected
> by a light shining through a corresponding series of images
> arranged on a continuous band of flexible material. (1971, p. 11)

Linden we remember (section 4.3) found film essentially dyadic; Cavell (section 4.3) stipulated it as a series of automatic world projections. For Linden the camera merely records; for Cavell the camera automatically records and the projector projects; for Sparshott the projector projects but the camera does not enter into it. As before, I ask, whatever happened to the invention of sound? The answer is: they forgot about it. How could they do that? Sound is very much more than a mere appendage to a primarily visual medium. Perhaps in asserting this I am in strong disagreement with them; perhaps that is precisely what they think. One definer has picked up on this and so, in Gerald Mast, we seem to get a blend of Cavell and Sparshott, plus sound: 'an integrated succession of projected images and (recorded) sounds' (Mast 1977, p. 111). The parentheses around 'recorded' make it look like an afterthought, which is probably not the author's intention.

So we have now two oddities. The first oddity is the decision to answer the question, what is film, by describing in a neutral language the machinery and its output. Cavell is the least explicit, but in his exegesis of the word 'automatic' it becomes clear that he wishes to incorporate in that word the machinery of image creation. The second oddity is that they all concentrate on cameras or projectors with the sole exception of Mast. Yet any close student of film knows that building and mixing the sound-track is as intricate a job as shooting and editing the visuals, and that unless the final marriage between the two is managed with skill each can spoil rather than enhance the other. We can not smell, touch, or taste movies, but we certainly hear them as well as see them.

But we also know that neither cameras, nor sound recording machines, are necessary to produce films. Norman McLaren has made films in which he drew both the visuals and the sounds directly on to the celluloid (c.f. Lackey 1973). Cavell, of course, can take the option of declaring these not movies. This seems simply to raise the questions, if they are not movies what are they and why not? Those machine-definitions that attend to projection evade the McLaren objection because we have yet to get movies that do not involve machinery.

But why machinery? What is the point of trying to pin down the movies by going into the processes of their production? Is there some implication that the processes of production make them what they are? And is that true? Let us take an analogue: books. First, what do we do with the question, what is a book? There are two strategies. If the question is a child's question, the child not having ever seen or heard named a book, then we would be sketchy, would we not? Depending on the child's vocabulary we might try, 'a book is a set of printed pages bound together for easy handling'. This answer is pretty unhelpful. A vocabulary adequate to it would undoubtedly contain 'book'. If the child was very young the question might naturally arise this way. It overhears one adult say to another: 'there's nothing to beat curling up with a good book'. Then, 'what is a book?' would evoke a quite different answer: 'you know, the thing with pictures and stories in it', nothing at all about the material composition.

If our interlocutor is philosophically inclined, however, 'what is a book?', is not to be answered that way. How is it to be answered? By some strategy like, 'a book is a set of evenly-sized pieces of paper on which are inscribed meaningful marks'? This would be too wide, embracing pamphlets and newspapers as well as theses, and too narrow, excluding books on film, fiche and xerox. But never mind refining it, would we go in this direction? Or would we perhaps say, 'a book is a series of inert inscriptions that when scanned yield various kinds of information, such inscriptions being impressed upon pieces of flexible material clamped together?' Are these sorts of answers any more than clever ways of talking? Clever because they attempt to characterize concrete things by the use of overlapping, abstract categories. How are such definitions better than describing a book as a means of storing and retrieving information? One answer is that gramophone records, computer tapes and notebooks are all means of storing and retrieving information too. So this does not distinguish books from other things with related functions. So now an underlying problem emerges: to characterize books in such a way as to distinguish them from other, related things. Why is this a problem? Does anyone confuse books with computer tapes, gramophone records, or handwritten notebooks? If there is no confusion, why the necessity of distinguishing them? What sort of word games are being played here?

Suppose we do come up with a form of words, a formula, that characterizes films, but not videotapes, computer tapes, gramophone records, film strips, silent movies, etc. What have we then achieved? Verbal formulae do have their place; for example, in schedules prepared by customs and excise it is often necessary to characterize goods by a verbal formula in order to decide whether or not an article is subject to one form of duty or another. But we are dealing with philosophers, not with the customs, and with works of art, not with commercial goods. Hence we may feel there is some futility in all this exercise, whatever its other problems.[2]

As I indicated at the end of the last chapter, the best rationale I can find for all this furious activity of defining by machines is that machines are concrete and tangible, so that if film can be tied to specific machinery, then it can to that extent be concretely distinguished from other things, such as photography or the theatre. Further, the material base may be thought to do two further jobs. The machinery to generate film makes it unable to do some things, and able to do others. The first are the limits or constraints of film, the second are its strengths. Thus there may be the hope that there is normative content in these definitions: film can and therefore should do (is well suited to) certain sorts of things, cannot and therefore should not do other sorts of things. Since its images are produced automatically, rather than by the real presence of actors to audience, film should not, we might think, photograph plays. The absence of the real presence makes a film of a play very undramatic and hard to watch. Such an injunction was a basic canon of thinking about film for decades.

Film machinery, it was reasoned, can in an instant take us to exotic places or allow us to view events from a position never possible in real life, therefore films should do these sorts of things.

Both these normative injunctions are derived from highly questionable specifications about film. Such a derivation is in itself invalid, as we shall see. For the moment I concentrate on the dubiousness of the mechanical facts. There are electrifying films of stage performances, and there are enervating films from exotic places and points of view. The material basis of film, after all, is not something that has remained fixed. Not only was sound added, but optical devices, special effects, patterns of cutting, speed and fidelity of film stock, shape of frame and so on have all been changed and developed over time. Many of us now see films on television or on VCRs where the image is produced by scanning. At the time of writing a further change in film technology has developed from this, namely digital storage of films that can only be turned back to something that resembles a film in experience by processing through a computer hooked to a television tube. We already have films stored on hard disks; soon they will be stored as sets of numbers in any format we want and so Sparshott's and Mast's definitions will come to grief. What about Cavell's though? Well, automatic will disappear. Because when we have digital storage audience manipulation of some of the values will become possible. Such technology is being developed as a way to store in a non-degradable form the presently very fragile celluloid image. Applications already discovered are that if a print has faded, but still is present, the computer can be programmed to build the image back up to the values it once possessed. Obviously, the next step is that if, for example, the glaring Technicolour of Fox musicals offends you, it will be easy to tone it down as, to an extent, it already is with the controls of your television set. VCR owners can already run through the dull parts of films at double speed, or slow them down to view them frame by frame. The world we allow them to project is less and less automatic, more and more governed by the human hand.[3]

The attempt to argue from the material basis of a medium towards normative questions concerning the strengths or limits of the medium is open to two clear philosophical objections. The first is that it does not follow that because the facts are a certain way that it is right or good that they are that way. This is the naturalistic fallacy. Yes, the reply goes, but 'ought' implies 'can'. If we think film ought to be different in some way, we must be able to show that it can be. Fair enough, but we must be careful not to make the assumption that the current technology and software in which films are embodied is fixed. Changes in technology and blending the technology with that of other media may alter the 'can' that 'ought' implies. With software the situation is even clearer. Rules and conventions of film making, like rules and conventions of any art, only seem to constitute strengths and limits. Their very existence stands as a challenge to some creators to overthrow or transcend them, to invent ways of working, even within current technology, that accomplish what orthodoxy implies cannot be. This is the second objection.

These arguments highlight the conservative aspect of essentialism, which essentialists are often blind to. 'What is film?' leads to various kinds of wild goose chases, but the most insidious is the idea that film has a fixed nature and that we do not 'know' what film is until we have pinpointed that fixed nature, whether directly by definition, or indirectly by approximating differences from other things. The whole line of thought pursues a chimera, but a deeply rooted one. What I am referring to is Plato's idea that what differentiates knowledge from delusive opinion is that knowledge is certain and unchanging, and if we are to have certain knowledge of the world then we must secure it to its categories. By his standards the history of science is a history not of knowledge but of changing opinion – as indeed it is. Where some of us differ from Plato is in arguing that if knowledge is certain knowledge then the only knowledge we have is mathematics, and mathematics tells us nothing about the world, only about the consequences of certain assumptions we may make. Otherwise, when it comes to the world, science is the best we have and science changes, so either the best is not knowledge, or knowledge changes.

Much of what I write here seems obvious and common sense, yet I know from experience it is often assented to by those who yet continue on futile essentialist quests for fixed categories prior to theory. Some twentieth-century philosophers, such as Cavell, try to identify knowledge with putting experience into words, a universal activity of humanity and hence something fixed and permanent. This claim has to be phrased just right, otherwise knowledge becomes part of linguistics, a science very much subject to change. The alternative, on my view, is to diagnose 'what is?' questions, to see whether they come from bad philosophy, in which case they should be ignored, or from some genuine underlying problem (as the child's), in which case the answer should be suited to the question, not to an attempt to capture the permanent essence of film.

We must beware of bewitchment by Plato's cave metaphor; it is a brilliant image but an antiquated and false picture of our epistemological condition.

Is there no way out of all this, no rationale for such definitions? Perhaps the impulse is very simple. Films seem like something new, a new medium or vehicle for artistic expression. Hence some rough characterization of this medium, in a way that differentiates it from existing media seems like a good plan. Or does it? Why differentiate something from something else? The effort would only seem worthwhile if there is some problem, let us say some confusion, between the two. And here we do finally come to a valid argument. Some confusion undoubtedly existed and exists between the legitimate stage and the movies. While early silent movie shows had content very different from stage performances, e.g. they had newsreels, reconstructions of prize fights, travelogue material, they also had filmed snippets of famous stage actors and, very quickly, short stories. Stories told dramatically, even in pantomime, naturally tended to be parasitic on the stage, for the simple reasons that the most ready source of material for them, personnel to make them, and conventions to frame them was the stage. There were ready-made ideas for plot and staging, and a reservoir of writers, directors and actors to make them. As the story form of film gradually became the dominant form, this hegemony of stage and ex-stage people became almost complete. [4]

But it does not follow from the fact that the origin of material and personnel was the stage that what they produced resembled stage work. It is the intellectuals rather than the film makers who forged the connection. While film makers, such as the slapstick comedians, were utilizing the film medium for purposes considerably different from those of the stage, intellectuals reflecting on the cinema often measured it by stage standards and dismissed it as inferior stage material. This explains why Munsterberg labours mightily throughout his book to compare and contrast movies and the stage, in this setting an example for many who were to come.

He quite rightly saw that stage and screen were very different, despite the origin of one in the other and the overlapping personnel. I would go so far as to offer the historical conjecture that it was the flexible ability to grasp the fact that film was a new medium that separated the (stagey) sheep from the (cinematic) goats among recruits from the stage.

Suppose, then, we accept that film is a new medium for communicating ideas, a new medium for stories, a new medium for art. Where are the ideas, stories, emotions coming from? The conventional answer is that they come from the artist, the creator. Provided we do not forget Munsterberg's clear thesis that the filmic result is a collaboration between the willing audience and the creator, if such there be, this is all well and good. Yet what an artist does is not well described as expressing himself. I express myself if I sing in the bathtub; such singing is a paradigm of non-talented expression. Exclamations – 'ouch' – are also expressive, and not art. Art, it seems to me, must take account of the audience; it is, so to speak, intentional: it is art only if it is art for some audience. There is no private art as there is no private language or private science. The artist is not so much in the business of expressing as in the business of communicating. So when in *The Sound of Music* Julie Andrews whirls around belting out the decibels to empty Alpine meadows we do not mistake this for bathtub singing, because at some level we know that although there is no audience on screen with her, we, through the camera, are the reason she is performing.

Setting aside these methodological questions, let us come to matters of substance, to the aesthetics of the photoplay. This is one field where there is a large literature, considerable dispute, and two excellent surveys (Andrew 1976; Tudor 1973), as well as three bulging anthologies (Cohen and Mast 1979 *et seq*; Nichols 1976, 1985). Hence it will not be necessary for me to guide the reader through the work of others in chronological fashion. Although the surveys ignore Harms and Adler, there is a continuous tradition of discussing the art of the film that probably begins with Lindsay (1915) and Munsterberg, continues with the work of the film makers Eisenstein and Pudovkin, and includes Balazs, Arnheim, Spottiswoode, Rotha, Jacobs, Manvell, and many others (Jarvie 1970, p. 338). They argue for the legitimacy and autonomy of film, and elucidate its artistic means by comparisons with language. Another tradition, largely French, branches off into a study of semiotics (signs), onto which is grafted all kinds of material from Marxism to psychoanalysis. In all this Munsterberg stands out because he makes his problems clear; he allows for active participation by the spectator. Furthermore, his mistakes are clear to see and, by reflecting on them we perhaps avoid making some of our own.

Munsterberg (1916) disputed with those who think art is the imitation of reality (mimesis) and the photoplay a poor substitute for the stage. Instead, he offered the idea that art transforms material; it isolates, selects, shapes and combines, not to imitate but to construct a work or a world complete and harmonious and satisfying in itself. '*The work of art shows us the things and events perfectly complete in themselves, freed from all connections which lead beyond their own limits, that is, in perfect isolation*' (p. 64). The work of art must not point beyond itself.

Various arts employ various means, but all must eliminate the indifferent, select the important and heighten it. Art must also be 'sharply set off from the sphere of our practical interests' (p. 69) otherwise it cannot be self-contained. Each art uses means particular to it to overcome the chaos of the world and render a part of it in a perfectly isolated form in which all elements are in mutual agreement. The photoplay is not music, drama, pictures, but an art of its own. What are its particular means?

Coming at this question, Munsterberg reiterated what he called the true thesis of his book: '*the photoplay tells us the human story by overcoming the forms of the outer world, namely, space, time, and causality, and by adjusting the events to the forms of the inner world, namely, attention, memory, imagination, and emotion*' (p. 74). As the theatre used the proscenium arch to distance the action, so, 'The screen too suggests from the very start the complete unreality of the events' (p. 75). Then, too, screen actors do not speak, they pantomime. But, 'The really decisive distance from bodily reality, however, is created by the substitution of the actor's picture for the actor himself' (p. 76). Not just that we see living persons in photographic form but rather that we see them in flat form; bodily space has been eliminated by a picture which yet 'strongly suggests to us the actual depth of the real world' (p. 77). Light, flitting immateriality, has replaced the heaviness, solidity and substantiality of real space. Time, too, has been discarded, past and future being interwoven into the present or elapsed time of the film show. But this freedom from material constraints results in a heavier burden of aesthetic rules. They need unity of action, unity of character and no display of locations, furniture or fashions for advertisement.

Munsterberg thought the photoplay needed imaginative talent, collaboration between writer and producer, an original literature not copying plays or novels. Intertitles were a sign of clumsy and untrained scenario writing, for the purity of the photoplay art does not depend on words, nor on speech, so synchronized phonographic accompaniment was out of place. Musical accompaniment is essential, but sound-effects 'will have to disappear too' (p. 89). Colour photography compromises the essential condition of a far-reaching disregard of reality (p. 90). 'We do not want to paint the cheeks of the Venus de Milo: neither do we want to see the colouring of Mary Pickford or Anita Stewart' (p. 90). Contact with reality must be maintained, the illusion not destroyed. All topics are grist to the photoplay's mill.

Movies he described as classless, cheap, pleasurable, technically clever and vitally dramatic. But the richest source of satisfaction they provide is aesthetic feeling. Their power is also a source of danger: lessons in low morality, crime, vulgarity and bad taste. Yet their power can be used for remoulding and upbuilding. So their mission may be aesthetic cultivation, not moral preaching. Canned, machine-made and unreal, said the critics. Munsterberg hoped his book was a rebuttal of them.

None of the constraints Munsterberg saw as essential to the purity of film, from the unities, through to no colour or sound, has survived. Films have altered their material base drastically, gaining thereby new means of evoking what Gombrich calls representation. Munsterberg's mistakes were superb rationalizations of the limits of the technical means of what confronted him. Like a good Kantian he argued they were inherent: synthetic *a priori*, much as Kant thought Newton's physics both *a priori* and synthetic. Neither turns out to be *a priori* necessary and one wonders whether Munsterberg noticed the contradiction between Kant's view that his (Newtonian) categories were necessary and the fact that the films project a world very un-Newtonian indeed.

This much said, we can now further sharpen the problems to be tackled in this Part. 'Movies as an aesthetic problem' is a title broad enough to allow us to range over a cluster of questions that debate has centred about. In its broadest formulation the problem is this: is the film medium a legitimate vehicle for art? That there is a medium, possibly a medium distinct from other artistic media, is little disputed. Rather is the problem whether this film medium can take its place alongside the older-established arts as capable of embodying some of mankind's most sublime endeavours, of providing the possibility of aesthetic experience. When, in a paper delivered to an aesthetics conference, I ventured to suggest that the argument about the artistic legitimacy of film as a medium was the central thread of much of the 'theoretical' literature on film I remember a reaction of incredulity. No-one, it was said, argues about that any more. Even if that were a true observation, this lack of present argument would establish that there was a great deal of argument about it in the past, and possibly even in the quite recent past. Be that as it may, I persist with a much stronger claim. Most of the philosophical literature on the art of the film only makes sense if we place it in the context of dispute over the legitimacy of the medium for art. The entire effort to specify the film with its mechanical apparatus, begun by Munsterberg but greatly elaborated by his successors, is a prelude to a line of argument which we might call 'outlining the expressive resources of the medium'. Paralleling my earlier remarks about expression we could rephrase this as 'outlining the communicative resources of the medium'. If, the thinking goes, a case can be made that this medium has powerful resources for conveying narrative, ideas and feelings, resources comparable to those of the traditional arts, and if it is distinct in its means, then it can claim to be a vehicle for art, and a new vehicle at that.

Film's legitimacy as a medium of art has been contested along three main lines. First, there is the problem of its newness; the arts in general are often treated like wine, they need to ferment and mature before taking their place as classics. When we think of a medium not a work the same thought applies. Secondly, there are doubts about the medium itself, whether, that is, its expressive (read communicative) resources are such that it can deal with issues in sufficient depth to be taken seriously. And finally there are doubts about the social matrix of movies, those who make them, those who consume them, their mass appeal. This latter

162

makes them very unusual among the arts, and perhaps out of place.

My reading of the literature leads me to divide further the problems of newness and one of the capacities of the medium into four sub-lines of argument, thus making nine sub-sections in all. In each I shall endeavour to state the case against film as a medium of art as strongly as possible, and then assess and criticize that case before turning to the next.

7

ARGUMENTS AGAINST FILMS AS ART

7.1 NEWNESS

7.11 *Less Than One Hundred Years Old*

What we declare to be the exact age of the movies depends upon what criterion we adopt for something to count as a movie. The generic term 'motion pictures' names an invention claimed by various parties, in various countries around 1893, but not publicly exhibited much before 1895. Standardized public exhibition, the Nickelodeon, is usually dated from 1905. Attentive readers of this book will, however, know that the generic 'motion pictures' is not something I will accept as the equivalent of movies. A lot more had to happen after the invention of the machine before the medium matured. Even Munsterberg discusses such devices employed by the photoplay as the cut-away and the close-up, each of which had to be discovered and implemented, and these devices in combination are the things that make possible the replication of mental effects on the screen that is for him the movies' unique feature. At a minimum I would demand 'mature motion picture technique' as the precursor of the medium of the movies. Such a criterion cannot be specified with precision and the decision to assign a date to the beginning of movies is a judgment call.

But there is another objection to dating movies to the 1890s that is just as radical, and which explains my suggestion that even 'mature motion picture technique' is only a precursor to the medium of the movies. The factor I have in mind is sound. When sound arrived there were many theorists who realized that a new medium had arrived. Far from welcoming it, they argued that it was a regressive development, pushing movies back towards their stage origins, particularly because of the dependence on words. Words created strong ambivalence in theorists of the silent screen, because all too often intertitles could be a way to avoid using imagination to get a point over visually, or 'filmically'. Films, it had always been argued, were powerful partly because they transcended the need for literacy, or the need to know foreign languages, both of which were barriers to the communication of literary art across class and national boundaries. Further, and less clearly, there was the analogue that film resembled a language; it was a visual language in the process of development, with resources as yet untapped and, like any new language (mathematics would be a good example although to my recollection no writer on film ever cited it), it would be possible to say and do things in that language that were not possible in other languages.

It is not surprising, then, that into the 1930s many writers on film lamented the arrival of sound, took every opportunity to crow over the stiff and theatrical look of some of the new talkies, and cherished the forlorn hope that because of the vast investment in vaults of silent films the two media would at least co-exist (Adler 1937, p. 516). An advocate of this from within film making was Charlie Chaplin, whose films of the sound period were virtually without dialogue until *The Great Dictator* (1940).

In one respect these antiquarians were right: sound films are a different medium from silent motion pictures. It is also true that in the rush to produce sound movies in the years after 1926, many horrible false starts and failed attempts were made. But here again we may attend to the film makers as much as to the theorists. The former were not all baffled or spoiled by sound. Alfred Hitchcock, whose staure is quite considerable, made, in *Blackmail* – his first talking picture – advances with the use of sound that make it today still possible to experience the film as bold and effective. He had shot the film silent before it became clear sound was going to come in, so, in a rush, he set about re-doing it for sound in mid-production. Not only was his imagination not constrained, it was, if anything, unleashed by the new dramatic possibilites (Truffaut 1967).

So, the upshot of this line of thought is that the medium the aesthetic problems of which I am interested in discussing is the sound movie, the talkie. What has the age of the medium to do with its claims to be a vehicle for art? I'm not sure that the argument is a very tight one, since it is both historical and inductive. It might seem to go like this. There are traditionally six classic arts: literature, painting, sculpture, music, dance and drama. Each of these existed fully fledged in Ancient Greece. Hence, treating them as vehicles for art is something hallowed by time and has important consequences we shall explore in sections 7.12, 7.13 and 7.14. How can we possibly expect to decide on the potentiality for art of a medium whose most generous defenders claim it to begin in 1893, not to mention those more conservative, like myself, who would opt for something nearer 1930? After all, the origin of these Greek arts was somewhat other than art, art being a category possibly not known in earlier societies. Much of what we now think of as art had its impulse not in artistic expression in the modern sense, but in religious rituals and representations. Our rather secularized view of the arts is of very recent origin, as are the associated notions of leisure time and entertainment. These art forms, then, emerged slowly from a complex background of which we know rather little, and this process took a great deal of time. Less than one hundred years after the invention of motion pictures, scarcely fifty years after the invention of talkies, *it is early days to say what it is we have here.*

When the movies arrived it was widely predicted that they were a substitute for the stage and it was predicted that the days of live theatre were numbered. This prediction seems to have been falsified. When the sound movie came along as a substitute for the silent movie it was predicted that they might co-exist: this, to all intents and purposes, was falsified too. When television appeared in the years after the second world war and began its period of rapid growth, it was widely predicted that the days of the movies were numbered. This prediction also seems to have been falsified. Current changes involving cable television, satellites, video recording systems and large-screen television sets have led to new predictions of the demise of the talkies. So far at least these seem premature. But previous failures of prediction are no argument for expecting future failures. Each prediction relates to an independent set of events, and the outcome is uncertain.

Let me sum up the structure of the argument. Historically, the arts emerged slowly from diverse backgrounds, but history need not repeat itself. Inductively, all the arts that now exist emerged slowly. But what happened to the first six need not apply to the seventh. Nevertheless, in its short life the medium of the movies has altered its form radically once, and has been involved in various other sorts of change. Were current predictions of the movies' demise to be correct, we might continue to find sound motion pictures being used, but with no claim to be vehicles of art. They might, for example, find it their destiny to be useful in scientific recording: the only films made could well be those involving microscopes, slow-motion or time-lapse. Much film would be shot, all the technology of talkies would still be used, but little or no attention would be paid to any aesthetic values.

What does this argument show? It is not conclusive. It is cautionary. It says: perhaps it is too early to tell whether movies are more than a brief phase as a medium of choice for art, much like *camera obscura*, peripatetic storytellers, medieval minstrels, town criers and other media for the communication of information that flourished once upon time but no more. The significance of their being no more is not that they never were vehicles of art, but that they are no longer. One effect of their being that no longer is that they are rarely, if ever, revived and hence works created for them have an absence of that permanence which we associate with art. Art should be lasting, as the works created by the Greeks in literature, painting, sculpture and drama.

What is to be said of this argument? It is what philosophers call a sceptical argument. That is, it does not establish a point but raises awkward questions intended to cast doubt on a point someone else is making: in this case that movies are a vehicle for art. The strategy of dealing with scepticism adopted by most philosophers from time immemorial has been to rise to the bait. The sceptic claims to cast doubt on your points, so try to ground or establish or guarantee or justify your points beyond doubt. There is a very simple flaw in this strategy: no claim on any subject whatsoever can be grounded to avoid all doubt. This was already made clear by Descartes, who needed the *deus ex machina* to assure him that ultimately there must be some point where doubt broke down. In this Descartes was mistaken: sceptical resources are limitless and a deceiving God or even no God at all does not tax those resources

167

very much. How, then, should we answer a sceptical challenge, or should we, indeed, answer it at all? Acknowledging the sceptic's resources of doubt, the best we can do is to be cautious and moderate in our claims. In effect the sceptic's challenge is to say: you can not be sure movies are a medium of art. Instead of arguing to show we can be sure, especially by such a device as analysis of the mechanical basis of the movie medium or an extended comparison of film and theatre, the only successful strategy is to acknowledge that no, we are not and cannot be sure. This defuses the sceptical challenge altogether. To admit we are not sure of something is not to agree to its contradiction, namely, it is not the case that films are a vehicle for art. It is to admit only that we are not sure films are a vehicle for art. Were someone to affirm that films definitely are not vehicles for art then all the arguments deployed by Munsterberg, Cavell, Sparshott and others could be utilized in a sceptical attack to show how unsure we should be of that proposition.

The proper conclusion of this section, then, should be this: while we cannot be sure, their newness is not sufficient reason to doubt that in sound movies mankind has developed a distinctly new medium for art.

7.12   *Lack of Settled Canons*

There is next to no agreement among those who speak of movies over the canon of movies to which their speaking must be accountable and by which standards are thus far set against which to weigh worth; nor over the cinematic grounds there may be in terms of which to argue worth or worthlessness.

(Cavell 1979, p. 164)

A work is canonical if it is authoritatively part of the tradition; e.g., the canonical books of the old testament as opposed to those which were left out. There are in each of the older arts substantial bodies of work and hence, by extension, numbers of artists, whose work defines the field in general, and exemplifies the standards of quality in particular. If a Bach fugue is not music then it is unclear what is; furthermore, if certain specified Bach fugues are not exemplary of the highest quality music ever written then again it is unclear what is.

The function of canonical works is not often enough made explicit. The motto on page 140 quotes Gombrich as saying there is no such thing as art with a capital 'A'; there are only artists. It can be argued that there are no Artists with a capital 'A' either. In fact to call oneself an artist is as presumptuous as to call oneself an intellectual. These are designations that only come appropriately from others. Art is not created by artists; artists are created by art. That is, someone is an artist because he or she has produced work judged to be part of the canon. The canon thus is not added to by artists. Rather are the ranks of artists swollen by those whose work is admitted to the canon. So: there is no Art with a capital 'A'; there are no Artists with a capital 'A'; there are only works of art.

In two papers on this matter (1967, 1981) I made the importance of the canon explicit. I argued that the elevation of a work to, and its general acceptance within, the canonical works of an art medium is a process that takes place over time, usually rather slowly, is subject to correction and change (expulsion and inclusion), and is a matter of rationality, not a matter of subjective taste or arbitrary authority. Arguing that in the arts we create standards by arguing about them, I tried to show how the subjective matter of *response* differs from the rational and objective matter of *evaluation* (of which more below). Few, if any, of the arguments we deploy in disputes over artistic evaluation are knock-down-drag-out, but then such arguments are rarer in supposedly harder-nosed subjects than they might appear to be.

My further thesis was that the standards we develop are not embodied in one form only, namely rules or rule-like statements of what is to be done and what is to be avoided. Such rules are at best rules of thumb which many an artist treats as challenges; rules to be broken with impunity rather than dogma to be violated at peril. Another form in which our standards are expressed is in the canonical works. Such standards are implicit rather than explicit, and separately and together the canonical works may stand as a challenge to be defied as much as an example to be copied. But it is the existence of canonical works that is our final court of appeal; the acknowledged classics of the arts embody what the arts strive for, or nothing does. But their canonical character is not merely a product of a public opinion poll: their status can be explained, explicated, and debated.

My papers pressed parallels between the articulation of scientific assertions and artistic 'assertions'. Each is an answer to a problem, each is tentative, and each is subject to argument and to test. Surviving 'assertions' are not thus established, verified, justified; they are simply the surviving assertions, the best we can do for the moment.

Perhaps the most contentious part of the parallel is not these methodological points, but the comparison of scientific assertions with what are aesthetic judgments. This is contentious because scientific assertions are cognitive; they make knowledge-claims about the world and it is widely held by contemporary philosophers that aesthetic judgments are non-cognitive. Here I part company with my fellow philosophers, since I believe that there is aesthetic knowledge just as there is moral knowledge. Neither aesthetics nor morals being mere matters of subjective taste, in my view, reasoned argument being possible in both, the question is, what is the subject of dispute? My view: claims about what is true and false, claims to knowledge in morals and the arts.

Bertrand Russell says somewhere that he finds it impossible to accept that 'cruelty is wrong' is merely a matter of subjective taste, yet he does not know any way to convince someone who is sceptical about it. This is what I have called the classic way to go down to defeat by the sceptic. 'Cruelty is wrong' is a moral hypothesis, a claim to moral knowledge to which those who disagree can produce counter-examples of competing principles and complex situations that allow us to discuss the hierarchy of our moral values.

The same goes for the arts. 'Bach wrote some of the finest music of all time' is no caprice of musicologists, but a claim to know something, in particular to know something about musical value. And it is a strong claim too, since the bulk of the population would either not know whether the assertion was true or not, or would flatly deny it since their musical universe is largely made up of popular songs and light orchestral pieces.

Let me sum up. Despite the well-known objections to cognitivism in art and morals I see no reason not to persist with it. Reasoned argument, tentativity and revision, and the pursuit of these processes over time are what we engage in to assess scientific ideas. The result is some ideas about what should be avoided in the arts and what should be done, and a set of works in each field that are widely taken to be canonical. Canonical works are neither fixed there for eternity nor are all of them accepted by everyone. But even those critical of the inclusion of this or that are nibbling at the edges, wanting a change here or there but not of the whole canon and, moreover, not of the whole idea that there is and must be a canonical set.

It is time we came back to movies. To say there are no canonical movies is not to deny that there is a candidate canon, or that there are lobbyists urging candidates upon us. In a sense all critics are working away at that all the time. But there is no decision procedure and hence the arguments advanced are not very strong. For example, John Simon, in an intelligently argued and sensitive book, declares that Ingmar Bergman is 'the greatest film maker the world has seen so far' (1972, p. 41). He goes so far as to put that proposition to Bergman face to face and ask him if the responsibility does not weigh him down. Why would he do this? Is he not afraid that to increase Bergman's self-consciousness about his status might inhibit his ability to work? Luckily Bergman has a down-to-earth attitude to talk of art and artists that may prevent any damage (see below, p.321). Would Simon have the temerity to say, even after long and careful consideration, who is the greatest composer of music or painter in oils the world has seen so far (Simon being Simon might well)? And how are we to know that his opinion is 'carefully considered' when he presents no alternative candidates (Welles?, Kurosawa? Ozu? Ray?), and hence does not marshall any arguments in favour of his candidate and in rebuttal of counter-claims thus articulating some of the criteria he has in mind? Apart from proclaiming that he has carefully considered the matter, the most that Simon says is that movies are both a visual and an aural medium and that Bergman is strong in both. Since I have castigated other writers for forgetting the sound-track this dual emphasis is welcome. But as an argument selecting out Bergman from rivals, it is weak. Indeed, at best, it is a minimum or necessary condition for achieving great film work in the period of sound movies.

Simon's whole book could be construed as a sustained argument of a different kind, namely from the films not the film maker. The book's centre is a close examination of four of Bergman's films

171

trying to show the power and depth of the achievement of each of them. If these works are truly great, by criteria of depth, universality, permanence, or whatever, then their maker, Bergman, may be considered great. Reasoning from the status of the works to the achieved status of the film maker is certainly the direction I prefer; the Hegelian move of ascribing status to the person who then transmits it to the works is absurd. Above all, if a film maker has contributed work that enters the canon his status is enhanced.

The problem is, there is no canonical set of movies; no established set of movies that embody the highest achievements of cinematic art. When I set about writing this book I thought long and hard about the use of films as examples. Most film books, I reasoned, proliferate film titles far beyond the experience of most potential readers. This could be explained as a form of showing-off or name-dropping. More charitably, it could be explained by the fact that few or no movies embody all the qualities that writers on movies are looking for and hence they must cite example after example, each a partial exemplification of quality in work. Not for a moment does this situation prove there are no canonical works. Proof is not sought, anyway. My solution to the problem of examples was to minimize them, to cite only a handful of films with any frequency and to make up that handful from works that are as near to canonical as any.

How to defend the assertion that there are no canonical movies? Their lack in the literature is not sufficient. True enough. One rough and ready way to find out which are the canonical works in music would be to read the writings of critics and musicologists, and to talk to them. This has been made simple with movies because the British journal *Sight and Sound* carries out decennial polls of critics in many countries to compile a list of the ten best films of all time. Recently, for the journal's fiftieth birthday, they reprinted all their polls. The results (see Tables 7.1 and 7.2) were astonishing. Films at the top of the list in 1952 were obliterated from the list of 1982; mixtures of silent and sound in 1952 were no longer present in 1982.

Let us pause for a moment over these lists, and those from Monaco (1979) of the decade 1965-75. The top film of 1952, *Bicycle Thieves*, directed by Vittorio De Sica and scripted by Cesare Zavattini, slipped to seventh place in 1962 and disappeared without trace thereafter. Two Chaplin films listed that year also disappeared, although Chaplin still got votes as director. Even more astonishing, the only film by Griffith in any list was *Intolerance* in 1952. In a way it is equally surprising that Eisenstein had the staying power he had, especially for the rather laboured *Battleship Potemkin*. The most consistent choice is Jean Renoir's *La Règle du Jeu*, at the bottom in 1952, but near the top ever since. It is surpassed only by Welles's *Citizen Kane*, not listed in 1952 but at the top ever since. One notices the eclipse of the reputations of Carné, Flaherty, Lean and Clair as well as De Sica, then of Visconti and Vigo from the 1962 list, of Bergman and Dryer from 1972. In 1982 Bergman is not listed among the directors; there are two Welles films, a Ford, a Hitchcock and a musical. None of the films in the 1982 list is included in Monaco's list (Table 7.2) of the best European films of the decade, although *2001* is in the best American films of the decade. (Our fascination with ten-year time slices is very puzzling. [1])

From any of these lists it would be very hard to infer a coherent set of criteria that would explain why any of their members should be included. Where, for example, is Satyajit Ray?

It would be cheap to mount a methodological attack on Monaco's poll. Its sampling basis, the scatter of age, sex and nationality, questions of the availability of older films, the entire notion of reducing art to a ten-best list, etc. These lists are symptomatic, not a conclusive argument. The lists show how, given the chance of specifying a small hard core of canonical works, a selection of the world's experts cannot come up with one from decade to decade. Would not the results in music, literature, and the other arts be very different?

An explanation of the phenomenon might be the lack of time. Films, as we discussed in Section 7.11, are not more than fifty years old, scarcely enough time for a body of work to be assembled that will win unanimous or even majority support as of the highest quality. Furthermore, films have come into being at a time when all the arts have been racked by the revolution of modernism, a revolution connected with radical change in the social position of art and an increased self-consciousness.

But the best explanation seems to be something else. Films are new and the problem is that we do not yet know what is the best: we are ignorant, and we flounder and make mistakes of the most

Table 7.1: *Sight and Sound's* poll of the ten best films of all time

1952

Bicycle Thieves		*Greed*	
De Sica 1949	25	von Stroheim 1924	11
City Lights		*Le Jour se Lève*	
Chaplin 1930	19	Carné 1939	11
The Gold Rush		*Passion of Joan of Arc*	
Chaplin 1925	19	Dreyer 1928	11
Battleship Potemkin		*Brief Encounter*	
Eisenstein 1925	16	Lean 1945	10
Lousiana Story		*Le Million*	
Flaherty 1947	12	Clair 1930	10
Intolerance		*La Règle du Jeu*	
Griffith 1916	12	Renoir 1939	10

1962

Citizen Kane		*Battleship Potemkin*	
Welles 1941	22	Eisenstein 1925	16
L'Avventura		*Bicycle of Thieves*	
Antonioni 1960	20	De Sica 1949	16
La Règle du Jeu		*Ivan the Terrible*	
Renoir 1939	19	Eisenstein 1943–46	16
Greed		*La Terra Trema*	
von Stroheim 1924	17	Visconti 1948	14
Ugetsu Monogatari		*L'Atalante*	
Mizoguchi 1953	17	Vigo 1933	13

1972

Citizen Kane		*Passion of Joan of Arc*	
Welles 1941	32	Dreyer 1928	11
La Règle du Jeu		*The General*	
Renoir 1939	28	Keaton 1926	10
Battleship Potemkin		*The Magnificent Ambersons*	
Eisenstein 1925	16	Welles 1942	10
8½		*Ugetsu Monogatari*	
Fellini 1963	15	Mizoguchi 1953	9
L'Avventura		*Wild Strawberries*	
Antonioni 1960	12	Bergman 1957	9
Persona			
Bergman 1967	12		

1982

Top ten

Citizen Kane		*L'Avventura*	
Welles 1941	45	Antonioni 1960	12
La Règle du Jeu		*The Magnificent Ambersons*	
Renoir 1939	31	Welles 1942	12
Seven Samurai		*Vertigo*	
Kurosawa 1954	15	Hitchcock 1958	12
Singin' in the Rain		*The General*	
Donen & Kelly 1952	15	Keaton & Bruckman 1926	11
8½		*The Searchers*	
Fellini 1963	14	Ford 1956	11
Battleship Potemkin			
Eisenstein 1925	12		

Runners-up

2001: A Space Odyssey		*Jules et Jim*	
Kubrick 1968	10	Truffaut 1961	9
Andrei Roublev		*The Third Man*	
Tarkovsky 1966	10	Reed 1949	9
Greed			
von Stroheim 1924	9		

Directors

Orson Welles	71	Akira Kurosawa	33
Jean Renoir	51	Federico Fellini	32
Charles Chaplin	37	Alfred Hitchcock	32
John Ford	34	Jean-Luc Godard	30
Luis Buñuel	33	Buster Keaton	30

Source: *Sight and Sound*, vol. 51, no. 4, Autumn 1982

basic sort. In particular, striving to legitimate and establish a new art form we eagerly respond to new work, overestimate it and create waves of fashion that skew our judgments badly. Let me give two examples from my own experience.

(1) *Antonioni*. In common with many *cinéastes* I was completely bowled over by Antonioni's 1959 film *L'Avventura*, which I at once elevated into my ten-best-films-of-all-time list. The film was unusual in construction, featured a fascinating new actress (Monica Vitti), and generated powerful affective response in the viewer. Twenty years later the film is interesting, but slight, contrived in a certain way and dripping with the fashionable existential angst of that period. My essay on the film (1961) I now treat as a report on a state of mind rather than a compendium of true assertions about the film and its director. I have this

Table 7.2: *Monaco's survey of critical opinion*

THE BEST AMERICAN FILMS OF THE DECADE

The Leaders: More than 5 votes each

The Godfather/Coppola 1971–4	14
Nashville/Altman 1975	12
Petulia/Lester 1968	9
Annie Hall/Allen 1977	9
Mean Streets/Scorsese 1973	7
2001:A Space Odyssey/Kubrick 1968	6
The Wild Bunch/Peckinpah 1969	6

5 votes each

American Graffiti/Lucas   1973
Badlands/Malick   1973
Taxi Driver/Scorsese   1976
McCabe and Mrs Miller/Altman   1971
Chinatown/Polanski   1974
Barry Lyndon/Kubrick   1975

4 votes each

Blume in Love/Mazursky   1973
The Conversation/Coppola   1974
Midnight Cowboy/Schlesinger   1969
All the President's Men/Pakula   1976

THE BEST EUROPEAN FILMS OF THE DECADE

The Leaders: More than 5 votes each

My Night at Maud's/Rohmer 1968	7
Scenes from a Marriage/Bergman 1973	7
Claire's Knee/Rohmer 1970	60
The Conformist/Bertolucci 1970	6
Amarcord/Fellini 1973	6
The Sorrow and The Pity/Ophuls	6

5 votes each

Lancelot du lac/Bresson   1974
The Mother and the Whore/Eustache   1973
The Discreet Charm of the Bourgeoisie/Buñuel   1972
Le Boucher/Chabrol   1970
The Passenger/Antonioni   1975

Source: James Monaco, *American Film Now*, New York:
Oxford University Press, 1979

overvaluation of Antonioni in common with a great many others. [2]

(2) *Woody Allen*. This I have in common with very few other *cinéphiles* indeed. Later in this book I shall treat Allen and his work with the greatest seriousness and respect. Although I shall not rashly make claims about his ultimate merits, alert as I am to the mood of the times, of oneself, and to the need for a distance from works before making strong pronouncements, nevertheless it will be clear that I am close to placing a high valuation on Allen's work. When I try this move out on colleagues and peers the reaction is rarely less than one of incredulity and so I realize that for that reason alone, I must marshall my arguments carefully.

These illustrations of the problem of the canon do not establish it, still less do they solve it. They are intended to show that with the best will in the world we can be misled by fashion and by our own intellectual ingenuity in explicating and defending fashion. There is no simple, remedial measure. In my articles I compared the situation once more to that in science where much confusion is created by talk of objectivity. Popper has argued in many places and, I hold, quite decisively, that objectivity is not an individual attitude. The individual is logically and psychologically incapable of detaching himself from a point of view. In place of attempts to purge the mind and 'be objective' Popper locates objectivity in scientific results, in their progress towards truth. The engine of this progress is provided by the social institutions of science, particularly the institution of mutual, friendly-hostile criticism. This means criticism of the ideas, not of the persons.

Similarly, I reasoned, the foundation of a cognitive approach to the arts had to lie in the institutions: in the tradition of critical exchange between those concerned with value in the arts. The main difference between responses (viz., 'I like it') and evaluations ('This work is of value') lies in whether they are putative candidates for rational dispute. Only our psychiatrists will challenge the assertion.'I like *Annie Hall*'; whereas, '*Annie Hall* is a great film', is open to challenge and discussion by anyone who has seen the film.

In section 7.11 I did not accept the conclusion that the newness of movies precluded us deciding they are a medium for art, although I acknowledged some of the arguments had force. At this stage a further concession seems to be in order. The evaluative critical process as I envisage it – putative evaluations considered, criticized, improved, overthrown, replaced, and so on – is one that takes place over time. By my own criteria, movies are little more than fifty years old. They are thus not slightly younger than the six classical arts; they are immensely younger. Perhaps as a result their canonical judgments are astonishingly unsettled. No matter what sampling method we use it is clear we will find radical disagreement about membership in the canon. We thus lack the first of many things needed to establish films as being capable of supporting art, namely something exemplary, some implicit embodiment. Until we have that, sceptics can go on trying to browbeat us with the negative existential statement: there does not exist an uncontroversially great film. Not until one is produced are they refuted; but even then not silenced. A one-shot is a notoriously weak basis on which to argue. That is why we need a canon, a body of work about which serious controversy has died down. Not one fixed for all time, no member of it displaceable; merely one that as a whole has continuous existence.

7.13   *Movies have no Established Criteria of Merit*

Having announced my allegiance to Gombrich it will be necessary to proceed cautiously here. Gombrich has made explicit and powerful *reductio* arguments against claims that there are articulable standards in the judgment of works of art. What he has in mind are sophisticated versions of those old art teacher injunctions about balance, about points of convergence, about combinations of colours, etc. He does not bother with such simple-minded examples, but only with higher-powered versions of the same thing. Rather than quote Gombrich, whose examples are from painting, I shall illustrate his method from Cook, a widely-used and recent textbook. After summarizing the plot of *Rashomon* and telling us it is about truth (see p.ix above), Cook issues a judgment, then explains it:

> Cinematically, *Rashomon* is a masterpiece, and its release marked the emergence of Kurosawa as a major figure on the international scene. Each of the four tales has a unique style appropriate to the character of its teller, but the film as a whole is characterized by many complicated tracking shots, superbly

paced editing, and thematically significant composition of the frame in depth. The camera seems to be almost constantly in motion, much of it violent, and Kurosawa uses many subjective shots to represent 'reality' from the perspective of the individual narrators. (Cook 1981, p.568)

This passage is quite typical of the less pretentious kind of critical writing about movies. I would subscribe to everything it says. The film is a masterpiece and its director is a master; each story is treated differently; the camera and composition are used to considerable effect. But I subscribe only on the face of it. What statements say is contained not just in what they mean on the face of it, but also in what they clearly imply. What a Gombrichian might fasten onto in the quotation above is the logic of it, the implications. Surely, he would say, there are many films that have 'complicated tracking shots' (e.g. *The Longest Day*) that Cook well knows are not masterpieces; there are many films with 'superbly paced editing' (e.g. *Jaws*) that are also not masterpieces. The same point could be made about thematically significant compositions and the use of the subjective camera. Furthermore, just as the presence of any of these features is insufficient to make a film a masterpiece, their absence is also not sufficient to prevent a film being a masterpiece. Some masters are known for their plainness of style.

As I interpret Gombrich, he believes that the futility of the attempt to explain why a work of art has merit by appeal to general standards or principles implies that we can abandon the search for those principles. He exemplifies this in his own writing which has the following prominent characteristics. It is consistently historical, placing works and their makers in the social and artistic context of their time, and making connections between earlier and later work, especially as regarding different solutions to problems of representation. Second, it is flush with the discussion of ideas. Gombrich pays great attention to what artists have written or said about the work of others and about their own endeavours. Third, Gombrich passes very few straightforward value judgments. The principal way value is conveyed to the reader is in the richness and density with which Gombrich explicates a work and the features of it that he picks out. One might caricature his method by saying it is their presence in his writings which shows that an artist and his work are to be highly valued. An aside about something atrocious only highlights the attention given to the valued. Both in *The Story of Art* and *Art and Illusion* Gombrich gives very little space and very brief exegesis to non-representational art. He gives a historical account of its emergence, and a little explanation of what the painters think they are doing, but he indicates that it is not altogether to his taste. The man of learning here engages in canon consolidation (Gombrich 1979, pp. 167-83) by mentioning and not mentioning, presumably as the connoisseur buys and does not buy, the critic reviews and does not review, and so some things survive and others do not.

Canonical works, thus, are implicit standards in Gombrich's critical practice and he consciously resists those who try to develop explicit standards. His relative lack of attention to abstract art has a deeper significance. In general, Gombrich does not much pontificate about the new. He is an art and cultural historian more than an art critic. One does not find him writing about the latest exhibitions in the newspapers or magazines. My guess is that Gombrich takes the test of time to be an important criterion in art, one that cannot be applied to the new. Once time has passed a work has become familiar; much has been disclosed about it by historical research and critical discussion and, above all, it has become embedded in the context of art. What does this mean? Well, art is a continuous tradition that feeds and builds upon itself. Artists are influenced by past art, positively and negatively. They work within conventions established by others; they place their work in relation to that background as they create it. This is not clear when the work is new. Indeed, one of the most characteristic of response chains is the following. A new school (or artist) appears on the scene and proclaims itself to be a radical departure from all that has gone before. Great excitement surrounds its works and creators. Considerable publicity and talk is generated. Time passes and what once seemed radical and new now looks completely continuous with what went before, perhaps, in some cases, a quite conservative continuation.

Films, being entirely new, are not yet settled in the general context of the arts themselves, nor have they had much time to create their own context against which to see the continuities and radical departures of their own tradition. So whether we concur in Gombrich's opposition to all attempts to formulate standards –

that is, to judge works of art by general principles – or whether we hold that some tentative standards may be found, discussion of movies is affected by their newness.

Other reasons besides newness explain the lack of standards in discussion of the movies: one is the problem of the alleged uniqueness of a work of art; another is the craft status of film making; a third, which will be segregated for discussion in the next section, is the irrationality of the tradition of critical discussion of films.

The argument from uniqueness goes together with the attack on general principles. What sense does it make, this argument goes, to seek general features of good art when what is so often cherished are those things that make a work of art different from everything else, including other works of art?

There is a logical flaw in this point. We can generalize about differences as readily as we can generalize about similarities. Hence, uniqueness is not a barrier to general standards. Every human being, we generally hold, is unique. It does not follow that we cannot characterize human beings by generalizations of similarity and difference. A work of art of merit will belong to some class, let us say portraits. There may be standards of portrait painting which it exemplifies. But then again there may be features of it seen nowhere else, and which are generally thought to contribute to its special value. So much for the uniqueness objection.

My point about film making being a craft is probably not clear. What has this to do with general standards? My answer is that the more rationally organized the recruitment into and teaching of a subject, the more likely it is that explicit standards have been developed. The reason is that even hands-on teachers have from time to time to say things, have to specify some dos and don'ts. Where an apprentice system prevails such injunctions may be uncritically passed on; whereas the establishment of training schools and courses, degrees and specialisms, exposure to other examples than the work of the master, encourages critical thought about knowledge and standards. If movies in their present form are only fifty years old, film schools, degrees, textbooks, are not more than twenty-five years old. Twenty-five years ago recruitment to the industry was haphazard and nepotistic; creators, where organized, formed craft guilds that taught by apprenticeship. Even today almost every film school is deeply split between the production side, with its anti-intellectual emphasis on hands-on teaching, and the history-criticism-theory side which has to struggle to legitimate its status. Such divisions are not healthy for mutual learning.

So although Gombrich pooh-poohs such notions as proportion, or line, or composition as standards of excellence, there is in his critical practice the use of canonical works to which to compare other works, and there is the standard of making historical sense of paintings. If, when we think of standards, we think of the Paris metre then our argumentation will be naive. 'Standards' means material criteria for assessing the strength of an argument. We have made a rough and ready distinction between two kinds of standard or criteria: (1) response; (2) evaluation. The difference is this: in the case of (1) a work is judged by the reaction of its consumer. If that reaction is positive, the work is good, and to the same extent; if it is negative, vice versa. (2), by contrast, looks to standards that are fulfilled in properties somehow possessed by the work itself; thus, if a work has proportion, or good composition, then it has passed muster. (2) can easily be subdivided into two kinds of properties of works, what might be called their formal and their thematic properties. Formal properties are what we have mentioned so far – proportion line, balance, etc., thematic properties look past the form of the work and its perfection, or lack of it, to the subject matter or, rather, to what it says about the subject matter. Few critics reject subject matter as such, even when it is a gory torture, crucifixion, or anatomy lesson, rather do they look to what the artist is saying about it. Then the question arises, is what he is saying: true or false, good or evil, banal or profound? If it is the wrong side of any of these disjunctions then . . . . Then what? Here is fierce disagreement. Suppose a novel was written that celebrated the devil and the triumph of evil and pictures this with relish. There are some critics who would automatically condemn the work, others who would ask, more subtly, does it do a good job of presenting its point of view? If it does then it deserves praise.

To be schematic: we have form *versus* content; then, within form, truth, or virtue *versus* diversity. My former student, Dr. Brian Baigrie, has suggested caricaturing these as the Platonic and

Aristotelian positions, respectively; that is, art as teacher (of the correct) versus art as explorer.

Many of the divisions in these matters go back to disputes in the older arts, paralleling the dispute in philosophy between a preference for Russell and a preference for Heidegger. Heidegger had some things to say, although far fewer than Russell, but he sounds incomparably deep as he goes about it. One will find many literary critics siding with Lawrence and Joyce and with very little to say for Shaw or Maugham. One looks long and hard in Russell, Shaw or Maugham for a sentance that is unclear or hard to grasp and, although they all grapple with the deepest problems, they somehow, to some critics, do not sound deep. So, true and good must also be deep-true and deep-good. If we extend the discussion a little further, to politics, it gets muddier.

The tone of film criticism has always been left-progressive, as explained elsewhere. Hence, Soviet silent films, with their mythification of Russian history, their agit-prop content, and their general lack of humour, have always found a willing audience in progressive circles. When, however, the Third Reich began to turn out watchable films, there was consternation in film circles. How could films in aid of bad causes, the worst of causes, be good films? After the war the intellectual problem continued to be debated, even though the USSR turned out ossified Stanlinist vehicles, and the West produced diverse kinds.[3]

None of these issues is clear and, although I have my preferences, they do not solve the dilemmas. In the face of confusion one has to rely on clarity and logic. If it is all right for Lawrence, Proust and Yeats to preach reactionary ideas and still be giants of literature, then it has to be the same for films. At each of the forked choices above one demands that critics be consistent across the different media. Similarly, if they regard Shaw or Maugham as facile, they must beware of their favourite films being subjected to the same charge. My own ideas are most clearly expressed when I consider what philosophy does, and what can be hoped for from philosophy on film, in the section on popularization (Chapter 10).

Meanwhile, some logical analysis is called for. What is the logical role of standards, whether of response or evaluation, whether of form or content? Are standards there for artists to absorb and then fulfil in their work? Or are standards there for the audience to apply to the works? (Or both?) Then, is it sufficient for a work to fulfil these standards, or is it merely necessary, that is, a minimal condition? We might compare the elevation of works to the canon, or their satisfying our standards, to the situation in cognition where we have candidates to be considered as knowledge and we try to decide about them. All classical epistemology takes it that knowledge is fixed and certain and that we exercise our reason in the search for what Bartley has called justificatory arguments, arguments which authoritatively ascribe cognitive status to a candidate. The non-justificatory epistemology of Popper and Bartley, by contrast, uses rational argument differently, namely to eliminate candidates. Candidates left over after the elimination process are not authoritative knowledge, they are no more than what remains – the best guesses we can currently make.

Can we now apply this epistemological move to assessment of the arts? Regardless of what art is, there exists a body of work handed down by tradition that we count as art – the canon. There are contemporary works making a bid for inclusion. Perhaps our search for standards is a search for arguments of elimination: that is, arguments, whether from response or evaluation, whether from form or content, from truth or politics, that we offer as reasons for not adding certain works to the canon of excellence. It does not follow that works possessing whatever it is are thereby added to the canon, merely that they are eliminated from candidacy. This model allows, indeed stresses, the centrality of rational argument about the arts not as a play-thing of intellectuals but instead as an essential mode of constitution. We are engaging in canon-making in such dispute, not merely art discussion. The discussions are open-ended; there is no final authority. Even the tradition of received works is open to sifting and challenge as well as addition as recent work enables us to see art where it was not seen before. 'Art', like 'science', is an honorific, and there is always dispute about the worthiness of applying an honorific to this or that. The history of science is a wonderful illustration of the confusion engendered when attempts are made to settle issues once and for all. Agassi (1963) has explained how some philosophers view only the latest science as science and all that went before as pre-science: the self-created problem becomes, what to do when the latest science changes? Others consider science to be what scientists do, which creates problems when, like Newton, they tinker with a lot of queer religious ideas. Still others, arguing science cannot come from nowhere, look for precursors to every scientific idea, but this incrementalism eventually ties in science to everything else. Let us look at how this line of thought applies to films.

Linden, in his paper (1971), lists ten questions which 'if a film were to fulfill them all, I am confident that it could be judged a good film if not a great one':

(1) Is the projected world pictorially plausible? (2) Does this seemingly real world really seem? (3) Is the experience always fresh? (4) Do the visuals and aurals work together? (5) Does it move? (6) Is it merely a recorded stage play? (7) Does it make you see more? (8) Are its symbols natural to their situation? (9) Is somebody in charge? (10) Is it indefinitely sentimental? (p.73)

Finding counter-examples to such lists is so easy we can treat it as knock-about fun. Here are a few troublesome ones: any Busby Berkeley dance sequence; Ingmar Berman's *The Magic Flute*; *Richard Pryor in Concert*; *Casablanca*; *The Atomic Café*; *The Rocky Horror Picture Show*; *Taxi Driver*. Indeed, it is easy to go through his list one by one, negate his criteria and come up immediately with a film of merit that fulfills the negation. But, it might be objected, Linden says that if a film fulfilled *all* his questions, *then* it would be judged a good film. This objection invites us to be pedantic. In what would the fulfilment of a question consist? Leaving that issue aside, is Linden saying that his list is *sufficient* for a film to be good? This makes the finding of counter-examples a little more difficult. Some of my examples above strike me as such global counter examples; I leave the reader to consider which they are, and to devise further ones.

Haig Khatchadourian (1975) presents only four, much more vaguely worded criteria: formal beauty: expressiveness; aesthetic and human significance of the action, characters, ideas and situations; fitness of form and content to purposes. Perhaps these are so attenuated that they fit any film; equally, perhaps, almost any film is a counter-example.

To speak diagnostically, these philosophers' efforts are bedevilled by their own high-browism, their selective viewing and lack of appreciation of just how diverse is the set of candidate films for the canon. The other problem comes from failure to separate the problem of legitimacy (is film a medium of art?) from the problem of standards (what makes a good film?). The two problems can be connected, but they are logically separable. Even if films were an industrial craft and not an art there would be a place for the question of what makes a good film. Equally, film could be declared an art with as yet no meritorious exemplars.

Finally, I sense confusion coming from the demotic character of movies, and their being made by committees. Since they are presented to us under the auspices, primarily, of commercial institutions, the kinds of preliminary sorting that cultural instit- utions do in the traditional arts is lacking. In this way institutions in the traditional arts embody standards; many institutional filters work over candidates before they obtain access to the public. [4] These filters are purely profit-oriented in films, or *post-hoc*: that is, after films have been shown, the magazines, classrooms and archives get to work on deciding whether they are fit for preservation as art.

When the institutions of film art get to work, what sorts of standard do they apply? Are they really as sophisticated as Linden and Khatchadourian? Maybe, but not to begin with. I contend that the basic standard that is applied time and again is 'I like it'. There is a fundamental tendency to trust to *response* as a first approach. If that reaction is not good you are unlikely to persist with the work. Yet implicit in this reaction has to be some such premise as 'and if asked to give reasons, I could'. Only this thought saves Sesonske (1980), in my view. In the course of a thick book about the French films of Jean Renoir, which he obviously adores, he never once advances an argument that would respond to a sceptical challenge, such as from someone who says that they did not respond to Renoir's films.

My suspicion is that such a challenge would be met by an argument of the form, if you cannot *see* the merit of Renoir's films then you lack either the taste or the cultivation to appreciate film art. The implicit premise here is that some people's reaction of 'I like it' is more authoritative than others: we might call these the connoisseurs. While he may acknowledge education and training, scratch an aesthete and you will usually find the idea that some people have taste and sensibility and some do not. Just as some people are colour blind, some tone deaf, some unable to distinguish good wine from plonk, the institution of the connoisseur is premised on the idea of a superior and authoritative taste. Polanyi (1958) even flirts with suggesting some such taste (more cultivated than innate) is essential to science, too. The connoisseur rationale stands behind the best film lists of Tables 7.1 and 7.2. How to establish a canon? Poll those who know best. This is a poor argument: who says these are the people that know best and how do they know; and is it logical to use numbers for the final selection?

In the traditional arts, especially painting, the situation is eased by the existence of two things: the art market and the length of the tradition of painting. These provide means of judging a connoisseur: if his taste coincides with eventual market value and/or if his taste is vindicated over time by the emergence of the canon. There is no market of taste in films, museums usually acquiring them gratis, collectors being few, trade being restricted because of copyright not being embodied in a print. And of course the whole time depth is too shallow. If taste and sensibility are largely acquired rather than inborn then the absence of a canon is an absence of means of cultivation.

A second standard often applied but little discussed is the aggregate version of 'I liked it', namely popularity. One measure of this is box-office revenue. This is slightly problematic because it does not reveal preference (*pace* the economists to whom it is a 'revealed preference'): what you paid for may not be what you like. One could cross-check by polling but, if the principal cause of popularity is word-of-mouth (Jarvie 1970), then high correlation of box-office and preference is to be expected. Linden, concentrating on the personal film, Khatchadourian concentrating on the art film, seek to exclude the demotic sense of the aggregate and then to rationalize connoisseurship. Worked out in detail this shows itself as a preference for foreign films over American ones, so one may harbour legitimate suspicion.

A third standard, and by far the most frequently invoked of all, is comparison – with other films, other work by the same person, group or firm, other versions of the same work, on stage, in print, with other arts generally. This is where the canon is so important, since the canon is a concrete embodiment of standards against which to compare the work under consideration. And yet always the logic of such comparison is in jeopardy because a comparison may lead not to rejection of the work under consideration, but to a rejection of the canon or the standard being used. Indeed, this process of feedback and correction is characteristic of the discussion of the arts through time.

To sum up: there is a lack of standards for the discussion of the aesthetic merit of films. If one takes the position that the value of such standards for the traditional arts is questionable, then this charge against films is vacated. If, however, one acknowledges the importance of one special form of standard, however inchoate, namely the existence of a body of work that has, over time, come to be thought of as exemplary of that art and of excellence of work in that art, then the charge sticks. Film lacks an agreed canon. Those writing about film can be thought of as engaged in the arduous and long drawn-out process of attempting to establish a canon, However, their not being aware of this makes them uncritical, hence their employment of criteria that are difficult to defend: connoisseurship, liking, popularity (whether generally or by connoisseurs) and comparison. Even if we reverse the position and concentrate on arguments for eliminating films from consideration as possible canonical works neither these standards, nor formal standards, nor vague general prescriptions, nor political considerations are any less contentious and inconclusive. There are here serious obstacles to any efforts to treat films as art.

7.14   *Shallow Traditions of Critical Discussion*

We come now to the last of the reasons for the movies' lack of standards: the impoverished state of critical discussion. For contrast, let me sketch a healthy tradition of critical discussion, that in natural science. Scientists engage in the solution of problems about the natural world. To accomplish this they propose hypotheses or theories. These theories are tentative and subject to review. Flaws typically sought in the review process are these. Theories may, when worked out in detail, prove to contradict other, well-established theories. They may fly in the face of some of the available evidence. And they may yield predictions which are contradicted by the test results. Disclosure of any of these contradictions creates a serious intellectual problem. A contradiction forces us to choose, in this case between the theory being considered and the statement which contradicts it. The choice itself is a meta-hypothesis, subject in its turn to the same sorts of review.

Notoriously, scientists are as likely to be in love with their theories as with their problems and to prefer the meta-hypothesis that their hypothesis is correct to the meta-hypothesis that the criticism is correct. Yet this scarcely fazes the progress of science. How is that accomplished? Simply, by not entrusting the critical process to the interested individual. Scientific training does teach a critical attitude and doubtless scientists try to internalize it. But the effective checks are external. Here are some of the places where institutions ensure exposure to criticism. Most scientists work in laboratories or in teams where they constantly chew over the progress of their work with co-workers. Money for the research is given on the basis of proposals that are carefully reviewed by independent judges. Results of work are presented at local, regional, national and international conferences where the format provides time for reaction and discussion. Papers are written and submitted to journals where editors have them assessed by highly-qualified referees on the basis of whose reports the decision about publication is taken. There is a plurality of journals. Published work is diffused around the world and journals make space available for comment and criticism, and even for retraction. It is as serious a responsibility of senior scientists to check each other's works or the works of graduate students, to respond to calls for assessment from sister universities, journals or granting agencies, as it is for them to do research and to teach classes.

None of this ensures that science will progress; none of it ensures there is not shoddy or even dishonest work in science. To demand that science ensure something is too strong. Yet such sense of progress as we have is largely, I would maintain, to be explained by reference to the operation of these institutions. One of the principal reasons so many scientists oppose secrecy is because they rely on public exposure and discussion to save them from error. The only component absent from much scientific discussion that is present in other traditions of rational discussion

189

is history. Scientists operate with a surprisingly short time-depth. The roots of current debate may be in a literature no more than thirty years old. There is, however, good reason for this. Science's progress is only partly incremental; it also is partly a matter of fits and starts – of scientific revolutions. While a historian can find long-lasting continuities in the history of the subject, in practice the aftermath of a scientific revolution is often that the terms of the science, the approach, the machinery and equipment are all different and hence historical depth is only occasionally relevant. [5] Yet it is instructive that the very greatest minds of a field are often well-versed in the history and philosophy of their subject.

So far as I am aware, no other field has as well-developed machinery as science does for the exposure of work to colleaguial criticism. One or more of the features I have listed is missing from other fields or, where present, is not taken so seriously. Philosophy is a case in point. Its practitioners tend to work in solitude. They belong to schools of thought which criticize other schools more severely than they criticize their own work. And, moreover, that work itself lacks the dimension of prediction and test – acid tests in science. Far more than science, philosophy is dominated by fashion and the ephemeral and it has a uniquely bad feature: unintelligibility is presumed to cloak depth.

Bearing in mind critical discussion in science, let us bring the discussion back to movies. What is the situation in the movie field? So far as I can see, deplorable indeed. Instead of Stanley Cavell carrying on debate with Hugo Munsterberg, he totally ignores him. Instead of explaining and criticizing André Bazin, he alludes to him while writing what is in most ways a monologue. Moreover, it is a monologue that takes care to be only partially intelligible. Writers on film characteristically make free with references and allusions to films which they have not the slightest reason to suspect their readers know. Writers on film characteristically drop the names of, or even quote from, their own favourite gurus (e.g. Heidegger or Lacan). Nearly all name-drop shamelessly. But worst of all is the general irrationality of their procedures. This is highlighted in two ways. The first way is that their prose is almost never organized around a clear and systematic discussion of one problem at a time, with the thesis spelled out and the array of supporting argument and the rebuttal of opposing argument easy to discern. The second way is that the predecessor literature is all

190

too often not surveyed and consciously addressed. It is thus only with the greatest difficulty that the student comes to appreciate that discussion of films is a battle between deeply divided positions.

Perhaps the most intellectually energetic discussions of movies in the 1970s came from a group of critics we could call Marxists. Their very existence, and even more their growth and influence, was astonishing. Just as astonishing is that they never hint that the principal ideas of Marx and Marxism were refuted long ago, so that continued adherence to them smacks of religious commitment. As indicated earlier, it is my thesis that the engine of intellectual progress and the very possibility of any kind of objectivity comes and only can come from cooperative endeavours of a community that engages in mutual criticism. This is no mere plea about attitude, it is a call for the construction and maintenance of institutions. The standards we ought to have, the canon we need to develop, can come only from such cooperative endeavour. Yet the institutional split in film education (production vs. studies), the paucity of refereed journals, the reduction of criticism to response, to undiscussable matters of taste and discrimination, are all bound to increase confusion and disarray. Marxism seems better precisely because of this confusion.

Before turning to other matters, two comments, one about reform, the other about newness. Challenged to come up with measures for reform and improvement it is pretty obvious what I should say. Foundation of more journals, reorganising the academy, changes in training are all indicated. The field is not centralized, however, so no such reform programme is likely to be implemented.

About newness. The institutional short-comings which impoverish the tradition of critical discussion in film studies may, if we are feeling charitable, be explained by the newness of the whole field. The institutions that characterize the more rationally organized field of science were not invented and put into place in fifty years. It is true that we can learn from past experience and accelerate development somewhat. But science is only in its most general respects a model for the organization of other subjects. No-one, least of all myself, would want film study to copy-cat science. Rather should science be an inspiration for us to find institutional arrangements adapted to the peculiarities of film studies, that will

191

do the job of improving and deepening the tradition of critical discussion.

7.2   THE NATURE OF THE MEDIUM

7.21   *Mechanical Reproduction*

Earlier, hints have been dropped about this particular line of objection to according the status of art to the movies. All the fine arts are immensely old, dating back not only to before the Industrial Revolution, but to a time before the present-day European languages existed, to a time about which we are still speculating. Livelihood was gained in those societies by a few very basic devices: agriculture, crafts and trade. It was this society, a society without industry and without science, possibly permeated by religious sentiments impossible to reconstruct, that nurtured the predecessors of the art media we have today.

For thousands of years no problems arose for our version of the arts. They were not added to, and their social matrix changed very little. A sea-change in human social organization did come, however, with the industrial revolution and its consequence of spreading industrialization (Gellner 1964). The traditional ways of making a livelihood came to seem slow and pedestrian, their products exquisite, perhaps but labouriously produced. Above all, industrialization has two features: mass production of identical objects; and reduction of complex or idiosyncratic processes to simple and standardized ones.

Consider mass production. Instead of each person attending the boot-maker's to have his feet drawn, to choose his material, to pay a deposit, then returning for a fitting and, finally, possibly after several days, for the finished product, a person now repairs to a large and well-stocked store where, off the shelf, can be obtained a replica of the shoes seen yesterday on someone else, moreover a replica adapted to the size you need. You spend less time buying them, maker and seller between them spend less time producing them than did the craftsman of yore, and while the hand-crafted object could be exquisite to feel and to look at, it would cost more than today's shoe, and might be less hard-wearing.

What is the application of this to movies? Well, movies seem to be mass-produced. Stamped that is from the same die, they in this resemble a printed reproduction of a painting. Aesthetes are sometimes hard on those who have prints of famous pictures in their home, some even intimating that it is better to have a genuine second-rate real work of art than a reproduced first-rate work of art. Such an attitude to movies would make no sense.

My view is that we should reject this argument altogether as muddle-headed. To begin with, films are not alone in being mass-produced. Long before films we had Gutenberg whose boon to mankind – movable type – at last enabled machines to mass produce books for all who could read to own and to study. This invention itself was a leading incentive for people to become literate; it was a skill useful in livelihood, and also in art and leisure. Also before films came along Edison had invented the phonograph recording which, once it was improved with high fidelity, enabled something very precious to be recorded and widely distributed: sound, especially musical sound. While we have to guess at what Greek, Roman and even medieval music sounded like, such guessing need never be the case with the music of our time. It has been captured forever. [6] So too have music and voice become available to people whose situation in life makes it too difficult or too expensive for them to get access to things 'live'.

Try as I might, I find it very difficult to discern the rationality in objections to the reproduction of painting or music. No doubt to own a Great Master, or to attend a live concert or, even better, to play music oneself, are aesthetic experiences of great value. But not just money and location are overcome by reproduction. Young, old, handicapped and ill people can enjoy listening to music. And there are many things to be gained from studying a print of a Great Master, much more than from a second-rate original. Indeed, especially when it is photographed on to a slide and projected at full size, a fine reproduction of a great painting can compare to the original. So, what does it matter that film is reproduced thousands of times over? Is it not like a book rather than a gramophone record or a reproduction? A book, no matter what its type, or binding, is the same book as long as the text has integrity (which is not to minimize the problems of establishing a text, as with the pre-Socratics or even Shakespeare). Thus, a film, too, given an integral text, correct photographic and sound values, is indifferent to the proliferation of its reproductions. To object to movies because they are mass-produced is mere muddle.

The other horn of this dilemma about mechanical reproduction is that it makes things too easy, even automatic. It is very hard to learn an instrument or to draw and paint, but very easy to have stereo technology fill your room with gorgeous music, or a slide projector show the world's greatest art. Is there perhaps yet another snobbery at the core of this objection? Music is written to be listened to, not only to be played; drawings and paintings are made for viewers, not just for apprentices or other artists. Film, furthermore, while relatively easy to project, is not thereby rendered very easy to make. Here we come I think to an implicit premise that needs to be articulated. Some people think that mass-production, automatic production, means simple production. They are both confused and, in the case of film (as of book production and sound recording), gravely misinformed. It is as hard to learn the skills and arts of making films as it is to learn those of recording sound or printing books, comparably hard, perhaps, as writing the music to be recorded or the books to be printed. I write 'perhaps' only because I suspect serious comparison would be silly. And films are like books in that the true object is distributed through, and hence available in, every copy. The novel or poem (in) itself is present in every true copy of its text. No-one thinks to assert that only the hand or type-written original is the work itself. Similarly, neither the cutting copy nor the answer print is the film itself. Every true copy is.

Unfamiliarity with their process of production may explain much of the muddle that is written about films as mechanical. So far from their creation being mechanical, one can argue that films are hand-made (see note 3, Chapter 6), being put together in tiny pieces over many months of work, much of that work direct, hands-on labour, as in design, lighting, staging and cutting, none of which is the slighest bit automatic.

Is the problem for many commentators that the very proliferation of copies of films somehow dilutes their claim to be hand-made art? We have seen that this would be absurd if applied to books. That does not mean there are not those who entertain such absurd ideas. Remember De Tocqueville:

> When none but the wealthy had watches, they were almost all very good ones; few are now made that are worth much, but

everybody has one in his pocket. (1835-40, vol. 2, Book I, ch. XI)

Films, being produced with the help of machinery, are more like watches, it could be said, than they are like poems or paintings. Hence the argument from analogy will not hold. But, I counter, neither will the objection. The illuminated manuscript or hand-copied book is a craft separate from the verbal content: when we print them they are in important senses identical through all the transformations.

So far, then, while granting that the age of machines involves a sea-change in human affairs, and that in it the arts have a different social position, I am not ready to concede that a medium that is a product of the machine age, a medium, that is, that has as its minimum conditions the precision engineering and chemical engineering of the nineteenth century, is not thereby a legitimate vehicle for art. It was never connected to religion. True. It has not grown out of, nor can it sustain, craft or folk aspects (unless we stretch the notion to include home movies). If it is a vehicle for art then it is something new, not quite comparable to anything that has gone before. [7]

There is yet another line of thought to be explored if we are to get to the bottom of the idea that film's mechanical origins in some way jeopardize its potential as a vehicle for art. This is the very general contrast of art versus machinery, of things that are products of human hands versus those that require no hands. The idea here is that machines are soulless, cold, the opposite of human and creative. Limit cases which test this contrast are the machine that creates, such as the robot or computer; and the analysis of the human being as a machine, clear in Hobbes and no-nonsense empiricists like La Mettrie, not to mention Descartes – who simply added a ghost to the machine. [8]Perhaps it is the presence or absence of this ghost, the soul, or mind, or human spirit that is being invoked by those who stress the contrast, who want to separate art from machinery. The very word 'mechanical' used in an aesthetic context means that a work is without creativity.

A frontal assault on this doctrine, ridicule of the idea that there is a ghost in the machine, will obviously not persuade those adopting it. They are convinced there is a contrast, a presence that is essential, and they are not open to contestation. Instead I want to offer criticism along two lines: the first that there is at work here a romantic conception of creation; the second that there is a logical error in thinking that the manner of creation is relevant to the question of art at all.

'Inspiration' is a word whose structure tells us something of the theory of creativity beneath its surface. To be 'inspired' is to have breath: the soul was identified with the breath and was thought to escape the body with the last gasp, the death rattle. The idea was that genuine creativity comes from the soul, and indeed is itself a little piece of the soul. Machines have no soul and cannot create and cannot reproduce the soul and so their reproductions are soulless, uninspired. Creativity is what gives the work of art its uniqueness and its power, which makes it, so to speak, what it is.

If what we appreciate in art is beauty, then we have the problem that beauty is not confined to created work; sunsets, mountains, men and women can be beautiful and no-one created them (leaving aside the hypothesis that Mother Nature or God is responsible). It could be retorted that in attributing beauty to natural objects we are projecting. This is a good reply, and such extensions of the notions may be out of order. However, the reverse could also be maintained.

Coming now to the second argument, the irrelevance of origins: how art is created is not relevant to whether it is art, or to whether it is good art. Origins do not explain the present. Consider a parallel point with science. Much confusion has been caused in the philosophy of science because people have sought to legitimate science by showing it has appropriate origins. If such security is to be sought in scientific method, let us say that of observation and experiment, it has been thought to be sufficient to show that some science originated in observation and experiment. Regrettably, it can be shown that much pseudo-science – by anyone's criteria – is also grounded in observation and experiment. Conclusion: the origins of science do not legitimate it as such. Science has come from cranks, from induction, from apples falling on people's heads, from dreams, and, no doubt, from data generated by observation and experiment. None of these amounts to a USDA Grade A Stamp because each of these origins has also been the womb of utter rubbish.

In science, we can say, what counts is not the origins of ideas but how they are assessed, how, in the present, they are subjected to tests. Popper says that the process of discovery has no logical bearing on whether or not something is science, only the process of testing has. And testing, obviously, can only take place after the idea has been discovered. The checks on work putatively taken as science are: can it be tested? Has it been tested? And, how do things stand with it after the tests? Negative reports on any of these three are grounds for it not taking scientific status.

Why can we not apply exactly the same reasoning to art? The creative individual is not sufficient and may not even be necessary – who can say what form art will take in the future? Obviously training in art school does not legitimate. Such a criterion would be both too narrow and too wide. Too narrow in that all primitive and self-taught artists would be ruled out; too wide in that many well-trained hacks and their work would be included. Indeed, I noted earlier that to say art is produced by artists may be to reverse the proper order of things. 'Artist' may more appropriately function as an honorific awarded to those who have produced art. We speak of 'the unknown artists who painted Lascaux', not envisaging some bereted caveman creating, but rather some painters who had no idea of what posterity would make of what they wrought. If origins are irrelevant, then whether art comes from a machine, from the soul, or from daubing by unknowns does not matter in the slightest. What matters is: can we treat it as art? Can we criticize it as art? And does it survive both processes?

So far the verdict on film is not in. Some think it has passed these tests. Others think it fixed at the level of good trash. As I shall argue at the end of this Part, the best resolution is to treat art as an essentially contested concept.

7.22   *Variety of Forms and Uses*

Whether or not film can be a vehicle for art, it certainly has been a vehicle for a great many other things, including the making of money, a matter we shall segregate in section 7.23. Film theorists and historians like to say that the spectrum of possible uses and forms for film was discovered almost at once and the poles are the work of the Lumières and Méliès. Whereas the Lumières were inventors in the photographic field, and they first used film to record such mundane events as a train entering a station or their workers leaving the factory. Méliès was a stage magician who used the film medium to create fantasy and delight: a voyage to the moon, for example. Let us call such a film as the entry of a train into the station an actuality, a record of some real event. Let us call Méliès' efforts a fiction. There are variants of both these forms. Méliès employed camera tricks, such as stopping the camera, to make people disappear. These can be applied to actual records of real events. The camera can be attached to a microscope, or put in a submersible, to photograph things never seen by the human eye. Or, more radical still, exposure of single frames over a long period, or of many frames over a short period, can enable us to see plants growing to maturity in a few seconds, or to study, at a speed more readily absorbable by our eye and brain, a motion that is very fast in real time. On the other hand, material that begins life as actuality, whether for scientific or newsreel purposes, can be taken by a film maker and cut together in such a way, and have such sound added to it, that it becomes a travesty of the real events, or propaganda. It is not long since a series of films called 'The March of Time', which consistently represented itself as actuality, would restage scenes it had been unable to photograph, not by any means always alerting its customers to the fact that what they were seeing was re-creation. At the time this device was scarcely ever commented upon. Seeing the films now it becomes the main issue (Fielding 1978).

In addition to its various forms, film has concomitantly various uses. For scientists it is a recording tool and an analytical tool. For politicians it can be a persuasive and propagandistic tool. For schools it can be an educational tool. For amateurs it can be a hobby and a means to family solidarity. This is indeed a wide range of forms and uses, additional to the possibilities of making art as such, and without denying the possibility of an aesthetic dimension to each of these uses.

One of the more conservative claims that is often made about art is that it is not useful, it is not a tool. That is, that the work of art exists in and for itself, *ars gratia artis*. My patience with this sort of claim is, I must confess, very short. It seems ahistorical in its view of art, and excessively romantic in its view of the artist. Most of us would not go so far as Plato did when he argued that poets should be compelled to write verse that fostered the interests of the Republic, by praising heroes or lauding combat. Yet many of the so-called works of art that have come down to us began life as political tracts, religious objects, services to vanity or worldly glory (portraits), hack work undertaken for money, and so on. To romanticize art and suggest that it is only produced when the high aims of art and creativity are at work is not only to fall back into the fallacy of origins but is also crude psychology. The artist may produce his best work under pressure for money and with no thought for posterity, and his worst self-indulgence when he works for his muse. It is not always so, but it is sufficient for the argument that it sometimes is.

But perhaps the simplest way to deal with the problem of variety of forms and uses is this: all are equally true of drawing, painting and sculpture, not to mention language. Just as language, which can be used to create art, can also be used for law, for propaganda, even for philistine attacks on art, so have drawings and paintings their uses for scientific recording, for political posters, for giving expression to religious and other superstitions . . . .

The things in the category we presently call art are in fact a grab-bag of this and that, diverse sorts of objects that had all kinds of functions and origins and intentions behind them. Only in the last century or two have the objects collected as art become solely that – things not intended for any other purpose than to be art and to deliver the properties and pleasures that art is supposed to deliver (whatever those may be, a contentous area yet to be ventured in this discussion). Films may well have come into being only in recent years, but that does not mean that they are destined to be any less diverse and multiple-functioned than any of the other media of art. It also does not mean that film's potential for art is at all diluted or corrupted by its employment in addition to, or instead of, more mundane purposes than art.

7.23 *Collective Authorship*

An imperative of the romantic view of art is that art must be created by an artist. There must be a person, perhaps a rather special person, who is inspired, through whom the Muse speaks. This Artist, or Creator, or Genius or whatever he is called, is essential to the romantic view since that view believes that what makes something art is that it is created by an Artist. Recalling my motto from Gombrich, not only am I critical of this view, but am tempted to regard it as the opposite of the truth.

In the case of films the romantic view is in immediate and obvious difficulties. For one thing, which we shall consider at length in section 7.3, the sheer cost of films more or less ensures that no single person ever gets control. At this point I want to consider the more limited matter of how films are made, cannot but be made, and the trouble this makes for the romantic view of creation. In doing so it should be recalled that I am engaged in going through arguments that have been used to make a case against film being a medium of art. Stated simply, the case is that a medium that has no creative controller, a medium that is collective, may be a craft or engineering, but not art. Yet there are adherents of the romantic view who want very much to make the case for films as art and so they have come up with a solution to this problem.

The technology of the six classical arts is so familiar to us, so widely diffused in our society, that it seems almost to be zero – not to be technology. To create literature all you need are pencil and paper, and the abstract technology of a literate knowledge of the language. Painting, dancing and drama also seem to require little technology, although technology can be deployed in them. With music the instruments and with sculpture the materials and tools are not such that everyone has them in the back of the garage. But still, some of them can be procured readily, if not by any means all. To write music does not require stave paper, but it does require musical knowledge or someone with it.

With more than 2,000 years of experience with these arts we have a tendency to minimize their technology, to see it as invisible or even non-existent. This is of course false, but plausible on the face of it. And while the pigments and oil paints today's painters use are in fact the product of advanced chemical technology, they need not be; painters could conceivably get by with less.

Here, then, is something of a decisive difference between films and the classical arts. Perforated celluloid, silver salts, developer and fixer, aniline dyes are all very advanced forms of chemical technology that demand armies of skilled workers and vast arrays of machinery and know-how for their production. Similarly, lenses, claw mechanisms, quiet and light-proof cameras, tripods,

cranes, lights, tape recorders, tape, mixing equipment, microphones, wiring are all indispensable to the film maker and are,
and always have been, possible only in a society with advanced
industrial technology. To this day poorly industrialized third world
countries have to import many of these things from advanced
countries.

While it is never done, it is by contrast possible for the single
unaided individual to burn his own wood for charcoal, dry his own
papyrus for paper, and to crush plants for pigment and so be the
sole creator of a painting. No single person could in a lifetime
create all the materials required to make a simple film, starting
from scratch. Thus the division of labour in the other arts (buying
paper from manufacturers) is an option; in film-making it is a
necessity. A society organized by means of the division of labour is
utterly different from one without it, as theorists from Adam
Smith to Emile Durkheim and as recently as Raymond Aron and
Ernest Gellner have vigorously argued. Not only are the products
exchanged in such a society different, but the sorts of relationships
that men must forge between themselves for such a society to work
are quite different from what went before.

The obvious objection to this is that it is irrelevant. That an
artist relies on others is no matter; if the artist selects them and vets
their product then he can still claim the responsibility and hence
the credit or discredit. This seems to have been true of the great
painting workshops. Division of labour no more detracts from the
painter than it does from the film-maker. This reply is helpful and
true. It shows us that the problem is not the division of labour in
general but the particular kind of confusion the division of labour
brings to films. It confuses us on the very question at issue: who is
the film-maker? Or, even more strongly formulated, is there any
one person who can be labelled 'the' film-maker?

In this book I have written from time to time about directors, as
though it were straightforward that films 'belong' to directors.
Now it is time to correct that impression. In the real world there is
a running argument between different claimants to the honorific of
'creator of the film'. Besides the director, the case has been made
for the screenwriter, the creative producer, and possibly even the
studio. Some Marxist analysts of ideology attribute films to
capitalism – they being part of its ideological apparatus. So many
sires for such a child, there must be a gravely tempting inheritance

201

at stake? Not really. Furthermore, these arguments are by and large irresoluble, in fact resoluble only piecemeal. For certain purposes MGM films can be lumped together and discussed; for other purposes the work of a producer, director or writer can be. Or does this sound anodyne? It is not intended to. The trouble is we are off on a hunt for the creative artist, the hand (hidden or otherwise) to whom the work should be attributed. The division of labour argument goes to the point that such attributions are hard to make. This argument cannot be dealt with unless we attend to what we are trying to discuss and what criteria of authorship and responsibility we have in mind.

Let us, since they are both mass-produced, compare films to books. We do not normally judge a book by its typography, because typography is usually no part of the writer of the book's bailiwick. [9] Do we say the same of a film's photography, is that equivalent to typography? Not really, since exactly how a shot is photographed adds important information and nuance, so it is more like a quality of the prose in a book. What is the equivalent of typography? Well, the celluloid is. So if a film is jerky in projection, or there is a sudden change in the image colours, for this we do not blame or praise the film maker. In discussing books we want to find out who authored the strings of words that make it up. Paper, print, binding, price are not relevant. But since the strings of shots and sounds which make up the film cannot but be generated by many, how shall we assign authorship?

Since the problem is insoluble, arbitrary answers have to be given and defended *ad hoc*. I know of two, one well-known, the other a cliché. The well-known one is the *politiques des auteurs* developed by French critics for dealing with the studio-factory output of Hollywood. Knowing full well the division of labour and responsibility in Hollywood, but believing that serious art needs an artist, they decided, as a convention, to attribute the meritorious and stylistic continuities in Hollywood films to the directors and, in turn, to seek out such continuities in the work of named directors (Sarris 1968).

The cliché was named by me the committee theory, the idea that the author of the film is a committee; that a film is like a committee report signed by all its members; even if drafted by the secretary, it will have been overseen and rewritten by the chairman and anyone on the committee powerful or assertive enough. Inside knowledge tells us of some reports that they were actually written largely by x or y; others are well-known to be agonizingly forged/cobbled together compromises between conflicting opinions and forces within the committee.

Each of these solutions is available, but one test of them seems not to have been thought out and that is their attitude to empirical evidence. Can we say that there should be as little argument as possible about facts, that where empirical evidence can settle issues it should do so, so that we can concentrate our energies where they are needed, where the discussion takes us beyond facts? If we can grant this assumption then it seems reasonable to say that the somewhat arbitrary ideas of the *politiques* come off worse than the cliché idea of the committee. Increasingly, we have access to empirical information about the making of films. Ever more studio files, out-takes, and personal papers of film makers are open to scholarly inspection. Hence this or that scene, or quality of a film that has attracted praise or blame, can be tracked down through these chains of paper so that we can pinpoint where it originated, how it was modified, and whether the director can be saddled with the responsibility of its presence. As matters of fact it can sometimes be shown that certain directors, while working at certain studios, were not allowed to spread their responsibility beyond the studio floor. Salaried like writers and editors, they could be called in when all pre-production was complete, and moved to another project as soon as the on-the-floor shooting was done. Hence scripting, casting, editing, sound, music, inserts, special effects and second unit work were all out of their hands. At another studio it might be shown that boundary-maintenance between roles was poor and that preferred directors managed to impose their wills on many aspects of the films they made, from the budgets to the publicity campaign. So the situation in both cases is more like that of the committee report where we attribute it to x when there is good evidence, and in the absence of such evidence we attribute it collectively. To attribute it to the secretary of the committee in the absence of evidence strikes me as arbitrary in the extreme and liable to create a quite false illusion of the career of the named person. [10]

If this argument goes through and we have to conclude that the best answer we can come up with to the question of who is the author of a film is a committee, how can we make sense of film in

203

terms of the traditional arts? This question poses no special problems. Cave paintings were undoubtedly collective works and we discuss them as art. But we have to hand two art media not, curiously, included in the six classical arts, namely opera and architecture, which everyone admits to be collectively authored. Composer, librettist, performers and producer are all required in an opera. But at least it is feasible for one person to oversee them all. Such is also true of architecture, although engineering aspects are usually delegated to the engineering contractor. But in the past such one-man oversight of architecture was literally impossible. Some of the great cathedrals, palaces and other buildings of the old world took two or more centuries to build, so everyone connected with their inception was dead before they were done. Furthermore, plans were sometimes revised or added to as ideas and conditions changed. Yet some of these are masterpieces of architecture, masterpieces we can attribute either to nobody, or to some known general planner at best, or to a committee the membership of which may or may not have been known, and which may never have convened at one time and place.

Films have often been compared to medieval cathedrals and that is something I think should be stressed rather more. [11] It follows that if they are an art, films are so in ways that differ drastically from the six traditional arts. And, however pretty the parallel with architecture, it is no more than that. Films resemble mainly themselves, and the problems of creative attribution appertain to them in unique ways. In analysing them we have to find criteria of creativity that will make sense. Here is a moderate proposal. As a first approximation attribute creative hegemony and hence appreciated touches to the director. But, and take note, check all available evidence, and where the studio, the producer, the writer, editor or actor can be shown to have contributed, bring this out and address the question of the extent to which the director had a choice in acceding or not to the suggestion.

Despite the architectural parallel, we are forced by the collective nature of film authorship to conclude that if the film is an art it is, once again, non-traditional. It is collectively authored, designed for collective consumption, capable of being reproduced innumerable times without loss. Neither the works, their manner of production, their status in society and the status of those who make them, resemble the parallel situation in the six classical arts.

As we shall see, admitting film to the temple of the arts may involve us in a redefinition of the rules of membership and, more important, of the religion practised within.

7.24 *How related to the Older Arts*

This subtopic deserves treatment at length on its own.

> With the rise of the moving pictures has come an entirely new independent art which must develop its own life conditions. (Munsterberg 1916, p. 60)

Extended discussions of the parallels between film and the other arts, such as are engaged in by both Munsterberg and Cavell, are not easy to understand. Their words may be clear enough but their purposes are buried in unexamined philosophical practice. We rarely bother comparing, say, novels to music and asking what the relation is. Not that we never make comparative remarks, like comparing the structure or rhythm of the one to the other; but we do not reach for systematic comparison in order to come to terms with one or the other. One rather obscure reason why these exercises are indulged at all is the influence of Kant: the idea that the mind operates with a limited number of categories and that the arts somehow are to be arranged under them. Music, it will be said, exists in time but not in space; painting, it is said, is not in time and is only in two-dimensional space; sculpture, it will be said, exists in space but not in time. More or less elaborate variations can be suggested for dance, literature and drama. For the non-philosophical reader, unaware of the curious goings on in and hence aftermath of the philosophy of Kant, this will either sound quite profound, or, equally, quite unilluminating (e.g. Kovach 1970).

What other purpose can be served by comparing film to the older arts? What about legitimation? There is a strong body of opinion sceptical of the claims of film to be a vehicle for art. One way of rebutting this scepticism is by the following sort of reasoning. Consider the classical arts. If it can be shown that film takes up and goes further with the means of one of those classical arts then may it not claim legitimacy by kinship? More elaborately: if we can assign the classical arts among the categories of time, space, motion and causality, and then can find a gap in the possibilities and fit film into that gap, have we not legitimated film by the same means we use to legitimate and differentiate the classical arts?

When, in the title of this section, I animadverted to relations to the other arts, I had in mind to deal with arguments of this general type. Before closely examining such strategies of legitimation, however, consideration of the problem of legitimation itself may be helpful. How seriously should we take sceptical arguments about the aesthetic legitimacy of film? What is the purpose of such scepticism, what is the purpose of our advocacy? Is the problem intellectually serious, or merely one of tidying up our classification system? Tidying up is neither serious nor urgent, and is different from the problem posed by awkward boundary-cases and counter-examples. It is here that film is important. Despite its newness, despite its mechanical aspects, since at least the *Birth of a Nation* in 1915, the case has been made that film was a new vehicle of art, not thought of and hence classified by either Plato or Kant, which, if it is to be accepted as such, may involve some revisions to the philosophical schemes for placing the arts devised by those great thinkers and by hosts of lesser ones.

The very notion of a new art form is itself troubling. The classical arts are ancient and hence ageless, as we have seen. They seem like permanent comforts in the human condition. What will become of our ways of organizing our thought about the world if something new comes along? If film is admitted to the arts then the possibility arises that it will not be the last newcomer. Perhaps the forms of the arts will start to proliferate. How can we construct a philosophical framework that is open-ended? The forms of time, space and causality are limited; once they have been fully permutated and parcelled out, what room will there be for newcomers, or will they have to displace present occupants?

I hope it will not be too cavalier to say that all this strikes me as not intellectually serious. That something new is troublesome for an existing intellectual scheme of things I take to be a sign of progress, a consummation devoutly to be wished. It is by exploding our neat schemes of the world, our theories and their attendant classifications, that we learn how the world is not, and so are galvanized into applying our ingenuity and imagination to the devising of new and better schemes. Kant's philosophy, which is a magnificient intellectual achievement, was predicated on an idea that is less readily taken for granted today. The idea, that is, that Sir Isaac Newton had more or less once and for all deciphered the scientific truth about the world (Popper 1963, chs 7 and 8). If he had, it followed only that we needed to tidy up the philosophical implications of his ideas. How was it, Kant asked, that the human mind has come to final and secure knowledge of the nature of the physical world? His answer was to the effect that in some way the world must be mind-like. The way in which the world is mind-like is specified as follows: the world is mind-like in that we are able to impose upon it our understanding, to categorize it with the apparatus of our intellectual equipment. This is not to deny that other kinds of intellectual equipment, such as that possessed by God or by E.T., might not be able to impose themselves upon it too. But human beings have a given categorial equipment with which they can make sense of the world. It remains only to analyse that categorial equipment and show how it does its work, in science, mathematics, religion and art.

This is the problem-situation as many writers on the arts see it, and into which film intrudes as a newfangled difficulty. Sceptical attacks on film rarely come from epistemological sceptics. They usually come from traditionalists who think aesthetics can be all wrapped up neatly in some modified Kantian forms if only the pesky newcomer can be disposed of. It is not hard to show that their view of the problem-situation is quite false. However great the achievement of Kantian philosophy, the problem situation with it is quite different: the premise on which it was erected is false. Newtonianism is no longer considered the last word on the nature of the physical world. Hence the problem of how come we have been so successful, how has the mind managed to do such a good job of getting the hang of the world, is a pseudo-problem. The mind has done no such thing. Rather the problem is, how was it that Kant convinced himself that Newton had solved the problems of physics once and for all? How was it that he thought the mind had triumphed?

Already by Kant's time it was well-known that Newton's optics were in trouble. Kant had read Berkeley, who had made devastating criticisms both of Newton's physics and his mathematics. In common with most readers, however, he seems not to have taken these criticisms seriously. Various problems were unsolved for

207

Newton, the perihelion of mercury and the many-body problem, to name but two. These were brushed off until the end of the nineteenth century when Newtonian physics began to collapse and the new ideas of relativity and quantum theory supervened. So long had Newtonian ideas had a hegemony that great efforts were made to conceal the fact that the new physics destroyed the old, that a totally different picture of the world and its workings was being put in place and that the continuing success of Newtonian calculations was covering up the end of the Newtonian world-view.

Philosophy of science was born of this world-view change, because clearly not the success of, but changes in, science were what needed to be understood. Hence Kant's problem was altered from, 'how have we managed to understand the world?', to, 'how do we continue to improve our understanding of the world?' The hypothesis that the world is mind-like is a very unpromising one. As Russell put it:

> Kant spoke of himself as having effected a 'Copernican Revolution', but he would have been more accurate if he had spoken of a 'Ptolemaic counter-revolution', since he put Man back in the centre from which Copernicus had dethroned him. (Russell 1948, p. 9)

We no longer even see science as an interaction of mind and the world. Minds are just another part of the world, did we but know it. Science is itself not an unaided product of minds. Rather is it a social mechanism for developing even better knowledge to serve our needs and our curiosity. And to say of the social organization of science that it is in some measure world-like in order to explain its success would be simply weird. Resemblance plays no part.

This problem-situation in epistemology has it seems yet to filter through to the hermetic world of aesthetics. If Kant's epistemology is no longer a serious contender, then the rest of his system may also be obsolete. No neat scheme of the categories and the forms of experience including the aesthetic is defeasible; that means of ordering the relation of the arts and the sciences is no longer available. Its problems are many but they are no little localized difficulties to be corrected by tinkering. They stem from global counter-examples to the whole project and require us to re-think entirely our approach to the arts.

Munsterberg is in a way the last gasp of this approach. By

arguing that films have their own life conditions, that they shape the objective world according to the movements of the inner world, he tries to psychologize Kant. The mind is now the thing we think with and its operations are being externalized by film. This view has, however, one very unfortunate consequence: it is too grandiose. For clearly, if film externalizes mental operations, it has to be regarded as in some way the supreme or ultimate art form, on the road to which all the previous ones are stepping stones or approximations. The intellectual excitement of Munsterberg's book seems to stem from a missionary zeal of this kind. Although, like most early writers on the film, Munsterberg is a devotee of the classical arts and an anti-vulgarian, he discerns great promise and potential in the film, a capability of reaching the finest heights of any other art and at the same time being accessible to the broad masses of people. An intoxicating vision indeed, and one shared by a great many of the pioneer writers on film.

Why is this consequence – that films are the supreme or culminating art – awkward? For two reasons. First, if Einstein shows us that Newton was not the last word in science, then why, logically, should we assume film is the last word in the arts? Why assume there will be a last word? If film is not the last word then it is not the culmination. There is more to come. Second, is not the idea of film – this vulgar form of mechanical reproduction – as the supreme form of the arts in itself absurd and even repulsive? When the aesthete sits transported by the sublime delights of a late Beethoven string quartet is he likely to be receptive to the idea that such objects as *Citizen Kane* or even *Rashomon* are the wave of the future?

The arts, we have noted, are not progressive in every sense, and certainly not in a manner parallel to science, where new developments tend to make old science obsolete. Old works of art do not become obsolete, and new forms of art do not make old forms obsolete. So, however grotesque it seems to bring string quartets into the discussion of film, when a claim of culmination is made it is fair. And awkward. Unless and until there are films that rank in the minds of devotees of the arts with the supreme achievements of music, literature, etc., the claim to culminate will be embarrasing. The older arts may not objectify the workings of the mind, but they have yielded works that seem satisfying on so many levels it does not seem to matter.

Otherwise, exercises in comparison and contrast between this art and the next are fruitless. It is true that film is a new medium. It is also true that it developed in its early stages through recruitment of people and ideas from the stage (Vardac 1949). But it is also true that those stage people rapidly found out that, used as a substitute for the stage, film did rather poorly, but given its own development it proved able to do things that were quite different from the stage. Hence the tie to the stage was slowly cut, and stage personnel learned the hard lesson that while it was possible to work in both, they were very different and skills could scarcely be transferred.

Films are no more the culmination of the other arts than are combination arts such as opera or architecture. In simplest terms films offer new ways of communicating by telling stories and stimulating the imagination. Like any such new medium they have potential for various uses, enhanced by the wide distribution made possible by their mechanical reproduction. Other media that have come into being in this period are the gramophone record, which is a minor medium of art; the radio, which was also a medium and still is, but on a small scale; television, obviously; and latterly the computer. The possibilities of art on the computer are just being explored, much as are the possibilities of synthesizing music. No-one in their right mind would think of any of these as culminations of all the arts. One hears, happily, less scepticism about their potential than was expressed about film, and the aestheticians are obviously so baffled by their proliferation that they do not even undertake the obviously futile effort to tidy them up into their ruined Kantian aesthetic structures.

Summing up the argument so far: two basic sets of objections have been offered to challenge the claim of film to be classed as a vehicle for art, as a form with artistic potential. One set reasons from the newness of the medium, the other from the nature of the medium itself. We have not acknowledged the force of the objection in every case, but we have not been able to waive away the objection in every case either. Newness in and of itself, lack of settled canons, shallow traditions of critical discussion and hence lack of established criteria for merit certainly cast some question up against the claims of film to be considered an art medium. It is hard for any argument concerning potential to be definitive; so it is no answer to these points that they are not definitive. What seems fair enough to conclude is that these points are cautious, encouraging us to emphasize the tentative and fallible character of the claims we may want to make on behalf of film. It could well go the way of strolling minstrels and radio, and this would scarcely be intelligible if as a medium it was such an incredible consummation of artistic possibilities. Its intrinsic dependence on machinery, its variety of forms, its collective authorship and its unclear relationship with the other arts establish no more than that, as a medium, it is not easily as assimilable to the other arts. Hence, if it is a legitimate medium of art, it could well be that traditional ways of thinking about, and classifying, the arts are in jeopardy. We thus have a philosophical explanation of aesthetic interest in film: it is problematic; it does not fit. This explains why some aestheticians have written treatises on film aesthetics trying, without fully realizing why they are doing it, to stretch and devise categories to fit film. The utter silence of other aestheticians about the film can be explained the same way: unhappily, they do not know what to do with film, so they ignore it.

7.3   MASS ART

The third line of objection to considering film a vehicle for art, and the final one I shall consider here, goes as follows: art is a matter of refinement, of taste, cultivation and sensibility. It is undertaken for its own sake and is its own reward. By contrast, movies are in their origins and their essence a mass medium that proceeds by broad strokes, conforms to mass taste, and embodies a fundamentally vulgar sensibility. Movies are undertaken by men of business for the purpose of making money, [12] and are enjoyed by the public for the most trivially and immediately gratifying of reasons: sensual pleasure. All art is entertainment, as the saying goes, but not all entertainment is art.

This argument could easily be construed as little more than an expression of snobbery towards the pleasures of the masses. Without denying that some of its advocates entertain those sentiments, I want to attempt to deal with it as a reasonable argument that is not a mere expression of snobbery. There are, after all, a good many truths in the argument. From time immemorial the classical arts have involved the cultivation of sensibility; it has been held that commercial movies or even sensual ones turn both artist and audience away from that cultivation.

It is not necessary for the argument to lump films together indiscriminately, as in the formulation just given. The argument can be strengthened by allowing that there are good, bad and better popular films; the question is not whether the medium itself should be eschewed, but whether one can mention in the same sentence, without incongruity, films and string quartets, as one can mention in the same sentence popular songs and string quartets – without incongruity.

Films definitely have their origin in appeal to the masses. There are economic reasons for this. Substantial initial investment is required to make a film, hence there has to be promise of substantial return, hence there has to be a reaching out for popular appeal. Films were invented at a time when private patronage of the arts in aristocratic settings – the system which had served Europe so well for so long – was much declined, and patrons still sought the prestige of giving commissions to the classical arts rather than the newfangled machinery of films. Even now, people, families and corporations will commission official portraits, usually in oils, sometimes by a prestigious photographer, never by a film crew. Yet to have a permanent record of someone moving and talking would, on the face of it, seem to be the sort of memorial that should appeal.

No-one would deny the vulgar origins of movies. The argument has always been that despite the myriad uses to which it has been put, including that of providing broad popular entertainment, the medium has the potential to sustain art of the highest quality. Potentiality claims being so hard both to rebut and to establish, how should the discussion proceed?

One move would be to ask of the classical arts whether their origins display any more promising auspices than the movies do now. The answer will have to be speculative, since the origins of the classical arts are hardly well known. Some, like literature, seem to have derived from the desire to take inventory (writing) and collect taxes – unalloyedly commercial motives, and also from traditions of popular storytelling (poems and songs). Very possibly writing was connected with the machinations of the rich and powerful, literary forms with both the aristocrats and the common

212

people. Such an answer may be persuasive, but it has no logical force. No sceptic persuaded of the commercial vulgarity of the film need deny that literature derived from storytelling or that it presently sustains Harlequin Romances. The point is it also sustains Jane Austen and Charles Dickens and Leo Tolstoy and Fyodor Dostoevsky. If that point is pressed then we may have to moderate our claims for movies. To suggest that the movies have already found their *Pride and Prejudice* or *War and Peace* may be contentiously to claim more for the extant body of movies than they can sustain. It is no good overclaiming for the movies in a potentiality dispute.

One might argue another way. The distance the movies have come from *L'Arrivée d'un Train en Gare* to *Rashomon* is not negligible. Indeed, the distance between *Birth of a Nation* and *Rashomon* is considerable, not to mention *The Jazz Singer* and *Rashomon*. And film has yet to complete its first hundred years of existence by the most generous measure; it is barely fifty years old by the measure I propose. Always allowing that it may prove a transient phenomenon to be buried by later developments, is it so unreasonable to think that there is hope that the medium has not yet realized its potential? It has provided all kinds of more basic experiences to its audience; is it not now beginning to provide something we can call aesthetic experience? For any test of aesthetic experience – refinement, subtlety, nuance, poetic quality, elevation, unity, harmony, rhythm, cinematic quality, and so on – there are films that exemplify some, and some that exemplify all.

There is truth in the argument of the sceptic but there is also something false – a tendency to make of art a rarefied matter, accessible only to a few, not operating at any level other than that of the sublime. This narrows art intolerably. The works of Rabelais, or Catullus, or Jonathan Swift, or Raymond Chandler or a host of other creators who can and do operate on many levels, seem to me to have a legitimate claim to be art. Beethoven wrote musical jokes as well as his late string quartets; we must guard against a tendency to associate art only with the solemn or the ecstatic. So much of the art that has come down to us has an overriding religious purpose, and during the hegemony of the Catholic Church in Europe, religion was such a serious business, we need consciously to correct a tendency to associate art solely

213

with elevation, with refinement, with absence of contact with the sensual or the broad. Kenneth Clark argues boldly that the nude which does not evoke an erotic response is the lesser work for that (Clark 1959).

It is interesting that very early on in writing about the movies we see an extraordinary reversal of what we might expect among aesthetes, namely, lavish praise for the slapstick comedy of the silent period. Coarse, broad, sometimes brutal, always taking the opportunity to attack pomposity, authority and sanctimoniousness, these comedies flooded American and world screens until well into the 1920s. Key figures in them were a fat man, a cross-eyed man, a meek and bespectacled figure, a stone face, a tramp whose feet pointed sideways, partners — one fat and one thin — and others. Fights, chases, dousings, pies in the face, clothes torn off, female impersonation, the list of standard situations is almost endless. One cannot erase from the memory the bizarre and anarchic logic of such scenes as when Laurel and Hardy get into a quarrel with another man whose house they damage and he retaliates by damaging their car. The quarrel escalates until both car and house are demolished. Another film has them quarrelling with someone in a shop doorway and literally tearing the trousers off the opponent, who immediately retaliates. A hapless policeman attempts to intervene and is similarly treated, as are by-standers and kibbitzers until the entire street is filled with men in their underwear tearing the trousers off anyone in sight.[13]

As I say, surprisingly, given their broad vulgarity, these slapstick films are often praised by intellectuals and aesthetes writing about the movies. There is an element of condescension and romanticizing the proletariat, no doubt; the simple pleasures of simple folk and all that, and the parlour pink can enjoy them as a way of wearing his cloth cap. But I have tried to avoid any imputations of snobbery. The universal popularity of these films, their discharge of the powerful emotion of laughter, usually at bullies and authorities, also explains their intellectual appeal. The first real hero of the intellectuals was a man from the centre of this tradition, the late Sir Charles Chaplin. Like most of them a vaudeville comedian of some experience, he began his film work in the slapstick comedy factories of the West Coast, although it was not long before he owned his own studio and was pushing the comedy form far beyond simple slapstick. Whether or not one appreciates his later work, here is an artist of the vulgar, broadening and deepening the form, embodying in his work the potential of the medium. His work was widely appreciated by critics and intellectuals, as we saw in Table 7.1 and 7.20. Politicians and artists of world stature beat a path to his door in Hollywood as the pages and pictures of his autobiography (Chaplin 1964) make clear.

But let me not leave slapstick behind just yet. What is the significance of the intellectual popularity of movies in their broadest form? It is a suppressed theme that has continued. Musicals, when they came along after sound, and animated cartoons, from Felix the Cat and Betty Boop to Walt Disney, have also been the darlings of the intellectuals (with the conspicuous exception of Stanley Cavell). I am not looking for contradictions here. I have not checked whether the sceptical arguments about film's potential also came from those who like slapstick, although I am inclined to suspect they did not. What is problematic is how intellectuals, who take an interest in the arts, should divide so neatly into those who accuse films for not being string quartets and those who revel in the ways films are totally different from them.

We have, I suggest, something more going on here than an argument over specifics. It is not just intellectuals slumming. What we have is some responding to and some resisting an alarming new factor movies bring to the discussion of the arts. That factor is the masses. Silent film is accessible even to the illiterate masses no matter what their language. Sound film is accessible to any speaker of the language in which it was made. There is no tradition, no schooling, no patrons, no elite, no barriers or requirements between the audience and the medium. If started early enough, the process of cottoning on to films, of being able to understand and to enjoy what is going on, takes place with little apparent difficulty. Elaborate literary or drawing skills, refinement of taste and intellect, long study and cultivation all seem unnecessary for the immediate appreciation of the movies. How different from the great novels and poems, art galleries, classic theatre and so on. These are confined by their minimum demands to a smallish segment of the population that has the access through parental encouragement and economic circumstances to make the approach. Not so the movies. They are accessible and cheap.

If they are also a vehicle for the highest sort of art, then they

215

mark a new phenomenon in the arts: the mass art. Made for the masses, accessible to the masses, yet having no inherent barriers to aspiration towards the finest sorts of artistic achievement. But there are problems too. Much of what is made is very poor, by anyone's standards, yet it rubs shoulders indiscriminately in the cinemas with works that by many standards would be considered superior. We do not as a rule hang trash art in art galleries, or play bad music at concerts. This, of course, is not unconnected with the fact that there is broad ('canonical') agreement on what is fit for galleries and concert halls. Since commerce and mass taste determine what shall be shown in cinemas, there is no way the cinema can be a temple of the arts in the way an art gallery or concert hall can. Of course, all temples need to remind us of their consecration to the sacred by the presence not too far away of the profane. It is the boundary of where profaning the temple begins that alerts us to its status as temple. But cinemas are confusing. In the same building, possibly during the same programme, a work with pretensions to something more, such as *Birth of a Nation*, may be shown alongside a broad slapstick comedy and a cartoon.

This juxtaposition of the refined and the vulgar, the common and the elevated, the sacred and the profane has characterized the movies since their origin. It is also a feature of television and of much popular journalism. A magazine like the *National Enquirer* may contain in a single issue articles about religious experience, miracles, astrology and extraterrestrial intelligence, along with gossip about the sex lives of famous people, exposures of corruption, advice and educational articles, and both sober and sensationalized coverage of medical stories. Even those of us who have specialized in thinking about mass culture must, I think, admit to a certain bafflement at this assault on the usual categories we were trained with. Our tidy worlds of art and information (sacred), sensation and scandal (profane) are broken down in the forms themselves: they co-exist in those forms, are readily consumed together.

We are looking only at the tip of the iceberg. Several of the classical media have been approached by the mass media. Popular fiction now floods the book market alongside classics, frequently put out by the same firms. Popular music has in the minds of some become synonymous with 'music'. Dancing has come to mean what couples do in dance halls, or what chorines do in variety shows on television. Drama has come to mean soap opera; painting has come to mean 'chocolate box art'.

Without being portentous, I want to argue that the movies are a harbinger of a new development in the arts, arts that incorporate in themselves the potentiality for both the lowest and the highest, and which encourage their customers not to shop exclusively at one end, but to expose themselves to the whole range of what is available. Hence, one will find serious students of the film thinking hard about mass produced, episodic serials, perhaps even trying to make pastiches of them. One will also find them puzzling over films made by avant-garde novelists and thinkers whose work can at best mean something to only a handful of devotees. All of this is film study, all of these are part of the art of the film.

To those who vigorously resist the tendency, who argue that the segregation of the arts from the vulgar and the low must continue, I point to the flooding of the traditional media by the new banal mass products. This is not a tide which some aesthetic Canute can order to roll back. It is rather an asault on the former social position of the arts. Work that had religious significance, work that was the product of craftsmen, work that was passed down from tale-tellers immemorial, came to seem the exclusive property of the clerkly classes, the literate, refined and leisured. The philosophical justification for this was given by Plato, who made no apologies. His immense prestige and the convenience of his ideas gave them an influence down to our times, although those fully familiar with his snobbery and elitism felt obliged to be apologetic about what they thought of as his worst excesses (Popper 1945).

Industrialization has changed all this. Leisure and comparative wealth are far more generally available. Industrial society demands a degree of formal literacy from all its citizens. This ensures that the population at large can begin to enjoy some of the things we call the arts. However, it is a democratic age in which the purchase price rather than the social access is what counts, and the tools of mass-production have put on sale a far wider range of products than was authorized by the guardians of the culture. Plato's philosophy of art and society has come to seem repugnant even to threatened intellectuals, who vacillate between their ideals, which are democratic, and their shaky undemocratic status as taste leaders. The reactionary sentiments expressed by so many twentieth-century artists cannot be unrelated to the threat they sensed in the disappearance of their traditional means of support and the rise of the unknown and inchoate force of the masses (Ortega 1932). The same fear shows in the other tendency, to embrace a 'progressive' ideology, like Marxism — which promises a rosy future for the loyal intellectuals as the vanguard of the proletariat

The drift of these arguments is clear enough. Nothing has turned up to show that the medium of movies is inherently second-class when it comes to seeking its place among the traditional arts. There are some things it can do better, some worse, as with all the others. But equally, to see it as the culmination of all the arts, whether for Munsterberg's psychological reasons, or because it utilizes the materials of nearly all the traditional arts, is simply to go overboard. New arts do not incorporate and supersede all the others; 'new arts' as an expression is suspect. What is treated as art has, in this century, greatly expanded. The suggestion has even been bruited around that art is simply what the society treats as art. Now that there are repertory cinemas, governmental and private film archives, scholarly journals about films, and relatively few voices attempting to delegitimate it with what are anyway poor arguments, we might say that, though it is a potentiality issue, it is in theory settled. Films belong with the other arts. Their particular social situation, especially their high cost and the possibility of further technological change, renders problematic their continuation in their present form. But because frescos and mosaics are scarcely done these days it does not follow that they were not and are not now media of art.

An argument against film as art not so far dealt with is the following (Thomas 1982). Mass media can function is several ways. Art, by our Kantian understanding, is not functional. Hence, if a mass medium performs important social functions it cannot be treated 'for itself' as art. This argument rests most plausibly on the cases of movies and television. There was a time when the movies were a central mass medium, performing the Durkheimian functions of promoting social cohesion and socialization (Jarvie 1982). It is instructive that viewing film as an art was then the prerogative of a small minority. When television superseded movies in these socialization functions movies were freed to be treated as art, and meanwhile it is very awkward to try to think of television that way.

Implicit in this argument is an acceptance of the Kantian premises that art is something of value solely for itself, possibly also elevated or rarefied, possibly of restricted circulation. Such art can also demand fredom from most forms of social control and official interference. Any major form of socialization, on the contrary, is of urgent public interest and hence lacks these protections. Other institutions of socialization – the family and the school – are considered legitimate targets of public policy and hence discussion.

There are historical flaws in this argument. Music and painting were, while they still served a religious function (especially for the non-literate masses), yet allowed the status of art media. There are also sociological problems. Writing has been a vehicle of art since Greek times, but has also been subjected to intense scrutiny and many forms of control. A revolutionary state such as France to this day licenses the publication of each book! Perhaps the basic flaw is the idea that art is detached from urgent social concerns. That is how many partisans of art try to preserve their freedom of expression in this age, arguing that art should be allowed a degree of freedom denied more mundane activities. This was neatly highlighted by the US Supreme Court. The US Constitution, First Amendment, allows for freedom of thought and speech and the absence of prior restraint on them. In 1915 a case against censorship of movies was upheld by the argument that movies were a commercial product, not a serious vehicle for thought, and hence to be denied First Amendment protections. This decision stood for thirty-eight years.[14]

Those of us in favour of freedom of speech and publication should not confuse that with the specious argument that art qua art should have a privileged position, else we too easily lend assistance to the reverse position, Plato's, that art is so important and influential it should be strictly controlled.

8

FILMS AS ART

The starting point of all philosophy of art is the fact of aesthetic experience.

(Hospers 1946, p. 3)

If film is treated as a vehicle for art, then it follows from sections 7.1, 7.2 and 7.3 that many of the traditional characteristics of art will not be present. But age and form and refinement, while not unimportant, are perhaps not decisive either. It remains to attend to those things thought to be decisive characteristics of art. Most central of these, since Kant, has been the matter of aesthetic experience, experience of a work, that is, undertaken and enjoyed solely as an end in itself. Art, it is reasoned, may be contained in mundane objects such as books or canvases. When we confront it, however, we can experience it in all the usual ways we experience an object, but also in another way as well, which we can call aesthetic. This is a form of strong and pure experience, pleasurable in a non-sensual way, that marks true works of art. We can attempt to experience any object in an aesthetic manner, but most do not yield anything. When we contemplate nature as art we are aestheticizing it, that is, treating it as though it were an artifact, which it may not be.

This philosophy of art developed before the age of industrialization. It is not easy to make sense of it today. In particular, the notion that there is a separate aesthetic experience might seem like a rarefied way of describing something otherwise mundane. It is very hard to characterize aesthetic experience in a way that does not exclude most of mankind from having it, if not also from being capable of having it. Some of us, at least, are uncomfortable with such a consequence. If it is the case that film is an art, however, that does seem to suggest, as Munsterberg clearly argued, that aesthetic experience is accessible to the mass of mankind.

Aesthetic experience, its very possibility, and its particular attachment to this or that work of art is often said to be the essence of art, what makes an object a work of art as opposed to a mundane object. Our Greek heritage, and especially its essentialism, seems to be completely overtaking us here. Starting from the idea that there is art, or that some things can be treated as art, the reasoning is that art must be in some essential way different from other things – functional objects, natural things. Kant tried to pinpoint this as the capacity to be experienced in a manner that is an end in itself. Art is not for him therapy; it is not sensual pleasure; it is not a way of passing time; it has no practical purpose; it is a *sui generis* form of experience intrinsic to living the good life to the full.

To the sceptical temperament this smacks of mystification. There is similar talk in the annals of thought about religious experience, the love of, and union with, God. If there is no God such talk obviously has to be redescribed both as to its object and to its quality. The same goes for aesthetic experience. If one questions the whole idea of an elevated plane of experience called the aesthetic, indeed, the very idea of modes of experience itself, then the pleasures of art, the things we say we take away from it, can be demystified. We may want to say such quite unelevated things as that a piece of music stirs feelings in us that are strong yet inchoate; that as a work unfolds we find we are understanding it on more than one level; that structural features of the work lend to it a completion that is very satisfying; that exploring a new work and coming to terms with it induces an intellectual and emotional excitement similar to grasping a mathematical theorem or a scientific theory; that creating and completing a work of art may give an adrenalin high very comparable to that induced by the solution of a scientific problem.

Gombrich has tried to argue that what goes on in art is that artists work in a context of unsolved artistic problems – for much of the history of painting these are problems of representation.

With the advent of abstraction – a product of the problem situation within representational art of the time – it became harder to formulate the problem in those terms. However, with the decay of abstraction, it may once more be possible to reformulate the problem in those terms. Some music is representational in intent, yet Stravinsky argued vigorously that that was not of any musical interest to him. If Gombrich is right I think we can demystify the aesthetic experience into a problem-solving experience. Perhaps the most powerful form this can take is when the creator, struggling with the problem, finally cracks it. 'Perhaps' is inserted because of the sleepwalking argument: the creator may solve the problem not realizing he has until hindsight makes it clear (Agassi 1981, ch. 16). Be that as it may, the artist is thus in a comparable position to the scientist, who also confronts a problem situation that is pregiven, yet his attitudes and moves in relation to it are his own. To the audience the situation is the same. The better their grasp of the problem-situation, of what it is the artist or scientist is taking on, the greater the thrill and the satisfaction they will experience if the solution is indeed a good one. If they are unaware of the problem, they may impose one of their own on the work and, by misunderstanding, take something out of it. If the solution is a poor one, they will be disappointed to the degree they appreciate the problem and hence the dimension of failure.

In writing about artists Gombrich always endeavours to fill us in on the problem-situation as it was confronting the artist; this is an exercise in historical imagination. So art criticism and art appreciation are fused, and are intrinsically time-bound. The joy of the work of the past comes because the intellectual structure of the problem is there for all time, is part of Popper's World 3 (Popper 1972), and hence can be rediscovered by each generation and reappreciated. And since each present is related to a past period in a way that differs from each other present, it is no surprise that interpretation and appreciation shift about somewhat.

So Gombrich's method takes us back to the hoary set of questions we were taught in school when confronting the work of art: what is the artist trying to do; how does he do it; and how well does he do it? Translated, this reads: what problem confronted the artist; how did he tackle it; and was the effort by any standard successful? The need for talk about aesthetic experience, rarefied and valuable in itself, without ulterior end of any sort, is disposed of. The power of works of art does not come from some capacity to engender experience unlike anything else, but rather from our sense of the depth and challenge of the problem with which the work engages, and its success as a solution.

No history of films and no aesthetic treatment of films uses this kind of approach in any systematic way. There is an excuse for this. As noted, the exercise of deciphering the problem which confronts the artist is a historical one. The problem can rarely be read straight off the work itself. It requires an understanding of the tradition, the social conditions of the time, the education and situation of the artist, as well as the resources he had available. The more we know on any of these topics, the better positioned we are to reconstruct the problem-situation. Notoriously, our understanding of historical matters improves with distance, at least partly because relevant documents and materials become accessible only after the fact.

Two obstacles present themselves to Gombrichian students of the film: first, documents and other materials have been singularly hard to assemble and gain access to. By no means everyone in film making thought they were engaged in acts of artistic creation that would one day be studied through documentation. So the personal papers and even the authoritative copies of the film themselves, as well as their earlier versions and planning materials, have not always been preserved. And the studios were business firms, for a long time private companies who regarded their records as both disposable and privileged. What has survived is now being made available to scholars in some cases but not all, and what has survived is not complete. Second — and even more troubling since it is a problem of principle — whereas Gombrich is usually able to name a particular artist who was in the reconstructed problem-situation (and where he cannot it matters little), with films it is very hard to say who (or even what) was in the problem-situation and then trying to solve it. If the author of the film is the studio, then explaining how a studio solves a problem of art in a manner comparable to the solitary human being is a tough task.

As previously indicated, candidates for the primary creative role in making movies include the director, the writer, the producer, the studio and, sometimes, the film editor. To the extent that these claims are taken seriously, and to the extent that they can be tested against documentary and other evidence, they reveal that a film is the outcome of people working on a cluster of problem-situations. Take the extreme case of the film editor. He may be presented with a batch of celluloid that does not, as assembled, work. A case in point is the book by Woody Allen's editor, Ralph Rosenblum (1979). Time and again the problem Rosenblum faced was that although incidentally funny, the jokes on film would not hang together into a coherent structure that would build towards laughs, maintain tone and mood, and round off nicely. He records how, in the course of the editing, deliciously funny sequences were left out because of this overall problem-structure. He describes how, working increasingly closely with Allen himself, he sought for possible structures in the material, reassembled it, then viewed it to see how well that assemblage worked. Such is his craft that much of the time he could carve a movie out of the given footage. He explains how, in effect, Woody Allen was his apprentice, striving to master that form of artistic control called editing, and being remarkably sanguine about sacrificing footage. In the case of *Annie Hall*, which is discussed in Chapter 15, the film as released was completely different from the shooting script that was filmed, including the fact that additional scenes and voice-overs were added to smooth over the emerging new structure.

These problems of structure and rhythm faced by an editor and his director are obviously not the same sorts of problem that a writer may be facing who is, let us say, adapting a novel and trying to create a screenplay that will be similar to last year's hit but have some novel features and in some way extend the *genre* so that the audience will not feel it is a retread. These problems may remain unsolved through to the editing stage, but they are more characteristic of the writing and story-conference stage. The same goes for the director, who may have in mind both the scripting problems and the upcoming editing problems, while having to concentrate, day-to-day on the set, on problems of controlling the mood, pace, acting balance and point of view of the film. Over and above these creators stands the studio or its representatives who may engage with all of these artistic problems (Rosenblum reports being called in to fix up ailing footage) and add to them others: will the solution be saleable, hence will it be financeable (or within reason), how will it be marketed, are the talents being showcased adequately displayed, etc?

Arguing this way suggests to me that Herbert Gans's (1956)

classic analysis of the problems that are involved in film making is a trifle narrow. He concentrates on the creator-audience relationship. A film, to be successful, has to find its audience. The conflicts and negotiation that characterize the film-making process are, he suggests, a complex argument about different audience-images. Possibly the different creative personnel envisage a different audience for the film and they are trying to foist that image on to the other members of the production team. It is not a foregone conclusion whose image will eventually triumph, but rather something that is battled out until the moment of release.

This Gans model is narrow because not every problem that the creative group faces hinges on difference of audience. In the case of a Woody Allen film the (initial) audience is known: it is Woody Allen fans. That does not dictate automatic solutions to Rosenblum's problem of how to get a workable structure. Similarly, in wondering whether a developing project is adequately exploiting a new star, the studio people are engaged in building an image for the star. Trivially, one could say Rosenblum's problem spelled out was: how to get a workable structure that will work for Woody Allen fans; that the problem of image-building is a problem of building an image around which an audience can coalesce. Such a vindication of Gans glosses over the fact that each of these problems is not reducible without remainder to the problem of audience-pleasing. The problems of the work have a degree of autonomy, as the following argument shows. Even if the film finds no audience whatsoever, it does not follow that its makers have failed to solve the artistic problems with which they were engaged. Much later, in all the arts, works can be rediscovered and lauded. To say that they just now found their audience is vacuous. Trivially, of course they have. But in fact there was no intention of, and hence no success in, audience-creating involved. Rather is a later generation appreciating the problem better and hence the film as a solution to it. Problems and solutions exist in a realm of their own, not as a function of public opinion.

To press this matter of identifying autonomous problems separate from public opinion: I would suggest an *ad hoc* historical method. Every studio, every producer, every film-making team or committee is a unique historical object and disentangling the problem (or problems) that confronted them and their way of going about solving it (them) can be done piecemeal. A helpful parallel might be the historical study of scientific teams. In these cases the problem-situation is the determining factor, and that problem-situation is often widely grasped within science. Think of the Watson-Crick discovery of DNA. In his memoirs Watson makes very plain that there was a race for DNA's structure precisely because it was widely believed there was a solution to the problem, that many possibilities had been ruled out, and that various tests, both empirical and conceptual, were available to check any model. In Cambridge he and his team knew that others, elsewhere, were on the trail too, and that galvanized them (Watson 1968).

Science is uncontroversially cognitive, and highly progressive and so somewhat different from the arts. We might expect then that artistic problem-situations will be more dispersed and also more diffuse, especially in the parameters which govern possible solutions.

I see no reason to think poverty of records or plurality of creators is an insuperable problem for the problem-solving approach. What Munsterberg called the inner history of the film was a sketch of some of the problems film makers faced and the devices they invented in order to solve them. If Gombrich is right that perhaps the most decisive problem and solution in the known history of Western art was the invention of perspective, one might claim that the comparable invention in film was the addition of sound. It is true that silent films had gained great power to narrate and move, but they were inhibited in their presentation of ideas by the clumsy manner in which words had to be printed on intertitles, and these could easily test the attention-span of the audience if they were too long or came onscreen too often. 'Ideas' here means not only philosophy or politics, but also psychology. The way silent film indicated feelings was by metaphor, by the selection of visuals that somehow suggested states of mind or feelings. Words have the advantage that they can directly address ideas and psychology as well as encompasss metaphors. The stage drama uses words; opera and song blend words to music; paintings have titles; and literature operates entirely with words. Words are a resource for art as for science that makes possible – or at least easier – many sorts of subject matter. It would be false to say the films needed words, or were inevitably drawn towards them. That is Hegelian anthropomorphism. It might be truer to say that the ambitions of film makers, as well as the pleasing of the audience and hence good business, were more readily served by talking pictures than by silent. Hence it was that the two did not co-exist as media; the latter swamped the earlier.

The immediate group of problems for the art medium that faced sound film makers turned on this: how do we make talkies that are not stagey? The problem emerged from a discovery, namely, that films which utilized the devices and approach of the stage were boring and hard to take. What worked in a proscenium with live actors did not on the silver screen. This discovery was made twice. The first time, in the early decades of the silent movie, various attempts to film stage plays and to capture the performances of great stage stars were made. They soon lost popularity and this was explained by claiming that what caught and held the attention of audiences at moving pictures was different from live theatre. When sound was introduced the combination of a need for dialogue, and the cumbersomeness of the new sound equipment, made stage plays and players natural-seeming attractions. Again it was argued that the initial success was novelty and the emerging preference for musicals with elaborate fantasy and dance, and for fast-action, told something about the medium and its hold on the audience. A suspicion of and hesitation before too much onscreen talk became endemic in Hollywood, which took special care to make talkative pieces 'cinematic'.

Such technical or formal problems are not at all the only ones in terms of which film history and film criticism can be written. A sub-problem of the musical is this: how should a choreographer work with the camera and microphone when both are movable, so the point of view of the audience can shift in relation to the dancers, and the close-up can emphasize detail? Furthermore, virtuoso and trick effects impossible on the stage can be easily managed on film. From the backstage musicals of the early sound era through to *All That Jazz*, these perennial problems have, excuse the pun, kept musical film makers on their toes.[1] As each film maker offers a solution to the problem, he creates for his successors a meta-problem: how can I solve the problem in a new way, one that has an original touch? Some creative people become obsessed with this problem above all others and that, it seems to me, is a crucial philosphical mistake, rather like thinking you become an artist in order to create art, rather than vice versa. A desire to be original, not to copy, is fair enough, provided some perspective is kept. After all, different people and different time will ensure that your effort will be no replica, and for all you know may be highly original to the spectator.

In arguing that one should look at films as efforts to solve problems I am aware that I am intellectualizing art, and indeed my intention in Part III is to go much further in this direction. One of the premises of the aesthetic experience approach that I have been criticizing is that works of art are things in themselves to be experienced for themselves. A consequence that some draw from this view is that there is a unity to a work of art that cannot be decomposed into form and content. Hence, when we say of a film that, 'it solved this problem', we have to add, 'in this or that way'. The film does not contain ideas or themes that are separable from the manner of their embodiment in the work.

This anti-cognitivism seems to be a solution to two very simple problems: how can a work of art be ugly, and how can a work of art be false? There is a hidden connection between the two because many a philosophy has argued for the identity of truth and beauty, so perhaps also for the identity of the ugly and the false. Both positions seem to me philosphically unacceptable. However, to try to discuss them by beginning with a question such as 'what is film?', or worse, 'what is art?', would be most unpromising. Of course we can specify art in such a way that whatever troubles us is not 'part' of it. But the victory is verbal.[2] The problem, alas, is not verbal. There are forms of art, such as the novel, the sonnet, the tragedy and so on. There are also ideas which may be contained in those, especially if words are deployed. Ideas are distinguished from other uses of words by being true or false, corresponding or not corresponding to the facts.

In my view people find it hard to admit of a work (or a person) they admire that the things they are saying are false (or immoral). Writers on the arts can be forgiven this weakness since it is very widespread and also can readily be found in philosophy and in science. Plato's *Republic* is a philosophical work that operates on many levels, including being a masterpiece of Greek writing, and a powerful dialogue. The thought in it is rich, profound and full of insights that we readily assent to today. It also contains a social-political philosophy that legitimizes the rule of one social class over another and it furthermore argues that the souls of men are such that those with a base soul can never become precious souls — in effect, that slaves can never become guardians. This is presented as a myth or noble lie, the purpose of which is to reconcile everyone to keeping in their place in society. These are the ideas of a man whose work is so brilliant he was referred to as the Divine Philosopher. Popper (1945) has chronicled the melancholy spectacle of his admirers either championing his reactionary ideas for today, or else dissembling about what he meant and reinterpreting the text to render it harmless. What they seem unable to do is appreciate his genius and to acknowledge that he made mistakes (Agassi 1963).

It is just this policy that I advocate. Works of art do contain ideas, and ideas are true or false. It seems to me to amount to a failure to take them seriously to try to get round the question of their truth or falsity by introducing such devices as the unity of the work of art, or the fusion of form and content. Again we see something similar in science. Agassi has identified in histories of science the following chain of reasoning. So-and-so was a great scientist. Great scientists follow the correct scientific method. The correct scientific method leads to truth, so, so-and-so created science, i.e. truth. But the historian usually knows that so-and-so's theory is far from what is accepted today. So he backs off, reinterprets so-and-so's ideas to the limit and, where so-and-so is still off the mark, claims that so-and-so 'set us on the track' or 'made a contribution' to our present science. Agassi wonders why it is so difficult to say that a great scientist can make mistakes, great mistakes and silly little mistakes, and still be a great scientist. It involves giving up the idea of science as a steady progress down the road to certain knowledge. Once science is viewed as conjectures and refutations we can combine admiration with frank recognition of mistakes.

Great artists are no different from great scientists in this regard. They have most likely absorbed the science, religion, mysticism and political ideas current at the time, all of which may now be thought false; they sometimes advocate a barbarous morality (e.g. Dante). Why should we not reason as follows: if one wants an elegant and masterly presentation of that view, then the work of so-and-so is it; but if you ask me do I agree with so-and-so's ideas, I say 'no'?

I am here preparing the ground not only for the present

argument but also for that of Part III where I have the temerity to take seriously the philosophical ideas of films without for a moment agreeing with those ideas. That some such resolution of the issue was inescapable first occurred to me in 1954 when the debate about commitment raged in British film circles. For those of us as fond, if not more so, of *Kind Hearts and Coronets, Singin' in the Rain* or late Hitchcock (not a fashionable position then) than of *Battleship Potemkin*, or neo-realism, the demand for commitment sounded like a demand for devotion to leftish social films above all else.[3] The test case was *Triumph of the Will*, a lengthy documentary made by Leni Riefenstahl about the 1934 Nuremberg Nazi rally. At that time the film's circulation was limited and one wondered what in it so frightened the authorities that they had made it hard to see.[4] Remembering the premise that none of its defenders were Nazis, indeed, that they would all compete as to who was more anti-Nazi, there was a clear division between those of us who admired it as a piece of film making, surgingly powerful and calculated to the last detail, and those who, because its ideas were repugnant, convinced themselves it could not be taken seriously as art. Art was a unity and fascist-art was a hyphenation that could not be broken, so to say it was good art was to say it was good fascist-art which was to say fascism was capable of sustaining good art which was to say fascism was good. The entire chain of reasoning was suspect. Bertrand Russell long ago made the case that more wickedness has been done in the name of Christianity than in the name of any other doctrine; Solzhenitsyn has consciously compared the monstrosities of Hitler and Stalin and suggested the latter might in numbers at least be worse. Such comparisons of wickedness, or body counts, are repulsive in themselves. The argument does not need them; it is sufficient if we grant that behind much of the Christian art of past centuries, glorifying God and the Church, and behind much of the art of Soviet Russia, including its films, there stand regimes and ideas of monstrous wickedness and inhumanity. Will those on the other side deal as harshly with Christian and Soviet art as with fascist-art? To say that some of the greatest art of our culture embodies Christianity is not to say that Christianity is good; to concede that great films have come from the USSR is not in any way to hold back from condemnation of that regime. Indeed one may detest some of Dante's values and still find his 'Inferno' a profound expression of its point of view. Can the same reasoning not be applied to Nazi art? Will the same chain of reasoning go through? *Triumph of the Will* can be looked at as a powerful and instructive and in some ways beautiful representation of a set of utterly anathematized political and moral ideas.

This, anyway, will be my line of thought. Films, like many other of the arts, contain ideas; those ideas can be true or false, moral or immoral. The question of what one thinks of those ideas should be directly addressed. It does not follow, that one's dissent from the ideas entails dissenting from the value of the work embodying them or from the greatness of their creator. We can admire Galileo and Newton, while finding most of their science mistaken, and still appreciate the genius of each as a scientific expositor. Parallel distinctions can and should be made for art and artists.

One reason the issue of ideas is unavoidable is because films use words. In the silent era they used intertitles; in the sound era they added speech. Hence they are part of literature, the artful use of words. They also employ pictures, sounds and music which are at best metaphorically or analogically related to ideas. Alongside the prejudice that films are 'primarily' a visual medium, it has long been suggested that the best way to appreciate film technique, in the use of images, sounds and music, is to conceive of it as like a language. An even stronger version of this that became fashionable in the 1970s was to suggest film technique embodied not just a straightforward language, but a language that was in code — and hence had to be decoded. The topic of film as language has been touched on before; now it must be confronted.

From Vachel Lindsay (1915) and Munsterberg (1916) to contemporary continental theory, the analogy between written and spoken language and the language of the screen has been pressed. At times this has been done in a *literary* way, with the attention to metaphor, image, the poetic line, the sentence and the supposed equivalents of these in film; latterly more in the way of *linguistics*, especially structural linguistics and its attempts to explain the manner in which we order words to yield meaning. Both literary and linguistic comparisons between film and language are at best similes, similes about the value of which there is legitimate dispute.

In simplest terms the literary version of the simile goes like this. Language is compounded of arbitrary letters into meaningful words which, strung together and combined in phrases and sentences, make assertions, ask questions, etc. Then these sentences are built into paragraphs, chapters, books. A variant would be to go from words to the poetic line, from the line to the stanza, to the work and/or its sub-divisions. In film a single shot can be likened to a phrase or a sentence, a sequence to a paragraph, a scene to a chapter.

The reason this literary simile is no longer popular is obvious: there is a clear difference between the manipulation of words and the manipulation of moving pictures and sounds. Letters and words are simply abstract marks on paper. They 'mean' things only because of a system of arbitrary and conventional rules which govern the direction in which they are to be read, and the manner in which they can be combined. A description of a person written or spoken in English bears neither a visual nor a causal relationship to a description of the same person written or spoken in the Cantonese dialect of Chinese. However, a film of that same person, whether made by an Anglophone or a Cantonophone might be recognizably the same. Only onomatopoeic words in any way resemble their referent, whereas images always do, otherwise we have to offer special reasons for speaking of x as an image of y. Words, then, are symbols of their referents; images and sounds are icons − to use C. W. Morris's terms.

To analyse the shot as a word, the scene as a sentence and the sequence as a paragraph is very neat and begins one on the task of thinking of films as something artfully constructed, as language is, and hence demanding skill as a basic requirement and, where skill is mixed with imagination, the possibility of art. The linguistic critique of the literary simile turns attention away from this straightforward move towards art. Films, like language, are sign-systems and the manner in which they work has to be studied independently, drawing on the language simile only when it is helpful. Such film semiotics or semiology sets out to understand, no less, the general question of how films mean. This is a preliminary to the specific question of discerning the meaning of this or that film, which, it is supposed, is hidden. At this point even the attentuated form of the simile has broken down. When we study the system of signs known as language in order to find out how it works, how words mean, we start from the fact that they do mean and we understand what they mean. Hence the problem is how arbitrary

232

marks governed by conventional rules do that. Linguistics does not seek out the hidden meaning in language. Film scholars, though, talk of film as being in a 'code' and imply that it is their job to 'decode' the messages for us. It is as though we were on the telephone through which was coming morse and someone offered to help us decode it. Yet film-goers are, I should hazard, largely unaware that they have any problem discerning the meaning of the films they see.

What, then, is the logic of this claim that films are in a code which conceals their meaning? Perhaps a simple illustration would be the discussion, in the Introduction, of *Casablanca*. Paraphrase A and paraphrase B (p.9 above) are examples of the meaning of *Casablanca* as it might be reported by the audience. But the claim that Victor and Louis are projections and exaggerations of sides of Rick's character, or the disentangling I offered of the film's complex messages about the contradictions of bourgeois society, these required much work on the structure of the plot, the deployment of images and sounds, the exposure, if you like, of hidden meanings. And so we begin now to discern what is going on. Once we are past the simplicities of paraphrases A and B there is an alarming possibility: a film like *Casablanca* can be interpreted as meaning a great many different things. One way of reducing this variety and hence of lowering the sense that such interpretation is arbitrary is to attach oneself to a theoretical system that offers well-defined 'readings' of a sign-system. Hence the popularity of Marxism and Freudianism, both of which offer all-encompassing interpretation of the world and hence of how to read sign-systems under those interpretations. Even this is a little arbitrary, however, because here are two such systems, and each sub-divides into variants, not to mention religious interpretations, pagan symbolism and what not. An unfortunate response is sometimes to try to blend all these interpretative systems together, which results in the strange spectacle of feminists relying for interpretations on the sexist Freud and trying to blend him with the anti-psycho-logistic Marx, etc.

Semiology comes with a different promise. The cinema sign-system may be, like the language sign-system, decipherable into determinate meanings that are correct or incorrect, not a function of any overall interpretation of the world. A recent monograph has it:

If films are texts and texts presuppose codes, we will want to know what the basic characteristics of the codes organizing the signs of the cinema are. (Nichols 1981, p. 11)

The movies are not (*pace* Bazin-Cavell, *et al.*) some straightforward mechanical reproduction of reality − that much Nichols has learned well from Gombrich − but rather the encoding of information about the world into a sign-system. Nichols labels an image of a horse an iconic sign, a sign where there is a real rather than a conventional resemblance between the thing represented and the image. Where a sign bears an 'existential' relation to what it represents, by which I think Nichols means 'causal', it is called indexical. If a picture of a horse is an iconic sign for a horse, then a gramophone recording of neighing and hoof beats would be an indexical sign for a horse, although the causal chain may be imaginary if the sounds were produced by coconut shells and trumpet. Some images have an arbitrary meaning as with Metro-Goldwyn-Mayer's Lion or Columbia's lady with a torch − these would seem most closely to resemble the functioning of words and be symbols.

Reasoning in this way, a vast apparatus of distinctions and labels can be built, as we find exemplified on pp. 302−3 of Nichol's book where he diagrams the ideas of Christian Metz. This diagram is intended to help understand Metz's system (the 'Grand Syntagm'), and yet the diagram itself uses the arbitrary signs of words and brackets. The question is what is its purpose, what are we supposed to be learning from all this, other than the jargon? In his discussion (1982, pp. 278 ff, see also 1965) of the question of the analogy between language and visual images Gombrich tries to show that both Socrates' position as shown in *Cratylus* and his own impulse (1960) to stress the element of the arbitrary in visual images go too far. Then he backs down and admits that perhaps the language of visual signs is more conventionalized than the discussion usually allows. This could be argued in any number of ways. But basically it stems from this situation.

What we see or what we hear contains an infinity of information that it is possible to represent, summarize or sketch in an infinity of possible ways. The conventions of visual representation do not consist of the extreme arbitrariness of attaching this or that image to things, actions, qualities and so on. It is rather a convention of selection; what a painting does is to deploy partly 'given' means of suggesting aspects of the visual world to us. A photograph may appear to involve a different process: it simply records all that is before us. This is a superficial analysis of a photograph. Every choice of lens transforms three dimensions into two in a different manner; if the photograph is in black and white we know the colours of the natural world are being similarly transformed into a limited range. But this is true of colour photography as well, every patented process of which gives different results, different 'values' as we say, to the colours of the world. The focus of a camera is different from that of the eye. And so on. It is an illusion to think photographs capture inherent or essential features of the visual world by mechanical means, they merely operate a different kind of machinery to the pencil and hence make somewhat different representations of our world.

What this leads to is a critique of the distinction between conventional, iconic and arbitrary signs (c.f. Hudlin 1979). In the course of *Art and Illusion* Gombrich argues convincingly that there is no such thing as 'resemblance'; there is only what we decide to take for or accept as resemblance. Thus, we can be taught to see a resemblance not at first apparent to us. Resemblance is a product of our point of view, the theories we hold about the world (Popper 1959, new appendix[*]x). This is obviously so with indexicality: if resemblance is a matter under the control of our theories, causal connection is even more so. It is easy to be superficial about this too, and to think that the states of the world are as clear as the balls on a billiard table with one crashing into another and causing it to move. Hume performed a sceptical attack on this very image itself, arguing that we see a ball A hit ball B but we do not see any other thing which we can call 'cause'. So he concluded that cause is no more than the regular and seeming-connection of events (Hume 1777, Section IV, Part I, Section 25). It is not along these lines that I would make the case for causal connection being a function of our theories. It is from the idea of connectedness itself. When our comb discharges a shock to pieces of paper we see no billiard ball-like collisions; without a theory we would not connect the hair-combing with the sparks at all.

In his analysis of what we do when we give a causal explanation, Popper brings theory centrally into the matter by saying a causal explanation is one in which we connect a singular event with one or more universal laws. Between the event and the law are intermediate conditions said to be 'the' cause of the event. So, the physical world is not the cause of the photograph; the cause is rather the condition of the world at that instant, including the set-up of the photographic apparatus. Just as any variations from camera speed to projector speed will distort the real time-lapse of the film, so use of infra-red sensitive film, distorting lenses and so on (all parts of the physical world) succeed in altering what we see on the photograph. The same, only more so, goes for the film where the photograph moves, there are cuts, and sound is added.

Hence I end up pretty much where Gombrich ends up on this matter: language is an effort to articulate and hence communicate our experience, whether to others, to posterity, or to ourselves. Film is analogous to language not because in some way it emphasizes the iconic and indexical at the expense of the conventional, but rather the reverse. Its indexical and iconic features conceal a deep reliance on conventions (c.f. Carroll 1987). The history of film is a history of the gradual proliferation of the technical and other means that have been discovered to articulate experience and hence to serve all the various functions for which people want to use film. Film with words is much better at doing most things than it was without words; words (and other sounds) are therefore part of its repertoire and not something inimical to its nature. Film is, to sum the point up, not primarily a visual medium. It is a medium that operates on two of the five senses at once, and it is an uninteresting question to discuss whether or which one of these senses is dominant.

Gombrich has slightly modified his views on signs over the years, coming to reject the view that representation is wholly conventional. He argues (1982) that since animals are not indifferent to the environment, there are configurations and perhaps colours (he could have added sounds and smells) which convey meaning almost universally. To revert to an illustration of my own: red, being the colour of blood and one of the colours of fire, is always strongly emotional in its effect. More specifically, there are facial expressions that are universally friendly, or hostile. In so far as art draws on these, it utilizes rather than controls the viewer's reaction. Clearly influenced by evolutionary episte-mology, Gombrich does not, it seems to me, circumscribe his concession sharply enough. It is true that the environment is not wholly neutral, but it is also true that it is largely neutral. 'Danger', 'attractive', 'food' are a small and limited number of reactions, and the vast majority of visual images we have represent none of these. We must beware of the Pavlovian fallacy. Pavlov got animals to salivate at hearing bells and thought he had achieved a conditioned reflex. But he was not able to condition their blinking, or to condition them to react to a pat or kind word instead of food; animal trainers do not use Pavlovian methods. Processes central to survival have a power and urgency that is general over our response-range that should not mislead us into thinking we react so specifically to other stimuli.

At the very elementary level of teaching people to think about how films work it is useful to give them the parallel with language, and to discuss the way imagery can be indexical, iconic or arbitrary. But such comparisons very soon exhaust their usefulness. Film is not primarily visual or verbal or anything else. If the arguments for its autonomy have established that autonomy then it will resist any characterization beyond noting that its effects are a composite of different means, the weight of which will differ from film to film and from scene to scene within films. At times the dominance may be musical, as in musical films, or in those sequences in *Jaws* when we are seeing shots moving through the water which we interpret as shark's-eye-view because the rhythmic shark theme music is in our ears. The shots themselves could be taken from a Cousteau diving documentary; the music is a banal riff. The combination is enormously suspenseful in that film. In a film to be discussed later, *Persona*, one of the characters describes, in words, a casual sexual encounter on the beach. All we see is her talking with her listener in the background. What we hear is Swedish; what we read are subtitles. Yet it is one of the most erotically charged moments in the movies, an effect produced by an intricate combination of means, including the extremely subtle skills of the actresses. To say of Woody Allen's films that they are primarily visual, aural or anything else would blunt discussion of them altogether. And so on.

There has been no attempt to conceal, in my discussion of aesthetic questions about film, radical differences of background and temperament from most authors who have written on these matters. Training as a social scientist could explain why I find much writing about the arts sorely lacking in a sense of what problems are sociological rather than aesthetic, or, rather, which aesthetic problems are disguised sociological problems. A second training in the philosophy of science could explain how a seemingly-narrow specialism can alert one to the many philosophical problems that are disguised discussions of the nature of scientific knowledge. In my remarks on mass art I think some of the sociological concerns come through; in my discussion of aesthetic experience some of my interest in science comes through. Before turning to the discussion of the philosophical content of films which has been promised for Part III I want to summarize and point up my argument.

The newness and mass character of film does not, I believe, reduce its potential as a vehicle for art; that granted, I do believe that film is the first genuinely new medium of art to have established itself in industrial and post-industrial society. The first but not the last. It forces us to reconsider our notions of the social position and functions of art and, as a consequence, our notions of the nature of artistic creation, and of the nature of aesthetic experience. My inclination is, it must be confessed, towards an extreme form of cognitivism, namely that what artists are engaged in is the construction of imaginary worlds, what philosophers call possible worlds, as forms of thought-experiment. Here, following Edward Davenport (1983), I would look to the story as being a central vehicle for the consideration of 'what if' situations. Such worlds are not inherently plausible or implausible; making them so, engaging our imagination and cooperation, is a matter of art. Also, such fictions are not only in the future. They can also be set in the past or the present. They can also be aware of themselves as films. A hidden text in all films utilizing stars is that among their 'what ifs' is the series, 'what if we made a movie in which star X, meets star Y and they . . .'. Such sub-texts are not available where there is no star system (e.g. the USSR); but then for the star system to be sustained in this manner we need the ramified machinery of promotion to alert the film-goers to the stars and their blended on and offscreen personae, so that when the 'what if' unrolls it has, shall we say, resonance (c.p. Jarvie 1970).

Cartoons are cases of 'what if animals could . . .', or 'what would it be like if animals . . .?' I can see that some would argue that many fictional films refer in a very direct way not to possible worlds but to this world now: all those that deal with current matters, wars, social issues, and so on; those that are biographies of real people. This counter-example is easily disposed of. All of these are 'what if' plot premises, even if they stem from slightly earlier real-world questions like 'why do you think . . .?' A more intriguing counter-example to the possible worlds cognitive model is the documentary film. Here are films of considerable artistic power − I have already instanced *Triumph of the Will* − which trade on audience knowledge that what they are seeing is authentic footage of actual events and which counter incredulity by stressing that actuality in various ways, and which are saying, it would seem, not, 'what if . . .' but 'this is the way it is . . .'. Bill Nichols has, I think, argued cogently that, examined closely, documentary deploys a great many devices of art, the purpose of which is to convince viewers that what they are seeing is what is there; as he puts it, we are seeing what would be there if the camera and recorder were not. As soon as this is stated its absurdity stands out. Movie equipment is never small enough, nor those filmed cool enough, for what we are seeing to be genuinely a view on to what was there even if the movies were not. (An exception might be hidden surveillance and bugging equipment, but very few films come out of that.) Furthermore, what comes out of the camera and recorder has to be arranged and mixed to present something coherent to the audience. Much deception is involved, such as cutaways to simultaneous events, which are impossible; subliminal shortening of apparently continuous time scenes, and so on. Nichols's idea is that narrative film creates a spatio-temporal universe 'plausibly maintained in its autonomy', whereas documentary film, which is concerned with exposition not narrative, needs to sustain its 'domain' of exposition. As he puts it:

> Exposition does not require the fabrication of an imaginary spatio-temporal universe so much as the fabrication of an imaginary rhetorical universe where demonstration, apparent or real, takes place. (Nichols 1981, p. 184)

The 'universe' metaphor is a little out of hand, but the frank acknowledgment that documentary seeks to show something to be the case is helpful.

My own argument is slightly different. Not believing there are uninterpreted facts, I believe the basic premise of documentary, that it trades in hard facts, is deceptive − self-deceptive. All that any film, whether of fiction or of fact, can do, is reflect the collectively arrived at point of view of the committee that made it (the limiting case being where the committee has or approaches having a membership of one). Hence, documentary films are presentations of a point of view, more or less well argued for (mostly less). Film is not particularly flexible as a discursive medium, since it has only rudimentary devices for keeping us in mind of the fact that we are following through the consequences of some assumptions, as opposed to confronting some realities. So film tends to disguise and thus to fudge the interpretative and propagandistic character of most documentary (see Jarvie 1978a, ch. IV; and 1983).

An amusing interstitial case between fiction and fact which highlights the problem, is pornography. Nichols (1981, pp. 183–95) maintains that all films tell a story, function on what he likes to call the plane of diegesis — even documentary.

> Two impossible identities often propose themselves for our consent in documentary and ethnographic film. (1) What you see is what there was. (2) What there was is what there would have been. The first proposition invites us to believe that our access to the pro-filmic event is complete and unmediated. The diegesis, constructed to minimize the signs of its construction, except those that signify 'This is authentic documentation', matches the event like a template; and if there are gaps, the 'diegesis' — the plane of rhetorical ordering supporting the exposition — papers them over. The second proposition invites us to believe that what occurred in the presence of the film maker(s) would have occurred in their absence as well; that the process of observation had no significant effect upon the situation or event. (Nichols 1981, p. 241)

Very well, but let us assume there is reason for such construction of possible worlds, namely in order to carry out thought-experiments or contingency plans. Human experience can be divided into two forms: actual experience and the rest. The rest includes indirectly reported experience, remembered experience, dreams, imagination. Actual experience is only present for an instant of time. Almost immediately it becomes recollection. Yet, clearly, for our ability to function in the world we need to know whether we are in an instant having actual experience, or are in the presence of a report that may be a report of previous actuality, or a report of the imaginary. Whatever it be, it is grist to our mental mill that thinks and anticipates and feels.

How does pornography enter in here? Well, as far as I can understand it, as follows. Pornography endeavours to populate the imagination with fantasies, fantasies that are sexually stimulating. Sexuality is so pleasuable that many people want to indulge it even in its mild forms of stimulation and recollection. In the past fifteen years the feature-length pornographic film has evolved into a stable product. It offers a set of conventionalized fantasies, such as voracious women, or of multiple encounters, or of great stamina, or of beautiful bodies, all of which are to a degree fantasy, or at least their ready supply is. Furthermore, these fantasies exist within a bizarre context. Western myths about sexual coupling are that it is forbidden between certain classes of people and in certain modes, hence these are exciting. Marriage should be based on true love, and sexual fulfilment should flow from that. Unlike these myths, people in fact overwhelmingly marry those of their age, class and culture, who provide a very safe form of sexual release. Moreover, the society encourages child bearing which, to say the very least, involves considerable disruption of fantasy-style sex life.

Pornography has to combine fantasy with a sense of the real. That is, every other regular film has characters kissing, getting into bed, rolling around. What marks pornography off is that the camera does not turn away, the nudity is not discreet, but instead we are able to gaze fixedly at people and their acts of sex in a way that is virtually unreproducible in everyday life. Unflinchingly we can examine the genitals and body of the actors and actresses as they perform intimate acts in full colour in extreme close-up. We do this in a manner that resembles nothing in our experience. And what is special indeed is that '*they are really doing it*'. In early pornography the main problem was how to bring the couples together and get over the approach stage so that the film can get on with the (sexual) action. Hence the flimsy plots of window cleaners, plumbers, peeping toms, and so on. These are not the main problems now. The diegesis of pornography is to sustain the idea that the viewer is seeing a genuinely sexual universe; real acts are being performed and they are being *enjoyed*; in other words, we are in the presence of real sex. As Nichols would say 'what you see is what there was' and 'what there was is what there would have been' (1981, p. 241). It is notable that Hollywood films with powerful sex scenes in them − *Boxcar Bertha, Don't Look Now, Bad Timing, The Postman Always Rings Twice* − are seriously debated in newspapers and the popular prints as to whether the actors and actresses were actually *doing it* on the set. Preposterous though this supposition is, a parallel discussion rages in the pornographic film magazines about the following: did the participants really enjoy doing it with the other partner? How do they *really* feel about such matters as fellation, swallowing semen, anal sex? And, above all, of the women it is asked whether they are always faking it or do they sometimes really 'get off'?

What is going on here? A fictional form is authenticated and rendered the more powerful for the viewer if he can be convinced that genuine sexual experience is being recorded. The most obvious device for creating such conviction is the male erection − widely believed to be unsimulatable − and, of course, ejaculation. Ejaculation shots − cum shots in the trade − are also known as 'money shots' because it is conjectured that these constitute a major customer satisfaction; a consumer guarantee or USDA Grade A stamp that what they are seeing is genuine; the diegetic plane is authenticated. Such shots are often very prolonged, even in slow-motion, and the actresses, who may be play-acting despite their writhing and bodily flush, are encouraged to play with the penis and the semen in various ways, signalling, I suppose, genuine appreciation. So although it is only a possible world, everything is done to encourage us to think it has been realized. This seems directed at enhancing arousal, the film-goer plays with the thought that his play-thought is real.

With apologies for these somewhat indelicate intrusions into a work of philosophy, let me make the argument plain. The audience at the pornographic movie is being fooled in a manner no different from in the everyday Hollywood movie. If you see a Hollywood film set in a foreign country you have to be very careful before you dare to say it was shot there. When you see an act of sex on the screen in a pornographic movie you have to be very clear that most likely nothing much resembling the act you see assembled on the screen ever took place (c.p. Jaehne 1983, pp. 14−15). In a not untypical film I counted twenty-five camera set-ups for one act of intercourse, with cutbacks to several of the set-ups. Even with hand-held cameras and possibly multiple cameras such a series of set-ups would take much longer than the sex act depicted. Only in legend do people perform for hours. In reality each set-up requires repositioning the actors, relighting, touching up make-up and the set, instructions from the director, possibly reloading the camera, and so on. Skimpy though pornographic budgets are, their present quality could be achieved in no other way. Sex acts on the pornographic screen are artifacts, as interviewed performers never tire of emphasizing. Yet it seems essential for their success that every possible device is deployed to suggest the opposite and invite the film-goer to feel he is a genuine voyeur:

> in seeing a film of a desirable woman we are looking for a reason. When to this we join our ontological status − invisibility − it is inevitable that we should expect to find a reason, to be around when a reason and an occasion present themselves, no matter how consistently our expectancy is frustrated. The ontological conditions of the motion picture reveal it as inherently pornographic (though not of course inveterately so). The million times in which a shot ended the instant the zipper completed the course down the back of the dress, or in which the lady stepped behind a shower door *exactly* as her robe fell, or in which a piece of clothing fell into the view of a paralysed camera − these were not sudden enticements or pornographic asides; they were satisfactions, however partial, of an inescapable demand. (Cavell 1971, p.45)[5]

Apart from a certain looseness of his use of 'pornographic', which he seems to equate with seeing the private or forbidden, rather than the stronger notion of it as graphic depiction of sexual acts, there is much here to agree with. The film viewer sitting in front of the screen becomes an invisible man, someone able to approach as near as he likes to other people, violating the conventional boundaries of close contiguity (Goffman 1963), precisely because he is in most films invisible, transparent. The people onscreen look past and through the camera as though it were not there. Actors develop a very careful technique of apparently natural eye movements that yet never catch the camera's eye. But not to exaggerate: this point of view of intimate invisibility, like all rules, is there to be broken; hence the many films in which the camera is directly addressed, deliberately covered up, or becomes, subjectively, the point of view of a participant in the onscreen action.

This seems to me not pornography so much as voyeurism: taking satisfaction from being able to get close to the lives of others without their becoming aware of us, we thus have a privileged access to the world as it is without us. Most of the time we act, react and interact; we are anything but invisible players in our own and other people's lives. This is an immense strain, which we relieve by reverie, by taking time by ourselves. How wonderful, then, that films enable us to be very close to human interaction yet free of the strain of being present, being noticed, being forced to participate. It is a rare oportunity for vicarious learning.

Whether voyeurism or pornography, it is clear that film as art is a very different order of things from the traditional arts. In particular, sensual pleasure is clearly intrinsic to their success. Furthermore, self-consciousness seems intrinsic too. It is often recalled that in a very early American narrative film — *The Great Train Robbery* — the film ends with one of the robbers facing the camera and firing his six-shooter right at us, the audience. This is in 1903. There almost never was a time, then, when film makers forebore drawing attention to the fact that this was a film the audience was watching and, in some sense, while usually ignoring the audience/camera, it was within the bounds of possibility that they could turn their attention to it.

Earlier, I instanced cases where films play with the idea of the audience being able to step into the screen world, and the same goes for the reverse. Some early cartoons play with the notion of the artist and his pen tussling with the creature they have created on the drawing board, and failing in their attempts to erase them. That watching a film is in itself a form of elaborate joke by the film makers on the audience, by the audience on itself, perhaps makes films rather different from the six classical arts in another way. It does not seem to me that music, literature, drama and so on are inherently jokes, inherently involve fooling us, yet a fooling which is, because we collaborate, not fooling us. It is true of painting, which has revelled in such styles as *trompe-l'oeil*, and the works of Margritte and Escher. Our conjoint awareness that movies are a form of sleight of hand, involving us in a world we collaboratively create and take seriously yet which is not there, creates a heightened awareness in the attentive viewer of the fact that they

244

are being made to experience something unreal yet seemingly real, rather than swimming in the flux of actuality.

These hints at how films can involve transformations in our attitude to art and its experience are only confirmed by the immense influence film has wielded on the six classical arts. This young upstart whose aesthetic status is permanently under dispute has nevertheless radically affected all the other arts. Christopher Isherwood's drastic wish for the writer to be 'I am a camera, with its shutter open' is only the most naive form.

When once I presented these ideas to an audience it was bluntly put to me that the problem of film's legitimacy as art was a question settled long ago and not worth serious discussion. My answer was that is false as a statement of fact, since such disputation continues. What I was unable to articulate at that time, but can now, is a somewhat stronger thesis: the status of film as art is an essentially contested concept. Since, if film is an art then we must needs revise our concept of art, and since if we start revision there are going to be many parties to the dispute and many sorts of considerations brought forward, we see at once how the dispute is going to become part of the discussion of art.

An essentially contested concept is one (Gallie 1956; Gellner 1973) with multiple criteria for its application; the criteria are evaluative; there is dispute about what weight to assign each criterion; the participants insist only one concept is in dispute; and such dispute is of the essence of the concept, not an accidental annoyance. To be a filmic work of art is, then something of an achievment, and achievements are normative things, hence there is bound to be dispute. The dispute is not solely about this or that judgment, but about the criteria themselves, and hence about the nature and boundaries of the concept.

All this is expressed somewhat in the mode of analytic philosophy, so perhaps I should translate it into a more rational idiom. The question cannot be resolved conceptually because it is a social rather than a conceptual question. Whether films are or can be art is to a considerable extent dependent on whether in our society they are regarded as and treated as art. If they are, then they are legitimated; if they are not, then a verbal struggle for legitimacy is only the tip of a struggle for treatment as such. But it is a feature of social life that such questions are not settled once and for all. We may utter pieties and cut off grants; we may take films seriously in one way and unseriously in another. The forces at work which have stakes in the outcome constantly change and so, thus, does the answer.

So, while I find none of the aesthetic problems of film intractable, I do end this Part on a tentative note. Writing about specific films as I now propose to do is to engage in the on-going debate about what is art, and what is the art in film. Since my focus is on philosophical content, however, my arguments will be tangential to the main lines of debate.

PART THREE

PHILOSOPHICAL PROBLEMS ON FILM

9

PHILOSOPHY

Philosophy is an academic subject with ancient roots, considerable intellectual prestige and, latterly, a highly technical manner of
going about its business. That business has been described here as a
continuous tradition of grappling with a small number of rather
abstract and general problems. Philosophers grapple with these
problems in various ways, but most characteristically by argument – a word with two distinct meanings. An argument is a
chain of reasoning towards a conclusion. It is also, in common
speech, a quarrel. Philosophers engage in both chains of reasoning
and quarrelling. Indeed, rubberneckers from other disciplines are
often shocked by philosophers' penchant for vituperation and
polemic. There is method to their madness. Most philosophical
problems do not lend themselves to mathematical or scientific
treatment and, therefore, disputes can only be handled by testing
the strengths of rival positions. This is done by pitting them against
each other, probing for weak spots, delivering low blows. Most
philosophical writing and speaking is done with the invoked
presence of at least one other, the Opponent or Critic. At times a
philosopher will simply marshal objections to his own view and
deal with them. At other times he will indicate how the objections
stem from a reasonably coherent alternative to his view. At still
other times he may conjure with two or more views, testing them
against each other and not clearly side with any.

These brief remarks about the rhetorical texture of philosophy
are not redundant havering. They are an attempt to capture some
characteristics that will not be found in films. Let us call this

argumentative, combative quality of philosophy 'discursiveness'. The film medium is not especially suited to the discursive mode of address. This may sound surprising. After all, films contain dialogue, so why should not the dialogue be given a philosophical content? We would then have a pitting of two or more characters representing different philosophical positions against each other in both speech and dramatic action. There would then be no reason why Plato's dialogues should not be filmed. So far as I know they never have been — presumably on grounds that so much talk is unfilmic.[1]

There are two other reasons, besides their being unfilmic, why Plato's dialogues are unattractive to film makers: their detachment and their closure. Consider Plato's detachment. Strictly speaking, in Plato's dialogues Plato does not appear. Although he is the author of the texts, he never steps forward and addresses us *in propria persona*. Scholars believe, no doubt rightly, that the character 'Socrates' is Plato's spokesman. Even so, the device of not being present in one's own work is used in important ways in philosophy. One use is to disguise or even hide the author, whose views may get him into trouble. Another use, much more important, is to detach the author from the problem and his ideas, enabling him to face the weakness of his position. Detachment has a further use: it emphasizes that the business of philosophy is not solely, or primarily, the advancement of the author's views: the business of philosophy is striving for the truth. The methodological detachment of the dialogue allows a philosopher to advance views in a very strong form, yet not quite to endorse them. That is, not to endorse them beyond admitting authorship of the dialogue.

The dialogue form thus embodies a philosophical stance that Popper has characterized as 'Conjectures and Refutations'. Starting from a problem, a philosopher can pose various solutions to it, perform destructive and adverse tests upon them, and end by in effect saying that that is as far as he can go for the time being. This detachment, this ending on a question mark, with your inclinations clear but your commitment denied, has an emotional elusiveness and lack of substance that is anti-dramatic.

Besides detachment there is closure. Some of Plato's dialogues will wrestle with a problem, advocate a solution but end with a hint that the debate will continue. Thus their stories have no ending, and any dramatic ending would smack of an arbitrary cut-off, like

250

those lines used by television interviewers as they regretfully, over swelling end music, tell their guest that time is up. It is not a question of happy ending or sad ending, but, rather, no ending at all. Where to call a halt? In the 1960s there was a brief period when quite a few films had an anti-dramatic structure and ended on question marks or with a 'things go on' scene. Many film-goers found this infuriating, the nearest they ever came to demanding money back at the box office. So much, then, for the dialogues as film material.

The present book is philosophy that exemplifies the virtue/vice of lack of closure. Far from resolving all the problems raised, the clear intention in several cases has been to raise issues and then take them only so far. One such issue is the present one: the aptitude of films for philosophy, especially for philosophy viewed as discursive practice. What films do most readily, it seems to me, is perform thought-experiments on particular solutions to philosophical problems. That is, they can portray one persuasive and one less persuasive alternative, and they can allow a dramatic triumph of one over the other to take place. From time to time they can also toy with a question mark ending, although this rarely involves challenging the entire basis of what has gone before. When it is such a challenge, then we have, I think, powerful works of philosophy on film – powerful not so much dramatically, but rather in translating philosophical dialectic into film.

Nothing has been said so far about what *sorts* of problems philosophers (hence philosophical films) consider. Academic philosophy is usually divided up in the following way. There is a foundational technical branch called formal logic. For the rest there are two approaches: the historical and the topical. The historical approach attempts to limn the tradition of philosophy by studying its classics and the ideas of its great men. (As noted in the Introduction, it is often said that philosophy is footnotes to Plato.) The topical approach concentrates on the problem of knowledge: the problem of existence; the problem of morality; the problem of art. Uneasily straddling both approaches is the existence of philosophical schools or classifications, such as empiricism, idealism, nominalism, and such like. So philosophy courses will often focus on schools and study phenomenology, or existentialism, or eighteenth-century empiricism, or neo-platonism.

This sketch-map is provided to indicate the range of problems in philosophy and hence the range of what we might expect to discover in philosophical films, if such there are. Films, of course, are not university courses; they are not book-length contributions to thought. It is a very slim book that can be read in the two hours or less of an average-length film. At best a film might manage to have the weight of − say − an article in a learned journal; at best be a fragmentary treatment of a problem, a topic or a school of thought.

Remembering the self-denying ordinance against lists of films and allusions to films, I avoid now finding films to fit all the sub-divisions of philosophy. Instead it might be an amusing exercise for the reader. I shall discuss a very small number of films, mostly classics, but including some surprises that should encourage the reader to break away from conventional lists and catgories. The selection will not 'cover' the field of philosophy, but, being few, can be examined in some detail, maybe avoiding that glibness which disfigures so much writing about films. The examples will ignore the borderline sometimes drawn between philosophy and psychology because I do not accept a rigid separation of these two fields. My guinea pig films will be *Citizen Kane, Rashomon, Persona* and three films of Woody Allen. *Kane* examines the question of explaining human conduct; *Rashomon* discusses truth and point of view; *Persona* is simultaneously about identity and facade in people and in films; Allen's films reveal a preoccupation with autonomously sustaining both personal integrity and good human relationships in the absence of tradition and authority.

10
POPULAR PHILOSOPHY

Philosophy is an academic subject; it is also an attitude to life. There is a third understanding of it in the public mind: elevated thoughts about basic human problems – in many ways quite indistinct from religion. Professional philosophers like to shy away from this responsibility, but they cannot if we are to make sense of films as philosophy.

Philosophy is not co-extensive with what is taught in universities, nor with the classics of the field, nor with any other stipulative definition of this kind. Philosophy is much more. Popper's way of putting it is to argue that virtually every person has philosophical views; has, that is, received or assumed ideas of a metaphysical and moral character that are exemplified in speech and action. People may be unaware that they have these views, which is all the more reason to acknowledge their presence and submit them to criticism, because such common-sense philosophy, like much of common-sense everything, may be out of date and false. A good example would be psychology. It is essential to our functioning in the world that we have general ideas about how other people work. Whatever the detailed criticisms that can be made of Freud and his successors, it can be argued that on account of their work, common-sense psychology, of others and of ourselves, is incomparably better than that of previous generations.

For quite disreputable reasons to do with the guild mentality, professional philosophers are given to denying the relevance of philosophy to anything whatsoever, to restricting the notion to current technical concerns, and to maintaining, for example, the absurd idea that there is nothing resembling what they are prepared to call philosophy in the cultures of India, China and Japan. Such 'occidentocentrism' and 'intellectocentrism' is absurd. There are no legitimate monopolies on philosophy. I prefer a liberal construction of its scope. Hence films about the meaning of life, films about the virtue and value of love, films examining the nature of duty in war, or responsibility in command and in the individual, all these are philosophical and should be exposed as such and subjected to the severest tests our forensic skills can devise.

An important part of philosophy when liberally construed is popular philosophy or popularizing philosophy. This scarcely existed until both widespread literacy and mass-produced books made it possible. Plato wrote for a very restricted audience, although the directness of his style makes the works readable to a broad range of people today. But some of the great philosophers of the recent past directed their work to professional colleagues, while others have sought a broader audience, and still others have written for both. This situation continues. Popular philosophizing is not the monopoly of Will Durant or Mortimer J. Adler. Two of the most important figures of the twentieth century in academic philosophy, Bertrand Russell and Jean-Paul Sartre, contributed esoteric and technical work, as well as popular and even popularizing work, to the general canon of philosophy. It is sheerest snobbery to think any the less of them for that. Who are we to look down our noses at what these men took to be perfectly legitimate concerns of the philosopher? Especially as, in Sartre, we come very close to our present subject: films. Several of Sartre's works have been rendered into film, sometimes with Sartre working on the script. To show philosophy at work in those films would be very easy, yet hardly of much use in making the case for philosophical content in films that have no connection with academic philosophy.

The search for literary forms and vehicles for popular philosophy — popular, that is, both in its broad appeal and in its addressing widely felt concerns — continues. Plato chose the dialogue, some of his predecessors and successors chose the poem; others have chosen the novel; still others, such as Sartre, the theatre. Bertrand Russell utilized adult education textbooks, popular histories, illustrated history, the popularizing non-fiction essay, short stories, radio lectures, newspaper articles and television interviews. Unike his contempories, Shaw and Maugham, he seems never to have considered theatre or the movies.

If we are interested in the problem that we call philosophical, interested in the sense that we want to see them solved, then the choice of form becomes one of appositeness: if the purpose is to reach a wide audience a popular form is indicated. It is absurd to imagine that only minutiae in the philosophy trade journals are to be taken seriously. As the editor of a trade journal I hope I can speak with inside knowledge. Trade journals are an essential mode of communication for modern academics. But one would do well to see them as part of philosophy rather than as its consummation. Philosophical ideas, like scientific ideas, are not solely for the benefit of the guild members. Many people are interested in getting at the truth. If the guild is convinced that they have come across the truth, a crucial further test of the ideas consists in their translation into an idiom accessible to those outside the guild, and a rational discussion with those outsiders, including answers to their doubts and objections. If esoteric knowledge is not translatable into a public idiom in this way, it carries a more or less permanent question mark against it. Possibly it is a *folie des spécialistes*, to coin a phrase.

In part one, I indicated the grounds for such a case when I argued that the objectivity of scientific work stemmed not so much from some demonstrated connection between the world and our ideas (via the senses, for example) but rather in the institutional arrangements for checking and criticizing our ideas. Sooner or later even the most esoteric of scientific ideas, whether of physics, chemistry or biology, are translated into forms that are taught in schools or embodied in experiments and devices that the public can scrutinize. That scrutiny occasionally leads to finding the scientists mistaken. Why should it not be so in philosophy, which concerns itself, despite guild claims, with general problems that every person can be brought to understand, partly because they already have views whether they realize it or not?

Films are, it seems to me, an excellent vehicle for popular philosophizing. If Popper can find great philosophy in Churchill, as he can (1972, pp. 42–3) so can I find interesting philosophy in films. This will not please the more uptight of my professional colleagues. Moreover, I shall not always find philosophy with which I agree or that I hold to be true. Allegiance to Popper's ideas puts me in conflict with almost every classic of philosophy, so why not with most philosophy in films? Be warned, then, that great or interesting art does not always contain great or true ideas.

Although many films are works of popular philosophy, this is not a conscious intention of their makers. To say that all men are philosophers includes the idea that they address, and hold solutions to, philosophical problems, without knowing it. Lack of awareness may make them somewhat uncritical, but then again it may not. It may seem improper to attribute to a film philosophical content when nothing could have been further from the creators' minds. My answer is that the question is logical, not intentional. If the best interpretation of a film connects it to what are nowadays taken to be philosophical matters then that is one of the things it is about. The implications of our views are contained in them. Learning what those implications are may be so startling that we deny them; that does not make them any less the implications.

To forestall certain other kinds of objections it is important, before turning to philosophical discussion of films, to indicate how my interpretations are not to be interpreted. Unlike Stanley Cavell, I do not use films to trigger musings about my own philosophy, such as of marriage, or of the film. This involves reading into the films in a strong sense. We usually mean by 'reading into', seeing something that is not there. The interpretations I want to make are all undeniably there. How to defend such a claim? How does it differ from Cavell's readings of films as about marriage, the relations between the sexes or the nature of film?

One strategy when faced with the question, 'how do you know?, is to reply, 'I don't know, I only guess'. Then the further questions will be pushed as to whether the guesses are interesting and whether a case can be made for them. A guess is interesting if it illuminates something puzzling; a case can be made provided we have some idea of the kind of objections to which the guess is vulnerable. And that means having some sort of idea of how it can be criticized.. Since Cavell does not explain how his philosophical interpretations are arrived at, and since he grounds them in his own experience, we reach an impasse. If we challenge his interpretations of the film he can fall back on that being his experience of the films. Another tack would be to criticize his actual philosophy of marriage, relations between the sexes and of film. Were one able to show, for example, that his philosophy was incoherent that in itself would be a good argument against reading it into a film. This is convoluted and would be greatly simplified if the issues involved in interpretation were made more explicit. That will be done in Chapter 11.

Interpreting films in a philosophical manner is not to claim all films are philosophical, except in a trivial sense;[1] neither it is to claim that these films are philosophical *and nothing else*. They may be many other things besides philosophical. Other works of mine have concentrated on sociological interpretation of films (1970, 1978a, 1982). This is a rich vein, since it too is sometimes conscious and, more often, not conscious, in its makers. To avoid confusion, I suggest the reader mentally preface all my interpretations with the qualifying phrase, 'if we read the film philosophically . . .'. Then it becomes clear that no other way of interpreting the film is being ruled out, and no claim for the domination of philosophy within the content of the film is being made. Films, like most cultural products, subsist in many interpretative dimensions at once and our concentration on one is a selection for purposes of analysis; other purposes, other analyses, could make different selections.

One kind of abstract thought is inextricably involved with much film making. I have in mind film criticism. People who work in films sometimes deny that they read what critics write about their work. Such a denial is not always disingenuous. But it is a fact that when film people get together they engage in a great deal of shop talk. Increasingly, in the last generation, that shop talk has not only been of technical matters or money matters but also of ideas about films and film making. Film makers, whether they think of themselves as critics or not, engage in a great deal of discussion of their own and others' films.

Now that a generation that was educated in film schools and in film criticism has entered the industry, in America and in other countries, philosophies of film, philosophies of the artist, philosophies of politics, are quite common currency in film-making circles. One can see, for example, in many of the socially critical

257

commercial films of the last fifteen years, the unmistakable thumbprint of the paranoia of the American left. So that whereas a vintage American director like John Ford could disdain interviews and describe his philosophy as, 'I take a script and just do it', one now finds great readiness to talk and to explicate. If modernism is the revolution of self-consciousness of the last one hundred years, achieved only after countless centuries of unself-conscious tradition, movies have recapitulated this whole development in less than a century.

But even in anti-intellectual Hollywood there were and are plenty of creators who in one way or another knew they were doing philosophy; we have only to consider the series of biographical films about scientists.[2] These touch on philosophy of life, the nature of natural processes, the morality of truth-telling, tests of truth, attitude to mistakes, and so on. If we turn from such conscious but implicit philosophizing to the more explicit, we could in Hollywood think of those films that expressed that 1960s philosophy of The Movement,[3] or we could look to the works of the Europeans Robert Bresson, Eric Rohmer or Ingmar Bergman. These film makers are conscious philosophers whose works have 'something to say'.

In considering which philosophies reach the screen, fashion is an important factor. At any time there are philosophies that get wide public airing and can be said to be fashionable among the book-reading public, and they tend to filter down in a certain way to students of other subjects and hence to have influence.[4] An outstanding example in the United States was the influence of John Dewey. In the 1930s and 1940s in Britain a very fashionable philosophy among the more daring was logical positivism, and A. J. Ayer's exposition of it, *Language, Truth and Logic*, was a best seller. Soon after the war the fashion was existentialism, perhaps the first of the successive waves of invasion from the *rive gauche*. Other more diffuse philosophies such as cynicism and nihilism have been fashionable among restricted groups. Obviously it says nothing about the value of a philosophy that it is fashionable and it would be altogether too glib to seek the philosophy of a film by checking to see which philosophies were fashionable at the time it was made any more than it would make sense to seek Heideggerianism in *A Little Romance* because the teenage protagonists both confess to a taste for his *Introduction to Metaphysics*.

11
ON INTERPRETATION

To fulfil earlier promises a final preliminary set of remarks before discussing particular films. The idea is to make explicit questions of method and of interpretation. In considering the films philosophically, I am going to impose upon them interpretations; I am going to give them cognitive readings, such as that *Rashomon* concerns the problem of truth. This is undertaken in full awareness of the earlier argument that to cognize works of art is to do violence to their unity of form and content. My answer was to diagnose that claim of unity as coming from a superstition that beauty and truth go together and so, if one appreciates the beauty of a work of art, one must also hold that it contains truth, possibly deep truths. However, truths are not truths because they are beautifully expressed. They are truths because they correspond to the facts. The problem of truth is one of the knottiest in philosophy and not one to be entered here. It must suffice to say that I shall adopt a relatively widely-held view (associated with Bertrand Russell and Alfred Tarski) that 'truth' is a relationship between *statements* and *the world*. When a statement is true it is said to *correspond* to the facts; when it is false, it does not. We can assess truth claims only of statements, hence some method must be found of extracting statements from works of art, statements that can then be defensibly attributed to those works, to the characters in their drama, or to their creators. Hence my earlier insistence that the doctrine of the unity of a work of art must yield when we wish to analyse.

The usual method of extracting statements from narrative works is by paraphrase. The paraphrase is not a neutral factual report on the film, but is itself permeated by the interpretations of its author. Even one-line paraphrases of a film have difficulty in corresponding to the facts of what is in the film or in corresponding with one another. Interpretation, then, is prior to, not based upon, paraphrase. Recapitulation of the plot or of particular scenes serves to illustrate an interpretation not to establish it. There are several ways to criticize an interpretation; scenes that do not fit it; disagreements over what in a film looms largest; evidence about the creator's intentions; the internal consistency of the interpretation; its consistency with the interpretation of other works by the same hands; its consistency with known facts; its consistency with current science. Any of these would need detailed exposition and defence.

To interpret a film, I take it, is to try to make sense of it, that is, to integrate it into some context wider than itself. Not that a film, treated naively, does not make sense; of course it does. It tells a story and the story has shape. But when we ask what does it all mean, or when we notice elements of the film — casting (why Bogart?), style (why romantic?), plot twists (why is Ugarte killed off?) — that seem optional, and ask why they are there, we have to look beyond the film for answers. Obviously, then, a film is not adequate as its own context. To be brutal: works of art are not self-sufficient.

Interpretation, then, comes to fill the gaps, answer puzzles, resolve inconsistencies. The main question is: are interpretations comparable? In my view they are when they seek to bridge the same gap, solve the same puzzle, resolve the same inconsistency; not otherwise. How can this be done? Well, by seeing how well an interpretation does its job. For example, a pretty interpretation like that which interprets Lincoln in *Young Mr Lincoln* as a phallus (Editors of *Cahiers du Cinéma* 1970), hence a castrated man, may make more sense of the curious sexual undertones (repressions) of the film than one which is content to describe them as undertones. Indeed, being fanciful as well as pretty, such an interpretation has the virtues of boldness and risk. Were it not that psycho-analysis is a bit on the fringe of current psychology (inconsistent with current science), and most likely false (inconsistent with facts), we could laud such interpretative ventures.

Once interpretations are admitted to be comparable they can be ranked by being criticized. Competing interpretations that cannot be shown to be false are not then equally good: there are at least two further tests; does one solve other puzzles the alternatives do not; and, does one cohere better with the internal and external evidence? If our aim is interpretations that solve the problems we set out with, and are in addition better than competing interpretations and are not clearly false, then this simple methodological procedure should suffice.

How best to go about this work of critical interpretation in Part III on specific films? One way would be simply to offer my own interpretations as well as some comments upon them to make explicit my aims and methods. This would disguise my aim of controverting other writers' methods of interpretation, such as those of Cavell. Their methods, I hold, inhibit rational disagreement because they do not make them explicit and because they hint that they are rooted in personal experience. Each of these is sufficient to create an impasse.

My approach will be different. I shall start by stating my interpretation succinctly in the sub-title of the section, then, after a few preliminary remarks, restate it at length in paraphrasing the film. Eager to criticize it and improve it, I shall consider some of the best interpretations of the film by other hands that I can find; try to expound these sympathetically; use them to criticize mine; and then subject them to critical scrutiny. Their inadequacies constitute problems which my own interpretative forays aim to solve; inadequacies in mine may not be in them.

It should be clear from this that my overall aim is something very akin to what in philosophy of science we refer to as the growth of knowledge; here, the growth of interpretative power. The purpose of controverting previous interpretations is to be able to give a better one. And to those who wonder whether a better one means simply one stemminng from a superior or more cultivated sensibility I would answer that I mean something different. A better interpretation means one that makes sense of all the elements of a work that its predecessors made sense of, and also makes sense of at least some elements none of its predecessors could. If this new interpretation is not more true than its predecessors, it is, at least, less manifestly false.

When trying to promote the growth of knowledge in science philosophers have offered recipes ranging from mental purges to scrutiny of their own thought processes. The approach I favour is social: namely, attempting to formulate and implement methodological rules that will discourage behaviour inimical to the growth of knowledge. Such rules (a summary of which is given on page 293) will be largely negative in character, since they are aimed at our bad habits. Positive rules are likely to be anodyne for the obvious reason that if there were recipes for success we should follow them and not then need rules to keep us away from bad habits. Unfortunately, then, in order to develop some rules for the growth of interpretative power that in any way parallel the rules for the growth of scientific knowledge, we shall have to look at negative cases, that is to say, at interpretations that are not progressive, possibly even retrogressive. Among these it will be my aim to concentrate on the best and most plausible, rather than the weakest and easiest to demolish.

Popper writes, 'it is obvious that we must try to appreciate the strength of an opponent if we wish to fight him successfully' (1945, p. ix). Under such a rule the opponent becomes an abstraction: possibly no flesh and blood writer ever formulated the doctrine in its best form. In improving it one evacuates personal polemics and displays clearly that truth is being pursued by an adversary method that pits ideas, not authors, against each other.

Let me, then, try to formulate 'Popper's Rule':

Popper's Rule } (PRI)   Formulate interpretations in their most fully-developed and logically strongest form.

What aim does such a rule serve? Answer: the logically strongest version of an interpretation says the most and hence is incompatible the most with evidence, hence is most readily criticized. What is the point of saying things that are maximally criticizable? Answer: growth of interpretative power, like growth of knowledge comes from detecting error and falsehood. We may treat an interpretation as a conjecture intended to make sense of some material, a film. This conjecture may not fit every aspect of the film; this forces us to refute it and seek a replacement.

The easiest way to modify an interpretation is simply to adjust it slightly to handle the awkward evidence. This we can call an *ad hoc* manoeuvre. Making such a move is defensive and so violates Popper's rule of considering interpretations in their strongest form. Let us now formulate these rules:

(RI 1)   Prefer the interpretation which makes sense of more scenes in the film than its rivals.

(RI 2)   When an interpretation clashes with some scene or element do not revise it *ad hoc*.

(RI 1) merely urges us to check our interpretations against the 'text' of the film. It can usefully be paired with a similar rule that specifically directs attention to problematic scenes or other elements of the text. This rule I take from the distinguished historian of science, T. S. Kuhn. Here is what he says:

> When reading the works of an important thinker, look first for
> the apparent absurdities in the text and ask yourself how a
> sensible person could have written them. When you find an
> answer . . . when these passages make sense, then you may
> find that more central passages, ones you previously
> thought you understood, have changed their meaning. (Kuhn
> 1977, p.xii)

The qualification 'important thinker' is unnecessary, especially as film 'texts' are collectively produced. Yet Kuhn's Rule is one of great use-value. Let us formulate it:

Kuhn's Rule $\Big\}$ (KRI)   Making sense of absurdities in the film may alter understanding of central passages.

Rule (RI 2) is my version of a general prohibition Popper suggests for the growth of science, namely, avoid all conventionalist stratagems. What is a conventionalist stratagem? That defence against criticism which renders the interpretation true by manipulating its meaning. Logically, it is possible to render any doctrine true by convention, that is true by virtue of special definitions of its terms, or the addition of auxiliary hypotheses. If we want to avoid such pyrrhic victories for interpretations of films then *ad hoc* adjustments of them, the addition of auxiliary interpretations, and the redefinition of terms must be discouraged. If we were to formulate this rule, a generalization of (RI 2), it might be this:

(RI2^1)   Avoid all conventionalist attempts to protect an

These initial Rules of Interpretation might find ready acceptance.

They place what contemporary critics, borrowing a word from texual hermeneutics, call 'the text' in a decisive position. Earlier in the book I did stress that establishing such a text in the case of movies can be highly problematic; but that, the hermeneuticist would say, it is problematic of the practice not of the theory of interpretation. However, I wish to develop a much stronger notion of interpretation, one which acknowledges each film as an historical reality, possibly part of an *oeuvre*, nested in a context of a national cinema and culture. I want all these matters to have a bearing on the testing and hence selection of interpretations.

Each movie is produced over time and hence has a specific history, so:

(RI 3)   However well an interpretation fits the film, if it does
         not fit the known and discoverable facts about its
         making that is a grave objection to it.

I was once present at a scholarly meeting where the paper turned on the interpretation of a very slight movement of the camera between two successive shots of the same street. The film was a very old one. A scholar in the audience pointed out that cameras in those days had magazines of small capacity and that it looked to him as though they had had to reload before the shot could continue, and that the shift of position was most likely due to a slight jarring of the camera while reloading. He was right. Alas, a beautiful 'creative' interpretation of a shot was destroyed by an ugly little historical fact!

(RI 3) may look innocuous enough, but it is in fact highly controversial. What it suggests is that the interpretation of a cinematic text can be challenged from materials that are outside that text. It says that if someone sits through a film and interprets it, their interpretation can legitimately be criticized by the citation, for example, of the documents from studio archives. To adopt rule (RI 3), then, is once again to challenge the doctrine of the unity of a work of art. This doctrine is sometimes put in this form:

Question: What does this film mean?
Answer: It means just what it says.
Question: Why don't you explain it to us?
Answer: If I could have said it any differently I should not have
            chosen to make this film.

264

In other words the claim is that the text of a work is a self-sufficient unity; it contains within it all that its maker wanted it to say. Let us call the text and its components the innards of the work, and historical documents, oral histories and such like, external materials. (RI 3) demands that interpretations be tested not just against the innards of the text but also against the external related materials. As a general rule this could be formulated:

(RI 4) In seeking and checking interpretations (and
problematics) all sources of information about the film
are to be explored.

While I deny that the creator of a work (especially the non-specified creator(s) of films) has privileged access to what a film is about and what the film 'says' about it, the ideas of the creators should be given a hearing. If they clash with or do not fit the film as examined, that provides an intriguing problem of explanatory exegesis, more scope for conjecture, criticism and refutation.If what they say about the film fits it very well, as do the comments of Bergman, for example, then we have for once a good source to help us in our understanding. Hence I do not at all believe the text is self-contained and should be examined and re-examined as though it lacked contexts of procreation, affinity, earlier inter-pretation, commentary, etc. All these matters are part of what makes it intelligible in the first place and so are hardly dispensable excess.

There is a tendency to want the text − filmic or otherwise − to be self-contained. This has to do with superstition about the unity of the work of art criticized earlier. However, other work of the same creator(s) is a different matter. In all the traditional arts we look to exhibitions, retrospectives, anniversary concerts, collected works and so on to illuminate the individual work. Thus, although it is obvious that a single work must not be incomplete, leaving the audience unsatisfied, it does not follow from this that the richness of our interpretation cannot be increased by exposure to previous and subsequent work by the same artist. Thus at some point we may invoke another rule:

(RI 5) An interpretation of a work that is at odds with what is
known of its creator's other works must be very
carefully argued for.

Thus, were we to find that one work of a notorious relativist was amenable to an absolutist interpretation, we should have to argue that very circumspectly.

As to still broader checks on our interpretative imagination, we come to the film culture and indeed the national culture in which they are nested. Once the American movie industry became located in Hollywood, a small town on the remote West Coast far from the traditional American centres of culture, it developed a peculiar film culture all its own. Prominent among the institutions of that culture are the *genre* (such as horror, western weepie, gangster, musical, etc.) and stars. Our knowledge of these two institutions is also relevant to our interpretation of a film. The culture may embody expectations that control or limit the interpretations that are appropriate. One reason for not interpreting *The Green Berets* as a satire on the Vietnam war is the presence in it of John Wayne. One problem with *Apocalypse Now* is that there are elements in it of Joseph Conrad, but also of the rip-roaring western. It is interesting that, ten years before, its director (Coppola), then a writer, scripted *Patton* in which elements of the western, the nature of good and evil, and a mystical side were all present. Imposing a coherent interpretation on these films, then, may have to take account of evidence that goes far beyond the text. Film texts are not self-contained.

(RI 6) The film culture and the national culture are contexts
with which the interpretation of a film must cohere
unless strong reasons can be given why they need not.

One type of strong reason for an exception to (RI 6) might be that the film was experimental, anti-establishment. This would not be a convincing argument because works made in reaction to an establishment require account to be taken of that establishment if they are to make sense. The effect of making a film in which John Wayne   put on top hat, white tie and tails and did a tap dance would have with the film culture.

These eight rules are very general and by no means exhaust those that I wish to recommend, and to comply with in my interpretative work that follows. However, since the discussion in this book is anyway rather abstract, I shall formulate the later rules not at this point but after we have considered some interpretations of the first film under consideration, *Citizen Kane*.

12
CITIZEN KANE AND THE
ESSENCE OF A PERSON

Welles: I always begin with the dialogue. And I do not
understand how one dares to write action before dialogue. It's
a very strange conception. I know that in theory the word is
secondary in cinema but the secret of my work is that
everything is based on the word. I do not make silent films. I
must begin with what the characters say. I must know what
they say before seeing them do what they do.

(Gottesman 1971, p.10)

Citizen Kane, perennially in the all-time top ten film lists of the
world's critics,[1] is a black and white sound film that was released in
1941. It was the first feature film directed by Orson Welles, a boy
genius of the theatre and radio. Actor, producer and impresario,
he brought many members of his talented Mercury Theatre
Company to Hollywood with him and took his time to learn the
ropes before venturing into his first film. For his writer he used
Herman Mankiewicz, a veteran screenwriter and former journal-
ist; for cinematography he had the services of an adventurous
young cameraman, Gregg Toland.[2] He himself played the leading
role.

If one knew nothing of the power of the press and the breed
known as press barons, i.e. wealthy men who controlled newspapers, magazines, radio and television stations, it is doubtful if
the opening of the film would make much sense. It is in two parts;
first, over menacing music, the camera climbs a fence signed 'NO
TRESPASSING' and moves, by means of lap-dissolves, towards a

267

distant castle with a single lighted window. When we arrive in the room we see various distorted scenes, a glass globe with a snow scene inside, a pair of lips whispering 'Rosebud', the glass shattering, and a nurse pulling a sheet over a corpse, the light in the window masked. Without warning, so that we jump, the scene becomes the opening of a newsreel, 'News on the March', blaring out martial music. This newsreel proceeds to deliver an obituary on a newspaper millionaire called Charles Foster Kane.

Much of the richness of the material has to do with the resemblances between the fiction on the screen and the audience's knowledge of such real-life press barons as Henry Luce and William Randolph Hearst.

The following scene sets the outline for the rest of the film. The newsreel ends and we see that it is being shown not in a theatre but in a small projection room at the newsreel company, because a group of shadowy figures in the semi-darkness of a projection room talk in a way that indicates these are the men who made the newsreel. One voice expresses dissatisfaction with the newsreel, that it is all surface and does not tell what made Kane really tick, and it is mentioned that his last words were 'Rosebud' — what can that signify? A reporter is singled out and detailed to track down key people in Kane's life and the film then divides into the reporter's interviews with each of these people: Kane's ex-wife, now an alchoholic club singer (refuses to talk, but does so later in the film); the diary of Kane's deceased guardian; Kane's Jewish business manager; Kane's best friend; Kane's valet. Each episode dissolves into a flashback to the episodes recalled, as the reporter tries to find out what made Kane tick. After all these interviews the reporter expresses frustration at not having got to the bottom of Kane's character, and that 'Rosebud' was probably without significance. The camera then roams over a stock room where junk from Kane's house is being incinerated and we enter the flames to watch a sled being burned which had on it the word 'Rosebud'. It is the sled the boy Kane was playing with when he inherited a fortune and was taken away from home to be looked after by his guardian. The film leaves it ambiguous as to whether this was Kane's last happy moment, or just a trivial piece of the bric-á-brac of memory. The opening approach shots are reversed, and the 'NO TRESPASSING' sign is shown once more.

The newsreel narrator suggested that Kane was all things to all men; to the right he was a communist; to the left a fascist; a man of the people who consorted with the rich and powerful; a foe of corruption who was himself corrupted by power; an amiable man with a stubborn and ruthless devotion to his own views. The successive stories embroider on this dual aspect of Kane: depending on who is talking he can be seen either way. His ex-wife finds him solely concerned with getting his own way; his best friend finds him corrupted by egotism; his business manager sees him as a creative and dynamic boss; his guardian as a dangerous and headstrong ne'er do well; his valet sees him as a man with feet of clay.

Now to philosophy. In the late 1930s when this film was conceived and written Freud was peaking in intellectual fashion. In the popular mind, and by that I mean outside the technical psychoanalytic community. Freud meant two things about the understanding of the human being: check out childhood and check out sex (and of course check out sex in childhood). *Citizen Kane* has little or nothing to suggest about either. Kane marries an heiress, has a child, has a mistress, is not indicated to have any sexual problems. It is indicated that he has difficulty giving love, and eagerly seeks it out. *Kane* also skirts childhood as a formative process, but hints that the abrupt cessation of childhood is a loss from which the boy never recovered.

One could then read the film as a criticism and repudiation of the very idea that there are deep childhood and sexual clues to a person. That rummaging round in people's memories of Kane does not turn up some vital clue to what makes him tick. That he eludes the best efforts of an investigative reporter. That a person is an enigma. The only real clue they have, 'Rosebud', is nothing more than a sled, which is perhaps a random memory on a dying man's lips.

All points of view are shown in the film. The boss of the newsreel sends out his reporter to answer a question. Various of his interview subjects think they know what made Kane tick. Yet just before we, the audience, find out what 'Rosebud' means, someone remarks to the reporter: 'if you could have found out what Rosebud meant, I bet that would've explained everything'. Thompson, the reporter, replies:

No, I don't think so. No. Mr Kane was a man who got everything he wanted, and then lost it. Maybe Rosebud was

something he couldn't get or something he lost. Anyway, it
wouldn't have explained everything. I don't think any word can
explain a man's life. (Kael 1971, pp. 419–20)

If we can identify the reporter with us, asking questions on our
behalf, then this speech tells us that there may be a presumption in
our questions that there is something to be discovered, when in
truth there is not. Yet this speech quoted above continues: 'No, I
guess Rosebud is just a piece in a jigsaw puzzle, a missing piece.' Is
it the missing piece that finally shows us what the pattern is, or is it
merely a missing piece we do not need if we are to complete the
rest? The ambiguity of the jigsaw image may or may not have been
clear to the film's makers.

(Identification with the reporter is problematic because he is a
shadowy figure and because, although we look over his shoulder,
so to speak, we are also privy to things he did not see – the
opening and closing views and the revelation that 'Rosebud' is a
sled. Carringer (1978, p. 387) found a direction in the second draft
of the script, missing from the shooting script, although effected:

> It is important to remember that only at the very end of the story
> is Thompson himself a personality. Until then, throughout the
> picture, we only photograph Thompson's back, shoulders, or his
> shadow – sometimes we only record his voice. He is not until
> the final scene a 'character'. He is the personification of the
> search for the truth about Charles Foster Kane. He is the
> investigator.

Thompson, then, while not representing us consistently, plays that
role so long as the question of the truth about Charles Foster Kane
is our question and his. Before he takes it up, and after he drops it,
we continue, perhaps to a conclusion not unlike his.)

In defence of this philosophy of presenting answers of the on-
the-one-hand and on-the-other-hand type it could obviously be
said that this is how things truly are. People naively suppose there
are hidden clues to the whole essence of a person which, when
disclosed and deciphered, reveal all. In truth, a person is an
enigma, not transparent to himself or to others, and things which
seem to be clues can equally well be dead ends. If *Citizen Kane* is
read as a statement of that philosophy it would have to be judged
rather weak. There is a good deal more to Freudian conceptions

270

than what I have just said about them. It is interesting that Kane is not shown as aware of having any problems that may be responsible for the dissatisfactions of his life. Hence the script does not explore an attempt on his part to cope with such problems.

An objection to what I have just written is as follows: it is unfair to criticize a work of art for what it does not try to be. Art is governed by its aims, and the creator has the right to single out these aims and not those. In general this argument is fair enough. Yet in philosophy we do find it fair to argue thus: the author fails to confront a glaringly obvious objection to this position, that goes as follows . . . It is assumed, in rationalist philosophy, that the advocate of a position, in the course of adopting it, expounding it and defending it, will cast around for the objections that can readily be anticipated. Philosophers regularly formulate these objections themselves, as I have done throughout this work, and try to answer them.

If, then, *Citizen Kane* is to be read as a critique of the naive theory of human identity, namely that there are clues to it which can be deciphered and so make sense of much of what a person does, it is a valid philosophical criticism to point to obvious objections to this view and wonder why the film makers failed to explore these. A fancy name for this criticism would be 'a failure of imagination', By and large this book avoids aesthetic evaluations, although the films I have selected are all, in my view, examples of movies at their very best. Hence, when I criticize the first suggested psychological/philosophical thesis of *Citizen Kane* — personal identity and motivation are enigmas — this does not detract, for me, from my evaluation of it. Rather would I say *Kane* is an admirable dramatization of this very plausible view. The demand that great art teach or preach the truth is, as I have argued, as unreasonable as the demand that the great work of science speak the truth. Galileo's and Newton's works are incomparably good, yet neither speaks the truth. And just as, by reconstructing the problem-situation that faced Galileo and Newton, we can appreciate their work as attempts to solve those problems, so, by reconstructing the intellectual situation of 1940, we can appreciate *Kane*. As a corrective to the glib view that psychology would enable us to penetrate and understand a man's life it is excellent. Ending with the suggestion of an enigma it poses a problem for other film makers: can you dramatize plausibly the view that despite the difficulties, we can make some progress towards understanding persons? The challenge is powerful. Each of the films I shall discuss below attends, to one degree or another, to the problem.

The form of *Citizen Kane* is that of a mystery: we have one clue ('Rosebud'), one gumshoe (Thompson), and various attempts at theories. It was quite characteristic of Hollywood at this time to make mysteries so complicated that no-one could follow them, but the audience was caught up in the exciting events nevertheless. Hitchcock invented a word for this, suggesting the plot mystery, or the object of everyone's attention, was a 'McGuffin'. It seems at the centre of things but it is actually irrelevant. This makes for a better defence of *Kane*. The alleged mystery of what makes Kane tick may be merely a McGuffin, a plot device to enable us to follow this reporter back into various people's memories. The interaction of the people on screen, the events that happen to them, become the point of the movie, and the hunt for the McGuffin slips into the background; then, in the incinerator scene, it is rounded off neatly, but cynically. For we see the smoke pouring out of Xanadu's chimneys, scattering this albeit meaningless clue to the winds.

In commenting on *Casablanca* and, now, *Citizen Kane*, I have noted that a principal methodological device is the plot summary. It took little argument to show that any given paraphrase will be informed by an interpretation. Can we criticize and improve on this approach? My criticism is that, unless we can criticize it, it is dogmatic. To avoid this danger I have in the case of *Casablanca* and shall, in the case of *Kane*, paraphrase the film repeatedly — as we say in logic, any set of facts is compatible with an infinite number of theories.[3] (When in a previous book, *Movies as Social Criticism*, I did this without explaining it, my point was missed.) With this in mind we may then get better at paraphrase, less authoritative about what a film means, more hypothetical, more critical.

From among the vast literature on *Kane* I have selected a widely-used and admirable recent textbook (Cook 1981), the monograph by Bazin (1950), a widely praised and anthologized critical essay (Bordwell 1971) and a monograph by Pauline Kael (1971). The latter three are highly influential thinkers well worth engaging for their own sake; Cook's work is so widely diffused that attending to it is service to generations of students.

Paraphrase J

Citizen Kane ****US 1941 119m bw RKO (Orson Welles) A newspaper tycoon dies, and a magazine reporter [*sic*] interviews his friends in an effort to discover the meaning of his last words. A brilliant piece of Hollywood cinema using all the resources of the studio; despite lapses of characterization and gaps in the narrative, almost every shot and every line is utterly absorbing both as entertainment and as craft. See *The Citizen Kane Book* by Pauline Kael and innumerable other writings.

w Herman J. Mankiewicz, Orson Welles d Orson Welles Ph Gregg Toland m Bernard Herrman ad Van Nest Polglase sp Vernon L. Walker

Orson Welles, Joseph Cotten, Dorothy Comingore, Everett Sloane, Paul Stewart, Ray Collins, Ruth Warwick, Erskine Sanford, Agnes Moorhead, George Coulouris, William Alland, Fortunio Bonanova.

'on seeing it for the first time, one got a conviction that if the cinema could do that, it could do anything.'

(*Penelope Houston*)

'What may distinguish *Citizen Kane* most of all is its extracting the mythic from under the humdrum surface of the American experience.'

(*John Simon 1968*)

'Probably the most exciting film that has come out of Hollywood for twenty-five years. I am not sure it isn't the most exciting film that has ever come out of anywhere.'

(*C. A. Lejeune*)

'At any rate Orson Welles has landed in the movies, with a splash and a loud yell.'

(*James Shelley Hamilton*)

'More fun than any great movie I can think of.'

(*Pauline Kael 1968*)
(*Halliwells Films Guide*)

David Cook, in the course of devoting twenty pages to the analysis of this one film, offers only one paragraph of interpretation. He treats the philosophy of the film as thoughts out of the blue, not related to any problem-situation in psychology, or to the treatment of biography in previous films, plays or books. Cook takes us through the plot of *Citizen Kane* scene by scene, mentioning each time the content of what we are told about Kane, and suggesting the visual and aural means by which this is supplemented. Here is a sample:

> 'Rosebud' is clearly inadequate to account for the terrible
> emptiness at the heart of Kane, and of America, and is meant to
> be. Its power as a symbol of lost love and innocence lies in its
> very insufficiency, for the 'missing piece' of the jigsaw puzzle of
> Kane's life, the 'something he lost', turns out to be an inanimate
> object, and a regressive one at that. In its barrenness, 'Rosebud'
> becomes a perfect symbol of Kane's inability to relate to people
> in human terms, or to love, and the ultimate emblem of his futile
> attempt to fill the void in himself with objects. In the film's two-
> hour running time we have seen Kane from several separate
> perspectives – those of the newsreel, the five narrators and the
> concluding reprise – and we probably have come to know more
> about the circumstances of his life than the man would have
> known himself. We know what he did and how he lived and
> died, but we can never know what he *meant* – perhaps, Welles
> seems to suggest, because, like 'Rosebud', he was ultimately
> meaningless, or perhaps because reality itself is ambiguous and
> unreliable. In any case, it is the quest for meaning rather than its
> ultimate conclusion that makes *Citizen Kane* such a rich and
> important film. (1981, pp. 364–5)

Neither of the statements, 'people's lives are meaningless', nor, 'reality itself is ambiguous and unreliable', seem to be philosophies attributable of the film. The mystery is unresolved because it is impenetrable, or perhaps it is phrased in too simple-minded terms, but that lives are meaningless or reality treacherous seems to me nowhere essayed in this film. So in Cook's twenty pages we get one unsupported paragraph, not well thought-out, lacking a structure of argument, waving its hand at symbolism, and showing no awareness that interpretation is undertaken responsibly only when argued out and defended against possible objection.

Cook's book is a textbook, and, like any textbook, attempts to summarize the state of the art of understanding a film at the time, as well as exemplifying the state of the art of film criticism. What lesson do nearly twenty pages of plot summary teach? That a valid way to argue is to disguise your argument as a descriptive paraphrase, thus setting the reader up for the brief summary interpretation at the end. Having built it into the description little elaboration is necessary. This is the commonest way of arguing interpretation and it is a poor way. All description involves theories and interpretations and has itself to be approached in a tentative manner, and be subjected to critical discussion. Consider two points in Cook's description. As I noted in my opening paraphrase, a 'NO TRESPASSING' sign is seen in both the opening and closing shots. An obvious interpretation of this sign is that it means that what lies inside − Kane's castle in the filmic space, Kane's life in the filmic content − is someone else's property. If we trespass we do so at our own risk. That a man guards his privacy may also indicate he has something to hide. Either way, we are being warned that our quest is out of order, an intrusion, and may do us no good.

Another scene Cook likes is when Kane has brought his wife's opera troupe to Chicago where his former best friend Leland is drama critic. Leland gets drunk, begins a bad notice, and falls asleep. When he is awakened, Kane is at the typewriter finishing the notice, the way Leland had begun it, as a bad one. The implication is that Kane will write as good a bad notice as Leland could; that Kane knows what is wrong with his wife's operatic talents and nevertheless imposes a career on her, and her on the public, as a kind of exercise of will. Here is a hint that a man is what he makes of himself, not a puppet of the strings going back to childhood deprivation.

Neither shot, of course, can be used as an argumennt to the conclusion Cook wants to make, quoted above. Significantly, his comments on them are largely 'cinematic', i.e. illustrative. Expecting a textbook to be uncritical, to chastise it with (PRI) or (KRI) would be unfair. So let us leave textbooks and turn to other kinds of writing, and especially, since he is so influential, to Andrè Bazin.

Bazin had immense influence on his compatriots as film critic and, as we saw in Part one, even on such as Stanley Cavell. His monograph of Welles (1958) tells us:

Citizen Kane [is] . . . a childhood tragedy. The last wish of
Kane . . . his 'fundamental project', as the existentialists would
say, is completely contained in a glass ball where a few artificial
snowflakes fall on a little house . . . The film ends on the word
with which it began; 'Rosebud', whose significance in Kane's life

the investigation seeks in vain, is nothing but the word written on the surface of the child's sled. . . . Isn't it with the sled . . . that he violently strikes . . . the banker who has come to tear him from his play in the snow and his mother's protection . . . he takes revenge on the frustration of his childhood by playing with his social power as a monstrous sled. . . . Unmasked by his best friend and by the woman he thought he loved the most, Kane admits before dying that there is no profit in gaining the whole world if one has lost one's own childhood. (Bazin, 1958, p. 65−6)

It may be instructive, as we enter into this controversy between different views of *Citizen Kane*, to re-emphasize methodology and procedure. My method, in the opening pages of each film considered, will be to describe the film in a manner that illustrates the philosophical interpretation I propose for it. Having isolated that interpretation I shall treat it like any other piece of philosophy, looking at its merits and demerits as such, and at the strengths or otherwise of the structure of argument meant to support it in the film, including the descriptions that serve it. Rather than proceed simply to imagine alternative readings of the philosophy of the film I shall then dip into the literature which has surrounded the film, using them as criticisms of my own. Recall: I have chosen only a handful of films because there is no canon and, except for the Woody Allen films, those I have chosen come as near as any to being in the canon. Second, there are no deep traditions of critical discussion, so I have chosen carefully some films that do have an extensive literature. And, third, there are no standards but, by examining what literature there is, we may begin the task of bringing standards into being.

In attending to the literature of interpretation and criticism that surrounds a film I shall be as interested in the methods by which the author makes his case, as in the content of that case itself. Philosophers always argue about two things: the actual position you take, and its rights and wrongs, and also the case you make, the arguments, including evidence, you marshal. Often dispute is hardest hitting about the latter, for being right for the wrong reasons is almost as heinous as being wrong.

The structure of Bazin's book is very odd. It was a slim little paperback in its first appearance, with no chapters or headings. Its preface, by Jean Cocteau, one of France's leading writers and film makers, sketched his relations with and attitudes to Welles. The purpose of such forewording is usually to legitimate the work of the lesser-known writer. It says, 'attend to this new young person because I, a more established person, bid you to do so'. Translated into English it now has chapters and sub-heads supplied by the (French) publisher. The book is sprinkled with stills, but it is not said if these were Bazin's selection, and the English translator has added footnotes correcting Bazin and supplying additional references. Most surprising of all, a new Foreword by the French director Francois Truffaut, almost one-quarter as long as Bazin's text, fronts the English translation. All this apparatus is there to tell us how important Bazin is. Two distinguished people front for him; the translator corrects him (thereby telling us he should be studied despite making factual mistakes).

And then there is the shape of the writing. Most of the book is an 'artistic biography', that is, an outer history of Orson Welles's career from theatre and broadcasting, through Hollywood, on to his years in Europe, ending back in Hollywood with *Touch of Evil* (1957) − which Bazin was able to discuss before his demise. This biography is interrupted by a discussion of the first two films beginning with the idea that Welles is obsessed with the theme of lost childhood (c.f. (RI 4) and (RI 5)). This is projected into *Citizen Kane* as I have quoted, and then

> If one had any doubts, on the evidence of a single film, about the obsession with childhood in Welles' work, *The Magnificent Ambersons* would provide a decisive confirmation. (Bazin 1958, p.66)

Look back at this argument. First, we are invited to take Bazin seriously by Cocteau (the other apparatus came after Bazin's death). Then Bazin sets us up for his interpretation by displaying familiarity with the external events of Welles's career. Then he offers an interpretation of Welles's thematic obsession and suggests our doubts will be decisively overcome if we consider his second film. (The sentence quoted above is grammaticaly ambiguous, since on the face of it what is decisively confirmed is our doubts. The context makes clear Bazin means the reverse of this.) He does not deny that there may not be other meanings of the film (c.f. (RI 10) below), but feels those he has singled out impose 'themselves on the author's imagination' (p. 67) in ways of which he could not be aware. He instances the repeated use of snow, with its childhood association of play.

It would not be difficult to be very harsh about this (RI 5). Doubts about the interpretation of a work cannot, logically, be resolved by consideration of another work. That another work may yield to the same interpretation is an argument for trying out the interpretation on the first work. But unless evidence from the first work resolves doubt a linking premise has to be introduced, something of the order, 'two separate works by the same hand are as likely as not to display the same thematic obsessions'. Such a premise, however worded, would seem to me highly contentious. There are authors who both at the conscious and at the unconscious level display sharp breaks between the thematic obsessions of their works. More serious, obviously, for film studies, is that the premise assumes an answer and, I have earlier argued (Part II, section 7.23), the wrong answer to the question 'who is the author?' The answer I suggested was that in fact a committee is the author. In practice we can attribute authorship to an individual but only if we keep the attribution under constant review. Hence, to validate a claim that Welles is obsessed with childhood and that this shows in his films, it would be necessary to discuss in detail the collaborative process of making his films, to show the possibility that his obsessions would surface, and that the obsessions visible in the films are his. Possibly this could be done, but Bazin does not do it.

Logically, as well as factually, Bazin has the situation backwards. Doubts are not resolved by single confirming instances. Single confirming instances add up to no more than: single confirming instances. More important, what are the criteria for imposing and defending the interpretation of a work, the attribution of meaning to it? Here we enter a vexed subject. Writers from a literary background too often proceed merely to offer their own relatively free associations as evidence that an interpretation is all right. Their writing thus becomes a disguised way of talking about themselves. Bazin is saying: 'when I see Welles' films I notice how many times snow figures in the scenes; snow for me meant games with sleds and snowballs so Welles' films have that association'. What is wrong with this? The answer is that it is parochial, even egocentric. There are, believe it or not, people in the world who have never seen snow and who hence will not associate snow with any of the things Bazin associates it with. Hence the resonance he takes from the film passes them by. Less extreme, there are plenty of people in northern climes to whom snow is no more than the condition of winter, as is greenery the condition of summer, and as one frolicks in the snow one season, one frolicks in the grass the next. Snow has no special overtone of childhood, and moreover no special overtone of frolic. In North America it is one of children's chores to shovel snow, and they do not all have happy associations with that hard work. One is reminded of the urbanized intellectuals who romanticize rural life, which to rural dwellers is more about rising with the dawn to milk cows, and being bound by the movement of the seasons, than it is about clean air and contact with nature, so-called. At the risk of going on too much about snow, two further points need making. The first is that snow comes in winter, a particular season of the year. It has much stronger associations to that than to childhood. The second point is this: in a black-and-white film snow is very photogenic. Everything stands out in its glare. One reason film makers like it is because it gives wonderful photographic effects, yet does not demand colour.

We can now begin to formulate some further Rules of Interpretation to carry forward the work of Chapter 11. The first eight rules (PRI, KRI and RI 1−6) enjoined that interpretations should be strong, non-*ad hoc* and comprehensive, that is, fit as much as possible of the information given. We can distinguish two kinds of information, that internal to the text (RI 1), and that of the contexts external to the text, namely historical (RI 3, RI 4), other work (RI 5) and of the culture (RI 6). In addition to this internal and external comprehensiveness some still more basic requirements have yet to be formulated: if our aim is to improve interpretative power by criticism then our interpretations in the first place need to be tentative, testable, tested, rationally handled, and contain a minimum of assumptions. Let me expand these desiderata into rules in the course of explaining their value.

(RI 7) An interpretation should be tentative.

Like scientific theories, which are conjectural, interpretations are putative solutions to problems. The problem interpretations are usually thought to address is, 'what does this work mean?' 'Mean'

279

here is very vague, because it can be translated as 'mean literally', 'mean sociologically', 'mean at the box-office', 'mean in its popularity', 'mean for the future of movies', etc. The kind of answer we would give to each of these translations (or interpretations) of the problem, 'what does this work mean?', is completely different. When we are looking at a film philosophically the sort of specification of the general problem we have in mind is something like this: is there an interpretation of the philosophy behind this film that fits all its parts into a coherent whole? It should now be clear that only our ingenuity sets limits on the number of answers there will be to this question. Hence, we should advance our answer in a tentative manner since we do not know whether or not a better one has been devised by others, and since we have yet to test our answer against argument. Neither tentativity nor reasoned argument is a prominent feature of much literary study, or literary-derived film study. Intuition and insight are greatly lauded there, which is fine, but not if an uncritical acceptance of intuition and insight is also encouraged.

(RI 8) An interpretation should be testable.

Clearly, if interpretations are to be held tentatively and tested by argument, they should be testable. How would one test the 'Terrible emptiness at the heart of Kane' (Cook), or Welles's 'childhood obsession' (Bazin)? Cook is simply redescribing with evocative prose something that may or may not gibe with the reader's reaction, Bazin may be saying that Welles's films often treat of childhood, which is easy to check, and that this is highly significant, a sign of obsession, which is less easy to check. So much of the interpretative argument is carried by description and redescription of the film, and description is so loaded, the problem of testablility might seem intractable. One solution would be to compare different descriptions of the same scenes. The description I offered above (pp. 267−8), for example, was highly schematic, much more so than the five page 'Content Outline' in the *Focus on Citizen Kane* volume (Gottesman 1971, pp. 149−53). Cook offers twenty pages of such descriptions, and I have re-examined two shots using them to raise questions that challenge his interpretations. The force of the exercise is related to (RI 1), the demand that an interpretation fit all the elements of a film, not just bits of it.

One could, of course, reply that it is possible a film is not coherent, that no one interpretation will fit all of its parts. Such a thesis could draw support from the manner in which films are made, with many hands contributing at different stages. Why should we demand that interpreters make a film seem coherent when in fact it is not?

This challenge raises basic questions, and must be addressed with care. (RI 1) does not assume that films are coherent. It recommends that we treat them as such, and render them as near-coherent as possible (PR 1). This even at the cost of overriding the stated intentions of the makers: artists are not authorities on how their works are to be interpreted, although they are privileged. If our efforts fail, that is, if there are scenes (not necessarily the same ones) that prove recalcitrant to whatever interpretation we try, we may conclude that the film is, indeed, incoherent. Other things being equal, an incoherent film is less desirable than a coherent one, because what it means to say of a film that it is incoherent is that it does not make sense. Strictly speaking, we are saying, 'we can't make sense of it'. This is a confession of defeat, and should be seen as such. Incoherence, not making sense, is not the same as being deep or ambiguous. Only if it is coherent can it be either of those.

(RI 9) An interpretation should be tested.

It follows from the demand for tentativity and testability that interpretations should be tested against logic, fact and theory. We should not foist on a film an inconsistent or manifestly false interpretation. The purpose of testing is to modify and improve (remembering RI 2^1) and, if necessary, jettison and replace our first efforts at making sense of the movie. Interpreting films, like learning about the world, is an incremental learning process of trial and error in which we collaborate with our fellows. Until we have tested our ideas we have no business offering them to the public; if they are decisively criticized by an opponent our responsibility is to reconsider, possibly retract. Rare indeed is this event in film studies (c.p. Bordwell 1971 below).

The demand for rational treatment of interpretation has more to do with conduct than with formulation of the interpretation;

(RI 10) Interpreters should controvert each other and seek means of rational argument.

Popper sometimes describes the rationality of science as consisting in the practice of friendly-hostile mutual criticism. Recognizing that our efforts to be self-critical will never be enough, he argues that science is a cooperative endeavour although not necessarily one suffused in a glow of brotherly love. On the contrary, rivalry and competitiveness may be as common as friendliness. In either atmosphere the controlling passion is to get it right, and each offering is scrutinized to see if it does. If it does not, that clears the ground for rivals to come forward. Where there are already several offerings in rivalry they will have their partisans, each of whom will be trying to eliminate the others. Hence there is cooperation, but it need not be friendly. Scientists' motives can be pure and disinterested; but they can also be ambitious, even venal. Motives, however, do not determine the ingenuity and force of the ideas and objections advanced, and it is those qualities that carry the day.

There is greater individualism and isolationism in the arts, both in creation and in critical interpretation, than in science. Perhaps this is a pity. Artists can learn from each other and from their critics, as can critics learn from each other as well as artists. The fear and suspicion so often expressed, especially by the creators of the critics, is an expression of insecurity. All of us are stimulated when critics controvert each other in journals, anthologies and the correspondence columns of the intellectual magazines. It is in those places one sees the greatest effort to sharpen up what the issues are and to present clear arguments to the point. This is also why interviews with artists, such as film makers (or the *Paris Review* interviews with writers) are so absorbing: because usually they centre around points of controversy. Not to listen to others seems to reveal a lack of willingness to learn, a lack of self-criticism, which is fundamentally anti-rational.

As to the number of assumptions an interpretation makes: this is a quasi-logical requirement. The more intellectual baggage an interpretation carries, the more vulnerable it is to criticism and confutation.

(RI 11) An interpretation is stronger the less elaborate or
esoteric the theoretical systems it draws upon.

If an interpretation draws upon a highly contentious theoretical position, as for example psychoanalysis or Marxism, then that interpretation is vulnerable to all the objections launched against those systems. When two such systems are combined and each repudiates the other that further increases the objections. Since so many film critics, as I have explained earlier, are partisans of these two systems of ideas (and of mixtures of them), perhaps my example should be different. Consider another widespread system of ideas, namely Christianity. Most narratives can be interpreted so as to illustrate the 'deep truths' of Christianity, from its emphasis on brotherly love, through to the symbolism of threes. Never mind for the moment how many of the Rules of Interpretation it would violate, consider *Citizen Kane* as a tragedy of the Imitation of Christ. What criticism could be made?

First, much of the world is not Christian. What, then, does the film mean for them? Second, Christianity is a bewildering mosaic of sects and interpretations, many of them mutually contradictory. Whence, then, the 'deep truths'? Third, Christianity is open to a great many serious philosophical objections as to its truth and morality and this makes the film vulnerable to them too (RI 6). A quite different case could be made by looking at the film as a criticism of Nietzsche's theory of the *übermensch*; and so on. If the film maker's testimony or other evidence foists such interpretations on us, that is one thing; to *choose* them is to invite unnecessary complications. Some of Bergman's early films seem to be religious allegories; Robert Bresson's *Journal d'un Curé de Campagne* certainly is. *Three Faces of Eve* and *Freud* are clearly Freudian; Fassbinder's work is generally Marxist; Riefenstahl's Nazi. Our interpretations of these films cannot but assess the films as expressions of those points of view, points of view likely to be very different from our own (RI 6).

If I were to assess Bazin by the eleven rules laid down so far, his grades would be mixed. Some of the rules are followed and some are not noticed. Since Bazin died in 1958 there would seem to be some injustice in applying these rules retroactively to him. Very well. But these rules are relatively common-sense and their backward projection is not totally out of order. Even so, they should be used with a light touch.

This becomes harder with another couple of writers on *Citizen Kane*, David Bordwell and Pauline Kael. Each gives interpretations that are suspect and each deploys argumentative techniques that are fundamentally scandalous, by anyone's criteria. Bordwell's essay on the film (1971) is only twenty-two pages long,[4] yet in the course of it he makes the following allusions (a partial list): Griffith, Murnau, Renoir, Berkeley (Busby), Keaton, Hitchcock, Lang, Clair, European film, Renaissance, Elizabethan, Flaubert, Pasolini, Godard, Bergman, Fellini, Bresson, Antonioni, Lumière, Méliès, *Caligari*, Naturalism, Eisenstein, avantgarde films, Brecht, Henry James, T.S. Eliot, Freud, Coleridge, Hawks, Marlowe, Shakespeare. What does such display tell us? 'Look what a well-read literary chap I am, look what a wide range of films I have seen.' Or, 'because I am so knowledgeable you should take my work seriously'. This sort of claim, the claim to intellectual expertise, is a fundamental form of intellectual pretence not confined by any means to film studies.

Instead of such pretence, an intellectual case should be made by precise and pithy formulation, buttressed by sound arguments, and by plausible rebuttals to counter-arguments. Who is making the case, what standing they have in the eyes of their colleagues or themselves, what they can allude to, are logically irrelevant. Besides efforts to impress, Bordwell offers such as this:

> Dying, he can only clutch the icon of love and innocence: his last moment becomes a final assertion of imagination in the face of the ultimate reality of death. (Bordwell 1971, p. 120 — all page references to the Gottesman 1976 reprint)

What does this sentence say? It spins words together obscurely (icon of love) and in cliché (ultimate reality of death). It makes mistakes. Kane does not clutch anything in dying. When he dies he drops the glass ball. A moment does not (cannot) 'become' an assertion; Kane's last *word* is 'Rosebud', but a name is not an assertion. Perhaps Bordwell means something like this: '"Rosebud" stands for love, innocence and imagination'. If so, why not say it? If not, how are we to know in writing like this? If the assertion of imagination in the face of death is being made by the film, not by Kane, this could be said without the mixed metaphor.

The attentive reader will not have failed to notice that in the last two paragraphs I have violated Popper's Rule of Interpretation (PRI) since Bordwell's view is not formulated in its logically strongest form. These paragraphs discuss not *Citizen Kane* but Bordwell's interpretative essay on the film. (PRI) is intended to apply, *mutatis mutandis*, to a text like Bordwell's as much as to a film: both need interpretation and paraphrase before discussion. My violation consists in plunging into discussion of Bordwell before presenting his ideas in their clearest and strongest form. This illustrates our need of rules: to try to live up to them ourselves. So let me begin again, reminding myself that Kuhn's Rule (KRI) can lead me back to troublesome passages later.

Bordwell's interpretation is that *Citizen Kane* is a film about what goes on in the mind, showing us various events and how we see those events, namely, variously, depending on our point of view. Such an interest in what happens in the mind he takes to be a characteristic of the art of the modern age, hence, 'modernist'.

What is Bordwell's procedure? He begins with a remark to the effect that Kane should not be valued solely for its technique but because it controls technique for artistic ends. Those who value *Citizen Kane* for technique are not named and their position is not set out and buttressed by argument. Bordwell violates (PRI) despite quoting a version of it stated by Welles himself: 'I believe it is necessary to give all the characters their best arguments . . . including those I disagree with' (1971, pp. 109–10). This is not Bordwell's procedure. He often bounces his own ideas off those he disagrees with, but they are not given any chance to speak:

> *Kane* should not be seen as a Rashomon-like exploration of the relativity of fact. (p. 110)

> The sled isn't really [sic] the cheap Freud some (including Welles) have claimed. (p. 111)[5]

Bordwell continues with some general remarks about the historical development of the movies and their two poles of potential: that of reproducing reality; and that of expressing the (poetic) imagination. *Kane* is something new, a 'monument in the modern cinema, the cinema of consciousness' (p. 104). Its

> great achievement, then, is . . . its rich fusion of an objective realism of texure with a subjective realism of structure.
> Welles . . . not only shows what we see, but he symbolizes the way we see it. (p. 105)

So the two poles are fused. How? '*Kane* explores the nature of consciousness chiefly by presenting various points of view on a shifting, multiplaned world' (p. 105).

This is a little confusing. Is Bordwell saying that the world is multiplaned or that the world of *Kane* is multiplaned? A nice ambiguity is compounded by the arcane metaphor of the multi-plane, a technical name for the animation camera developed by the Walt Disney studios in the 1930s.

These preliminary excursions still do not bring us to grasp the originality of the article. Bordwell does more than offer the interpretation previously stated, but what this is he never really states in the article, although it is hinted at in the quotation about technique. Most of the article is a recapitulative description of the film drawing attention to ways in which these stated artistic ends (a modernist fusion of the real and the subjective) are contained within the framing, cutting, camera movement, lighting, and, very occasionally, sound. Bordwell's thesis, then, is a variant of Bazin's, namely that a single imagination, Welles's, informs the making of *Citizen Kane*, every nuance of which involves a fusion of content (the interpretation) with technique. This is an exemplary implementation of (RI 1). If Bordwell's interpretation can be shown to agree even with details of technique this is a strong buttressing argument for it. What is weak in Bordwell is the backhanded dismissal of alternative views (RI 10), hence a lack of tentativity (RI 7), and no discussion of the weakness of his own case (RI 9).

Bordwell contends that the problem posed in the film, namely what makes a man tick, and, narrower, what did his last words mean, has no final solution. The problem has, however, a meaning rather than a solution: 'the film proposes that action becomes an egotistical drive for power when not informed by love' (p. 111). Because the film opens and closes on a 'NO TRESPASS-ING' sign it 'restore(s) a grandeur to Kane's life, a dignity born of the essential impenetrability of human character' (p. 111). Now we are getting somewhere. The film is, then philosophizing in ways that can be paraphrased in words, in ways that are permeated through its visual and aural texture But instead of some (technical-based) arguments about this interpretation and the extent to which it is warranted by the film we get a reversion to:

Thus the clash of fact and bias, objectivity and prejudice, interweaving through the history of a personality, creates a

world that is nearly as complex as reality and yet as unified as
great art. (p. 13)

It is hard to reconcile this with:

> At no point does Welles suggest that Kane's story is being
> distorted, wilfully or unconsciously. . . . There is . . . no doubt
> about the *facts* which are revealed. (p. 10)

Contradictions, or even seeming contradictions, are a reason
one demands a text be as pithy and as clear as possible, because
length and vagueness are the usual ways people conceal contradictions. What *Kane* has, in Bordwell's terms, is not facts and bias,
but facts and interpretations of why these are facts. This problem
goes back to Bordwell's fundamental philosophical view of the
film. He argues that in clashing the sombre opening shots, a
private, poetic image of Kane (p. 106), with the public, documentary side of him in the newsreel.

> Welles immediately establishes the basic tension of *Kane* (and
> cinema itself): objective fact versus subjective vision, clearness
> and superficiality versus obscurity and profundity, newsreel
> versus dream (p. 106).

Put more pithily: *Citizen Kane* is a movie about movies; a movie
about our consciousness of the problems posed by movies. Having
begun this book at the beginning the reader will be well aware of
my basic agreement with part of Bordwell's thesis. Munsterberg
and Cavell argued along the same lines (see Part I). Film draws
some of its potency from self-conscious reminders to us that we are
watching a film, and that the film world is part of, but not
continuous with, the real world. Precisely because I agree with so
much of what Bordwell writes do I feel free to criticize him.
Bordwell's pairs in tension will not do. Films do not trade in 'facts'
and 'subjectivity', they are inter-subjective, conventional.
Furthermore, clearness is not the same as superficiality, any more
than obscurity is a sign of profundity. I hope that these pairs are
not reflexively intended by Bordwell as a defence of his own
practice of writing obscurely, thinking that this is profundity.

These methodological and philosophical animadversions aside,
though they are essential preliminaries in such a chaotic field, what

of Bordwell's actual interpretations of *Citizen Kane*? My view presented earlier, that the human character is an enigma and that trespassing inside it may be tempting, but is liable to be futile if pursued in the spirit of getting to the bottom of things, fits most of the material Bordwell deploys and so is tested and passes the test (RI 8, RI 9). He offers several subordinate readings. Let us look at those first: action not informed by love becomes an egotistical drive for power; 'Rosebud' stands for love, innocence and imagination; *Kane* explores the nature of consciousness.

'Rosebud' can indeed be said to stand for something Kane had lost, or longed for, as the dialogue of the film makes quite clear. One for Bordwell. Does any action not informed by love become an egotistical drive for power? Does this film make that argument? Kane, like writers of articles on films, has a strong ego as a boy (look at his mother), and gives it full rein when he is of age: his main conviction is a confidence in his own rectitude, even when he is misbehaving. David McClintick's book about Hollywood, *Indecent Exposure*, is full of characters with the same trait. There is in *Citizen Kane* the idea that absence of love is what explains Kane, but the film's structure is not such that we are asked to believe it; moreover the drive for power and abundant love are shown co-existing in the another Hollywood film, *The Godfather Parts I and II*. Both cannot be true. So here we will unpack from (RI 9) a new rule:

(RI 12) Other things being equal, do not foist a false
proposition on a work as its interpretation.

Now we begin to see differences between the approach I propose and Bordwell's. Reading between the lines, I sense that Bordwell thinks not only that *Citizen Kane* 'proposes that action becomes an egotistical drive for power when not informed by love', but also that this is true. So Bordwell proposes and Jarvie disposes, for this philosophy has just been shown to be possibly false. That in itself does not show that it is not 'proposed' in *Citizen Kane*. On the contrary, I have stressed repeatedly that we neither need agree with an interpretation nor hold it to be true to attribute it to a film. Yet once it is under discussion, the question must arise as to whether it is true or false. And the phrase 'other things being equal' is in (RI 12) to suggest that we only attribute a falsehood to a film if no equally viable interpretation can be found that is not false.

It is no accident that Bordwell sees in *Kane* a philosophy that attracts him and yet he does not notice that it is not endorsed. Probably such empathy is basic to the attraction of certain works: they are amenable to our projections. Indeed, this seems to me the entire procedure of Stanley Cavell's 'readings' of films. But if philosophy is more than musing or conversations, namely an activity regulated by the search for truth, we may face the fact, as has been mentioned earlier, that a work we admire nevertheless proposes a possible falsehood.

Now to our major disagreement: if *Kane* explores the nature of consciousness then Bordwell explores the nature of philosophy, i.e. they are equally preposterous. There is nothing about consciousness in the film. Indeed, in a certain way, the film is anti-psychological, offering only the most passing hints as to what is going on in Kane's mind. He is an enigma who, we are left feeling, is large on the landscape, yet very far from transparent. NO TRESPASSING is a warning that the voyeur will find plenty to occupy himself, but would be deceived were he to think that this inside information offers any better clues to what makes a man tick than what is publicly available. That this idea is not new, not profound and not true detracts very little from the film despite (RI 12).

En passant let us notice that Bordwell backhands Welles's own ideas about the film, even though he refers constantly to Welles as the author of the things in the film he is interpreting. Having criticized the uncritical use of such authorship-attribution while discussing Bazin, I want to now propose a further rule of interpretation:

(RI 13)   While the author may not have privileged access to what his work means, in working towards a viable interpretation the *prima facie* case has to be that offered by the author.

There is an objection to this rule that constitutes a kind of limit case: what of the director, author or piece of evidence that suggests a film has no interpretation at all? Logically, the other limit case is evidence suggesting that a film will bear any interpretation whatever. To deny that a film has an interpretation, like denying that one has a philosophy, is an interpretation, is a philosophy. How do we handle the anti-philosophy philosophy? Usually by showing the anti-philosopher that he has presuppositions that his anti-philosophy is denying he has, and that such a contradiction is intolerable.

There are quite a few Hollywood creators who are on record as denying that their films will bear interpretation, that they are not sending *any* messages, still less philosophical ones. Before we come to the obvious point that, since we are not always conscious of what we do, we cannot then be conscious of all that what we are doing means, and that hence our denials of significance can be discounted, we can note that such an anti-philosophical stance seems to be the case with Ford, Hawks and Hitchcock, three of Hollywood's most prominent figures in the golden age. Ford argued that he simply took a script and did it, and so all questions of conception were turned aside (Anderson 1952). Hitchcock expressed bemusement when confronted with his Jansenist philosophy by Rohmer and Chabrol (1957).

Does this mean, then, that (RI 13) requires that we do not offer any interpretation, since it flies in the face of the denial of interpretation? I do not think so. These are limiting cases, which must be handled with special care in order not to foist untenable interpretations on the films and their makers. First of all, if no pattern of preoccupation emerges in a work or a body of work, one may then well decide to say that putting interpretation on it is forced. After all, why bother to interpret *Hopalong Cassidy* westerns, or the films of efficient technicians like Terence Young? If, however, a pattern emerges in a work, one may then attribute the interpretation not to the director who disavows it but to the writer, the studio, the star, whoever. One may even attribute the interpretation to the *Zeitgeist*, as when considering stereotypes, sacred cows, pieties, etc. When a plausible pattern emerges over several works by the same hand (writer, director, star, whatever) the attribution is defensible shorthand.

The solution to the problem of who the author is can be left aside, because attribution of, or claim to, authorship is enough. Bazin quotes Welles:

Thompson . . . decides that a man's dying words ought to

explain his life — maybe they do. He never discovers what Kane's mean. But the audience does . . . five people . . . tell five different stories . . . the truth about Kane, like the truth about any man, can only be calculated by the sum of everything that has been said about him . . . the point of the picture is not so much the solution of the problem as its presentation. (Bazin 1950, p. 58)

This interpretation, which is pithy and precise, testable against the facts, and so on, I read only after I had written my own interpretation. This was an accident of research procedure, not an attempt to avoid bias. I too have suggested that what *Kane* poses is a problem: how to understand and explain something that is enigmatic and elusive. However, Welles's assertion that the truth about a man can only be calculated by the sum of everything that has been said about him is intriguing. It of course applies to Welles, as to Kane. It does not mean everything said about someone is true. Perhaps a historian would say that you cannot make an informed judgment about a person (calculated) until you have read all the documents, the evidence. *Citizen Kane* shows us the complexity of some of that evidence and withdraws from the responsibility of making a judgment. If its makers started out to attack William Randolph Hearst, they were sidetracked along the way. Pauline Kael suggests that in fact the writer Mankiewicz both admired and despised Hearst and that the portrait in the film need not be read as a condemnation, but as showing that he may have had his reasons but we do not know what they are.

To me the controversial aspect of her much controverted book — which centres around Welles's claim that 'the only film that I wrote from beginning to end and was able to complete properly was *Citizen Kane*' (Bazin 1950, p. 134) — is her summation of the film's value: 'The conceptions are basically *kitsch;* basically, *Kane* is popular melodrama — Freud plus scandal, a comic strip about Hearst' (Kael 1971, p. 74). Her view is that it is a great film, a masterpiece, but a *shallow* one (p. 4). I do not dispute her idea that a great work can be shallow, although I have my qualms, any more than I dispute that a great work can be false or immoral. What does worry me rather is her argument purporting to show that *Citizen Kane* is shallow. The film's basic problem and philosophical ideas seem to me good enough. They are thoughful and provoking and I mistrust a criterion of shallowness that demands more in the name of depth or profundity. Kael's mode of argument is this. This is a shallow work. How so? Answer: it was written by a shallow but facile hack writer. Buried in this argument are two hidden premises. One is that Welles, not Mankiewicz, claims to be the author of *Kane*. Much of the book and much of its scandal has to do with her reasoning to deny that proposition.The other hidden premise is more interesting: shallow things are shallow because their authors are shallow. This strikes me as plainly false. I doubt whether one should ever be as categorical as to call a person 'shallow'. But even allowing that, it is no explanation of why a work is shallow to say its author was shallow because this begs the question of, 'what is shallow about the work?' Here Kael's argument is a long discursus on literary life in New York and Hollywood in the 1920s and 1930s, and the flourishing of a slick and journalistic cleverness, a tradition which produced plays and screenplays with a clever but shallow aspect. Still we want to know, 'what is shallow about the work?', but answer comes there none. It is shallow to talk of shallowness in this way.

The irony is that Kael may be right. If what *Kane* proposes is the philosophy found there either by Cook or by Bordwell then the film is indeed shallow. Why such ideas are shallow takes me a little further into lessons in philosophy than I care to go. On the other hand, if Welles is right that the philosophy of *Kane* is merely to pose the problem, or is that plus showing how no good solution is to hand, then it need not be shallow because the problem of understanding why persons do things is not a shallow problem. It could still be a shallow film, but not because its problem was shallow, Moreover, if Welles is right, the film makes an interesting claim to contribute to discursive philosophy, not simply illustrating or dramatizing a point of view, but rather exploring the ramifications of the problematic.

In discussing *Kane* I have been critical of Cook, Bazin, Bordwell and Kael. Yet it should be noted that I have used their work to move myself forward to a better interpretation of *Kane* and a better understanding of the work of interpretation itself. That is why it is not hypocritical of me to say, though I criticize their work, that I found it interesting and thought-provoking; in short, I learned

---

Aim: criticism and growth of interpretative power

Methodological rules

(PRI)   Formulate interpretations in their most fully developed and logically strongest form.

(RI 1)   Prefer the interpretation which makes sense of more scenes in the film than its rivals.

(RI 2)   When an interpretation clashes with some scene or element do not revise it *ad hoc*.

(KRI)   Making sense of absurdities in the film may alter understanding of central passages.

(RI 2')   Avoid all conventionalist attempts to protect an interpretation against criticism.

(RI 3)   However well an interpretation fits the film, if it does not fit the known and discoverable facts about its making that is a grave objection to it.

(RI 4)   In seeking interpretations (and problematics) all sources of information about the film should be explored.

(RI 5)   An interpretation of a work that is at odds with what is known of its creator's other works must be very carefully argued.

(RI 6)   The film culture and the national culture are contexts with which the interpretation of a film must cohere unless strong reasons can be given why they need not.

(RI 7)   An interpretation should be tentative.

(RI 8)   An interpretation should be testable.

(RI 9)   An interpretation should be tested.

(RI 10)   Interpreters should controvert each other and seek means of rational argument.

(RI 11)   An interpretation is stronger the less elaborate or esoteric the theoretical systems it draws upon.

(RI 12)   Other things being equal, do not foist false propositions on a work.

(RI 13)   While the author may not have privileged access to what his work means, in working towards a viable interpretation the *prima facie* case has to be that offered by the author (if there is one).

(RI 14)   Attempt to assist your critics (including yourself) by indicating what sorts of argument or evidence you would accept as damaging to, or overthrowing, your interpretation.

from it. Intellectual activity, scientific or critical, is a form of leap-frog, and in jumping over someone's bent back one may deliver a painful blow or a crushing weight.

Popper sometimes says that we should, as we work at our writing, be our first audience and our first critic. In seeking to criticize our own work we need to consider the question of what will count as criticism, especially what will count in the limit case: what will refute our ideas. So perhaps we can strengthen (RI 10) as follows:

(RI 14)   Attempt to assist your critics by giving some indication
          of what sorts of argument or evidence you would
          accept as damaging or overthrowing your
          interpretation.

This rule may be toughest of all to implement. We all love our own ideas, and we are all corrupted by the mystique of the 'insight'. That is why this rule is so important. It concentrates our mind wonderfully, forces us to stand outside our own views and look for their weaknesses and then to point them out.

What would count against my interpretation of *Citizen Kane* as an argument for the idea that a man's life is an enigma? One possibility is a new interpretation that fits the film as well as mine. The existence of such an alternative is a challenge. Another challenge would be scenes or lines from the film that deny the enigma thesis. Yet another one would be evidence about the intentions of any of the film's makers that would contradict the enigma thesis. None of these is a possible refutation; that would emerge only were the enigma thesis to be found internally inconsistent.

13

RASHOMON: IS TRUTH RELATIVE?

One doubts very much that Kurosawa was deeply interested in objective truth in this or in any other film. This is because the *why* is always implied. And in none of his pictures is Kurosawa even slightly interested in the why of the matter. Instead, always, *how*. This offers a clue. The level of objective truth is not the truly interesting one. Much more interesting is the level of subjective truth. If the truth searched for becomes subjective, then no-one lies, and the stories are wildly at variance.

Truth as it appears to others. This is one of the themes, perhaps the main one of this picture. No-one lied. They all told the story the way they saw it, the way they believed it, and they all told the truth. Kurosawa therefore does not question truth. He questions reality.

(Richie 1969, pp. 224).

First a declaration of philosophical intent. If *Rashomon* articulates a philosophy of relativism, if it says that truth is unobtainable, or relative to the point of view of a person, then I shall want to criticize it for promulgating a false philosophy (Jarvie 1984a). To be critical of a view, however, is not to denigrate it. It is not necessary to agree with a philosophy to appreciate it, especially to appreciate the manner of its presentation and defence. It does not tell against a work of art that its philosophy is mistaken. This goes in reverse too. That one agrees with the philosophy of a film is not sufficient for one to appreciate its presentation and defence. Perhaps the most common dilemma for today's film-goer is to see a film which impeccably embraces the right outlook and which succeeds in being offputting because it complacently slants the presentation so that all of us will know when we can congratulate ourselves for holding the right views. When you notice your own philosophical positions being presented, the natural tendency is to sigh with relief and relax; this is fatal. It is precisely in that situation where we should endeavour to be most critical. To be right for the wrong reason is, to a critically-minded philosopher, as gross a sin as being wrong.

So, if *Rashomon* turns out to be a relativistic film, the fact that I do appreciate and esteem it is something of a test case for my philosophy of film.

Although it is my impression that *Rashomon* is a highly regarded film, there is relatively little published on it in English compared to *Citizen Kane*, doubtless because it is Japanese.[1] There are abundant materials and possibly even a copy of *Citizen Kane* in most public library systems; this is not so of *Rashomon*. Nevertheless, my method in this discussion will be to describe it in more detail than was necessary or appropriate for *Citizen Kane*. Besides Scheuer's and my own paraphrase, I shall quote the plot synopsis *in toto* from Richie (1972). No description is neutral, but each should serve to highlight the point of view of the other.

When the film won the Golden Lion at Venice in 1950 it was the first Japanese film widely seen in the West since pre-war days. Its maker, Akira Kurosawa, was immediately hailed as a great film maker. The same instant acclaim had been accorded Orson Welles, but *Citizen Kane* was his first feature film and he was but 26. *Rashomon* was Kurosawa's twelfth film, and he was aged 40. The success of Kurosawa's film led to each successive film of his being exported to the West and eventually the mounting of retrospectives of his work, including the earlier films. He is still active as this book goes to press, was profiled in the *New Yorker*, has published his autobiography (1982), and gained financing for films from Russia (*Dersu Uzala*) and the USA (*Kagemusha*).

It is puzzling, to me at least, that *Rashomon* is not on any of the lists on pp.174–6. *Seven Samurai*, a film Kurosawa made four years after *Rashomon*, and which spawned two Hollywood copies, *The Magnificent Seven* and *The Return of the Magnificent Seven*, is in the 1982 list. This film is long, exciting and brilliantly made. Perhaps, however, it is its philosophy that puts it on the list. This remark is meant ironically, for the philosophy of *Seven Samurai* is a straight, humanist message, namely that warriors may come and go, but the farmers, the salt of the earth, go on forever. To discuss that philosophy in detail would expend space I wish to conserve for *Rashomon* (or risk the book becoming longer than I wish), but I cannot forbear remarking that by a philosophical film I do not mean one which endorses liberal and humanist values, however nicely, as in *Seven Samurai*. Taking positions, or preaching, is not philosophy; or perhaps I should be less categorical and say it is not *interesting* philosophy. Philosophy that tells you what to believe gets the priorities wrong. Philosophy that is interesting is philosophy that tries to get at the truth. What you believe in the face of the truth is not something philosophy can do much about and so should not bother with.

To return to Kurosawa's discovery by the rest of the world. His success performed a very important service for Japanese films and for those of us who appreciate them. Since prizes and money were to be made in the West, Japanese companies began to market their films there. So, on Kurosawa's coat-tails, as it were, the films of Mizoguchi, an older master, Ozu, Ichikawa and others circulated outside of Japan. Again, glancing at the lists of best films, we see that in the eyes of the sample of critics canvassed Mizoguchi seems to have eclipsed Kurosawa for a time (1962 and 1972), but that the balance has shifted back to the younger man.

So much for preliminary remarks. Now to the film itself.

Paraphrase K

Rashomon (Japan, 1951 [sic]) ***Toshiro Mifune, Machiko Kyo. The good but overpraised film that introduced Japanese cinema to the Western world. The story of a man and his wife who are surprised by a bandit while crossing the forest is told by each participant as well as by a witness, and the theme is the unknowability of truth when all human beings are naturally liars. (Dir: Akira Kurosawa, 90 mins)

(Scheuer's *Movies on TV*)

Paraphrase L

Three men, a priest, a woodsman and a commoner shelter from the downpour under a massive wooden gate. Full use is made of the possibilities of wood, rain, and the positioning of sitting figures to create powerful compositions. Loud naturalistic sound is overlain with music that blends Western and Japanese instruments. At the end of the film we will return to this location, the disagreements between the men will become sharp, the rain will stop and a philosophical suggestion will be made. Meanwhile, the men fall to discussing a recent case of rape and murder. We are in the middle ages, when the costumes were traditional, travel was by foot and horseback, and there was a sharply differentiated class hierarchy in Japan. Each of the men has heard something of the incident and undertakes to tell it, and the woodsmen surprises us all at the end by confessing to being an eye-witness.

The agreed facts are limited. A samurai, journeying through the forest with his wife, is attacked by a bandit. By the time the encounter is over, the samurai is dead and the wife maintains she was raped. Three people could have killed the man, the bandit, the wife, and himself – suicide. The wife could have been raped, could have enticed the bandit, or could be lying. The story could be a simple tale of a footpad and his victims, or a complex one of psychology involving pride, machismo and class. There has been a trial, and so both the woman's story and the bandit's have been heard. But, through a medium, so has the dead samurai's. When the woodcutter eye-witness adds his two cents, we realize that he may have been involved too. Not one of these contradictory versions is endorsed, but when we leave the flashbacks to return to the gate it happens that a foundling baby turns up. The only one of the men who will take responsibility for it is the poor woodcutter, who already has many children, but who regards the imperatives of the baby's needs as overriding all considerations of poverty or of philosophical reflection on who's responsibility it is.

Paraphrase M

Rashomon is a collection of versions of the truth about an attack, a rape, and a robbery, all of which occurred during the middle ages in the old Japanese capital of Kyoto, then called Miyako. These stories are being discussed by three people – a woodcutter, a commoner, and a priest – at the gate, Rashomon, where the three have gathered to shelter themselves from the rain.

They recount the various versions. The woodcutter says originally that he merely found some articles at the scene of the crime. He then relates the story that he heard the bandit, Tajomaru, tell the magistrate. The bandit said he had tied up the samurai husband and tried to rape the wife, only to find that she was quite ready to give in to him. Later, however, he said he had been forced (by the unfaithful wife) to fight with the husband and he had won.

The priest next gives the version that he heard the wife tell the magistrate. It is quite different. She said that after she had given herself to the bandit her husband hated her, and, distraught, she had killed him herself.

The next version is probably told by the priest. It concerns the dead man's story, told through the lips of a medium called in by the magistrate. It too is different from the others. The samurai said that after the seduction his wife had tried to have the bandit murder him. In this she had failed, but he had killed himself with a dagger.

At this point the woodcutter is made to confess that he did not tell the whole truth, nor did he complete his story. He says that the husband indeed no longer respected his wife. She, in fury, goaded the two men into fighting and the husband was killed. She fled from the bandit. He was left alone and eventually captured.

The three comment upon these various stories. Unaccounted for in any of them are the murder weapons. The bandit had said that the sword was sold; and the dagger is also missing. An amount of suspicion falls naturally upon the woodcutter, who had not told his whole story the first time, and the suspicion of theft is deepened by the possibility of murder.

None of this is resolved, however. The three are distracted by the cry of an infant abandoned in the attic of the old gate. The commoner wants to strip it and sell its clothes.

Now 'the *Rashomon* problem' – I owe this phrase to the anthropologist Marvin Harris, who writes as follows:

> In this movie the viewer witnesses four different versions of the 'same' scene. The principal actors are a man, his wife, a stranger, and an onlooker hidden in the bushes. Each of the actors narrates a different version of the lived experience, and each version appears on the screen as the lived reality. Manly heroism in one version is abject cowardice in another; chastity in one is carnal heat in another; and so on. Each narrative unfolds as a graphic, vivid reality, and the audience is left on its own to decide which version, if any, actually represents the event – or indeed, if there ever was an 'event' to begin with. (Harris 1979, pp. 321 and 327)

Harris further comments that there are two obvious solutions to the *Rashomon* problem; one is that one of the versions is true and the other is false; the other is that all are false.[2] He then adds a gratuitous, naughty, and quite accurate backhander. To phenomenologists, he remarks, a third possibility presents itself: all are true.

We have already seen (p. ix) that David Cook, author of a recent and widely used textbook, drew this relativist conclusion from the film: if there are several versions of a story, then the truth about the events eludes us – either because each person has his truth; or, truth is relative to point of view; or, there is no such thing as truth, only reconstructions of events. This conclusion can be criticized philosophically, but also from the film. There are matters on which there is agreement. No suggestion is made that the samurai did not exist and hence is not dead; that the wife has not lost her husband; no pretence is made to deny that the bandit was up to no good; and the woodcutter, priest and stranger do not doubt their existence. So this is not an idealistic film which says everything is in people's minds and there is no real world and hence no facts of the real world. If it has any relativist scepticism this is not general but rather pertains to the construction of events in human interaction.

Munsterberg, it will be recalled, argues that the artistic power of the film comes from its setting free the power of our minds. Both he and Cavell tell us how, if the film shows the undressing beginning, the mind will complete the process after the cut-away.

Rashomon: *Is Truth Relative?*

Munsterberg allows that the mind works strongly across the cut: if there is a shift of angle of view, or of setting, the mind leaps the gap without any sense of transition. Kurosawa's film is almost a conscious challenge to this thesis. So far from being able to leap gaps of point of view or of setting, he shows us how, in one setting, with three main characters and an onlooker, some chain of events can take place that our mind cannot reconstruct. If this is correct, it follows that the mind is enabled to do its work of completion over transitions by something the film maker does. If the film maker fails to do that, whatever it is, he can thwart the mind's power. Thus we discover something philosophically new about the film from this movie even as we consider the overt issue of truth and reality.

Let me then put on the agenda for further discussion the following problem: what does the film maker need to do to permit (or not to do to thwart) the mind's ability to close the gap of a cut? Technical answers about invisible cutting (on motion), eyeline matching, complementary point of view shots, seamless sound-track are all part of it. More is required. There has to be a withholding of the epistemological doubt that can very quickly be triggered in the film viewer. So far from our being fooled and swallowing the evidence of our two senses, I have maintained that we knowingly play with allowing and not allowing our selves to be fooled, thus our delight in the film makers' tricks, their jolting the audience – like the shock cut to 'News on the March' in *Kane*: the movie-goer is jolted from his movie-going reverie by a reminder of the transitions involved in movie-going as the feature gives way to the newsreel.[3]

Kurosawa deliberately gives us too much information: we cannot from this information assemble a coherent model of the putative events so we are forced to philosophize. Either one is true and the rest false; all are false; or all are true. The latter is absurd, since we have no general scepticism about truth in the film. Donald Richie, in the motto I placed at the beginning of this discussion, opts for them all being true by the following man-oeuvre: if truth is what people believe sincerely to be the truth, then everyone in this film tells the truth. Hence, the film is not about truth in the objective sense, but about reality. What 'reality' means for Richie is, I suspect, the world. The problem of the film for him, then, is how the world looks to different points of view.

This leaves untouched the question of how the world is, independent of all points of view. To a Berkeleyan idealist (c.f. Part I, Chapter 1) there is no such world, but it can be simulated if there is a Supreme Perceiver with His point of view. I doubt that Richie is that kind of idealist, and I doubt very much, on the basis of this film, if Kurosawa is too. Furthermore, I see no evidence that Kurosawa is engaging in deliberate mystification, such as in the intriguing Australian film *Picnic at Hanging Rock*.

The conflict of evidence in the film can be seen to create a problem. Not all the stories can be true. There is no warrant for the decision to back one and declare the others false. It seems to me that if the film points in any direction, it is that all are false. Now, to say that we can never altogether get to the bottom of an event is not a relativist idea. It does not say there is no bottom to be reached, or that all attempts to plumb it are equally useless, only that there will be no reaching it. This does not exclude a hierarchy of the false, in which we find each successive version less of a distortion than the previous, and so on. This hierarchy can be constructed and sustained without coming to the limit, namely, that this latter account is without distortion. Possibly the wood-cutter's tale is the least distorted.

It is important not to be carried away by this film, beautifully made and skilled though it is. A much more mundane American film of a few years later, derived from television, *Twelve Angry Men*, took up precisely the same problem, namely conflict of witnesses in a murder case. The *Twelve Angry Men* were jurors. That film tried to show how people's prejudices and personal interests coloured their attempts to reconstruct events from a welter of testimony, but how the conscientious persistence of one man devoted to the truth was able to identify the clues that made conviction impossible.[4]

It does not follow, to speak philosophically, that because there is conflict of evidence truth is therefore relative. Conflict of evidence forces a conscious decision on us as to what is the most plausible model to account for what happened. As in science there are in law elaborate procedures for checking – *Rashomon* is not a mystery with clues to the real culprit – and we need not assume Kurosawa is imputing a relativist message. It would be enough to say he is showing how difficult it is to assess what happens, even when you are an eye-witness.

Rashomon: *Is Truth Relative?*

So far it is clear that what we have in *Rashomon* is several versions of a series of events, versions which in some ways supplement and in other ways contradict each other. One resolution of these contradictions is relativism. Relativism amounts to saying that the contradictions are a function of trying to compile a single, true version of events. If, instead, we talk of truth relative to a point of view, we can say each participant in the events had his or her point of view and that, in describing it, they did not get involved in contradictions. A quite different way of resolving the dispute is ontologically: to concentrate not on point of view but on the world itself and argue that it lends itself to being described in ways that are contradictory. This seems to be what Richie has in mind in the motto. But for this argument to go through, the nature of the world – of reality – has to be modified too:

> Here, then, more than in any other single film, is found Kurosawa's central theme: the world is illusion, you yourself make reality, but this reality undoes you if you submit to being limited by what you have made. The important corollary – you are not, however, truly subject to this reality, you can break free from it, can live even closer to the nature you are continually creating – this occurs only in the later films. (Richie 1969, p. 227)

Richie strengthens his case for this by two strategies: one is by compiling tables of the various stories and who could be lying, arguing that this does not produce coherence (Richie 1972, pp. 76–82); his other strategy is to appeal to his (peerless) knowledge of Kurosawa's other work:

> In all of Kurosawa's pictures there is this preoccupation with the conflict between illusion (the reactions of the five and their stories) and reality (the fact of rape and murder). To do something is to realize that it is far different from what one had thought. To have done something and then to explain it completes the cycle, because this too is (equally) different from what the thing itself was. Given a traumatic experience, one fraught with emotional connotations (murder, falling in love, bankruptcy, rape), reality escapes even more swiftly. (1969, p. 225)

It has already been indicated how this idealism is both unsatisfactory in itself and not to be foisted on the film. The film could equally be treated, like *Citizen Kane*, as less one advancing a philosophy and more one that criticizes other philosophies and leaves us with a problem-situation. In this case the criticism is not of theories of the nature of the person, but rather of the eye-witness.

Gombrich (1982, pp. 252–3) has argued that the Greeks discovered the 'eye-witness principle' which demands that a painting show nothing that could not have been seen by an eye-witness to events. The eye-witness is assumed to be in a fixed position. This principle applies to films as long as they were made by single takes of all the film in a camera. But as soon as trick shots (stopping and starting the camera) and the cut were employed, there arose the possibility of shifting the point of view from one eye-witness to several. These constraints do not seem to have lasted very long, since, presumbably drawing from the stage and the novel, films quickly showed us some events from impossible eye-witness points, ubiquitous in time and space. In *Citizen Kane*, Kane's friend Leland describes the deterioration of Kane's first marriage, but the scenes we witness are their conjugal breakfasts over a period of nine years when no-one else was present, certainly not Leland, who did not live with them.

In *Rashomon* this same shift has taken place. Some of the stories are clearly narrated by someone, others not. In the synopsis I quoted on p.299 it says only the story told by the dead man through the medium is 'probably' told by the priest. Kurosawa does not, and need not, make it clear just who is speaking. And he nests all the stories into the eye-witness view of the film itself, which shows us the gate from a distance, the rain beating down, the figures sheltering under it, a viewpoint not belonging to any of the characters. The question of point of view is one of the most intriguing in movie construction. Our other films, *Persona* and *Annie Hall*, also reveal highly intricate manipulations of point of view.

Not being the scholar Gombrich is, I have no conjecture as to the origins of this freeing of cinema from the eye-witness principle, a freeing that allows it to be reinstated whenever the film maker chooses. It certainly is a means whereby movies come much closer to the freedom of the novelist than of the painter. *Rashomon*, then, could be looked on as *reductio* of the eye-witness principle. To show its absurdity you need two conditions: an event highly emotionally charged, and one involving several people. Allow some time to pass then try to reconstruct the chain of events and, however sincere the witnesses are, their stories will not be completely congruent. How, then, shall we decide on the truth of things? Perhaps we will never get to the bottom of it. But the bandit admitted enough to be executed; the woman is guilty enough to feel badly; and the woodcutter shows that this conundrum need not be used as an excuse for cynicism or inaction when dire emergencies arise.

What Harris's formulation of the problem overlooks is the baby incident at the end of the film. An abandoned baby, crying, is a helpless human being in need. No way exists for these people to identify who it truly belongs to and hence who should look after it. Besides, its needs do not wait for such decisions. The woodsman/onlooker who may have misbehaved, while bemoaning his poverty, is nevertheless the one who acts, who takes on the baby with the argument, 'what difference does one more mouth make?' The man of toil cuts through the knot of philosophizing to act in a humane and decent way. Something he did not do in the forest, that is, try to help the samurai and his wife when they were beset. For all the farrago of what really happened, is Kurosawa trying to direct attention to taking responsibility? Is he elevating action over thought? Is there an element of expiation by the woodcutter in assuming responsibility for the baby?

Can it be, then, that *Rashomon* is only on first glance an epistemological film, which turns out, on second glance, to be a moral film (as McDonald 1983 argues)? Perhaps a moral film with an immoral philosophy? It is easy to show that the elevation of action above thought is, as a generalization, foolish and immoral. It is also confused because, as I have argued elsewhere, thought is a form of action. That technical point aside, what of the elevation of action, practice? To respond to the urgent cries of a baby is one thing; to adopt it is another. The farmer needs to give thought to his wife and to his other children and what their views will be, not to mention the relatives of the baby. Its mother may have abandoned it, but what of the father, or relations of the mother's? They may be prepared to take it. Such speculation probably sounds absurd. It is not. It is an argument to show that because an urgent action needs to override contemplative thought, it does not follow that contemplative thought is vitiated. To take on someone else's baby is an act that has consequences for many other people and those consequences should figure in any final or long-term decision or action. Action is not exhausted by the notion of immediate response, it also has a longer-term sense. Both must be discussed in relation to thought.

All three men sheltering under the Rashomon gate are engaged in a quest for knowledge of what really happened. But this epistemological quest is framed in scenes involving shelter from rain, the discovery of the abandoned baby, the commoner's stripping it of clothes, the woodsman deciding to accept responsibility for it and so reviving the priest's faith in human nature and the sun breaking through, all of which suggest a moral, rather than an epistemological, quest as the film's thesis. What of attitude and general philosophical framework? The strangely Westernized music, a bravura camera style (much given to travelling shots of the back of the necks or of the sun seen through the forest canopy), tight compositions and a stylized acting style give me at least the impression that Kurosawa's attitude to events is detached, even playful. He slightly alters his style for each story, echoing the fact that each is a recollection by a different person. The framing story, however, is put over firmly, as though to carry the authorial signature. Since Kurosawa wrote the script as well as cast and directed the film, this point of structure can be interpreted as revealing of his attitude.

It only remains to say that, in accord with (RI 13), the testimony of Kurosawa is now available. Autobiography is a notoriously unreliable form, but cannot be ignored. Kurosawa tells how, before the film began shooting, three assistant directors of the Daiei company complained to him that they could not understand the script. Writing over thirty years later, he recalls telling them:

> Human beings are unable to be honest with themselves about themselves. They cannot talk about themselves without embellishing. This script portrays such human beings – the kind who cannot survive without lies to make them feel they are better people than they really are. It even shows this sinful need for flattering falsehood going beyond the grave – even the character who dies cannot give up his lies when he speaks to the

living through a medium. Egoism is a sin the human being
carries with him from birth; it is the most difficult to redeem.
This film is like a strange picture scroll that is unrolled and
displayed by the ego. You say that you can't understand this
script at all, but that is because the human heart itself is
impossible to understand. If you focus on the impossibility of
truly understanding human psychology and read the script one
more time, I think you will grasp the point of it. (1982, p. 183)

A moral tale after all, then.

On the philosophical framework of this film I shall say nothing.
It is a Japanese film of the immediate post-second world war
period, and my ignorance of the philosophical presuppositions of
Japanese culture is complete. Kurosawa is a somewhat Westernized director and it might be possible to explore the impact of
Western thought on him, on Japan and Japanese movies, but it
needs the talents of a Ruth Benedict.

What I have tried to show in these remarks about *Rashomon* is
that it is a highly thought-provoking film that should not be
convicted hastily of espousing the cheap philosophy of relativism.
It may do so, but, like its own plot, such a judgment requires the
marshalling of evidence and argument, and there may be no
conclusive demonstration possible, only a hierarchy of false
approximations. The really tough question is this: does the film
medium allow detachment? Can we allow Kurosawa to be at one
remove from his material (RI 1)? Can its philosophy be this: here
is an intriguing plot structure? A simple event which sustains four
discrepant versions. How can they be reconciled? One way is to set
aside thought and attend to human necessities. Is that a viable or
merely an issue-side-stepping strategy?

14
PERSONA: THE PERSON AS A MASK

> The people in my films are exactly like myself – creatures of
> instinct, of rather poor intellectual capacity, who at best, only
> think while they are talking. Mostly they're body, with a little
> hollow for the soul. My films draw on my own experience;
> however inadequately based logically and intellectually.
>
> (Bergman 1973, p. 190)

> I am intuitive, I have my radar. But when I have to talk and
> explain things, I think that I think. I am most of all intuitive
> and I have trained intuition; I trust it and I always use it in my
> profession, but I don't discuss with it. So my intuition is my
> best weapon and my best tool.
>
> (Bergman quoted in Simon 1972, p. 38)

> S. That was a very concrete image, visually; but what it meant
>   metaphysically was not quite so clear.
> B. To me that is not so interesting.
>
> (Simon 1972, p. 38)

When Ingmar Bergman's film *Persona* was released in 1966, to
almost immediate acclaim, the writer/director was already an
established figure in the international world of films. For a time, in
the late 1950s and 1960s, he was the darling of what the Americans
call 'the art house audience'. His 1956 film, *The Seventh Seal*, had
had considerable impact worldwide, and he was closely watched
after that. But in fact, like Kurosawa in 1950, Bergman already
had a substantial body of work behind him in 1956, when

'discovered' by the rest of the world, and *Persona* (1966) was his twenty-seventh feature film. Bergman was 48.

I have deliberately and unself-consciously written the preceding paragraph as though Bergman were unproblematically the author of his films. To an extent this is true. He mostly writes his own scripts, is completely in charge of casting, indeed declares that he cannot finish a script until he knows who will play the roles. Bergman himself compares film making to the building of medieval cathedrals, structures that may not be finished until several generations of contributors have died. This is not excessive modesty on his part, but a way of drawing attention to the special way he works in Sweden. An established writer and theatre director, and a famous man, he knows well most of the people in theatre and film. Yet time and again his key collaborators are the same: the director of photography, Sven Nykvist, and the editor, Ulla Ryghe, have worked with him on film after film. Over the years the other personnel change, but rarely with any abruptness. The manner of their collaboration suggests an admiration of, and respect for, his work that has to infect it and contribute to its success. His own comments show that what he is striving for in each script is discussed carefully with all the key people in the unit, including leading players, well before shooting begins. In *Persona* this manifests itself in an intensity of effect that is eerie because it is unspoken. I am not referring to the paucity of dialogue but, I suspect, to the lack of orders by the director. The film gives one the feeling of an intimate triangle of the director and the two actresses working on intuition to put together a completely disciplined film that is yet difficult to articulate in words.

Having dug myself into that hole, I now am ready for more words – what else? – to discuss the film. It has a simple plot.

Paraphrase N

Persona (Sweden 1966)**** Liv Ullman, Bibi Andersson, Gunnar Bjornstrand. Director Ingmar Bergman's masterpiece is less enigmatic today, seeming emotionally direct and thematically accessible. Ullmann is an actress who has decided to remain mute; her babbling nurse is played by Andersson as a surrogate for our decent impulses and petulant disappointments. There is no more moving expression of spiritual anguish in cinema. (81 mins)

(Scheuer's *Movies on TV*)

> ### Paraphrase O
>
> A famous actress is suddenly struck dumb in the middle of a performance of *Electra*. She is hospitalized and found sound in body and mind, she just won't talk. A young nurse is assigned to be her companion and to accompany her to a summer cottage on a remote island to see if the peace and quiet will effect any change. The two women at first develop a good relationship, but then severe tensions spoil it. They quarrel and part and it seems, although it is not quite clear, that in the final scenes the actress is back at work.

When I lecture about this film I ask my students how they think it was written. My own guess is that the writer was struck by certain images and situations and simply allowed them to develop in his imagination, forging a scenario that was not consciously plotted in advance. How encouraging, then, to find, in a 1973 book, Bergman confessing just this. Suffering from Ménière's disease, in early 1966 he was hospitalized and miserable for months and cancelled plans to film his script 'The Cannibals'. During an evening at his doctor's home he saw a slide of Bibi Andersson and the Norwegian actress Liv Ullmann sunbathing together and was struck by their likeness. He associates his giddiness (a symptom of the disease) with the idea of writing something in which two people lose their identities in each other. He spoke to his producer, who asked him what the idea is about. Bergman said, 'Well, it's about one person who talks and one who doesn't, and they compare hands and get all mingled up in one another' (Bergman 1973, p. 196). The idea of comparing hands had simply come suddenly to him, as had their wearing big hats.

Without asserting in any way that his authority is unchallengeable (RI 13), I would contend that Bergman in this one quoted sentence gives the best possible description of the film. There is an enormous amount going on in the film, between the two women, between them and the director and between the three of them and the audience, but it has very little to do with plot. For example, the running plot is not will Anna get Elisabet to talk again, even though she does try and does succeed. Rather are we sensitive to their isolation and dependence on each other, hence warmed by their initial good feeling and perturbed by the tension and develops between them and anxious to see it resolved.

There are two other layers to the philosophical problematic of this film that I want to separate: its framing, and critical reaction. But before that some more about Bergman himself. He confesses to being a nervous, hysterical personality, subject to moods and depressions. His films deal with the whole range of emotions, and sometimes utilize actors letting go in a way they seldom do in anyone else's films. And yet. . . . Yet Bergman is a playwright, an author, a theatre director and a film maker, at all of which he is prolific, and all of which are jobs that demand a certain kind of discipline and organization. The attitude that comes over in his biographies and interviews is of a high-powered but totally professional and unpretentious craftsmen:

> When I start writing a new picture, or start shooting or cutting it, or when I release it to the audience, it's always the first time, and always the last time. It's an isolated event, and I never think backward and forward; it's just that. Of course, I have amassed a lot of experience over twenty-five or twenty-six years and thirty pictures and, of course, I have a lot of hopes and desires about what I want to do with what is still far away; but my relation to my work, my film work and my theatre work, is completely un-neurotic. I'm just a professional; I'm just a man who makes a table or something that is to be used. Whether it is good or bad, a masterpiece or a mess, has nothing to do with the making, with my creative mind. So my reply is [to Simon's question as to whether it bothers him being the greatest film maker in the world – Simon's view]: I feel responsible only for the craftsmanship being good, for the thing having the moral qualities of my mind, and, if possible, for my not telling any lies. Those are my only demands. When I make my pictures, I never place myself in relation to the New Wave or to my other pictures, or to Fellini, or to the cultural situation in the world today, or to television, or anything else. I just make my picture. Because if I started to think this way and that, there would be no picture. So, I have all my difficulties, and get all my joy, just handling the material. (Simon 1972, pp. 11–12)

Attentive readers of this book, and those familiar with my 1967 and 1981 articles on objectivity and creativity, will be able to imagine my thrill on reading this passage. Here is a writer-director whose interest in people and feelings is intense, who toys openly with philosophical and psychological themes, who is a disciplined creator with a strong claim to be among the finest film makers yet seen, displaying a modest, professional and utterly rational attitude to his work. His whole case rests on a distinction that resembles one Popper makes between the logic of science and the psychology of science. Popper argues that thoughts and ideas are not science, hence questions of their origin or inspiration, while biographically interesting, cannot legitimate them as science. So whether they came in a dream, a brainwave, or were synthesized from data inductively, is all irrelevant to their scientific status. To achieve that they have to address a problem and offer a testable solution that improves on previous ones and survives testing.

Can we translate this argument to art? It is simple enough. Whether Bergman's work is art, whether great or not, whether he is the greatest film maker alive, are all logically irrelevant to him ('has nothing to do with the making, with my creative mind'). He works on his films to the best of his ability as a craftsman, dedicating himself to making it as well as he can. This does not make it either art or good. As in science, the decision as to the worth of a work, and hence the worth of the person behind it, takes place in the public domain, is a function of tradition and social institutions. If one becomes intimidated by one's reputation (or lack of it) paralysis may set in. Bergman's comments on other film makers are pithy and to the point. My own wish would be to ask him whether he thought Chaplin, for example, ruined himself by struggling to live up to his own internalized version of what was emerging as his reputation. Sudden access of fame and fortune create a crisis often enough; but so do praise and reputation with the peer group. It is notable that Bergman flirted with but rejected Hollywood offers, and only filmed outside of Sweden when forced to by a dispute with the government over income taxes.

In this manner Bergman keeps a perspective on his work as well as a perspective on life itself. Questioned about why he lives on Faro, he points out that things get out of proportion in the intense atmosphere of the capital city, where his every doing and pronouncement is hung upon, and he is constantly distracted by social life. Asked by Simon about death he gives the same answer, that to fear it is to get yourself out of proportion, but that on an isolated island you realize that things go on.

Reporting on himself Bergman notes that at other times he has been more neurotic and self-conscious and haunted by religious ideas and bad dreams. But he has found immersion in his work a self-cure needing to be followed by a further self-cure for workaholism.

With these background remarks out of the way I turn back to the film and its philosophy. One complete aspect of the film was not mentioned in my earlier sketch, Paraphrase O, of its plot and wordless theme. It opens in a most unusual way. The two carbons of an arc light come closer and a spark lights between them; the wheels of a projector start; film rushes through its gate; the camera shoots straight into its flashing light; and then we see a rapid series of shots that can be described but which, cut together, create a different effect on each viewer: 'You can interpret it any way you like. As with any poem. Images mean different things to different people' (Bergman 1973, p. 199).

Bergman says various other things about the film. That his intended title was *Kinematograph*, but his producer objected. That when he felt a bit better he completed the second half of the script in a fortnight! He had a lot of trouble when shooting began in the studio, with lingering fatigue and illness, but things went swimmingly on location and his idea of blending the faces of the actresses – the most famous image in the film – came there, when he was looking at shots with half of each woman's face in shadow. He also says clearly that the opening 'poem', which is resumed in the middle and concludes the film, was always part of it.

While I was working on *Persona*, I had it in my head to make a poem, not in words but in images, about the situation in which *Persona* had originated. I reflected on what was important, and began with the projector and my desire to set it in motion. . . . [Even projection is not automatic!]

But when the projector was running, nothing came out of it but old ideas, the spider, God's lamb, all that dull old stuff. My life just then consisted of dead people, brick walls, and a few dismal trees out in the park.

In the hospital one has a strong sense of corpses floating up through the bedstead. Besides which I had a view of the morgue, people marching in and out with little coffins, in and out.

So I made believe I was a little boy who'd died, yet who wasn't allowed to be really dead, because he kept on being woken up by telephone calls from the Royal Dramatic Theatre. Finally he became so impatient he lay down and read a book. All that stuff about The Hero of our Time struck me as rather typical – the overstrained official lying on his sickbed. Well, all this is trivial. But that's how it works – and suddenly two faces are floating into one another. And that's where the film begins. (Bergman 1973, p. 199)

My own memory is that the first images projected are upside-down cartoons, followed by a slapstick farce in which a skeleton is chasing a man in a nightshirt, who hides in bed; there is a spider, hands holding a lambs head while its throat is slit, hands rummaging in entrails, bringing the eye of the beast close to the camera; a hand holding another through which a nail is being driven, then bleak landscape shots of a wall, trees, railings, snow, rocks, then corpses in a morgue, a boy, an old woman, an old man; the woman's eyes snap open, the boy wakes to the telephone, tries to sleep, looks at the camera, puts on his glasses to read, turns and reaches for the lens, and we see he is touching a high key projection of a face, which is in turn that of each of the women in the film; these faces are interspersed with titles. It fades to white, and from white to the door of a hospital office through which comes nurse Alma to be given her assignment.

In the middle of the film, when the two women have quarrelled bitterly, one wounding the other, the image freezes, appears to burn as when the projector jams, then tears into whiteness. A few more shots from the slapstick film, the devil clearly seen, whiteness, the impaled hand again, a figure out of focus, which becomes Elisabet, a musical note on the soundtrack. At the end, as Alma leaves the cottage, we see a quick shot of Elisabet back in make-up as Electra, a shot fractionally different from the cut-in during Alma's interview at the beginning (as a comparison of the stills in Bergman (1973) p. 199, and Simon (1972) pp. 218, 285 makes clear), two men on a camera crane, Elisabet upside-down in the viewfinder. Alma leaves on the bus, the camera looks at the rocks, which lap dissolve to the boy reaching for the face, the film stopping in the projector, the arc breaking and the carbon rods cooling and fading. Over all of these scenes the sound-track consists of music and basically natural sound, mostly of the projector, or of the studio noises, or of the hammer driving the nail through the palm. The studio and projection noises return over the final sequence.

Persona is, of course, a film; indeed, to repeat, one Bergman planned to call 'Kinematograph'. Film as a subject, as its own subject, the magic of film to adult and child, clearly fascinates all film makers, or, might one say, that many film makers were drawn to film from a childhood fascination? Bergman has often told of his own delight at first playing with a projector. The cut-away in the middle, where the film breaks and burns, is reminiscent of how, in *La Ronde*, Max Ophuls has his narrator interrupt a sexy scene by holding celluloid in front of us and trimming out several frames as unsuitable viewing before letting the story continue.[1] Bergman's images have more intensity, but are equally related to what is happening on screen and both the film maker's and the audience's attitudes. The intensity of the conflict between the women is very hard to bear:

> The film snaps and the projector comes to a stop. Inspiration had suddenly dried up on me. That was in May, when I got ill again, and the whole thing had come to a stop. (Bergman 1973, p. 202)

Bergman, by the way, is recollecting the events surrounding this film in an interview three years later. *Persona* was made very quickly, shot in July and August 1966 and premièred in Stockholm on 18 October.

The boy, as we have been told in the quotation above, is Bergman; but then again he is us (reaching towards the screen) and the screen actors (when he reaches towards the lens). The entire set of these framing shots could be taken quite easily to distance us from the psychological drama, yet it does not do so. Just as we snap into a film as the lights dim and the titles roll, so we snap into and out of Bergman's drama as it starts, unfolds, stops, resumes, and so on. Eye-witness point of view, self-consciousness, scarcely disrupt our ability to 'enter in' to the movie.[2]

At this point we have enough background information to

undertake the major project, which is to look at the film as philosophy. In earlier writings on Bergman I have always been an admirer of his dramatic and psychological powers, and his film making skills (Jarvie 1959, 1963). But, when I wrote, his themes were reverting again and again to religion, a subject with which I have very little sympathy. Hence I was rather harsh on him as a philosopher, little realizing that I was criticizing interpretation of his films rather than the films themselves. This *mea culpa* out of the way, what of the film in general? What philosophical problem does it tackle? That of personal identity, I suppose. The problem is a vast one consisting of, among others, the following:

- Are there other minds?
- Are there other persons?
- A child changes into an adult, is it the same person?
- Can two people share the same identity?
- Is it a sign of ego strength to be uninfluenced by others, or to absorb that influence?

Impressed by the similar looks of the two actresses, Bergman began to write a script in which two very different women, a simple nurse and a famous, intelligent actress, begin to learn about similarity and difference.

> Elisabet is intelligent, she's sensible, she has emotions, she is immoral, she is a gifted woman, but she's a monster, because she has an emptiness in her. (Simon 1972, p. 32)

She feeds on Alma a little bit, and she can go on.

To concentrate their differences Bergman allows one to talk, the other not to. Both the psychiatrist and Alma are quickly alert to the egotism of Elisabet's silence, and her coldness to the distress it causes her husband and son. Yet Alma is no plaster saint: she blurts out an erotic tale of an encounter on a beach and the abortion that followed, only, towards the end of the film, to suggest that Elisabet also tried to abort her own child, failed, but then also failed to love it. The trouble in their relationship comes when Alma, too curious, reads a letter Elisabet has written to her psychiatrist. The immorality of her action is ambiguous: as a friend she should simply have mailed the letter; but Elisabet did not seal it, and, as her psychiatric nurse, Alma may need to know the contents (what is she telling the doctor of her progress?). She finds

316

the letter condescending, implying that Elisabet is amused by this simple nurse who is a little in love with her. In rage, Alma leaves a shard of broken glass in Elisabet's path and precipitates a confrontation. From here on their relations will be stormy. For Elisabet's immorality and emptiness has evoked echoes in Alma, who feels guilty and tries desperately to repair the friendship. To no avail. Haunted by Elisabet in dreaming and waking she seems to blend herself into the other. Later the therapy has worked; we see Alma coaxing Elisabet to say 'nothing' (a nice paradoxical play on her silence), and we seem to glimpse her back on the stage.

The film lends itself to many readings of its attitude, none of which it can be said categorically to assert, since not all of them are consistent with each other. This poses most acutely a serious methodological problem raised earlier: how can the critic avoid merely projecting his own preoccupations or free associations on to the film, so that it becomes not a film containing ideas that happens to trigger such-and-so ideas in the person experiencing it? Some might answer that that is all a work can ever do, but I am disinclined to accept this view as it would make it rather difficult to assess ideas that differed from person to person.

It is tempting, for example, to interpret the actress Elisabet as standing for artists or artistic endeavour (possibly for Bergman himself). Alma voices admiration for artists and concedes art is important as therapy. John Simon (1972) asked Bergman about this and the latter replied, 'For heaven's sake no' (p. 32). In accord with my basic methodological principles about not rejecting good evidence (RI 3, RI 13), I suggest this denial be taken at face value. Simon (on p. 304) has the temerity to reject it with no more argument than that he finds the theme of the relation between artist and audience running through several of Bergman's films, and Bergman may have a bad conscience about his personal and professional treatment of women. These arguments are not good enough. Both could be projections of the preoccupations of Simon rather than Bergman. Nothing in the film permits us to generalize from Elisabet to art in general, any more than from Alma to ordinary nurses in general.

Simon at least acknowledges that the film can be taken to be saying many things, and some that we are hard put to articulate. He denies that the film can be read as all in the mind of Alma, for there are two important scenes where we, the audience, are alone with Elisabet. In the first, she is in her hospital room and sees on television the self-immolation of a Vietnamese bonze. She presses herself into the corner of the room and whimpers. In the other she is alone at the cottage staring at a famous newspicture of German soldiers rounding up Jewish women and children in the Warsaw ghetto. Clutching her hands together she gazes at the picture intently and Bergman treats us to a brilliant photo-analysis of the picture and its details. Critics tend to read these scenes as anguished. It makes just as good sense to see them as Elisabet asking herself why she does not feel the things she thinks she ought. She has callously left her husband and son, has been unfeeling to Alma, refuses to talk to her and has been told by everyone that this is supreme selfishness. Bergman himself has commented that she is an empty person (p. 316, above).

Let me now analyse two sentences from Simon's essay which summarizes his entire reading of the film, and which highlight the grave weaknesses of methodology I have been concerned with. He is arguing that the whole film flows from the opening shots:

> In some sense, then, the crone's awakening into life, Alma's setting out on what seems to be a series of dreams or visions, and Elisabet's being photographed in a film within a film correspond to one another. Bergman seems to be saying that life, dream, and art are identical: that being born, having visions, creating a role or some other work of art are basically equivalent activities. (Simon 1972, p. 303)

The tentativity – 'seems' – is admirable (RI 7), the rest less so. The proposition, 'being born, having visions, creating a role or some other work of art are basically equivalent activities', strikes me as sheer equivocation. False, certainly; easily reinterpretable as trivially true; hence little more than a string of words used for effect. Everything is similar to everything else under one aspect or another, so to assert parallels is to assert very little except within a specific context. 'Equivalent' is much the same sort of slippery word: something is equivalent to something else not once and for all but only for certain purposes. What possible purposes could make equivalent birth, visions, art? The necessities of windy critical parlance, perhaps? To foist this vaporness on Bergman is an offence that comes oddly from an admirer who prides himself on his verbal skills and who has been priviledged to interview him.

But Simon is not intimidated by Bergman, as we have seen; finding no difficulty in setting aside Bergman's answer to Simon's questions, however categorical those answers be (p. 317, above).

I propose a different methodology (RI 4). See the film and amass all relevant evidence, including the views of the film maker, and try to interpret the film in a way that is consistent with all that evidence. The more evidence the interpretation can unify and make coherent the better it is; the more evidence that it cannot incorporate the worse it is. When Bergman says *Persona* is not about art and artists I take it that he means this was not a preoccupation while he was writing the script and that, having cut and viewed the finished film, it is not an interpretation he finds very illuminating. As a liberal he allows viewers to make of his work what they will. But the critic, writing about the work for now and posterity, needs to be a little more responsible. The evidence does not go away because the critic likes to free associate in certain ways. And to foist on an author, to say what he seems to be 'saying', and then to complete the sentence with high-sounding emptiness is unserious.

Robin Wood, a critic of a wholly different stripe, offers interpretations with which Simon disagrees. These amount to saying that the film is about the merging of two representative consciousnesses or the breaking down of the protective facades people erect to defend themselves from reality (Wood 1969, p. 147). Once more we approach the sort of thing to which professional philosophers are allergic. Alma is taken to represent normality, 'us'; Elisabet is taken to have a deeper and more acute 'awareness' (is awareness not transitive?). Thus Wood, the structure of whose argument is very similar to Simon's, namely a recounting of the film more or less in temporal order – with digressions to take in parallel scenes and in order to give interpretations – saddles the film with the message that it shows two people's minds merging. 'But Robin,' one wants to say to Wood, 'minds cannot *merge*, any more than an actor *becomes* his role or a film-goer *enters* a film. All this is metaphor, metaphor cut through by Bergman when he said simply that Elisabet is an empty person who has fed upon Alma and will be able to go on, but that Alma, not as weak as she had estimated, will go on too.' If our critical friends want a metaphor, a better one would be a blood transfusion, one that fits naturally to the scenes where Alma tears

319

her own flesh and Elisabet sucks the wound. The donor recovers, the recipient of the transfusion is able to go on.

Wood said something else, about people defending themselves from reality. Do they? And what is 'reality' in this assertion? Elisabet confronts some horrible events, but is not unaware of, or defending herself from, them. Alma seems very much in touch with herself and able to absorb the brutalizing entailed in this phase of her job. But Wood has odd standards: 'the fate of a Lear . . . is more endurable to contemplate than that of the slaughtered women and children of Vietnam'. This is breast-beating, of course, and has nothing to do with Ingmar Bergman. It is part of the opening of Wood's piece where he ruminates about awful things, such as napalming, and philosophizes about the twentieth century, which, he says, has 'discovered (or thinks it has discovered)' the meaninglessness and chaos of existence. This premise leads him to mistakes of interpretation that are quite clear cut. He says that in reaction to the burning monk on television and the photograph of the Nazi round-up, Elisabet recoils from the horror of existence itself in which such events have become *everyday* (p. 146).

It is hard to know where to start. Centuries, not being thinkers, do not 'discover' things. Meaninglessness and chaos are interpretations, not things, and so are imposed, not discovered. Elisabet whimpers at the television images but shows little reaction to the photograph (RI 1, KRI). The horror Wood feels is all his own. He has missed Bergman's point: Elisabet's inadequate reactions are in contrast to the audience's presumably more adequate reactions. Existence as such is not horrible, and monk-burning and genocide are not *everyday* (RI 12). Rather is it the case that changes in communication technology make the horrors of remote parts of the world quickly and widely known. Horrors of existence were far more everyday in medieval Europe than in the twentieth century.

Wood concludes by hailing Bergman for being:

sensitively (hence very painfully) alive to the pressures and tensions of the world we all have to live in, who has been able through his courage and intelligence to convert a private anguish into a universal witness, while remaining intensely human. He exposes himself fully to the despair and horror that man must confront if there is ever to be a possibility of passing beyond.

For all the anguish and the sense of deep hurt, there is a marvellously sensitive feeling, at once dynamic and compassionate, for human potentialities, for the development of consciousness. Toward the end of the film Alma, incoherently babbling nonsense-phrases, lets slip the words 'A desperate perhaps'. And that is exactly what *Persona* is. (1969, p. 67)

I can leave comment on such a passage to Bergman, who, after admitting he was making fun of Alma's reverent attitude to artists, says:

But it's just the sort of thing one hears. Where one feels most touched, and gets most furious, is when one hears people, decent people, who go toddling off to the theatre and fill the concert halls and go to evening classes, say: 'I've an enormous respect for artists and I love art and I think art is terribly important to people who're suffering'. There they sit patiently, patiently, waiting to be edified. But usually the artists, with their enormous vanity, are less interesting than the people who are sitting there waiting for them to edify them. I loathe the whole of this humble attitude towards artists, *who really ought to be given a kick in the arse*. (Bergman 1973, p. 211)

And perhaps critics too, Mr Bergman?

There is a huge literature on Bergman, even bigger than that on Orson Welles, and just as I separated out the layer of the framing devices of *Persona* and argued that their reconciliation with Bergman's own account was complete, I have also engaged with fellow critics on the grounds (RI 10) that this is what treating interpretation as a rational activity consists in. Once more, as noted in discussing *Kane*, and as should have been implicitly clear in discussing *Rashomon*, I have engaged with critics whose work made me think hardest and hence disagree most sharply. As a final address to the literature on Bergman I want to take up the most recently published monograph, one more closely argued and more wide-ranging in its materials than most.

Paisley Livingston's *Ingmar Bergman and the Rituals of Art* (1982) could be described as a literary-anthropological interpretation of Bergman. Bergman is something of a philosopher of culture and this explains why Livingston dips into those other sources of thinking about culture, anthropologists. The baneful presence in all philosophizing about culture is Hegel (Gombrich 1969), who Livingston avoids by treating us instead to doses of Adorno. Luckily, Bergman comes out as superior to Adorno, whose high-culture snobbery and conceit scarcely fit him to be discussed on the same page with Bergman. If there is anyone at whose arse Bergman's foot should be directed . . .

If Bergman is to be 'read' as a philosopher of culture – presumably 'our' culture in a sense that embraces Sweden and North America – then the first question is what are the problems of culture about which he is philosophizing? Here is where one risks being swamped in metaphysics. It seems that for Livingston there are two problems of culture; one is that our culture is in a crisis – specification of that crisis and proposals to deal with it are problematic. In addition to the culture in general there is a problem with culture in the narrow sense – where it is a synonym for the arts. This second problem could be formulated in one word: 'modernism'. Of all the isms in the aesthetician's vocabulary this is one of the most overworked. 'Modernism' is the philosophy of modern art. Modern art begins somewhere in the nineteenth century, possibly with impressionism, and is taken to be some sort of sea-change in art, a sharp break from all that went before, revolutionary or radical in all its aspects: form, content, expectation, social value. Again, specifying in what this modernism consists and figuring out the position of art and the artist is problematic.

'Cultural crisis' is of course a metaphor. What arguments are there for talking the metaphor seriously? This is an impossible subject to enter, since everything from industrialization to the rise of National Socialism has been held to be symptomatic of the cultural crises. Instead of treating it seriously my own inclination is to look at (not the problem of crisis in the culture but) the problem of why there is so much talk – among those in the culture business in the narrower sense – of culture crisis. My aim, were this treatment to be extended, would be to show that Bergman is virtually untouched by all this talk, despite having exposure to it, and that his work can be interpreted far less portentously.

If art comes from magical and religious origins, as Cavell tells us, and once had an organic place in the community, which was itself organic, as Leavis tells us (and Wood has a motto from

Leavis to his chapter on *Persona*), then there are two extensive social changes that have made a lot of difference. The first is industrialization. This altered the basic organization of social life and, since it has yet to spread throughout the globe, may not have finished with us yet. Industrialization displaced the classes among which artists used to dwell, and gradually eroded the patrons they serviced. By the late nineteenth century, plastic artists could no longer apprentice, had to seek formal education or self-educate, and were lacking the subject matter and patronage once supplied by the aristocracy and the Church. To some extent this involved downward mobility: the genius-starving-in-the-garret syndrome. Almost as a compensation device artists staked claims to being 'the conscience of the human race'[3] (Livingston 1982, p. 182), in other words not just to socially superior status, but to a morally superior status from which they would tell the rest of us what's what and what should be done about it.

Let us call this view the Artist as Pundit. To an extent the punditry was in the art, most obviously in works of literature. Music and the plastic arts often needed exegesis if their punditry was to be understood. Hence the growth of art that consists of artists pronouncing on what they are doing, why and how their work is to be interpreted (Wolfe 1975).

A naive reading would distinguish such commentary from creative work. It would be less naive to allow that creative input on the part of the artists goes into both the works and the, so to say, secondary works, such as manifestos, notes, interviews, proclamations, letters and so on. It is not just that the art needs explaining, it is that the explanation is part of the work of the artist, therefore part of the art. This enables a secondary industry to arise, namely commentary on the art. This is partly created by the artists and partly by a new class of pundits who go by the name critics.[4] Naturally, since livelihoods are at stake, there is a good deal of ambivalence in the relations between artists and critics, especially while both are living.

Notice that the machine side of the industrial revolution, whether in creating new art forms or in making cheap reproduction possible, is unimportant in this context. What is important is the social displacement of the artist and his loss of bearings. He not only does not know where his next crust will come from, he does not know what the subject of his next painting will be. Forced on to his own resources, he is also forced to keep up a running commentary in lieu of the expectations usually induced by tradition and convention.[5]

The other major change is also brought about by industrialization and that is change itself. Industrialization has not spawned a new society that has settled into place. Rather has it spawned a new society that refuses to settle. And by some measures the rate of change seems to be accelerating. Trying to get new bearings in a craft is not likely to be easy. Modernism thus becomes a portmanteau-word for all the turmoil and change and new experiments in art that have been going on for a century. Each new school comes and goes and is hailed and forgotten. Some of the work stands the test of time, some does not. To the artist the issues are urgent, since the question is what to do, what direction to take. To the spectator there is all the time in the world, since there is plenty of old stuff to occupy us while we try to decide if the new is any good, and we can complacently say to the artist that he has the cart before the horse. He becomes an artist by creating work; he is not an artist first with something to say coming later.

One way out of the dilemma of what to do is to make the question, 'what to do?', into part of, or the subject of, the art. Thus paintings can be about painting, music about music, novels and poetry about writing. Art becomes reflexive.[6] Movies are a cultural product of the modernist era. Although they are popular art, there are highbrow fringes, and both have been influenced by the approval of self-regard: in popular films this most often takes the form of satire on other movies; in highbrow movies it takes various forms. *Citizen Kane* and *Persona* are highbrow examples of the reflexive movie; *Annie Hall*, as I shall argue, is a blend of the popular self-conscious movie satire with highbrow reflexivity.

As I mentioned earlier, suspicion of language itself, the thought that putting things into words is inherently mendacious, is one of the most bizarrely influential thoughts of this century. Livingston suggests that the actress's silence in *Persona* is an awakening to the falsehood of her art to which her solution is silence. Some critics have gone on to argue that the problem is so deep and intractable that Bergman has embodied it in a film that is inherently enigmatic, without a definite meaning. Livingston airs these views with some care, and suggests that Adorno's formulation is the best. But he rejects all of them and says Bergman goes deeper.

Elisabet's silence, after all, is exposed in the film as just another role of which she will tire – and does. Furthermore, Bergman has not himself resorted to silence; he has made a film, a film which reminds us that it is a film.

Livingston's most original move is to connect art to other ritual activities and to think about the function of ritual in relation to the maintenance of social order. Ritual is a way of policing the boundaries, a way of marking off and keeping out dangerous and disruptive forces, whether sacred or profane, and those persons in threatening states, whether outsiders or insiders. He alludes to some French sociology but completely overlooks Van Gennep whose work would have shown him that rituals limit states as well as mark boundaries: states of pollution, transition, entry and exit, ecstasy, and so on. However, his conclusion is:

> Bergman's intuition is that the frames set by art and by other cultural forms are never wholly stable, and that the same imitative practices are pursued on both sides of their boundaries. (1982, p. 217)

He thus rejects the strong sense of Wood's view that all life is role-playing, while accepting that, in a weaker sense, imitating others and ourselves is something engaged in for purposes of social maintenance and mirrored in dramatic work.

> The modernist disruptions of the formal conventions of art are transgression mimicking the gestures of ritual without understanding their context or nature. (1982, p. 221)

So far as all this is decipherable, Livingston's claim is that artists do not and cannot stand outside society, cannot make special claims to seeing through or getting away from its constraints. Their resources are themselves social facts, indeed social facts that resemble those to be found among non-artists. Hence, there is no escape, no breaking out. Art is not a case of transcending the mundane so much as part of the mundane, at least for the artist.

The thought troubles me that after castigating others for treating films as excuses for hanging out their own musings on the topic the film treats, I may have used Livingston's interesting but hard-to-summarize book as a peg on which to hang some of my own musings. It is hard to read a work in which sociological understanding is dawning without pushing it closer to a full grasp.

With apologies to Livingston and this warning to the reader, it is now time to put up or shut up. Taking what Bergman says to heart, namely, concentrate on the work not the artists, and avoid fake humility before his edifying thoughts (which may be your own edifying thoughts projected), what to do with the interpretation and assessment of this very philosophical/psychological film? First and foremost to agree that reducing it to propositional form overall is very difficult. Bits and pieces yes, but not in general. Hence it is not to be taken to be uttering general truths. In fact, this is what has confused most writers. Religious and psychological ideas were part of Bergman's early films, but here they are absent. Beginning from some images and scenes he has fashioned a drama about a nurse trying to get at a troublesome patient. Doubting her own strength, and awed by the actress's distinction compared to her own ordinariness, she is delighted when a friendship begins to grow, despite the silent treatment. The disclosures of the letter, that her patient is a good deal less admirable than she seems, and her treatment of others not so easily set aside, precipitates some more painful interactions of a wounding character. At the end she has found herself not so nice as she once thought, has been haunted by nightmares and has precipitated a confrontation where she has repeatedly struck Elisabet.

Utilizing the distinctions developed in this book, what are the quest, attitude, thesis and framework of *Persona*? The problem as I have stated it has to do with the problem of human identity: two people may look dissimilar, have different character and personality, yet influence each other, even sense a certain identity beneath the skin. Strictly speaking this is a problem-area not a problem, a problem-area that the film is engaged in exploring rather than arguing about. Each of the two women in the film undertakes a quest in this area: Elisabet, unable to tolerate her roles in life (as actress, wife, mother, speaker), retreats to silence; Anna, competent and reliable, accepts the challenge of trying to help this famous woman. Elisabet does not want to be who she is; Anna finds her solid identity shaken but intact. Their quests have altered and strengthened both of them.

What sort of attitude does the film adopt to this encounter? A complex one. There are the poetic framing images, to which I shall come shortly, and there are scenes treated realistically, others treated either as dreams or hallucinations. The combination of all three in the same film suggests to me that the attitude of the film is aesthetic – we are invited to be present at some events we only partly understand but which are both beautiful and intriguing. We are intrigued not, it seems, by the rudimentary plot, but by the psychological probing of each woman and their feelings for each other.

All the framing devices can be seen as drawing attention to what movies can do; they come to an end and we leave them, and, like Alma and Elisabet, go on. Bergman seems to have created in a sleepwalking manner a powerful film that can stand as a metaphor for whatever the spectator chooses. Metaphors are not true or false but appropriate or inappropriate. We cannot allow ourselves to argue from the ideas we have of the meaning of the metaphor over to the assertion that this is what 'Bergman' says. Bergman seems allergic to 'Bergman'. Qualifying his cathedral-builder metaphor for Simon he says that un-neurotic creation is the best:

> which is why the nineteenth-century romantic notion of original genius strikes me as very silly, and as having nothing to do with real creation. (Simon 1972, p. 38)

There remains the film's thesis and its philosophical framework. To explicate these I turn back to the framing sequence and to the general use of such devices. My aim in selecting *Casablanca*, *Citizen Kane*, *Rashomon* and *Persona* as case studies for philosophy on film was to take relatively well-known films about which there existed a body of writing with which one might enter into some sort of dialogue. A striking feature of the selection, now that we have worked through it, is how each film has a frame around it: *Casablanca* begins in documentary vein, with maps and a voice of God narrator telling us how the events of the war have led to Casablanca being a way-station for those in flight. Untidily, the film does not revert to that framework at the end, merely having Rick and Louis walk off into the fog. But *Citizen Kane* brings us back to the newsman; *Rashomon* brings us back to the men sheltering under the gate; *Persona* brings us back to the images with which it opened. We will next consider three Woody Allen films, two of which, *Annie Hall* and *Manhattan*, also use 'frames'. I want to consider the interpretative significance of this device. First a confession: it is my guess that only a minority of films use such framing devices, although I concede that if we add flashbacks and parallel action, they may then be a large minority.

It was Munsterberg, we recall, who drew attention to the special ability of film to move us deftly through time and space, either to transport us elsewhere or, more strikingly, to give us a sense of simultaneity: two courses of action are parallel, or will converge, or some memories are being rehearsed in among the present action. This could be framed as an argument in rebuttal of those critics of classic Hollywood cinema who maintain that it conceals the fact that we are watching a film. The counter-argument would go that the use of titles and framing devices is the opposite: these are attention-getting devices used to draw on the audience's imagination, to direct them to construct highly counter-intuitive connections between the scenes on the screen (time and space are rigid rather than flexible). They are very complicated versions of the standard fairy story opening, 'once upon a time . . .', as Linden points out. His metaphysics is awry, but his view that films have their own distinct ways of narrating is correct.

These framing devices work quite subtly. At the same time they draw attention to themselves and hence to the fact that a film is being experienced, while offering us means of plunging deeper into the illusion of the film. Since framing devices are themselves conventions, they reveal a manner in which films do not pretend to transparency in order to foster illusion, that they do draw attention to themselves, make us conscious of what is happening.

When discussing *Casablanca* we noted that it was Kant's view that philosophy was thinking about how thinking about things was possible. These framing devices seem to be something similar: they are filmic devices by means of which we see how filmic devices work. They work not by obliterating the distinction between film and world, by fostering the illusion that we are watching the real thing, but, on the contrary, by reminding us of the boundaries or framework we are now inside that enable us to experience the world of this film.

Husserl used to like to think there was a kind of natural, unself-consciously lived world that had to be philosophically bracketed if we were to analyse the experience of it. If this state was ever true of any real communities, they disappeared a long time ago. Our present condition is rather one of permanent bracketing, es-trangement, or alienation, putting things we might once have taken for granted in some sort of distancing frame. This may make sense of Bordwell's idea that the modern cinema is a cinema of consciousness, of Linden's idea that films are of our time. A rational way to express this is to say that some films replicate in their structuring features devices that we employ in order to experience everyday life under industrialization. Industrial society imposes on our relations with others much abstraction in a world that is largely disenchanted. Our lived world is a world of framing devices, such as the separate locations of home and work, the different activities of work and play, the changing role relations involved, the adjustments we make when crossing national borders or oceans, or contacting people by telephone. Here there is an echo of one of my earliest assertions in this book (Part 1, Chapter 1), namely that cinema-goers play at and accomplish with ease what philosophers labour mightily at failing to understand: the construction and maintenance of what we might call multiple worlds. The world we actually inhabit consists of many other worlds nested within it, and we cross from one to the other not exactly effortlessly, but dextrously, with skill. Like all skills that look easy this one of ours is acquired after much rehearsal and practice, including that of the boundary and framework crossing involved in going to films and in deciphering them once there. Film already is old technology, and other forms of frame creation and frame crossing are taking over. Nonetheless, this is the general significance I give to framing devices in the medium of the film: they are revelatory of the cultural presuppositions of our age.

15
WOODY ALLEN AND THE SEARCH FOR MORAL INTEGRITY

> The worst thing in the world could happen and he could go into that room and write.
>> (Louise Lasser on Woody Allen (Lax 1975, p. 44))

> My one regret in life is that I am not someone else.
>> (Woody Allen (Lax 1975, p. vii))

> I don't want to sound pretentious but my depression is why I'm drawn to philosophy, so acutely interested in Kafka, Dostoevski, and Bergman. I think I have all the symptoms and problems that those people are occupied with: an obsession with death, an obsession with God or the lack of God, the question of why are we here. Answers are what I want.
>> (Woody Allen (Lax 1975, p. 45))

This final section on films as vehicles for philosophy breaks quite new ground. Firstly, it is not about one film only, but several, especially Allen's 'trilogy' *Annie Hall* (1977), *Interiors* (1978), and *Manhattan* (1979). Secondly, it takes seriously a film maker who has, in the critical literature, been treated entirely as a 'comic', i.e. comedian, a description completely inapposite. Thirdly, it somewhat widens the range of philosophical topics, since *Citizen Kane*, *Rashomon* and *Persona* have been interpreted primarily in their epistemological/psychological dimensions, while Woody Allen's films seem to have more to do with moral philosophy and the search for the good life.

330

Woody Allen is the creator of his films in much the way that Ingmar Bergman is. Beginning his career as a comedy writer, continuing as a night club comedian, breaking into films in the 1960s, Allen has several times been directed by others, notably in *Play It Again Sam* (1972) and *The Front* (1976), but since 1969 has mostly directed himself. Except for *The Front*, he has also written or co-written all his screenplays.[1] Since the early 1970s he has concentrated on films, plays and short written pieces, the latter collected in books. His nightclub and TV appearances have ceased, as has his cutting of audio discs.

Whether consciously or not, his life resembles that of Ingmar Bergman. He has written and directed plays and seems to have very close relationships with a small group of actors and actresses, around whose talents he writes his screenplays. Although in his screen self-portrait there is much talk of bumbling and confusion, everything he lets slip about himself bespeaks a person of strict work habits and strong self-discipline. One of the best such pieces of evidence is the memoirs of his editor, Ralph Rosenblum, who began working with him when he was very much a learner, and who stayed with him to a point where he could declare Allen to have grasped all he had to teach about editing (Rosenblum 1979). He reports Allen to be modest and eager to learn, fascinated by the whole process of film making, unafraid to reshoot or totally alter structure, able to discard excellent scenes that did not fit the final cut. His concentration and dedication to the work and his craftsmanship were total. Exceptionally revealing is the narrative of how the widely hailed and unique film *Annie Hall* was carved out of a much larger body of material shot from a script with the unpromising title of *Anhedonia*.

Allen's film comedy is much preoccupied with films themselves and with us as viewers of them. His stage hit *Play it Again Sam* features a film critic hero who is fixated on *Casablanca* and the Humphrey Bogart character, Rick. Inept with women, he conjures up a Bogart-figure to prompt him. He falls in love with his friend's wife then gives her up in a scene consciously modelled on the renunciation-parting at the end of *Casablanca*. Although it was Allen's stage play, in which he starred, the film version was directed by Herbert Ross (Anobile 1977). Several of Allen's films have filmic or literary antecedents. *Take the Money and Run* (1969) is a spoof of *Bonnie and Clyde* (1967), *Bananas* (1971) of

Che (1969), *Sleeper* (1973) of Rip van Winkle, *Love and Death* (1975) of Russian novels and Bergman films. In *Annie Hall* his hero refuses to enter a movie theatre after the film has started, repeatedly views *The Sorrow and the Pity* (1970), and fantasizes squelching a pretentious talker about films by producing Marshall McLuhan from behind a lobby display. It would be easy to make the case that *Interiors* is Allen's *Persona*, and *A Midsummer Night's Sex Comedy* is his *Smiles of a Summer Night* (1955).

My view is that despite his origins as a comedian, Allen is, like many comedians, deeply serious, using humour to get at, as well as round, painful topics. The films he has made beginning with *Annie Hall* are all highly philosophical and craftsman-like and bear endless re-experiencing. They articulate and develop perfectly straightforward ideas about the problems they treat and show their author maturing. The first film, *Annie Hall*, is about the pains of living: Allen articulates the view that the important emotion of love, which brings such joy, is inseparable from some pain; needing the first, our problem is to survive the second. The second film, *Interiors*, is a study of the relations between three sisters, the husbands of two of them, and their parents. Each daughter is a facet of their mother, a domineering woman preoccupied with beautifying the surface of things. Her suicide may be a liberation for them all. *Manhattan* reflects on the difficulty of behaving honestly in relation to others, both friends and women, and to oneself. *Stardust Memories* (1980), which greatly puzzled audiences, is about just that: how to keep integrity with your own development when the audience has other expectations. *A Midsummer Night's Sex Comedy* seems to be a hymn to the life force. In 1983 Allen released *Zelig*, a film declaredly about extreme identity loss: Leonard Zelig is a chameleon-man. In 1984 came *Broadway Danny Rose*, a film about the connection between guilt, niceness and being a loser. *The Purple Rose of Cairo* (1985) deals directly with the relation between the real world and the screen world, *Hannah and Her Sisters* (1986) with the search for love and meaning.

Following through on my standing prescriptions, let me present some attempts at a problematic for Allen. He is a Jewish comedian born and brought up in New York. He worked in television and nightclubs as writer and performer, was the author and star of a hit Broadway play, but declares he always wanted to

332

make films. He graduated from high school, but flunked out of college and went straight into joke writing. He himself claims that his self-education was undertaken in order to communicate with the kind of girls he was attracted to. He found he liked what he read and when something interested him he went into it thoroughly.

> I am a voracious reader now. You have to read to stay alive. I read existential philosophy because it mirrors my own anxiety. It's tough, but it has a disciplinary effect and I am trying to grow slowly. (Lax 1975, p. 38)

Humour is, of course, a standard response to anxiety. If all problems are dealt with by humour there may be something wrong. But if the humorist can joke about the problems and articulate them seriously as well – cope, as it were, in both ways – then that is a sign of health. I take Allen seriously when he says he is trying to grow slowly, specifically 'trying to advance in the direction of films that are more human and less cartoon' (Jacobs 1982, p. 127). And I see nothing funny in his affirmation (*loc. cit.*) that he would ultimately aspire to tragedy. Part of the roundedness of some creators is that they try all forms, as when Bergman does both comedies and tragedies. The choice to stick in one groove, as Welles or Kurosawa did, is not one for the audience/critic to make.

As a film maker Allen is acutely conscious of what I have called film culture. Whether to Groucho Marx or to Ingmar Bergman, his films are rich with references and allusions to other films. This is most spectacularly demonstrated in *Annie Hall*, where a bewildering variety of filmic devices are smoothly integrated into the structure. So his problematic has two sides: certain philosophical questions about life and about human relations, and certain aesthetic questions about how to treat these in the form of satiric and dramatic pieces – literary, theatrical and filmic. And, of course, the two sides blend in a modernistic question as to how someone preoccupied with these questions can continue to keep his audience with him and avoid narcissism.

The problems themselves, as I shall make clear in what follows, are easy to formulate: why are we here?, why bother with love when it always fades?, what sort of obligations should friends and/or lovers undertake towards each other?, should you chase success or listen to other voices?, how to cope with depression? These

questions are often buried beneath others, on which the plot turns.
For example:

> The connections between the artist and his art, and between the
> artist and his public, the meaning and value of comedy, the
> burdens of fame, the entrapment of the popular artist within his
> persona, the exchange between art and neuroticism. (Hirsch
> 1981, p. 197)

The problems Allen is addressing can be assembled both from
biographical and self-descriptive materials, as well as from the
filmic texts. In accord with (RI 3) I argue that interpretations of
him and his work are the better the more they reconcile all of this
evidence together. My own picture is not of an Allen conducting a
carefully planned campaign of finding an outlet for his seriousness
by the subterfuge of breaking into the limelight through comedy.
My thesis is that Allen dealt with his anxieties from an early age by
means of humour – almost a tradition among Jews. This was his
avenue of escape from his background and into show business.
Seeing other people perform and seeing other people mangle his
material, he tried and succeeded in performing it himself.
Reaching a point where he no longer needed to work on
commission to pay the rent, but rather could take time to decide
what he would do next, he found his range expanding, ideas
coming to him for anything but jokes, together with an increasing
confidence that he should try it and he might succeed. When he
was younger he was much encouraged by the critics, in every
medium he tried (Lax 1975, p. 167) and he considers that of great
value. As his professional competence built, his ambition
widened. We may see the seeds of later work in the earlier, but
not, I think, a plan.

Partly because there is very little serious discussion of these
films, and partly because I need to illustrate my argument in detail,
I shall follow the critical practice of such as Bordwell, Simon, and
Wood in this section by narrating each of these three films in such
a way as to bring out the interpretations I make of them and to
point my philosophical reflections along the way. This is pedestrian but necessary if I am to have any hope of sustaining my
claim that Woody Allen is probably the most intellectually serious
film maker presently working in the English-speaking world, with
a claim to be discussed alongside Welles, Kurosawa, Bergman, Ray.

15.1   ANNIE HALL

Paraphrase P

Annie Hall (1977) ****Woody Allen, Diane Keaton, Shelley Duvall. This is an absolutely marvelous film, directed and co-authored by the extravagantly talented Woody Allen. 'Annie' is not only one of the funniest and wisest film comedies ever made, it's also a courageous, poignant, perceptive and perfectly acted film. This is more of an autobiographical film than any of Allen's earlier entries. Our red-headed hero Alvy Singer has been in analysis for fifteen years, loves New York, and falls in love with Diane Keaton. Woody and co-author Marshall Brickman fire off an enormous number of comic salvos; the one-liners and the sight gags pay off brilliantly. A joy from start to finish! (Dir: Woody Allen, 94 mins)

(Scheuer's *Movies on TV*)

Annie Hall is framed by monologues. The film opens on Allen, face to the camera. He tells two stories, one about not wanting to belong to any club that would have a person like him as a member; the other about a lady guest who, while agreeing that the hotel food is terrible, also complains of such small portions! Although in the film Allen plays a comic called Alvy Singer, the fact that in this monologue and throughout no item of clothing or touch of make-up is used to make him look any different from Woody Allen, and the fact that the monologue precedes any introduction of character, makes it nicely ambivalent as to whether we are being addressed by 'Woody Allen' or 'Alvy Singer' on the subject of Life. In the middle of the monologue be begins to don character: 'Annie and I broke up. . . .' The film's closing monologue, a joke about not incarcerating a brother who believes he is a chicken 'because we need the eggs', is delivered voice-over while the camera holds on an empty street corner.

Opening so directly, Allen lets us see Alvy's quest, the quest for love or, rather, the quest to understand the place of love in our lives. Love here is narrowly conceived: it is sexual attraction and amiability between men and women. It is free from questions of family background (neither Alvy nor Annie has much understanding of the other's background), social class, or education. It is entered into for reasons of its own, not in order to have children and participate in the community. Such love is like the Kantian aesthetic, enjoyed for itself alone and no other purpose.

Being in the form of a comedian's stand-up monologue, the opening is also able to set the *attitude* that the film will take to Alvy's quest, namely, slightly detached, wry and humorous.

One should resist, I think, treating Allen's films as autobiographical.[2] Any creator draws on his own experience and is trying, through the work, to say something or other. Allen's ambiguity about addressing the audience in and out of character should be seen for what it is, part of the means deployed in the work, the work that is crafted to articulate ideas. What is important is the truth or falsity of the ideas, and the appositeness of the means of their articulation.

Between these monologues we follow a tale of Alvy's difficult relations with women. An anxious boy from Jewish Brooklyn (depressed by the universe expanding and hence falling apart) he is already attracted to girls in grade school. We learn that he has been married twice before he meets and falls for Annie Hall. Hesitant at first about her moving in with him, he watches her career flourish and their incompatibilities develop and, while he does not resist her moving out, he misses her terribly and makes a trip to Los Angeles to ask her to take him back; she refuses. She has changed considerably and we see that he misses her as she was, not as she has become.

This simple plot, without dramatic tension, was sufficient to support a film that was Allen's most successful at the box office, that won Academy Awards, and made his co-star Diane Keaton a major star in her own right.[3] It was well understood by the audience that Allen and Keaton had had a long-standing affair of which there might be echoes in the film. This, it seems to me, is of importance for only two reasons: (1) that in writing the screenplay Allen and his collaborator Brickman could have had Keaton in mind; (2) that Allen as director had an intimate rapport with Keaton that infused the film. Other than that a great many sub-themes are touched on and laughed off: anti-semitism; the West Coast versus New York; intellectual pretentiousness; liberal pieties; frigidity; psychiatry, and other things. None of these explains the course of Annie and Alvy's relationship. Annie suggests Alvy is self-contained, and that New York living fills his life so he has no need of her. His desperate plea to her expresses need, but the rueful ending of the film is that he is over her, that they remain friends, that his memories of her and that friendship are precious, are the eggs that make sense of the whole of living.

Let me articulate this more directly. The *thesis* of the film can be taken as: in reaching out to others for love and joy there will be the possibility of much pain. Not the pain of rebuff, which is trivial, but the pain of mistakes and the realization of mistakes. Alvy has been married twice, and those relationships failed. We see him involved with other women in the film, and these fail. And in the end his favourite relationship, with Annie, failed too. He does not know how to explain this, even on the psychiatrist's couch and through childhood events. But his final attitude is philosophical in the sense mentioned before, namely reflective and accepting.[4]

That this film was immediately popular both with the public and the critics is a phenomenon in itself. Part of the explanation has to be that it addressed, and presented a solution to, a problem of considerable current interest, part of the philosophical *framework* of our society. This is the problem of romantic love. Although Woody Allen and Alvy Singer are men in their forties, they live like, and seem stuck at, the young adult stage, the stage of having work, but having assumed no responsibilities of a familial or financial kind. Neither alimony, nor mortgage, nor children cloud Alvy's horizon; his offer of marriage to Annie is a desperation ploy that would in due course be regretted, and the old scenario of settling down for life does not seem to be in his mind. To the well-educated, urban, young adult movie-goers who are in the majority, all this must resonate. They are probably embroiled in the same problems, hear all the facile solutions, and instead find Allen saying, 'try to get a perspective and be philosophical'. As time goes by they may manage this and the film is a comforting portent of that possibility. Very few in fact will end up as Alvy/Woody, affluent, famous, and able to work out their problems on film. That, however, does not affect the structural parallel between the two conditions of life.

It is instructive to compare this movie to Bertrand Russell's great work of popular philosophy, *The Conquest of Happiness*. This will shock my professional colleagues. Was that not just a pot-boiler Russell wrote to finance work on important things like logic? That Russell sustained himself largely by writing is true; but to allege that he did not take his popular books seriously is to suggest an irresponsibility of attitude for which there is absolutely no warrant. Russell tried to help people in his books and was to an extent successful, if sales are any measure. Allen, too, is giving us his thoughts, but it is to be remembered that he is not a young adult but a middle-aged one and is not to be identified with his films. What makes sense in the life of Woody Allen, famous man, may not be feasible for others. If his films are to have any general appeal or universality they have to address problems well beyond the boundaries of Allen's personal life. The same was true of Russell, English aristocrat and professor. It is foolish to imagine that it is easy to be philosophical if you are a philosopher; the two, in my experience, very rarely go together, any more than being non-neurotic and a psychiatrist do. But there is no requirement that a person embody their ideas; the truth or falsity of the ideas is an independent matter.

Allen seems to me to have said something reasonably close to the truth: if you want the eggs (genuine contact with other people, love, friendship) then you have to pay the cost, pain. But over time, both the joy and the pain will lessen and exist more in memory than in the present. Such a philosophy is banal. Is that a criticism? Are the only truths worth telling new truths, startling truths, deep truths? These demands strike me as too strong. Allen's success stems from his new way of saying old things or banal things, a new way that is not itself banal. Partly because of his own originality and partly because he is recasting old problems in terms dictated by the current framework, his work seems fresh, lively and original.

By what means does he cue in his philosophical framework? His opening monologue uses his own appearance, unmistakably that of the 1960s and 1970s. The manner of speaking and the allusion to Freud also 'place' us. Most of the film takes place in New York; its characters go to psychiatrists as a matter of course; they are much interested in going to movies and discussing the etiquette of sexual relationships.

All films operate within a philosophical framework set by the time they are made, but they have the option to articulate those connections or to leave them unstated. In *Citizen Kane*, although the film is identifiably of the twentieth century, it is none too specific as to locale or as to the sorts of people it is dealing with. We have little idea of why Kane and his cronies engage in so little self-understanding, and no clue as to what Thompson and his colleagues do regard as the keys to understanding someone. *Rashomon*, similarly, is vague as to its philosophical framework. There may be clues there that the non-Japanese misses but they do not seem necessary to grasping the film. And lastly *Persona*. Certainly it is twentieth century; and certainly some acquaintance with depth psychology is assumed. But again these connections are vague, and we are offered no clue as to in what sort of a context the characters' problems would have to be solved.

Annie Hall, by contrast, is tightly tied to its time and locale, to certain sorts of preoccupations and hence to discussing its problems within given terms. Allen offers no new recipes to solve the problems of our modern condition, but a new form of a banal message, presented in a manner that is utterly contemporary, and yet distanced and ironic. The very use of humour itself, so integral to Allen, so peripheral or absent from the other three films, is that this is a principal device for gaining philosophical distance. Problems can be more easily overcome if they are satirized.

15.2 INTERIORS

perhaps the single worst movie ever made by a major American film maker.

(Foster Hirsch 1981, p. 88)

We have depended on Allen for more than ten years now as champion against just this particular sort of bad-faith artiness and the mid-cult sensibility from which it stems.

(James Monaco (cited in Jacobs 1982, p. 127))

One of the criticisms of *Interiors* was that all serious works that are worth anything have humour in them as well: Bergman's *Persona* is a truly great film, and there's not a comic moment in it.

(Woody Allen (Jacobs 1982, p. 127))

Interiors, which is not a comedy at all and in which Allen does not appear, silences any charges of adolescent outlook or of limited range. So far from ignoring responsibility and family, this film is solely about the dynamics within an extended family.

Paraphrase Q

Interiors (1978) **** Diane Keaton, E. G. Marshall, Geraldine Page, Maureen Stapleton, Sam Waterston, Richard Jordan, Mary Beth Hurt, Kristin Griffith. Woody Allen picks up the mask, and every character stands in for aspects of his psyche, though that is where the much-vaunted resemblance to Bergman ends. Their styles couldn't be more dissimilar, for Allen uses so many shop-worn art mannerisms that his style recalls chopped meat. Still, it's a seriously felt, sly film that encourages the viewer to overlook the howlers in the dialogue. Some of the acting, notably by Mary Beth Hurt and E. G. Marshall, is superlative. Uneven but often moving and involving. Few intentional laughs in this Allen homage to Ingmar Bergman. (Dir: Woody Allen, 93 mins)

(Scheuer's *Movies on TV*)

Paraphrase R

It opens on empty rooms and the father of the family reminiscing, and soon arrives at a breakfast table scene where an ageing Arthur (E. G. Marshall) declares to his assembled family that he wants a trial separation, to move out of the family home and live by himself for a while. We know he is dissembling because in the opening monologue he has described his life with Eve (Geraldine Page), his wife, as an ice palace: beautiful but cold. Eve has a nervous breakdown and is hospitalized after a suicide attempt. The unmarried actress daughter Flyn (Kristin Griffith) flies in for the father's remarriage to a warm, possibly Jewish woman, Pearl (Maureen Stapleton). The two married daughters are in their ways impotent: the poetess Renata (Diane Keaton) blocks and hallucinates, the other Joey (Mary Beth Hurt) changes jobs and vacillates. Renata's husband Frederick (Richard Jordan) drinks because his books are not good enough, he also tries to rape Flyn. Joey's husband, Mike (Sam Waterston) is involved in the impotence of theoretical politics. At the wedding Eve reappears then commits suicide. The family comes together to mourn.

Nothing much happens in the film. There are no jokes. Anguish is everywhere, above all in the tortured face of Geraldine Page as Eve. But that is because the film concentrates on the difficulties of human relationships: sexual, sororal, filial, marital. It shows a woman who substitutes order, beauty and control, for warmth and love. It would be very easy to inflate the theme and say it is Allen's challenge to Plato's idea that the virtues harmonize. Eve's taste is indeed exquisite, and the interiors she creates for her family would win prizes. She is herself a beautiful woman who tries to remain so in old age. She has a fragile dignity. What none of her daughters seems to have as part of their lives is love, a naturally welling up human warmth. 'Interiors' in another sense. Diane Keaton, as Renata the poetess, for example, has a little daughter. Yet she is just something there in the house, another nice piece. All three daughters are heavily introspective: Renata looking for her inspiration, Joey looking for her métier, Flyn bemoaning the well-paid rubbish she turns out and acknowledging her limitations. Each of them looks into themselves and finds nothing in the interior. This depresses them; there is no solid self to be, to give love, or to receive love.

The film is very Bergmanesque. In all sorts of ways Allen gives it a Scandinavian feel: in the sort of interior design Eve does, in the quality of the light, and in the selection of the actors. Pauline Kael's cruel question: 'is this family Jewish?' is on the ball. Obviously they are not (although probably Pearl is) any more than Bergman's people are. Allen even recapitulates the famous shot from *Persona* where one actress faces the camera and the profile of another cuts across: a shot he had previously parodied in *Love and Death*. He lines the three sisters up in profile at times, in a manner reminiscent of Bergman. This is not mere homage. *Interiors* does take up and develop some of Bergman's themes. Instead of masks, personae, Allen looks at interiors. The film looks not at people's surface, but at their interiors. This is all metaphor, and yet shows the 'visual' medium of film is not confined to how people look.

When the father announces he is to be married the sisters are upset; loyalty to their mother, snobbery towards Pearl, confused feelings towards their father, all surface. Yet when Joey, drunk, tells her mother that she is too perfect for the world and her mother walks into the waves, it is Pearl who performs mouth-to-mouth resuscitation on Joey, who has made a futile attempt to rescue her mother. In the final scenes Eve's death has not disrupted Arthur's marriage, and the last words of the two sisters suggest peace and tranquillity. We are not left feeling their problems are over, we are left feeling that Eve's exit leaves her legacy to her daughters untouched.

It is very easy and glib to dismiss the film as dollar-book Freud, to use Orson Welles's expression. That strikes me as snobbery. The film is popularizing psychology by suggesting an analogy between outer arrangements and inner states; how one can stultify the other even though it appears so beautiful and ordered. But in popularizing (i.e. not being clinical), the film is not offering recipes on how to get better in five easy lessons. If it offers any wisdom it would be along these lines: if you subordinate human relations and love to anything else, when raising children, the result may be to stunt their interiors irremediably. Or, more sharply, beauty and order are secondary virtues, love and warmth are primary.[5]

More schematically, referring back to my quest, attitude, thesis and framework labels, we can see the film as itself a quest, perhaps for the source of impotence and frustration felt by three women. In striving to make her family perfect, their mother has made all of them feel inadequate. This thesis is put forward in an intensely serious and direct way. The film does not stand at a distance from its people. Perhaps it was this attitude that so startled Allen fans, an attitude he caricatured in *Stardust Memories* by having people repeatedly praise the early funny films of his hero.

The framework for the film is the only indicator we have of how universal the problem and thesis can be taken to be. Once more it is set in New York and in the present time. Its characters are all well-educated and affluent. At most, then, it deals with contemporary urban people with time and capacity for introspection. By analogy it may be possible to project its problem of impotence in the face of demands for perfection to other places and times, where the metaphor of interior decoration and interior psychological states is changed. It is also possible to argue with the psychology – does such a drive for perfection always alienate? But the film is particularized; nothing in it suggests that kind of universalizability. Its feeling of depth and mystery have to do not with its marshalling a powerful theory but rather with its intense scrutiny of a set of clearly differentiated individuals. In ninety-three minutes of screen time Allen sketches in eight people, most of whom we feel we have learned a great deal about. This is deft writing, drawing on acting talent able to project strongly, and utilizing a studied style of directing (shots of empty rooms, or characters seen but not heard) that is, albeit, unobtrusive.

It baffles me that the film was greeted with so much derision and hostility, and I wonder if, had Allen released it pseudonymously (perhaps signing his real name, Alan Konigsberg), he might not have been greeted as a bright new talent. Certainly Pauline Kael's taunt about Jewishness, and a comment by Scheuer in *Movies on TV* that each character is a facet of Allen himself, suggests to me that in this case preconceptions have seriously interfered with the effort to confront the film with an open mind.

15.3 MANHATTAN

IKE. . . . An idea for a short story . . .about . . .people in Manhattan who . . . are constantly creating these real . . . unnecessary neurotic problems for themselves 'cause it keeps them from dealing with, uh, more unsolvable, terrifying problems about, uh, the universe . . . well, it has to be optimistic. Well, all right, why is life worth living? That's a very good question. (*Sighing*) Uh, like what? (*Sighing again and scratching his neck*) Okay. Uh, for me . . . (*Sighing*) or, I would say . . . what, Groucho Marx, to name one thing . . . uh, ummm, and (*Sighing*) Willie Mays, and um, the second movement of the Jupiter Symphony, and . . . Louis Armstrong's recording of 'Potatoehead Blues' . . . (*Sighing*) ummm, Swedish movies, naturally . . . *Sentimental Education* by Flaubert . . . uh, Marlon Brando, Frank Sinatra . . . (*Sighing*) ummm, those incredible apples and pears by Cézanne . . . (*Sighing*), uh, the crabs at Sam Wo's . . . tsch, uh (*Sighing*) Tracy's face. . . .

(Woody Allen (Four Films 1982, pp. 267–8)

Manhattan is the film that tempts me most to follow the example of Stanley Cavell. He took some 1930s comedies and read into them his own preoccupations about the nature of the relations between the sexes, and the conditions of there being a meet and happy conversation. I rejected his method (in section 4.2) without noting that I also thought he formulated the problem poorly and presented a solution with the consistency of mush. Yet I find in

Allen's films a matching of some of my own philosophical preoccupations so close as to be uncanny (since I have nothing in common with Woody Allen's background), and find his discussion of them to be at a very high level of intelligence and penetrating enough to embarrass some of his fans (c.f. the Hirsch and Monaco mottos at p. 339 above), as well as coming to admirably sane the conclusions.

Paraphrase S

Manhattan (1979) ****Woody Allen, Diane Keaton, Michael Murphy, Meryl Streep, Mariel Hemingway. Director Allen sublimates his gag bent into genuine drama in his most worthwhile film. He jettisons the sweetness of 'Annie Hall' and looks at 'himself' with a jaundiced eye – the womaniser he plays in this film is a wily manipulator aware of his prowess. I can't think of another movie in which New York has appeared so beautiful. Hemingway establishes herself as the best natural actress in a long time. B&W. (96 mins)

(Scheuer's *Movies on TV*)

Paraphrase T

Manhattan is a philosophical film about moral questions, rather than psychological ones. Its central character, Isaac, once more played by Allen, is a successful television writer who wants to give it up in quest of something more serious, but, as usual, he's allergic to pretentious phoniness about the arts. He is having an affair with a seventeen-year-old schoolgirl (Tracy) whose affection for him is quite genuine and uncomplicated. His towards her are complicated and guilty. Introduced to another woman, Mary, (Diane Keaton), by his best friend Yale (Tony Roberts), he does not get involved until Yale makes it clear his own affair with Mary is over. Isaac gently tries to ease himself out of the affair with Tracy by encouraging her to take a music scholarship in London. Things go quite well between Isaac and Mary, then not so well, and it transpires Mary and Yale have resumed their affair. Isaac is devastated and confronts Yale in his Columbia University classroom next to a skeleton: 'IKE – Jesus – well, what are future generations gonna say about us? My God! (*He points to the skeleton, acknowledging it at last*) You know, someday we're gonna – we're gonna be like him! I mean, y-y-y-y-you know – well, he was probably one of the beautiful people. He was

344

probably dancing and playing tennis and everything. And – and – (*Pointing to the skeleton again*) and now – well, this is what happens to us! You know, uh, it's very important to have – to have some kind of personal integrity. Y-y-you know, I'll – I'll be hanging in a classroom one day. And – and I wanna make sure when I . . . thin out that I'm w-w-well thought of!'

Confronting Yale with the problem of integrity, it dawns on Isaac that his own could be questioned. Tracy really cared for him and had the kind of integrity he sought, a faithfulness to one person, yet he dissembled with her. After the monologue quoted above as motto he tries to intercept her before she leaves for London. She tells him he hurt her and that she won't change her plans, and repeats back at him his 'line' that if they still love each other six months is not so long. He worries she will find someone else. 'TRACY: Why couldn't you have brought this up last week?' Look, six months isn't so long. (*Pausing*) Not everybody gets corrupted. (*Ike stares at Tracy, reacting. He pushes back his glasses*) Tsch. Look, you have to have a little faith in people. *Ike continues to stare at Tracy. He has a quizzical look on his face; he breaks into a smile.*' These are the last words of the film. Isaac has been put on the spot. Tracy the (now) eighteen-year-old is more sure and consistent and mature than he is. She may still love him despite the way he treated her. But she will not vacillate back and forwards at his whim, rather works out the logic of his own arguments that London will be a good experience for her and what's six months if they love each other? We are, of course, not at all sure if Isaac can control himself. He has no difficulty in meeting women and possibly what he is saying in the scene is not that Tracy will meet someone else, be corrupted, change completely, but that he, in six months, cannot say where he will be. He has listed Tracy's face among the few things that make life worth living for him, but will she still be in the list six months from now?

Uniquely for a Woody Allen movie, in this film the character he plays has a child, a young son from his marriage to Jill (Meryl Streep), who has left him for a lesbian and written a book accusing him of a merely narcissistic fear of death and of being full of complaints about life with never any solutions. We see him on his fatherly visits going to restaurants, playing ball, talking about women in a heterosexual manner, doing what he can, one suspects. A delicately funny sub-plot.

Isaac's quest for integrity in his work and in his relationships covers up – and this is the thesis of both the film and of his ex-wife – self-deception. Isaac is someone who demands integrity: a purity of feeling, a commitment to one person, a level of honesty of behaviour. But he is poorly self-aware. So although he does not begin his affair with Mary until he knows she and Yale have broken off, and is shocked when Yale conceals its resumption, he himself tries to ease out of the Tracy affair, having met Mary, by persuading Tracy to go away. So he is imposing a standard on Yale (honesty) that he is self-deceptively not living up to. Yet such is Tracy's purity that she does not spurn him out of hand, offering him instead a simple solution: you have to trust some people. Now the nice dilemma is, can he trust himself?

After the critical hostility to *Interiors*, *Manhattan* once more regained the loyalty of Allen's following. Isaac is sophisticated and urbane, but still has nebbish features. The attitude of the film to Isaac's quest and its own thesis is once more satirical and ironic. As its title indicates, New York is a central character in it. If *Annie Hall* was a romance with a woman, *Manhattan* is a romance with a city. Its opening voice-over finds Isaac seeking to express a character's love of New York, and the music consists entirely of George Gershwin tunes. Its framework is thus the same as *Annie Hall*, only with no excursus beyond the city (Annie was from Wisconsin). Whereas Alvy Singer is very up-to-date, Isaac is a little old-fashioned, nostalgic. Yale accuses him of being too demanding, self-righteous.

With *Citizen Kane*, *Rashomon* and *Persona* I have always faced the problem of assessing the truth of their philosophy or, where I could not get it into propositional form, admitting that. And also with those films I had to expend space sorting out the philosophy of the film from the competing interpretations offered. Woody Allen's films have been theorized about very little because he has yet to interest intellectual critics. Since the sympathies of those critics so often incline to radicalism and idealism, or at least to mystification, this is not hard to explain. Allen's films are approachable, readily yield up their secrets, and demand a perspective that includes a sense of humour. Are the problems they pose genuine? My own answer is 'yes'. There is a conflict in the contemporary ideology of romantic love between its individuation and intensity and what seems like a natural tendency to fade and re-focus on another person. This in turn leads to difficult problems in the notion of integrity, since honest attempts to confront this conflict are extremely painful. Even when a relationship has been held together by children and a loyalty to the family unit the feeling may still be there, and a decision to act on it may have shattering consequences (*Interiors*). A rueful and humorous attitude to all this is admirable.

In all three films the solutions posed to the problems are the same: the necessity of coming to terms with things the way they are, and accepting the consequences. Alvy assimilates his love for Annie into his memory and continues to befriend and appreciate her. Arthur and his daughters accept that Eve would rather die than tolerate their rejection of her urge to perfection. Isaac may have gained a little self-understanding, certainly enough to know that he cannot control Tracy and that whether their relationship will continue will depend on what happens to her in London and to him in Manhattan.

Not very deep and shattering, some will say, in fact rather common sense. When it comes to what we might term philosophy of life most of the results of philosophy are just that: simple and common sense, from the Delphic 'know thyself' and Socrates' 'the unexamined life is not worth living', down to Russell's *The Conquest of Happiness*. If one were to subject to scrutiny the works of the only professional philosopher to have been extensively filmed, Jean-Paul Sartre, one would find the same combination of the obvious, the common sense, possibly even the banal. When we think of the problem of how to live as being deep we need not mistake that for a kind of intractable intellectual depth, like quantum mechanics. It is, rather, a depth that has to do with being all-pervasive (affecting much of life) and blending intellectual questions with strong feelings. The obviousness or banality of a solution is no barrier to its truth and effectiveness.

Diane Jacobs in her study of Allen (1982) brings out the point that critical reaction to his films, from *Annie Hall* onwards, has been systematically bedevilled by a kind of love-affair the public has with 'Woody Allen'. This neurotic Jewish comedian from New York, half intellectual, half punk, irreverent and deflating, had become a national icon, meriting a *Time* magazine cover. All his early films are extensions of his comedy sketches, stand-up routines, television specials and magazine parodies. From *Annie* onward it has become clear that he is a film maker with more interests and range than this public realized. The last of his comic films was appositely entitled *Love and Death* and is, indeed, a philosophical film that both laughs at, and stands intimidated by, both these topics. He also showed himself as a film fan, devoted to *Casablanca*, Bergman, Fellini, Ophuls. There was always a mordant side to his comedy, and some of the quips steered awfully close to aphorisms.

In settling into film making Allen made a number of changes. He acted a straight part in someone else's film: *The Front*. He eventually ceased collaborating on the scripts with Marshall Brickman. He gradually ventured into new territory, even a serious film without himself in the cast. This has been a difficult transition both for him as a creator and for his fans. Since the fans are in love with 'Woody' they make two mistakes: (1) that whenever Woody appears on the screen he is going to play 'Woody', the 'Woody' they love, the comic, the clown, the nebbish; (2) they operate under the delusion that 'Woody' is actually the real Woody Allen. Thus they yap for him to go back to making us laugh, and not spring these new films on us that get further and further away from the 'Woody' they know and love (c.f. Hirsch 1981).

This is a new problem with old roots. All the old stars used to complain about type-casting and begged to be given a chance to do something else. The Front Office resisted not so much because they enjoyed enslaving their employees, but rather because a star persona served a particular function. A star was never just an actor (some were not even actors). A star was a presence reverberating with the echoes of all the previous roles in the audience's memory. This is why their films are so rich.

Woody Allen is suffering from a variant of this: the audience is type-casting him in his comedian persona and furthermore identifying that with the real him. Hence, for example, a great many people confusedly think that Woody Allen bares his psyche on the screen, that his films are autobiographical. Bergman says all his characters are like him. If we were to apply that to Woody Allen we might get bizarre results. For example, Tony Roberts surfaces in his films time and again, so this assumes there is a side to Allen who resembles Roberts. But the basic mistake is to think that the statement, 'an artist draws on his experience as well as his imagination', is the same as the statement that, 'to draw on your experience is to be autobiographical'. My guess is that what is autobiographical in Allen's films are the *thoughts*, the problems, preoccupations, the semi-aphorisms, the emerging philosophy of love and death.

That philosophy is pretty simple. Life, despite all its short-comings, is short. Love, despite all its pains, is wonderful. Indeed love is the only one of two ways to deny death; the other is through your work. But love is a disappointment because it does not last, the pain is coming. In Allen's films the question is raised, can you win love and, having won it, can you avoid the mistakes that end it? His own answer seems to be that it is not something anyone does, it just fades. The work in which you articulate this does not fade.

Various criticisms of this philosophy are obvious. It equates love with sexual love, downplaying friendship (although his characters always have friends) and family (mothers, in-laws are usually shown as trials; children are kept at a distance in his films). Again, some try to argue that love can last, but not without changing its form. Adolescent passion cannot be sustained between two people, but a permanent kind of pair-bonding can develop in which two people give a great deal to each other. Allen never creates a character who could live out this life. His Alvy, Isaac, Sandy (in *Stardust Memories*) are highly self-contained, wanting both fun and togetherness and solitude. Annie Hall tells him he is incapable of enjoying life, he is an island, and his life is New York City.

And, finally, one could argue that Allen does not dramatize sufficiently the satisfactions, in the face both of death and of love, of satisfying work. He himself is a prolific creator, with a very large body of work to his credit. This in itself is a philosophy.

He only addresses this directly for the first time in *Stardust Memories* where Sandy is a film director. In the course of a weekend retrospective of his films, many of the major themes of Allen's own work are rehearsed. He is torn between three women, one attractive and neurotic, one homely and devoted, and a new one, yet to be tested out. Old love, intense love and new love. He is preoccupied with mortality and whether life is passing him by. And he is in agony because his films have changed direction from comedy to tragedy and everyone is telling him to revert to comedy. In a filmic form highly derivative of Fellini's *8½*, a film I find unredeemingly boring and its fascination a mystery, he rehearses life's problem's through this retrospective; he takes stock, so to speak.

In particular he confronts some new problems. In all the previous films the character was successful but not especially famous. In *Stardust Memories* Sandy is well-known and distracted by fame. His fans are not content with his work, they want to possess him, going so far as to invade his bedroom. Sandy is very successful, but clearly fears and detests his fans as much as he loves them; just as they hate him while loving him. It is one thing to have satisfying work that leaves you some private space to live in, it is another to have satisfying work that brings you barrages of praise and fame as well as barrages of criticism and advice. As at the end of *8½* when Guido emerges from his retreat with the confidence to stage his new film, however crazy it all looks, so at the end of *Stardust Memories* Sandy has confronted his worst fears of misunderstanding, even assassination, and will continue. Significantly, Allen's next film was again a new departure. *A Midsummer Night's Sex Comedy* is a light and playful treat – of love and death – in which his main character does find love and happiness within a continuing relationship. It is modelled on Bergman's *Smiles of a Summer Night*, which was also a light comedy about straightening out sexual conflicts. A main character dies in it, but this is treated lightly (he is engaged in sex at the time and dies happy) and his spirit stays on with the characters (literally).

In 1983 Allen released *Zelig*, a film he had been working on for three years. Greeted with rapturous reviews, and enjoying some success, the film is in the form of a *reductio*. Imagine a person so empathic with others that he could change form like a chameleon. The result is an astonishing film that takes the one basic situation and hence the one basic joke and plays variation after variation on it. It simultaneously satirizes documentaries, feature films like *Citizen Kane* and *Reds*, and meticulously recreates the period between the wars. Allen has done nothing like it before, and neither has anyone else. I tell my students that if Allen were a Japanese he would long ago have been designated a Living National Treasure, as are the great actors of Noh and Kabuki.

In 1984 Allen released another black and white film, *Broadway Danny Rose*. This is a framed narrative. A group of stand-up comedians chatting in a deli swap stories about an agent they all know, Danny Rose (Allen). A small-timer, utterly devoted to the 'acts' he manages, no matter how bizarre, the centre of the film is an account of the adventures he has in staging the comeback of a

1950s Italian crooner, Lou (Nick Forte). The crooner is nervous and begs Danny to fetch his mistress Tina (Mia Farrow) from New Jersey. In doing this Danny visits a medium, is chased by the mafia and eventually caught, escapes and then is unceremoniously dumped as manager. At the end of the film Tina comes to apologize. After hesitating, he accepts.

This film is more audaciously philosophical than any before. It is a fast-moving comedy with everything Allen fans love (although Pauline Kael dismissed it because she thought it was written down to please the audience); its tone is warm and affectionate; it centres its plot line around a man-woman relationship. And yet it is directly a film about philosophy of life. At least three times the protagonists directly confront the issue of philosophy of life, kindness and help versus grab what you can get. At the end it is the hard-boiled Tina's plea that he live up to his own philosophy of 'acceptance, forgiveness and love' that leads to a reconciliation. Philosophy is neither the film's quest nor its attitude, but rather its thesis.

Because all of Allen's films are recent, and because reflection takes time, I have discussed them more briefly than previous ones. One feature I would like to comment on is the total integration in Allen's work of the content – whether serious or comic – and the filmic technique. Working always with the same cinematographer, Gordon Willis, Allen has developed a lean and self-effacing style as plain as his unadorned titles (invariably white on black). He has honed his editing technique to the point where scenes are cut with a precision and timing that bespeak enormous skill. Although he does not compose the music, Allen draws largely on standard recorded works, and so in a way the matching of music to visuals and cuts stems from his sensibility also.

CONCLUSION

I do not want to write a concluding summary of this book, rather I want to end in the midst of this discussion of Woody Allen as a philosopher. I have called Allen a popular philosopher addressing problems of perennial concern to everyone: love, death, happiness, fulfilment. He is not making films about himself. He is making films about problems. In each he dramatizes the problems

351

in different ways and considers the various solutions available. Work itself is not, it seems, enough if we are to judge by *Interiors* and *Stardust Memories*. It is something one wants to go on doing, but which is worthwhile as long as it is encased in a form of living that is satisfying; not otherwise. When otherwise it is likely to bring on creative impotence, commercial sell-out, or violence and addiction.

These propositions are food for thought. That, within the commercial American cinema, a writer-director has the opportunity to think about them in his work has much to do with the prior success Woody Allen had as comedian. So far, despite his failure to repeat the immense success of *Annie Hall*, his producers/ sponsors seem not to have withdrawn their financial and moral support as he moves forward in his quest. Allen's work develops and matures as it continues, and has a characteristic very precious in a thinker or a film maker: originality. Not a strident cultivation of being different or being experimental or being modernist, which are largely phoney forms of originality. The mark of his originality is different: you cannot predict what he will do next. Constant and delightful new surprises are in store, as he finds his way. Along that way he has already created three masterpieces (*Zelig* may be a fourth). Allen is a major artist because he has created a body of major work. I have offered some arguments to that point. But we must acknowledge the intellectual space for dissent. There is no point in demanding the answer once and for all, demanding to *know*. That rage for certainty is a false (meta-)philosophy. Testing these tentative assessments will take time.

NOTES

INTRODUCTION   ON THE VERY IDEA OF A PHILOSOPHY OF THE FILM: *CASABLANCA*

1 *Casablanca* has been reprinted as a screenplay three times: in Gassner and Nichols 1945; in Koch 1973; and by Anobile 1974. Also of some relevance are Koch's autobiography 1979, ch. 8; Francisco 1980; Wallis's autobiography 1980, ch. 8; Corliss 1974, pp. 103–16; Ingrid Bergman's autobiography, 1980; her interview in the Anobile book; and Rosenzweig 1978.
2 The inaccuracies in Paraphrase D are: (1) Rick's is a 'Club' not a 'Bar'; (2) Rick is not aiding a Resistance worker, he refuses to help; (3) 'tightly worked out plot' suggests coherence rather than inconsistency; (4) 'Play it, Sam', is said by Ilsa, not by Rick.
3 Arguments to show the priority of theory to fact are to be found fully set out and defended in Popper 1959.
4 Ferrari says, 'My dear Rick, when will you realize that in this world, today, isolationism is no longer a practical policy'. Later, Renault commends 'I stick my neck out for nobody', as a 'wise foreign policy'.

1   KNOWLEDGE AND EXISTENCE

1 'Requiring', postulating', 'having a place' and 'able to be made consistent with' constitute a weakening series of possible connections between a new theory and the existing stock of theories.
2 Persistence of vision as an explanation for motion pictures is decisively refuted by Munsterberg 1916, ch. 3, as noted by Anderson and Anderson 1980 (it is not mentioned in Vernon's survey, 1962, ch. 9); see Nichols and Lederman 1980, and Gibson 1979 for suggestions about how better to understand the physiological psychology of movies.

3 Stanley Cavell offers an odd third possibility:

> If we do not equate knowledge with the results of science [he
> nowhere argues why we should] but understand it as the capacity to
> put one's experience and the world into words, to use language . . .
> (1981, p. 74)

The equation (knowledge = experience put into language) neglects
the question of whether that 'experience' is of any epistemic value
(e.g., is it mere hallucination?). Cavell's 'linguisticism' is so obviously
unpromising, both too narrow (excluding science which is no-one's
experience) and too wide (letting in hallucination, memory lapse, etc.)
as scarcely to be worth extensive criticism.

4 We can even, like Elmer Rice 1930 and numerous others, satirize the
screen world and the supposedly off-screen world, Hollywood, where
it is manufactured. Among the first to catch on to this possibility were
the denizens of Hollywood itself, where the production of movies
satirizing Hollywood is a venerable tradition (Thomas and Behlmer
1975; Myers 1978; and Parish 1978) as is the writing of such novels
(Van Loan 1915, Wilson 1922 and Van Vechten 1928).

5 The best gisting of Berkeley available is the section 'Berkeley's
Considered Philosophy' in Wisdom 1953. Wisdom rightly interprets
him as a phenomenalistic idealist – indeed Mill is Berkeley without
the Supreme Perceiver – and not, as Russell does (1912), as a
subjective idealist. There is a considerable difference between the
monomaniac idea that the world is my dream and Berkeley's idea that
the world is God's dream:

> 6   Some truths there are so near and obvious to the mind that a
> man need only open his eyes to see them. Such I take this important
> one to be, viz. that all the choir of heaven and furniture of the earth,
> in a word all those bodies which compose the mighty frame of the
> world, have not any subsistence without a mind; that their *being* is
> to be perceived or known; that consequently so long as they are not
> actually perceived by me, or do not exist in my mind, or that of any
> other created spirit, they must either have no existence at all, or else
> subsist in the mind of some Eternal Spirit: it being perfectly
> unintelligible, and involving all the absurdity of abstraction, to
> attribute to any single part of them an existence independent of
> spirit. (Berkeley 1710, Part First)

6 One can ask of them, 'what becomes of things on film?' This is an
ambiguous question because it can mean, what becomes of real things
once they are filmed, i.e. how do they function and how do they relate
back to their originals? It can also mean what do we make of the
subsistence of apparent things in films that are yet truly artifactual?
Stanley Cavell (1978) seems to be havering away at the first, not
noticing the second. Disappointingly, his conclusion seems to be that
we must study 'the succession of films that matter to us' (p. 256) –
however they are to be defined.

2 PLATO AND THE CAVE

1 Interestingly enough the psychologist J. J. Gibson, when searching for a notion of the unchanging world that undergirds changeable appearance, resorts to the mathematical notion of a topological invariant (see Gibson 1950 and Topper 1983).
2 It is important, I think, to stress the delusional, projective nature of the idea that 'others' are being warped by things to which the speaker is immune. Intellectuals often adopt the most strenuous of stands against television (not having one, etc.) on the grounds of its cultural vapidity, yet prove themselves insatiable addicts when they are alone with it. Ordinary people, in addition to cognitive and affective discount, are also able more readily to turn away from television (c.p. Gans 1962).
3 Compare this with Edward Davenport's idea that literature is a form of thought experiment (1983) or Jay Haley's that films rehearse in imagination real-world problems (1952).
4 The logic of science, metaphysics, falsification and verification is discussed in Popper 1959.

4 FILMS AND ACADEMIC PHILOSOPHY

1 There is, to be sure, an affinity of art for idealism, for idealism elevates the work of the mind (which embraces the imagination) to the status of world-construction. This makes it possible to treat the worlds of art as having reality. (C.f. Cavell on films as more real, below.)
2 Northrop Frye, often praised for his vast learning, yet (1957) blithely discusses 'the growth of science on a basis of inductive observation' (p. 14), sees no serious conflict between science and myth and science and the Bible (pp. 66–7), and ridicules Sir James Frazer for thinking he was a scientist 'and hence was subject to fits of rationalism, which seem to have attacked him like a disease' (p. 35) so when he wrote, 'By myths I understand mistaken explanations of phenomena, whether of human life or of external nature', this was obviously part of an ideology designed to rationalize the European treatment of 'natives' on darker continents, and the less attention given it now the better (p. 38). Such are the facile misunderstandings on which Frye's huge apologetic structure is built.
3 For example, those contributing to this debating line ignore the following: the empiricist critique of Cartesianism; the empiricist critique of Hegelianism; the large and rather devastating literature criticizing Marx; the literature tending to show psychoanalysis to be pseudo-science; Marxist critiques of psychoanalysis; Marxist critiques of Althusser (O'Neill 1974; Santamaria 1983); the body of arguments suggesting that to compare films to language is to misunderstand both (Guzetti 1973; Harman 1977; Gaggi 1978; Worth 1975; Fuller 1983); and the general critique of the French intellectual tradition for

355

incestuousness, irrationalism and obscurantism, proneness to follow fashion, ignorance of science (Aron 1957, 1969; Revel 1957; Descombes 1980).

4 One of the best texts in the tradition, relatively understandable and not written in what Altman (1977) calls 'Frenchspeak', is Nichols (1981). Less sympathetic expositions in the course of devastating critique are Carroll (1982) and Salt (1983).

5 Mitchell (1983), in an article bristling with radical hostility, labels Munsterberg a reactionary tool of Taylor, the efficiency expert. It is true that he was one of the first industrial psychologists and that he, and many of his peers, laud movies for their capacity to take us away from reality. What Mitchell misses is the Kantianism. For Kant the aesthetic experience must be pure, enjoyed for itself alone. It is careless reading to see Munsterberg arguing the movies are a blessed relief from the assembly line, when what he is trying carefully to argue is that they are not a mere pastime but a vehicle for genuine aesthetic experience, perhaps the first form of aesthetic experience accessible to the assembly-line worker.

6 Walker followed up his 1966 essays on stars with a full-scale treatment in 1970. His theory that the offscreen activities of a star can infuse their onscreen performances and so heighten the audience's sense of intimacy with the character neatly complements the theoretical work of Horton and Wohl (1956) about the para-social intimacy cultivated by television 'hosts'.

7 This sense that while new art is not better than old art yet there is clear progress of means, both hardware and software, is a feature of Gombrich's 1950.

8 I have endeavoured to criticize film as a medium for discursive thought in my papers 1978b and 1983. One line of argument not touched on there, but perhaps of some importance, comes from the analogy of film and language. If film resembles language in that it can be used to make statements, there are two further requirements if it is to be suitable for discursive discourse. The first is some equivalent to negation (a capacity denied it by Worth 1975). The other is some equivalent of the conditional or the subjunctive, without which positions cannot be entertained for the purposes of the argument only. Each of these requirements is doubtful of fulfilment.

9 By extension one can detect in the occasional panic expressed about television fear that it so engulfs the passive mind that all normal socialization and social control mechanisms are by-passed. Hence television is supposed to lead to passive people who are more violent, intermittently attentive people who watch more television, politically pliable people who are more prejudiced, than the pre-television population. It is no surprise that such contradictory sorts of predictions have failed to realize themselves.

10 Imre Lakatos argued that the actual history of a debate may not correspond to its logical structure. If so, so much the worse for history,

which may be described as a caricature of its rational reconstruction (Lakatos 1962).

11 And, if he is a serious scholar, to indicate why he repudiates the critique of essentialism. Popper's is developed extensively (1945); Wittgenstein's is ably summarized in Pitcher (1964), ch. 9. See also Cohen 1965.

12 Dudley Andrew (1978) offers a sketch of the philosophical influences on Bazin, which he identifies as principally Sartre, Malraux and Teilhard de Chardin.

13 It is hard to resist setting one phenomenologist to catch another. Cavell has it (1971, p. 24) that the camera confines the senses 'leaving room for thought'. Barthes (1981, p. 55), by contrast, holds that because you cannot stop attending to movies for fear of missing something they are not conducive to '*pensiveness*'.

14 The first claim for the writer is Koch 1950; for the producer, Reisz 1951; and for the studio, Higham and Greenberg 1968. On the matter of the script the issue is troubling. No-one would say a good script is sufficient for a good movie; a botched job is too easy to manage. It would seem to be necessary but is not; there are films with poor scripts that are carried by the verve of the direction or even of a central performance.

15 Probably I have not stated this very well. A better attempt, more sympathetic, is by Shiner (1983) who quotes Cavell: 'what scepticism suggests is that since we cannot know the world exists, its presentness to us cannot be a function of knowing. The world is to be *accepted*; as the presentness of other minds is not to be known, but acknowledged'. Shiner says to deny the reality of the external world is to practise avoidance.

> Whence comes this certainty that the world is present to us? Here Cavell . . . asks us to meditate upon what it is to learn language, to become human. It is a process of learning how things are, of learning realities, not appearances. Initiation into the human form of life is initiation into the world, the real world. . . . Knowledge is . . . in the end secured by individual action in preserving our kinship from the threat posed by our separateness. (Shiner 1983, pp. 4–5)

16 Peter Munz (1984) savages and satirizes this conception.

17 I have in mind Gellner's notorious explanation of the hegemony of Oxford philosophy, advanced in his 1959. None of the reviews of Cavell is either appreciative enough or severe enough.

18 *The Wild Child* and *The Enigma of Kaspar Hauser*.

19 This phrase is from Kracauer (1965) and is his attempt to tell what the essence of film is and why its art ties it particularly tightly to the 'real world'.

5   ART AND SCIENCE

1 Two Marxist works of film criticism of recent vintage attest to how the
Marxist position feeds back into the philosophy of science. Terry
Lovell's *Pictures of Reality* is the most astonishing of the two. This one
hundred-page booklet was published under the auspices of the British
Film Institute, a publicly-funded body that runs Britain's National
Film Theatre and National Film Archive, and publishes the magazines
Sight and Sound and *Monthly Film Bulletin*. *Pictures of Reality*,
subtitled 'Aesthetics, Politics and Pleasure', refers only glancingly to
film criticism and to particular films at all. It seeks rather to convince
fellow-Marxists [sic] that Marxism, while committed to a metaphysical
realism, need not be committed to a realistic or social realistic art. It
labours through Althusser and other less well-known, latter-day
Marxists and concludes that the theory of ideology does not demand
that art is a form of knowledge. Most striking is the first chapter in
which the author explains how, despite Kuhn, a realist philosophy of
science is still possible, courtesy of Roy Bhaskar.

   Bill Nichols, in *Ideology and Image*, a book which purports to show
how to unmask the ideological content of film and other images
produced under capitalism, also offers a run-through of some current
philosophy of science, stressing the anti-positivist and even subjectivist
line that can be attributed to Kuhn and Feyerabend, as warrant for his
own debunking of the notion of the facts of an external world.

6   AESTHETICS AND ESSENTIALISM

1 The major exponent of the institutional theory of art is George Dickie.
Arthur Danto was once lumped with him, but his (1982) shows him
distancing himself from it. Noel Carroll (1979) has applied it to film. It
is criticized by Silvers (1975).
2 Not incidentally, such quasi-legal customs, specifications and definitions are bewilderingly elaborate, subject to disputed interpretation,
and constantly under revision to try to impose order on a changing
world.
3 Steven Spielberg has been quoted, on starting on a new film, as
lamenting the fact that despite their appearance of high technology,
films are in fact slowly and painfully hand-made.
4 The fascinating story of the emergence of movie forms from stage
forms is told in Vardac 1949 and Fell 1974.

7   ARGUMENTS AGAINST FILMS AS ART

1 Unless it is a degenerate survival of Hegel's view that nations and
cultures briefly flower and then are transcended and superseded, their
flowering being their 'age'. Hence the general notion that there are

'ages' or 'periods' in the history of art. And 'ten bests' like 'decades' are reminiscent of number-superstition.

2 A word more may be in order on this topic. Some critics (I suspect Cavell) think that criticism is no more than reporting on states of mind – putting experience into words, perhaps. The state of mind that interests me is when I am thinking of statements of the form, 'this film has value because of . . .'. The 'because of . . .' may consist of good reasons or bad ones. There is a difference: one can make mistakes. My new perspective on Antonioni partly stems from exposure to his other work. What seemed enigmatic and intriguing seems now to be obsessive and glib. The works have not changed. I do not know if I or my standards have changed. More plausibly, one extends a wait-and-see attitude towards something new, knowing the first reactions can be unreliable. But is this specific to film? Is one more indulgent to the new, more ready to wait until the one work can be situated in the context of an *oeuvre*? Do films provide the context for other films more than novels do for other novels? Is there a lack of self-containedness tolerable in films not tolerable in novels? Has this anything to do with their brevity and hence relative paucity of information?

3 The debate over the aesthetics of Nazi films was fuelled after the second world war by the fact that most copies of those films were in the hands of the occupation authorities who refused, for a time, to release them for public showing in Allied countries. The official reasons were the campaign of de-Nazification and the problem of who they belonged to. But some critics who had seen the films pre-war argued that fascist art is a contradiction in terms and so the films should not as film art be released to the general public. Eventually they were released, but argument about their value continues to this day (Sontag in Nichols 1976 and Winston 1981). See the discussion in Chapter 8 below.

4 George Dickie's (1974) institutional theory suggests that art is (and is no more than) that which is treated as art by the society in question.

5 The beauty of Kuhn's view of science is that it makes the indifferent attitude of many scientists to the history of their field rationally intelligible; the ugly aspect of his view is that he endorses their attitude.

6 It could survive all but the destruction of our planet. Indeed, since so much of it has been broadcast on electronic waves which escape into space, it is possible to claim that it exists forever.

7 This is the thesis of Benjamin's famous essay 'The Work of Art in the Age of Mechanical Reproduction' (1969, pp. 217ff). Attributing to traditional art works an 'aura' of authenticity only an original can have, Benjamin sees mechanical reproduction as reversing the function of art, instead of being based on ritual it is based on politics, the cult value of an art work is replaced by its exhibition value. Film, despite being a distraction, is possibly a progressive force:

Mechanical reproduction of art changes the reaction of the masses towards art. The reactionary attitude toward a Picasso painting changes into the progressive reaction toward a Chaplin movie. The progressive reaction is characterized by the direct, intimate fusion of visual and emotional enjoyment with the orientation of the expert. Such fusion is of great social significance. (1969, p. 234)

8 The best philosophical treatment of the man-machine issue is in Agassi 1977. La Mettrie's classic and Needham's critique (1928) are also recommended.

9 I write that typography is not usually part of the writer's bailiwick to allow for those authors who do involve themselves in book reproduction. Virginia Woolf ran a press, and the contemporary philosopher Robert Nozick boasted that the typography, layout and choice of paper were his for *Philosophical Explanation* (*New York Times Book Review*, 20 September 1981). He did not, however, claim that the typography affected the validity of his arguments. His concern then was aesthetic/decorative.

10 Helpful examples of this empirical approach are the introduction to the Wisconsin/Warners Script Book Series, a set of volumes chronicling the creative processes of classical Warner Brothers films. Equally instructive is a study of the work of David O. Selznick, see Behlmer (1972), Howard (1979), Haver (1980), Lambert (1973), Flamini (1975), and Selznick (1983).

11 Ingmar Bergman once made the comparison but tries, unaccountably, to withdraw it in Simon (1972).

12 In denying movies First Amendment Protections of Freedom of Speech the Supreme Court of the United Stated declared them in 1915 to be: 'a business pure and simple, originated and conducted for profit' (quoted in Randall 1968).

13 In this paragraph are described Roscoe Arbuckle (fat), Ben Turpin (cross-eyed), Harold Lloyd (meek and bespectacled), Buster Keaton (stonefaced), Charles Chaplin (tramp), Stan Laurel and Oliver Hardy (one thin, one fat). The demolition of the car and house is in *Big Business* (1929), the debagging in *You're Darn Tootin'* (1928).

14 See note 12 above. Carmen 1966, Randall 1968, Hunnings 1967 and Jowett 1976 chronicle the story of the struggle to classify films as speech and hence to entitlement to constitutional protections. Hunnings' is a comparative study that is much updated for the United Kingdom in Williams 1979.

8   FILMS AS ART

1 One of the best-informed of these discussions is by the dance critic of the *New Yorker*, Arlene Croce (1972), who carefully analyses the Astaire-Rogers musicals and the philosophy of dance-on-film they display.

2 In his (1982) Arthur Danto stretches 'art' so far that anything and everything is art, and *works* of art scarcely any longer exist.

3 The principal venue of the commitment debate was *Sight and Sound*, in particular Anderson 1956 and Taylor 1956–7. Anderson's argument, which showed traces of Leavisism, was that artistic film like artistic literature had to embody life-enhancing values. The Leavis school's use of the word 'life' in an evaluative context, as in 'life-affirming', was a neat verbal ploy that made it difficult to controvert them. How could one argue against 'life', or not value materials that affirmed it? Indeed to praise anti-life materials was a bit of a pragmatic contradiction.

4 See note 3, ch. 7, above.

5 C.p. Munsterberg's reflections on our automatic completion of such interruptions.

9 PHILOSOPHY

1 What is filmic and what is unfilmic seems to evolve with technique and 'exemplary achievements' (Kuhn 1977). Once Eric Rohmer made a success with his talky *contes moreaux* films, the way was opened for *My Dinner With André* (being forced to watch this is a vision of hell for many of the philosophers I know; it was popular despite us). Much earlier, Laurence Olivier overcame filmic prejudice against words with his Shakespeare adaptations (c.p. Khatchadourian 1978).

10 POPULAR PHILOSOPHY

1 The same trivial sense in which Metz says every film is a fiction film (*Screen*, vol. 16, 1975, p. 47); Sarris (See Barsam 1973, p. 2) also says every film is a documentary, and Heider (1976) that every film is ethnographic.

2 I have in mind *Dr Ehrlich's Magic Bullet* (1940); *The Story of Alexander Graham Bell* (1939); *Edison the Man* (1940); *Madame Curie* (1943); *Young Tom Edison* (1940); *Freud* (1962).

3 *The Strawberry Statement* (1970); *Zabriskie Point* (1970); *R.P.M.* (1970).

4 C.f. Ingmar Bergman's remarks about the impact on him of existentialism (1973, pp. 11–16).

12 *CITIZEN KANE* AND THE ESSENCE OF A PERSON

1 See also the lists given at pp. 239–40 of Robertson (1980).

2 The origins of *Citizen Kane* and the history of its making are matters of

some dispute, centring around the contribution of Welles himself. The dispute is referenced and discussed in Carringer 1978, 1985. A useful collateral source based on archival work is Jewell 1979.

3 Why, for example, do so many film scholars yearn to transcribe films fully and expend funds on frame enlargements? Answer: they want unassailable 'visual evidence'. An interesting trace of positivism.

4 Bordwell's essay, first published in 1971, is anthologized by Gottesman (1976) and described as follows: 'David Bordwell's resonant essay . . . sets a standard for all Welles scholars' – not, I shall show, a standard they should follow. When Bordwell's essay was again reprinted in Nichols (1976) he added to it a self-critical addendum. His principal anxiety is that the assumptions of his criticism were not spelled out and that the original essay was insufficiently formalist. He chastizes himself for adverting to 'reality' as something to measure the film against, and suggests there is a failure to look at ways form and content or different levels of structure in the film conflict with each other. One can only applaud the spirit of such self-examination and criticism, even if it hardly gets to the heart of the matter. That would be reachable only by beginning with the rather fundamental question of what the purpose of such exercises in criticism might be. From the answer will flow materials for self-assessment.

5 'The Rosebud gimmick is what I like least about the movie. It's a gimmick, really, and rather dollar-book Freud', Welles cited in Kael 1971, p. 49. Carringer's researches (1978) establish that Rosebud is definitely one of the script elements due to Mankiewicz.

13   *RASHOMON*: IS TRUTH RELATIVE?

1 The main sources are the screenplay *Rashomon* (1969), *Focus on Rashomon* (Richie 1972) and Richie's monograph of the director (Richie 1965). Recent publications are Kurosawa's autobiography (1982) and McDonald (1983).

2 Harris's 'nickname' has spread, as see recent papers by the anthropologists Frankel 1981 and Heider 1982.

3 When first I saw *Citizen Kane* I believed, for a second or two, that the projectionist had mixed reels of the feature with the newsreel.

4 It might be said that a courtroom drama of guilt and innocence is not about the same things as a film about reality and truth. *Twelve Angry Men*, however, is about truth rather than guilt. What the jury discovers is that a witness could not have seen what he claimed to see, hence his testimony was doubtful.

14   *PERSONA*: THE PERSON AS A MASK

1 In an interesting discussion of the film, Campbell (1979) tries to show how it constitutes a reflexive involvement of the audience in its own

construction. He overlooks the Ophuls precedent, however.

2 Thus, I never shared the distress Campbell (1979) reports at the interruption in the middle of the film. In general, serious critics miss the humour and playfulness in Bergman. See also Browne (1979a).

3 Livingston (1982) puts some quotes on the phrase: but I suspect he takes it seriously nevertheless.

4 In his otherwise admirable *The Painted Word* (Wolfe 1975), Wolfe overlooks the historic complicity of artists in the deluge of words – William Blake, etc.

5 This may explain why contemporary schools of art and artistic movements so often cluster round manifestos and articulated philosophies, rather than, as of old, around particular workshops, teachers, or cities.

6 Livingston, like others, persistently writes pleonastically 'self-reflexive'. As mentioned in Section 4.1 above, reflexive in logic means 'self-referring'; no prefix is possible.

15 WOODY ALLEN AND THE SEARCH FOR MORAL INTEGRITY

1 Allen's films are: *What's New Pussycat?* (w. Allen, d. Clive Donner), 1965; *Take the Money and Run* (wd. Allen) 1968; *Bananas* (w. Allen and Mickey Rose, d. Allen) 1971; *Play it Again, Sam* (w. Allen, d. Herbert Ross) 1972; *Everything You Always Wanted to Know About Sex* (wd. Allen) 1972; *Sleeper* (w. Allen and Marshall Brickman, d. Allen) 1973; *Love and Death* (wd. Allen) 1975; *Annie Hall* (w. Allen and Marshall Brickman, d. Allen) 1977; *Interiors* (wd. Allen) 1978; *Manhattan* (w. Allen and Marshall Brickman, d. Allen) 1979; *Stardust Memories* (wd. Allen) 1980; *A Midsummer Night's Sex Comedy* (wd. Allen) 1982; *Zelig* (wd. Allen) 1983; *Broadway Danny Rose* (wd. Allen) 1984; *The Purpose Rose of Cairo* (wd. Allen) 1985; *Hannah and Her Sisters* (wd. Allen) 1986.

2 Allen says they are autobiographical but exaggerated.

3 Each of them has received the accolade of a cover story in *Time* magazine, Allen on 3 July 1972 and 30 April 1979; Keaton on 26 September 1977.

4 Allen's own explanation is that much of this is 'traceable to bad choices in life' (Hirsch 1981, p. 91) and indeed the problem of choices in life could be added to the inventory at p. 316 above.

5 In light of the surprised comments about the magical moment in *A Midsummer Night's Sex Comedy*, Allen's 1982 release, film critics need reminding that in *Interiors* Renata has visions/hallucinations and that, when their mother drowns, the two daughters who are asleep suddenly wake up. In *Broadway Danny Rose* a medium is treated both satirically and seriously.

BIBLIOGRAPHY

Aaron, Daniel, 1961, *Writers on the Left*, New York: Harcourt Brace.

Adler, Mortimer J., 1937, *Art and Prudence*, New York: Longmans.

Agassi, J., 1963, *Towards an Historiography of Science, History and Theory*, Beiheft 2.

Agassi, J., 1964, 'The Nature of Scientific Problems and their Roots in Metaphysics', in M. Bunge (ed.), *The Critical Approach*, Glencoe: Free Press.

Agassi, J., 1977, *Towards a Rational Philosophical Anthropology*, The Hague: Nijhoff.

Agassi, J., 1978, 'Movies Seen Many Times', *Philosophy of the Social Sciences*, vol. 8, pp. 398–405.

Agassi, J., 1979, 'Art and Science', *Scienta*, vol. 73, pp. 127–40.

Agassi, J., 1981, *Science and Society*, Dordrecht: Reidel.

Altman, Charles, 1977, 'Psychoanalysis and Cinema: The Imaginary Discourse', *Quarterly Review of Film Studies*, vol. 2, pp. 257–72.

Anderson, Joseph and Anderson, Barbara, 1980, 'Motion Perception in Motion Pictures', in de Lauretis and Heath, pp. 76–95.

Anderson, Lindsay, 1952, 'The Quiet Man', *Sequence*, no. 14, pp. 23–27.

Anderson, Lindsay, 1956, 'Stand Up! Stand Up!', *Sight and Sound*, vol. 26, pp. 63–9.

Andrew, J. Dudley, 1976, *The Major Film Theories*, New York: Oxford University Press.

Andrew, J. Dudley, 1978, *André Bazin*, New York: Oxford University Press.

Anobile, Richard J., 1974, *Casablanca*, New York: Universe.

Anobile, Richard J., 1977, *Woody Allen's Play it Again, Sam*, New York: Grosset & Dunlap.

Arnheim, Rudolf, 1933, *Film*, London: Faber & Faber.

Arnheim, Rudolf, 1958, *Film as Art*, Berkeley and Los Angelos: University of California Press.

Bibliography

Aron, Raymond, 1957, *The Opium of the Intellectuals*, New York: Doubleday.

Aron, Raymond, 1969, *Marxism and the Existentialists*, New York: Harper.

Astruc, Alexandre, 1948, 'Le Caméra-Stylo', reprinted in Peter Graham (ed.), *The New Wave*, London: Secker, 1968, pp. 17–24.

Ayer, A. J., 1936, *Language, Truth and Logic*, London: Gollancz.

Baechlin, Peter, 1947, *Histoire Economique du Cinéma*, Paris: Le Nouvelle Edition.

Balazs, Bela, 1930, *Der Geist des Films*, Berlin: Wilhelm Knapp.

Balazs, Bela, 1953, *Theory of the Film*, New York: Roy.

Barsam, Richard B., 1973, *Nonfiction Film, a Critical History*, New York: Dutton.

Barthes, Roland, 1981, *Camera Lucida*, New York: Hill & Wang.

Bartley, III, W. W., 1961, *The Retreat to Commitment*, New York: Knopf.

Bartley, III, W. W., 1973, *Wittgenstein*, Philadelphia: Lippincott.

Bartley, III, W. W., 1982, 'Critical Study: The Philosophy of Karl Popper, Part III. 'Rationality, Criticism, and Logic', *Philosophia*, vol. 11, pp. 121–221.

Bartley, III, W. W., 1984, 'Knowledge is a Product Not Fully Known to Its Producer', in K. Leube and C. Nishiyama (eds), *The Road to Serfdom After Forty Years*, Munich: Philosophia Verlag.

Bazin, André, 1950, *Orson Welles*, English trans. of 1958 edition, New York: Harper & Row, 1978.

Bazin, André, 1959–62, *Qu'est ce que le Cinema?*, 4 vols, Paris: Editions du Cerf; Edition definitive, Paris: Editions du Cerf, 1975.

Bazin, André, 1967–71, *What is Cinema?*, 2 vols, Berkeley and Los Angeles: University of California Press.

Behlmer, Rudy (ed.), 1972, *Memo From David O. Selznick*, New York: Viking.

Benjamin, Walter, 1968 (1969), *Illuminations*, New York: Schocken.

Bergman, Ingrid and Burgess, Alan, 1980, *My Story*, New York: Delacorte.

Bergman on Bergman, 1973, interviews by Stig Bjorkman, Torsten Manns, Jonas Sima, New York: Simon & Schuster.

Berkeley, George, 1710, *A Treatise Concerning the Principles of Human Knowledge*, Dublin.

Blocker, H. Gene, 1977, 'Pictures and Photographs', *Journal of Aesthetics and Art Criticism*, vol. 36, pp. 155–62.

Bordwell, David, 1971, 'Citizen Kane', *Film Comment*, summer, vol. 7, pp. 38–47; reprinted in Gottesman 1976, pp. 102–22, and Nichols 1976, pp. 273–90.

Boudon, Raymond, 1982, *The Unintended Consequences of Social Actions*, London: Macmillan.

Browne, Nick, 1978, '*Cahiers du Cinéma*'s Rereading of Hollywood Cinema: An Analysis of Method', *Quarterly Review of Film Studies*, vol. 3, pp. 405–16.

Browne, Nick, 1979a, 'The Filmic Apparatus in Bergman's *Persona*', *Psychocultural Review*, vol. 3, pp. 111–15.

Browne, Nick, 1979b, 'The Spectator of American Symbolic Forms: Re-reading John Ford's *Young Mr Lincoln*', *Film Reader*, no. 4, pp. 180–8.

Campbell, Paul Newell, 1979, 'The Reflexive Function of Bergman's *Persona*', *Cinema Journal*, vol. xix, pp. 71–85.

Carmen, Ira H., 1966, *Movies Censorship and the Law*, Ann Arbor: University of Michigan.

Carringer, Robert L., 1978, 'The Scripts of *Citizen Kane*', *Critical Inquiry*, vol. 5, pp. 369–400.

Carringer, Robert L., 1985, *The Making of Citizen Kane*, Berkeley and Los Angeles: University of California Press.

Carroll, Noel, 1979, 'Film History and Film Theory: An Outline for an Institutional Theory of Film', *Film Reader*, no. 4.

Carroll, Noel, 1982, 'Address to the Heathen', *October*, no. 23, winter, pp. 89–163.

Carroll, Noel, 1987, 'Conspiracy Theories of Representation', forthcoming.

Caute, David, 1973, *The Fellow Travellers*, New York: Simon & Schuster.

Caute, David, 1978, *The Great Fear*, New York: Simon & Schuster.

Cavell, Stanley, 1971, *The World Viewed*, New York: Viking; second edn 1979, Cambridge, Mass.: Harvard University Press.

Cavell, Stanley, 1974, 'More of *The World Viewed*', *Georgia Review*, vol. 28, pp. 571–631; expanded as an appendix to the second edn of Cavell 1971.

Cavell, Stanley, 1978, 'What Becomes of Things on Film?', *Philosophy and Literature*, vol. 2, pp. 249–57.

Cavell, Stanley, 1981, *Pursuits of Happiness*, Cambridge: Harvard University Press.

Chaplin, Charles, 1964, *My Autobiography*, New York: Simon & Schuster.

Clark, Kenneth, 1959, *The Nude*, New York: Doubleday.

Clark, Terry Nichols, 1973, *Prophets and Patrons: The French University and the Emergence of the Social Sciences*, Cambridge, Mass.: Harvard University Press.

Cohen, Marshall, 1965, 'Aesthetic Essence', in Max Black (ed.), *Philosophy in America*, Ithaca: Cornell University Press, pp. 115–33.

Cohen, Marshall and Mast, Gerald, 1979, *Film Theory and Criticism*, New York: Oxford University Press.

Cohen-Séat, Gilbert, 1946, *Essai sur les principes d'une philosophie du Cinéma*, Paris: Presses Universitaires de France.

Coleman, Francis X. J., 1974, *The Harmony of Reason: A Study in Kant's Aesthetics*, Pittsburgh: University of Pittsburgh Press.

Cook, David, 1981, *A History of Narrative Film*, New York: W. W. Norton.

Corliss, Richard, 1974, *Talking Pictures*, New York: Penguin.

Cowie, Peter, 1982, *Ingmar Bergman, A Critical Biography*, New York: Scribner's.

Crawford, Donald W., 1970, 'The Uniqueness of the Medium', *The Personalist*, vol. 51, pp. 447–69.

Crawford, Donald W., 1974, *Kant's Aesthetic Theory*, Madison: University of Wisconsin Press.

Croce, Arlene, 1972, *The Astaire-Rogers Book*, New York: Dutton for Outerbridge and Lazard.

Danto, Arthur, 1979, 'Moving Pictures', *Quarterly Review of Film Studies*, vol. 4, pp. 1–21.

Danto, Arthur, 1982, *The Transfiguration of the Commonplace*, Cambridge: Harvard University Press.

Davenport, Edward, 1983, 'Literature as Thought Experiment', *Philosophy of the Social Sciences*, vol. 13, pp. 279–306.

Davis, Murray S., 1971, 'That's Interesting! Towards a Phenomenology of Sociology and a Sociology of Phenomenology', *Philosophy of the Social Sciences*, vol. 1, pp. 309–44.

Dayan, Daniel 1974, 'The Tutor-Code in Classical Cinema', *Film Quarterly*, vol. 28, Fall, pp. 22–31; reprinted in Nichols 1976, pp. 438–51.

de Lauretis, Teresa and Heath, Stephen (eds), 1980, *The Cinematic Apparatus*, New York: St Martin's.

De Tocqueville, Alexis, 1835–40, *Democracy in America*, ed. Phillip Bradley, New York: Vintage.

Descombes, Vincent, 1980, *Modern French Philosophy*, Cambridge: Cambridge University Press.

Dickie, George, 1974, *Art and the Aesthetic, An Institutional Analysis*, Ithaca: Cornell University Press.

Editors of *Cahiers du Cinéma*, 1970, 'John Ford's *Young Mr Lincoln*', *Cahiers du Cinéma*, No. 223, pp. 29–47; translated in *Screen*, vol. 13, 1972, pp. 5–44; reprinted in Nichols 1976, pp. 493–529; Cohen and Mast (second edn) 1979, pp. 778–831; *Screen Reader*, I, 1977, pp. 113–52.

Eidsvik, Charles, 1978, *Cineliteracy*, New York: Random House.

Ellis, John, 1982, *Visible Fictions*, London: Routledge & Kegan Paul.

Erens, Patricia, 1979, *Akira Kurosawa, A Guide to References and Resources*, Boston: G. K. Hall.

Fell, John L., 1974, *Film and the Narrative Tradition*, Norman: University of Oklahoma Press.

Fielding, Raymond, 1978, *The March of Time*, New York: Oxford University Press.

Flamini, Roland, 1975, *Scarlett, Rhett, and a Cast of Thousands*, New York: Macmillan.

Four Films of Woody Allen, 1982, New York: Random House.

Francisco, Charles, 1980, *You Must Remember This . . . The Filming of Casablanca*, Englewood Cliffs, N. J.: Prentice-Hall.

Frankel, Barbara, 1981, 'The "Rashomon Effect" and the Puzzled Ethnographer: On the Epistemology of Listening to Different Voices', unpublished.

Fredrickson, Donald L., 1973, *The Aesthetics of Isolation in Film Theory:*

Hugo Munsterberg, New York: Arno.

Friedson, Eliot, 1953, 'Adult Discount: An Aspect of Children's Changing Taste', *Child Development*, vol. 24, pp. 39–49.

Frye, Northrop, 1957, *The Anatomy of Criticism*, Princeton: Princeton University Press.

Fuller, Steve, 1983, 'The "Reductio ad Symbolum" and the Possibility of a "Linguistic Object"', *Philosophy of the Social Sciences*, June, vol. 13, pp. 129–56.

Gaggi, Silvio, 1978, 'Semiology, Marxism, and the Movies', *Journal of Aesthetics and Art Criticism*, vol. 36, pp. 461–9.

Gallie, W. B., 1956, 'Art as an Essentially Contested Concept', *Philosophical Quarterly*, vol. 6, pp. 97–114.

Gans, Herbert J., 1956, 'The Creator-Audience Relationship in Movie-Making', in B. Rosenberg and D. M. White (eds), *Mass Culture*, Glencoe: Free Press, pp. 315–24.

Gans, Herbert J., 1962, *The Urban Villagers*, Glencoe: Free Press.

Gans, Herbert J., 1973, '*Deep Throat*: The Pornographic Film Goes Public', *Social Policy*, vol. 4, no. 1, pp. 119–21.

Gassner, John and Nichols, Dudley, 1945, *Best Film Plays 1943–44*, New York: Crown.

Gellner, Ernest, 1959, *Words and Things*, London: Gollancz (second edn 1979, London: Routledge & Kegan Paul).

Gellner, Ernest, 1964, *Thought and Change*, Chicago: University of Chicago.

Gellner, Ernest, 1973, 'The Concept of a Story', in *Cause and Meaning in the Social Sciences*, London: Routledge & Kegan Paul.

Gellner, Ernest, 1975, *Legitimation of Belief*, Cambridge University Press.

Gibson, J. J., 1950, *The Perception of the Visual World*, Boston: Houghton Mifflin.

Gibson, J. J., 1979, *The Ecological Approach to Visual Perception*, Boston: Houghton Mifflin.

Goffman, Erving, 1963, *Behaviour in Public Places*, Glencoe: Free Press.

Gombrich, E. H., 1950, *The Story of Art*, London: Phaidon.

Gombrich, E. H., 1960, *Art and Illusion*, London: Phaidon.

Gombrich, E. H., 1965, 'The Use of Art for the Study of Symbols', *American Psychologist*, vol. 20, pp. 34–50.

Gombrich, E. H., 1969, *In Search of Cultural History*, New York: Oxford University Press.

Gombrich, E. H., 1979, *Ideals and Idols*, London: Phaidon.

Gombrich, E. H., 1982, 'Standards of Truth: The Arrested Image and the Moving Eye' in *The Image and the Eye*, Ithaca: Cornell/Phaidon, pp. 245–77.

Goodman, Nelson, 1976, *The Languages of Art*, Indianpolis: Hackett.

Gottesman, Ronald, 1971, *Focus on Citizen Kane*, Englewood Cliffs, N. J.: Prentice-Hall.

Gottesman, Ronald, 1976, *Focus on Orson Welles*, Englewood Cliffs, N. J.: Prentice-Hall.

Bibliography

Guback, Thomas, 1969, *The International Film Industry*, Bloomington, Ind.: University of Indiana Press.

Guzetti, Alfred, 1973, 'Christian Metz and the Semiology of the Cinema', *Journal of Modern Literature*, vol. 3, pp. 292–309; also in Cohen and Mast 1979, pp. 184–203.

Hale, Jr, Matthew, 1980, *Human Science and Social Order, Hugo Munsterberg and the Origins of Applied Psychology*, Philadelphia: Temple University Press.

Haley, Jay, 1952, 'The Appeal of the Moving Picture', *Quarterly Review of Film, Radio and Television*, vol. 6, pp. 361–74.

Harman, Gilbert, 1977, 'Semiotics and the Cinema: Metz and Wollen', *Quarterly Review of Film Studies*, vol. 2, pp. 15–24; also in Cohen and Mast 1979, pp. 204–216.

Harms, Rudolf, 1926, *Philosophie des films, Seine aesthetischen und metaphysischen Grundlagen*, Leipzig: Meiner.

Harms, Rudolf, 1927, *Kulterbedeutung und Kulturgefahren des Films*, Karlsruhe: Braun.

Harris, Marvin, 1979, *Cultural Materialism*, New York: Random House.

Harvey, Sylvia, 1978, *May '68 and Film Culture*, London: British Film Institute.

Hauser, Arnold, 1982, *The Sociology of Art*, London: Routledge & Kegan Paul.

Haver, Ronald, 1980, *David O. Selznick's Hollywood*, New York: Knopf.

Heath, Stephen, 1981, *Questions of Cinema*, Bloomington: University of Indiana Press.

Heider, Karl G., 1976, *Ethnographic Film*, Austin: University of Texas Press.

Heider, Karl G., 1982, 'The Rashomon Effect in Ethnography: The Problems of Contradiction and Replicability', unpublished.

Heine, Heinrich, 1833, *Religion and Philosophy in Germany*, English trans. Boston: Beacon Press, 1959.

Henderson, Brian, 1974, 'Critique of Ciné-Structuralism, II', *Film Quarterley*, vol. 27, pp. 37–46.

Higham, Charles and Greenberg, Joel, 1968, *Hollywood in the Forties*, New York: Barnes.

Hirsch, Foster, 1981, *Love, Sex, Death, and the Meaning of Life*, Woody Allen's Comedy, New York: McGraw-Hill.

Hirschhorn, Clive, 1979, *The Warner Brothers Story*, London: Octopus.

Horton, Donald and Wohl, R. R., 1956, 'Mass Communication and Para-Social Interaction', *Psychiatry*, vol. 19, pp. 215–29.

Hospers, John, 1946, *Meaning and Truth in the Arts*, Chapel Hill: University of North Carolina Press.

Howard, Sidney, 1979, *Gone With The Wind: The Screenplay*, New York: Macmillan.

Hudlin, Edward, 1979, 'Film Language', *Journal of Aesthetic Education*, vol. 13, pp. 47–56.

Hume, David, 1777, *Enquiries Concerning Human Understanding*, ed. L.A. Selby-Bigge, Oxford University Press, 1902.

Hunnings, Neville March, 1967, *Film Censorship and the Law*, London: Allen & Unwin.

Husserl, E., 1960, *Cartesian Meditations*, The Hague: Nijhoff.

Husserl, E., 1982, 'Ideas Pertaining to a Pure Phenomenology and to a Phenomenological Philosophy', *Collected Works*, Vol. II, The Hague: Nijhoff.

Jacobs, Diane, 1982, *. . . but we need the eggs, The Magic of Woody Allen*, New York: St Martin's.

Jaehne, Karen, 1983, 'Confessions of a Feminist Porn Programmer', *Film Quarterley*, vol. 37, pp. 9–16.

Jarvie, I. C., 1959, 'Notes on the Films of Ingmar Bergman', *Film Journal*, no. 14, November, pp. 9–17.

Jarvie, I. C., 1960, 'Bazin's Ontology', *Film Quarterly*, vol. 14, Fall, pp. 60–1.

Jarvie, I. C., 1961, 'Love, Death and Destruction, Antonioni and *L'Avventura*', *Motion*, summer, pp. 7–10.

Jarvie, I. C., 1963, 'Recent Films of Ingmar Bergman', *Film Journal*, no. 22, pp. 14–18.

Jarvie, I. C., 1964, *The Revolution in Anthropology*, London: Routledge & Kegan Paul.

Jarvie, I. C., 1967, 'The Objectivity of Criticism of the Arts', *Ratio*, vol. 9, pp. 67–83.

Jarvie, I. C., 1970, *Movies and Society*, New York: Basic, reprint 1983, Garland.

Jarvie, I. C., 1978a, *Movies as Social Criticism*, Metuchen, N.J.: Scarecrow.

Jarvie, I. C., 1978b, 'Seeing Through Movies', *Philosophy of the Social Sciences*, vol. 8, pp. 374–97.

Jarvie, I. C., 1981, 'The Rationality of Creativity', in M. Krausz and D. Dutton (eds), *The Concept of Creativity in Science and Art*, The Hague: Nijhoff, pp. 109–28.

Jarvie, I. C., 1982, 'The Social Experience of Movies', in S. Thomas (ed.), *Film/Culture*, Metuchen, N.J.: Scarecrow, pp. 247–68.

Jarvie, I. C., 1983, 'The Problem of the Real in Ethnographic Film', *Current Anthropology*, June, vol. 24, pp. 313–25.

Jarvie, I. C., 1984a, *Rationality and Relativism*, London: Routledge & Kegan Paul.

Jarvie, I. C., 1984b, 'Philosophy of the Film: Metaphysics, Aesthetics, Popularisation', *Persistence of Vision* forthcoming.

Jarvie, I. C., 1985a, 'The Social Experience of Movies', in 1985c.

Jarvie, I. C., 1985b, 'Methodological and Conceptual Problems in the Study of Pornography and Violence', in 1985c.

Jarvie, I. C., 1985c, *Thinking About Society: Theory and Practice*, Dordrecht: Reidel.

Jewell, Richard, 1979, 'A History of RKO Radio Pictures Inc., 1928–1940', Ph.D. dissertation, University of Southern California.

Jowett, Garth S., 1976, *Film: The Democratic Art*, Boston: Atlantic Little Brown.

Bibliography

Kael, Pauline, 1971, *The Citizen Kane Book*, Boston: Little Brown.

Kalin, Jesse, 1977, 'Ingmar Bergman's Contribution to Moral Philosophy', *International Philosophical Quarterly*, vol. 17, pp. 85–100.

Kaminsky, Stuart (ed.), 1975, *Ingmar Bergman, Essays in Criticism*, New York: Oxford University Press.

Khatchadourian, Haig, 1975, 'Film as Art', *Journal of Aesthetics and Art Criticism*, vol. 33, pp. 271–4.

Khatchadourian, Haig, 1978, 'Remarks on The "Cinematic/Uncinematic" Distinction in Film Art', *Quarterly Review of Film Studies*, vol. 3, pp. 193–8.

Klingender, F. D. and Legg, Stuart, 1937, *Money Behind The Screen*, London: Lawrence & Wishart.

Koch, Howard, 1950, 'A Playwright Looks at the Filmwright', *Sight and Sound*, vol. 19, pp. 210–14.

Koch, Howard, 1973, *Casablanca: Script and Legend*, Woodstock, New York: Overlook.

Koch, Howard, 1979, *As Time Goes By*, New York: Harcourt, Brace Jovanovich

Kolker, R. P. and Ousley, J. Douglas, 1973, 'A Phenomenology of Cinematic Time and Space', *British Journal of Aesthetics*, vol. 13, pp. 388–96.

Kovach, Francis J., 1970, 'Metaphysical Analysis of Film', *Southwestern Journal of Philosophy*, vol. 1, pp.152–61.

Kracauer, Siegfried, 1965, *Theory of Film, The Redemption of Physical Reality*, Princeton: Princeton University Press.

Kuhn, T.S., 1977, *The Essential Tension*, Chicago: University of Chicago Press.

Kuklick, Bruce, 1977, *The Rise of American Philosophy*, New Haven: Yale University Press.

Kurosawa, Akira, 1971, *The Seven Samurai*, New York: Simon & Schuster.

Kurosawa, Akira, 1982, *Something Like an Autobiography*, New York: Knopf.

Lackey, Douglas P., 1973, 'Reflections on Cavell's Ontology of Film', *Journal of Aesthetics and Art Criticism*, vol. 32, pp. 271–3.

Lakatos, Imre, 1962, 'Infinite Regress and the Foundations of Mathematics', *Aristotelian Society*, Supplementary Volume, XXXVI, pp. 155–84.

Lakatos, Imre, 1963–4, 'Proofs and Refutations', *British Journal for the Philosophy of Science*, vol. 14, pp. 1–25, 120–39, 221–45, 293–342; book version Cambridge: Cambridge University Press, 1976.

Lakatos, Imre, 1971, 'History of Science and Its Rational Reconstructions', in R. C. Buck and R. S. Cohen (eds), *Boston Studies in the Philosophy of Science*, vol. 8, Dordrecht: Reidd, pp. 91–135.

Lambert, Gavin, 1973, *G.W.T.W.*, Boston: Little, Brown.

Langer, Suzanne K., 1953, *Feeling and Form*, New York: Scribner's.

Lax, Eric, 1975, *Being Funny, Woody Allen and Comedy*, New York: Charterhouse.

Bibliography

Leary, Donald E., 1982, 'Immanuel Kant and the Development of Modern Psychology', in Woodward and Ash (eds), pp. 17–42.

Linden, George, 1970, *Reflections on the Screen*, San Francisco: Wadsworth.

Linden, George, 1971, 'Ten Questions About Film Form', *Journal of Aesthetic Education*, vol. 5, pp. 61–74.

Lindsay, Vachel, 1915, *The Art of the Moving Picture*, New York: Macmillan.

Livingston, Paisley, 1982, *Ingmar Bergman and the Rituals of Art*, Ithaca: Cornell University Press.

Lovell, Terry, 1980, *Pictures of Reality, Aesthetics, Politics, Pleasure*, London: British Film Institute.

McClintick, David, 1982, *Indecent Exposure*, New York: William Morrow.

McDonald, Keiko, 1983, *Cinema East*, Rutherford, N.J.: Fairleigh Dickinson University Press.

Mast, Gerald, 1977, *Film/Cinema/Movie*, New York: Harper & Row.

Merleau-Ponty, Maurice, 1945, 'The Film and the New Psychology', collected in *Sense and Non-Sense*, Chicago: Northwestern University Press, 1964, pp. 48–59.

Mitchell, George, 1983, 'The Movies and Munsterberg', *Jump Cut*, no. 27, pp. 57–60.

Monaco, James, 1979, *American Film Now*, New York: Oxford University Press.

Munsterberg, Hugo, 1915, 'Why We Go to the Movies', *Cosmopolitan*, 15 December, pp. 22–32.

Munsterberg, Hugo, 1916, *The Photoplay: A Psychological Study*, New York: D. Appleton.

Munz, Peter, 1984, 'Philosophy and the Mirror of Rorty', *Philosophy of the Social Sciences*, vol. 14, pp. 195–238.

Myers, Richard, 1978, *Movies on Movies*, New York: Drake.

Needham, Joseph, 1928, *Man a Machine*, New York: W. W. Norton.

Nicholas, Bill (ed.), 1976, *Movies and Methods*, Berkeley and Los Angeles: Nichols 1976, pp. 607–28.

Nichols, Bill (ed.), *Movies and Methods*, Berkeley and Los Angeles: University of California Press.

Nichols, Bill, 1985, *Movies and Methods, Volume II*, Berkeley and Los Cinema and Other Media, Bloomington, Ind.: Indiana University Press.

Nichols, Bill, 1985, *Movies and Methods, Volume 11*, Berkeley and Los Angeles: University of California Press.

Nichols, Bill and Lederman, Susan J., 1980, 'Flicker and Motion in Film', in de Lauretis and Heath (eds), 1980, pp. 96–105.

Notcutt, L. A. and Latham, C. G. (eds), 1937, *The African and the Cinema*, London: Edinburgh House Press.

O'Neill, John, 1974, 'For Marx, Against Althusser', *The Human Context*, vol. 6, summer, pp. 385–98.

O'Neill, William L., 1982, *A Better World*, New York: Simon & Schuster.

Ortega Y. Gasset, José, 1932, *The Revolt of the Masses*, New York: W. W. Norton.

Oudart, J. P., 1977–8, 'Cinema and Suture', *Screen*, vol. 18, no. 4.

Parish, James R., 1978, *Hollywood on Hollywood*, Metuchen, N.J.: Scarecrow.

Petric, Vlada (ed.), 1981, *Film and Dreams, An Approach to Bergman*, South Salem, N.Y.: Redgrave.

Pitcher, George, 1964, *The Philosophy of Wittgenstein*, Englewood Cliffs N.J.: Prentice-Hall.

Plato, *The Republic*, trans. G. R. H. Grube, Indianapolis: Hackett.

Polanyi, Michael, 1958, *Personal Knowledge*, London: Routledge & Kegan Paul.

Popper, K. R., 1945, *The Open Society and Its Enemies*, London: Routledge & Kegan Paul.

Popper, K. R., 1959, *The Logic of Scientific Discovery*, New York: Basic.

Popper, K. R., 1963, *Conjectures and Refutations*, London: Routledge & Kegan Paul.

Popper, K. R., 1972, *Objective Knowledge*, New York: Oxford University Press.

Popper, K. R., 1983, *Realism and the Aim of Science*, Totowa: Littlefield Adams.

Randall, Richard S., 1968, *Censorship of the Movies*, Madison: University of Wisconsin.

Rashomon, A Film by Akira Kurosawa, 1969, New York: Grove Press.

Reisz, Karel, 1951, 'The Showman Producer', in Cinema 1951, pp. 160–7.

Revel, J. F., 1957, *Pourquoi des Philosophes*? Paris: J. J. Pauvert.

Rice, Elmer, 1930, *A Voyage to Purilia*, New York: Cosmopolitan.

Richie, Donald, 1965, *The Films of Akira Kurosawa*, Berkeley and Los Angeles: University of California Press.

Richie, Donald, 1969, '*Rashomon* and Kurosawa', in *Rashomon* 1969, pp. 222–40.

Richie, Donald (ed.), 1972, *Focus on Rashomon*, Englewood Cliffs, N.J.: Prentice-Hall.

Robertson, Patrick, 1980, *Movie Facts and Feats*, New York: Sterling.

Rohmer, Eric and Chabrol, Claude, 1957, *Hitchcock*, Paris: Editions Universitaires.

Rosenblum, Ralph, 1979, *When the Shooting Stops . . . the Cutting Begins*, New York: Viking.

Rosenzweig, Sidney C., 1978, *Talking Shadows: The Major Films of Michael Curtiz*, Ph.D., University of Rochester.

Rotha, Paul, 1930, *The Film Till Now*, London: Jonathan Cape.

Rothman, William, 1975, 'Against the System of the Suture', *Film Quarterly*, vol. 29, no. 1, pp. 44–50; reprinted in Nichols 1976, pp. 451–9.

Russell, Bertrand, 1912, *The Problems of Philosophy*, Oxford: Oxford University Press.

Russell, Bertrand, 1927, *The Analysis of Matter*, London: Allen & Unwin.

Bibliography

Russell, Bertrand, 1940, *An Inquiry into Meaning and Truth*, London: Allen & Unwin.

Russell, Bertrand, 1948, *Human Knowledge, Its Scope and Limits*, London: Allen & Unwin.

Salt, Barry, 1983, *Film Style and Technology, History and Analysis*, London: Starword.

Santamaria, Ulysses, 1983, 'Marx et L'Economie Politique: Contre Althusser?', *Philosophy of the Social Sciences*, vol. 13, pp.1–16.

Sarris, Andrew, 1968; *The American Cinema*, New York: Dutton.

Schmitt, Richard, 1968, 'Phenomenology', *Encyclopaedia of Philosophy*, New York: Macmillan.

Scott, James F., 1965, 'The Achievement of Ingmar Bergman', *Journal of Aesthetics and Art Criticism*, vol. 24, pp. 263–72.

Screen Reader 1: Cinema/Ideology/Politics, 1977, London: Society for Education in Film and Television.

Scruton, Roger, 1974, *Art and Imagination*, London: Methuen.

Selznick, Irene Mayer, 1983, *A Private View*, New York: Knopf.

Sesonske, Alexander, 1974a, 'Aesthetics of Film', *Journal of Aesthetics and Art Criticism*, vol. 33, pp. 51–7.

Sesonske, Alexander, 1974b, 'The World Viewed', *Georgia Review*, vol. 28, pp. 561–70.

Sesonske, Alexander, 1980, 'Time and Tense in Cinema', *Journal of Aesthetics and Art Education*, vol. 38, pp. 419–26.

Shiner, Roger, 1983, 'Getting to Know You', unpublished.

Silvers, Anita, 1975, 'The Artwork Discarded', *Journal of Aesthetics and Art Criticism*, vol. 34, pp. 441–56.

Simon, John, 1972, *Ingmar Bergman Directs*, New York: Harcourt Brace & Jovanovich.

Sklar, Robert, 1975, *Movie-Made America*, New York: Random House.

Snyder, Joel, 1983, 'Photography and Ontology', *Grazer Philosophische Studien*, vol. 19, pp. 21–34.

Sparshott, Francis, 1971, 'Basic Film Aesthetics', *Journal of Aesthetic Education*, vol. 5, pp. 11–34.

Sparshott, Francis, 1982, *The Theory of the Arts*, Princeton: Princeton University Press.

Spottiswoode, Raymond, 1935, *A Grammar of the Film*, London: Faber & Faber.

Taylor, John Russell, 1956–7, Letter to the Editor, *Sight and Sound*, vol. 26, p. 164.

Thomas, Bob, 1970, *Selznick*, Garden City, N.J.: Doubleday.

Thomas, Sari, 1982, 'Introduction' and ed., *Film/Culture,* Metuchen, N.J.: Scarecrow.

Thomas, Tony and Behlmer, Rudy, 1975, *Hollywood's Hollywood*, New York: Citadel.

Topper, David, 1983, 'Art in the Realist Ontology of J. J. Gibson', *Synthese*, vol. 54, pp. 71–83.

Truffaut, François, 1967, *Hitchcock*, New York: Simon & Schuster.

Tudor, Andrew, 1973, *Theories of Film*, New York: Viking.

Ullman, Liv. 1976, *Changing*, New York: Knopf.

Van Loan, Charles, 1915, *Buck Parvin and the Movies,* New York: George H. Doran Co.

Van Vechten, Carl, 1928, *Spider Boy*, New York: Grosset & Dunlap.

Vardac, A. Nicholas, 1949, *Stage to Screen*, Cambridge: Harvard Unversity Press.

Vernon, M. D., 1962, *The Psychology of Perception*, Harmondsworth: Penguin.

Vidal, Gore, 1974, *Myron*, New York: Random House.

Walker, Alexander, 1966, *The Celluloid Sacrifice*, London: Michael Joseph.

Walker, Alexander, 1970, *Stardom, The Hollywood Phenomenon*, London: Michael Joseph.

Wallis, Hal, 1980, *Starmaker*, New York: Macmillan.

Watson, J. B., 1968, *The Double Helix*, New York: Atheneum.

Wasko, Janet, 1982, *Movies and Money*, Norwood, N.J.: Ablex.

Weiss, Paul, 1975, *Cinematics*, Carbondale: Southern Illinois University Press.

West, Nathaniel, 1939, *The Day of the Locust*, New York: Random House.

Wicclair, Mark R., 1978, 'Film Theory and Hugo Munsterberg's "The Film: A Psychological Study"', *Journal of Aesthetic Education*, vol. 12, pp. 33–50.

Williams, Bernard, 1979, *Report of the Committee on Obscenity and Film Censorship*, London: HMSO.

Wilson, Harry Leon, 1922, *Merton of the Movies*, New York: Doubleday.

Wilson, John, 1961, 'Film Illiteracy in Africa', *Canadian Communications,* summer vol. 1, pp. 7–14.

Winston, Brian, 1981, 'Was Hitler There?', *Sight and Sound*, vol. 50, pp. 102–7.

Wisdom, J. O., 1953, *The Unconscious Origin of Berkeley's Philosophy*, London: Hogarth.

Wolfe, Tom, 1975, *The Painted Word*, New York: Farrar, Straus & Giroux.

Wolfenstein, Martha and Leites, Nathan, 1950, *Movies: A Psychological Study*, Glencoe: Free Press.

Wollheim, Richard, 1968, *Art and Its Objects*, New York: Harper & Row.

Wood, Robin, 1969, *Ingmar Bergman*, New York: Praeger; page references to extract in Kaminsky 1975.

Woodward, William R. and Ash, Mitchell G. (eds), 1982, *The Problematic Science: Psychology in Nineteenth Century Thought*, New York: Praeger.

Worth, Sol, 1975, 'Pictures Can't Say Aint', *Versus*, vol. 12, pp. 85–108; reprinted in Thomas 1982.

INDEX OF SUBJECTS

t indicates that a term is explained

INDEX OF NAMES